NEW MEDIEVAL LITERATURES

New Medieval Literatures is a new annual of work on medieval textual cultures. Its scope is inclusive of work across the theoretical, archival, philological, and historicist methodologies associated with medieval literary studies. The title announces an interest both in new writing about medieval culture and in new academic writing. As well as featuring challenging new articles, each issue will include an analytical survey by a leading international medievalist of recent work in an emerging or dominant critical discourse. In order to promote dialogue, from time to time issues will include digests or translations of important new work originally published in languages other than English. The editors aim to engage with intellectual and cultural pluralism in the Middle Ages and now. Within this generous brief, they recognize only two criteria: excellence and originality.

New Medieval Literatures

7

Edited by
WENDY SCASE
RITA COPELAND
DAVID LAWTON

OXFORD
UNIVERSITY PRESS

OXFORD
UNIVERSITY PRESS

Great Clarendon Street, Oxford OX2 6DP

Oxford University Press is a department of the University of Oxford.
It furthers the University's objective of excellence in research, scholarship,
and education by publishing worldwide in

Oxford New York

Auckland Cape Town Dar es Salaam Hong Kong Karachi
Kuala Lumpur Madrid Melbourne Mexico City Nairobi
New Delhi Shanghai Taipei Toronto

With offices in

Argentina Austria Brazil Chile Czech Republic France Greece
Guatemala Hungary Italy Japan Poland Portugal Singapore
South Korea Switzerland Thailand Turkey Ukraine Vietnam

Oxford is a registered trade mark of Oxford University Press
in the UK and in certain other countries

Published in the United States
by Oxford University Press Inc., New York

British Library Cataloguing in Publication Data

Data available

Library of Congress Cataloging in Publication Data

Data available

ISBN 0-19-927365-0
978-0-19-927365-2

Typeset by SNP Best-set Typesetter Ltd., Hong Kong
Printed in Great Britain
on acid-free paper by
Biddles Ltd.
King's Lynn, Norfolk

Contents

Illustrations

The Medievalist's Tale

Wendy Scase

'I have decided to give it all up. I've decided I don't want to be a post-modern literary theorist.' . . . 'I need a life full of things,' I said. 'Full of facts.'

'Facts,' said Ormerod Goode. 'Facts.' He meditated. 'The rich-ness,' he said, 'the surprise, the shining solidity of a world full of facts . . . every established fact illuminates the world. True scholar-ship once aspired to add its modest light to that illumination. To clear a few cobwebs. No more.'

A. S. Byatt, The Biographer's Tale

THE TITLE of A. S. Byatt's recent novel, *The Biographer's Tale*, gestures towards her narrator's ancestry among Chaucer's pilgrim narrators, while her character Ormerod Goode, 'an Anglo-Saxon and Norse expert', typifies a long line of fictional medievalists, possessors of arcane knowledges and staunch believers in scientific truth. Seduced by Goode's promise of certainty, the narrator, Phineas Nanson, would-be biographer of Scholes Destry-Scholes, becomes increasingly enmired in the snares of textuality during the course of the novel. Arguably the narrative played out in Byatt's fiction haunts all of our practice, and all of the essays in this volume (one of them explicitly). Yet each of the essays also seeks to embrace, exploit, even challenge the endless replaying of this scenario. And each of them does so in ways that have come to typify the *New Medieval Literatures* essay. In this introduction I shall re-flect on the ways in which these essays may each seem to exemplify a de-veloping and distinctive practice, to write, as it were, The Medievalist's Tale.

The first three essays all make innovative use of unusual resources to offer new historical and theoretical perspectives on modern practices of medieval studies. In Trigg's, Ellis's, and Wakelin's essays, analyses of tourist guides, film, and modern and post-modern novels give rise to re-flections on practice. The work of professional medievalists in these three pieces is considered alongside the practices of a range of other inter-preters: modernist and medieval readers, heritage site managers, museum curators, archivists and librarians, parents, film directors, ancestral families, and traffic police.

Stephanie Trigg's essay, 'Walking through Cathedrals', reflects on the identities and scholarly practices of medievalists in relation to the identities and experiences offered by tourist practices at medieval sites. Trigg contrasts the visit to medieval religious buildings with reading a medieval manuscript in a library. Whereas medieval manuscripts are largely experienced only by scholars, in institutions whose aims are scholarly and conservationist, medieval religious sites are presented with plural uses and meanings. Canterbury, St Paul's, and Lincoln cathedrals, Westminster Abbey, St George's Chapel, and St Michael's Church, Stanton Harcourt, Oxfordshire, are all framed and interpreted in very different ways (ranging from the Canterbury Tales Visitor Attraction, through traffic control programmes, to the dynastic uses of chapel and parish church). However, all, Trigg argues, are illuminated by self-conscious post-modern simulacra—whether by the Cloisters Museum in Manhattan or the cathedral scenes in Brian Helgeland's film *A Knight's Tale*. In the library, the medievalist's identity as one able to distinguish the authentically medieval is affirmed by the context, whereas visiting religious buildings deconstructs the binary of authenticity and simulacrum, problematizing, even dissolving, the identity and practices of the professional medievalist. For Trigg, these experiences erase any distinction between medieval studies and medievalism: 'whether we like it or not, there is no "pure" medieval; there is only medievalism.'

The ironies and complexities of the Canterbury Tales Visitor Attraction are anticipated by Virginia Woolf's representation of the pilgrim pageant in her 1941 novel *Between the Acts*, as read by Steve Ellis in his case study of modernist medievalism, 'Framing the Father'. In *Between the Acts*, the Chaucerian pilgrims who frame the village pageant of English history represent anonymity and collectivity. Yet Chaucer is also the precondition (or 'foil') for the individual reader, whose 'journey of reading' begins with Sir John Paston's reading of Chaucer (in *The Common Reader*). The common reader is a private self, cut off from the world of collectivity of the pageant pilgrims, who is exemplified in *Between the Acts* (in an early draft) by the series of individuals who have read the copy of the *Canterbury Tales* in the library of Pointz Hall. If there is, as Trigg suggests, only medievalism, Ellis's essay reminds us that, none the less, medievalism is infinitely varied and complex. Unlike her male modernist contemporaries, such as Joyce and Eliot, Woolf is anti-medieval, yet even within her own work, Chaucer carries contradictory meanings.

The figure of the individual reader, emerging from collectivity through individual encounters with books, and the modern preoccupation with the history of this figure (in the history of the book and the history of reading), are the subjects of Daniel Wakelin's essay 'William Worcester Writes a History of his Reading'. Woolf's John Paston, individual reader, has much in common with William Worcester in Daniel Wakelin's account. A near neighbour and contemporary of the Pastons, voracious reader of many authors (including Chaucer), and persistent documentor of his reading, Worcester in Wakelin's description 'steps forward to assert his own role as one of the individuals of whom such communities [of readers] are constituted'. Yet, Wakelin turns to the post-modern female novel to invert the standard view of the relations between the individual reader as described in book history and the modern book historian. A. S. Byatt's *The Biographer's Tale* provides a model for Wakelin's reversal of the roles of Worcester and himself. Whereas, according to Ellis, Woolf fictionalized Sir John Paston as reader for her own ends, Wakelin locates the act of creating the narrative of the individual reader in Worcester himself. In making his annotations, Worcester becomes an early writer of book history, and Wakelin identifies himself no longer as practitioner of the new discipline of book history, but as his intended reader: as Phineas Nanson is to Destry-Scholes, so Wakelin is to Worcester.

This opening group of essays illustrates one genre which *NML* has attracted and cultivated: scholarship that self-consciously reflects on its own practices and histories by reaching for resources and perspectives outside and beyond the usual disciplinary confines. The second group of essays in this volume represents a second genre that has flourished in the series: historicist analysis. Whether they focus on non-canonical texts, deploying historicist method to animate neglected or despised materials, or read canonical texts in new, unfamiliar contexts, all of the essays in this group deploy historicist analysis to underpin broad-reaching revisionary or iconoclastic theses about medieval textual culture.

Mishtooni Bose's essay, 'Vernacular Philosophy and the Making of Orthodoxy in the Fifteenth Century', is both an exemplary instance of this genre and an exploder of it. Bose's essay engages with and critiques the 'vernacular theology' paradigm that has become an orthodoxy in late medieval English literary history. Shifting vernacular Wycliffism from the central place it has held in recent accounts of late medieval literary culture (but without giving comfort to sceptical or dismissive historians), Bose identifies the 'making of orthodoxy' as the central project galvanizing fifteenth-century opponents of heresy. Focusing on the little-known but voluminous works of Thomas Netter, Reginald Pecock, and John Ireland, she narrates a history of contestation, loose ends, and fragmentation in these writers' respective attempts to create an orthodox theological discourse. In Bose's analysis, despite this fragmentation, Ireland and Pecock are linked in parallel endeavours to create and defend a 'vernacular philosophy'. Both writers, she suggests, draw on scholastic defences of the use of rational method and argumentation in theology, applying them to create and defend vernacular theological discourse. Bose's essay offers a new theoretical framework for analysing the development of late medieval English writing. At the same time, it also signals the potential of a broader cultural framework. Bose demonstrates that the traditional, England-centred paradigm is too narrow: Pecock's comparators are drawn from French vernacular theologians (Jean Gerson and Jean Germain) and above all the Paris-trained Scottish theologian, John Ireland. Bose's essay, then, is at once about the construction of orthodoxy and a powerful demonstration of how orthodoxy can be challenged.

Another text that resists assimilation with the 'vernacular theology' thesis, Bose suggests, is *The Book of Margery Kempe*: as a vernacular text that transmits 'clerical priorities', the *Book* has affinities with Pecock's experimentation. (It is perhaps no coincidence that *The Book* is also fruitfully understood in the context of Europe-wide literary traditions.) Melissa Raine likewise offers *The Book of Margery Kempe* as a text that, when historically contextualized, challenges a dominant paradigm in medieval studies. Raine's essay, ' "Fals flesch": Food and the Embodied Piety of Margery Kempe,' analyses the many references in the *Book* to Margery's eating and feeding, both at home and on her travels in England and abroad, such as fasting, sharing meals, and almsgiving. Raine argues that Kempe uses such practices to negotiate and display her spiritual identity, and that their meanings are culturally specific, as is amply demonstrated by many parallel examples. Raine argues that recognition of the cultural specificity of food practices presents a challenge to Carolyn Walker Bynum's highly influential thesis in *Holy Feast and Holy Fast*, which, she suggests, rests on anachronisms, such as modern Western associations of breast-feeding.

Relationships of cultural and commercial exchange between England and the Continent are among the contexts that Lisa H. Cooper invokes to illuminate Caxton's *Dialogues in French and English*, and in particular, the identities which this curious text constructs for its readers. First appearing as a French-Flemish vocabulary written in Bruges around 1340, versions of this text survive in several languages, and in manuscript as well as print. Many puzzles remain concerning Caxton's version; we do not know who translated the Flemish part into English, the date of the translation, where Caxton got his manuscript, or the market(s) at whom it was aimed. Cooper's essay suggests that the solutions to this last problem are complex. The *Dialogues* teaches commerce, validates mercantile culture, and interests itself in craft skills and labour. In Cooper's analysis it speaks not only to 'the affluent householder', but also to 'the travelling merchant' and even to socially aspirant 'literate craftsmen'.

We turn from relations between England and the Continent to relations between the Eastern empire and the West in Seeta Chaganti's essay on Chrétien de Troyes' *Cligés*. Taking the Byzantine-influenced Stavelot triptych as an example, Chaganti shows that reliquary art problematizes relations between containing and being contained. Reading the many references to enshrinement in *Cligés* in this light ('[a] text preoccupied with the depiction of [Byzantine] artistic productions, such as tombs, shrines, and noble dwellings'), Chaganti suggests that Byzantine aesthetics provided a language in which Chrétien could have conceptualized the relation between *Cligés* and its intertext, the legend of Tristan and Iseut. This aesthetic troubles boundaries between verbal, visual, and material modes of expression. Chaganti suggests that it therefore offers a new mode of interdisciplinary interpretation, one that neither analogizes text and image nor posits relations of influence, but reads narrative and artefact in the same way.

All four essays in this second group, although identifiable with monolingual disciplinary traditions (English Studies, French Studies), seek to renew and reinvigorate those disciplines in their openness to alternative cultural and historical paradigms. The final pair of essays engages explicitly with the disciplinary traditions of medieval studies. Christopher Cannon reconsiders the validity and the characteristics of 'early Middle English' as a linguistic and literary period, while, in the volume's analytical survey, Clare A. Lees reflects on the current dynamics and possible re-mappings of Anglo-Saxon Studies.

Christopher Cannon finds that 'early Middle English' is a period characterized, paradoxically, by its unsettling of period categories: texts written in 'Old English' survive in manuscripts datable to the 'Middle English' period, or display literary features characteristic of Middle English texts. For Cannon, 'early Middle English' is a valid period descriptor, and the characteristics of this period are that it is one in which the distinction between Old and Middle English is 'annulled', and in which texts are not datable on the basis of their linguistic features. Cannon claims to rediscover the potency of a traditional disciplinary category, rather than to offer a new one; to make known what has 'long existed in linguistic and literary scholarship' but has remained concealed. For some, possibly, this move to reinvigorate the traditional (though hardly long-standing) English Studies category of early Middle English will prove contentious, not, perhaps, in that it seeks to breathe new life into periodization, but in that it seems to run counter to the methodologies and agendas of much recent scholarship (for example, the study of early English language in multilingual frameworks, or of language in relation to research on scribal practice).

In some ways, Cannon's proposals chime with the calls made by Clare A. Lees, in her analytical survey 'Actually Existing Anglo-Saxon Studies', for a rethinking of the 'before-and-after model of periodization' grounded in new work on the eleventh and twelfth centuries, and for later medieval scholars to incorporate Anglo-Saxon materials into their work. Yet, in seeking to reinvigorate an established English Studies paradigm, Cannon's proposals would also perhaps shore up the 'existing Anglo-Saxon Studies' in a manner that Lees critiques, rather than contributing to the kind of re-mapping that Lees calls for.

'Actually Existing Anglo-Saxon Studies', for Lees, is vigorously solipsistic. It is a discipline whose success in shoring up its boundaries is also its greatest weakness. One strength, which is also a symptom, is success with 'large-scale, multi-year' research projects. Lees suggests (quoting Nicholas Howe) that such projects tend 'to promote unexamined "fantasies of total knowledge" that haunt such scholarship'. A collective investment in traditional strengths is also exemplified, according to Lees, by the prominence of critical anthologies, readers, and companions as publication formats in this field. This vigorous publication record represents a victory in the face of the cruel economics of publishing for small markets, but it comes at a price, with the development of a rigid 'consensus about just what Anglo-Saxon Studies is'—and what it is not. Despite the appearance of fine theoretical and historicist work, in Lees's view, the companions tend not to offer 'any sustained encounter with modern critical theory', but to 'assimilate theoretical methodological approaches that actually contest some of the structural principles that traditionally shape the field'. In her final section, Lees sets out her vision of alternatives to existing Anglo-Saxon studies. This is her challenge, one might say, to the endless replaying of Byatt's Goode–Nanson scenario. She proposes that adoption of new paradigms and categories of knowledge would both end the discipline's solipsism and increase its strength by unlocking its potential to transform other fields of knowledge: thus Anglo-Saxon would take its place 'on the map of new medieval literatures'.

University of Birmingham

Walking through Cathedrals: Scholars, Pilgrims, and Medieval Tourists

Stephanie Trigg

> We no longer dwell in the Parthenon, but we still walk or pray in the naves of the cathedral.
>
> Umberto Eco, *Faith in Fakes*

THE INSTITUTIONS and practices of contemporary medieval tourism and heritage culture raise powerful questions for medievalists about the uses and significance of the medieval past. These questions take us far beyond our rarefied discussions of the interpretation and meaning of medieval texts and events, towards an interrogation of our role in perpetuating or challenging general understandings of tradition and heritage for particular communities. This essay takes its epigraph from Umberto Eco as a starting-point for a meditation on the experience of visiting medieval religious sites, in our various capacities as medieval scholars, as pilgrims, and as tourists. Eco contrasts the discontinuity of our classical heritage with the more active continuity that it is possible to experience with the medieval past: 'We no longer dwell in the Parthenon, but we still walk or pray in the naves of the cathedral,' he claims.[1] But such acts of walking—and indeed, of praying—are far from straightforward; nor are they reducible to the simple tropes of 'authenticity' or 'continuity', any more than the 'we' who walk or pray represent any kind of homogeneous collectivity, or that the selves who perform those acts are constituted in any single or simple way.

This essay examines a range of medieval religious sites, and aims to articulate the complex forms in which they are presented for a range of

---

[1] Umberto Eco, 'Dreaming of the Middle Ages', *Faith in Fakes: Essays*, trans. William Weaver (London, 1986), 68. Stephen Medcalf assumes an even stronger continuity: medieval culture is 'not utterly alien to us but continuous, ancestral, familial. We may speak a language descended from theirs, worship in their churches, share some of their presuppositions, religion and rituals—and all this without self-consciousness' (Stephen Medcalf (ed.), *The Later Middle Ages*, The Context of English Literature (London, 1981), 9).

visitors, in order to negotiate the potentially conflicting interests of those groups: worshippers, pilgrims, tourists, and scholars. Visitors are drawn to medieval religious buildings in part because they seem to represent an easy continuity with the past, in the repetition of familiar or stable religious rituals and practices on the same sacred site. The interior of the Gothic cathedral in particular, moreover, encourages the imagination to transcend present realities: its soaring columns and arches; its remarkable depth of field from every perspective; its play of light and shade, austerity and intricacy in its structural and decorative elements—all these aspects have the effect of diminishing individual or modern response in favour of an imagined collective, communal response, conceived, however vaguely, as 'medieval'. Visiting such sites is already a historicist project, for many visitors.

Historicism was not the original purpose or function of the cathedral, of course. Among others, Otto von Simson emphasizes that for the twelfth-century designers of Chartres and other cathedrals, ecclesiastical architecture was an intellectual exercise as much as it was an expression of faith:

Designed in an attempt to reproduce the structure of the universe, not unlike the great scientific experiments of the modern age in this respect, the cathedral is best understood as a 'model' of the medieval universe. That may give us a better idea of the speculative significance of these great edifices, a significance that transcends their beauty and practical purpose as a place of public worship.[2]

When considering modern responses to these medieval models, we must also consider the importance of the Gothic revival of the eighteenth and nineteenth centuries. The imaginative leap from modernity to the medieval period is significantly mediated and facilitated by the resurgence of Gothic as the predominant—even the naturalized—style for ecclesiastical architecture, especially in the nineteenth century. As Chris Brooks demonstrates, however, the semantics of 'Gothic' as a cultural and stylistic signifier are remarkably rich, mutable, and even contradictory.[3]

For example, the greatest and most prolific proponent of Gothic as a building style, Augustus Welby Pugin, described it tellingly as 'Pointed or Christian Architecture', believing that a revival of Gothic style would aid in the revival of the Catholic faith. This programme of design and archi-

---

[2] Otto von Simson, *The Gothic Cathedral: Origins of Gothic Architecture and the Medieval Concept of Order* (1956; 2nd edn. New York, 1962), 35.

[3] Chris Brooks, *The Gothic Revival* (London, 1999), 4–6, 23–48, and *passim*.

tecture was intimately linked to medieval forms and the belief that the external form would produce the appropriate religious sensibility:

> Restore the old reverence, and gladly will men welcome the old things—arch and aisle, and pillar and chancel, and screen, and worship as their fathers worshipped, who now sleep in Christ; and the green bough will twine in the tracery, and the tapers sparkle round the rood, and surpliced clerks sing in chancel stalls, whilst the saints shine bright in the mullioned lights—*venit hora et nunc est*—when the old glory of the sanctuary will be restored and solemnity revived with returning faith.[4]

Unfortunately for Pugin's programme, it was not the Catholic but the Anglican Church and the English establishment that had the resources to build so spectacularly in this style.[5] The fashion for Gothic architecture in this period was also strongly mediated by the twinned romantic preoccupations with the Sublime and the Picturesque, as Brooks demonstrates.[6] In this sensibility, however, medieval religion is less important than subjectivity or, rather, the delicious abeyance of the self. Coleridge's remarks can stand as representative here:

> But the Gothic art is sublime. On entering a cathedral, I am filled with devotion and awe; I am lost to the actualities that surround me, and my whole being expands into the infinite; earth and air, nature and art, all swell up into eternity, and the only sensible impression left is, 'that I am nothing!'[7]

Whereas Coleridge is transported beyond the material 'actualities' of style and architecture, Pugin affirms much stronger associative links between Gothic architecture as style and medieval Christianity. In the same way, Gothic architecture in Australia would later conjure up a complex set of familiar and nostalgic associations with Englishness.[8]

Modern visitors may experience a residual trace of Coleridge's Sublime when entering Gothic cathedrals, but the dominant perspective of the twentieth and twenty-first centuries is surely that of heritage culture. Accordingly, many visitors enter medieval cathedrals looking for traces of the medieval as a historical period, however imperfectly or generally

---

[4] A. Welby Pugin, 'Catholic Church Architecture', letter to the *Tablet*, 9, no. 435 (2 Sept. 1848), 563, quoted in Brian Andrews, *Australian Gothic: The Gothic Revival in Australian Architecture from the 1840s to the 1950s* (Melbourne, 2001), 9.

[5] Andrews, *Australian Gothic*, 9–10.

[6] Brooks, *Gothic Revival*, 140–52.

[7] Samuel Taylor Coleridge, 'General Character of the Gothic Literature and Art', in Thomas Middleton Raysor (ed.), *Coleridge's Miscellaneous Criticism* (London, 1936), 12.

[8] Andrews, *Australian Gothic*, 2–6.

conceived. Conversely, for the imaginative re-creation of the medieval to take place, the architecture itself need not be perfectly or exclusively 'authentic'. For many of us who live outside Europe, our first experience of walking in a Gothic cathedral took place in nineteenth-century buildings.

Most medieval buildings and religious establishments do not survive unmodified as medieval buildings, of course; they have distinctive histories of discontinuity, disruption, and violent destruction, especially in Protestant countries, which have left material structures and traces. Moreover, these are often narratives of problematic intersections between religious, political, national, and social interests. In the contemporary social and local sphere, churches also have ongoing responsibilities to their parishioners, and the broader spiritual community, while for many, their greatest source of income comes from the heritage tourists and culturally minded visitors who may be little concerned with those spiritual or social missions. The visitors who pass through the doors of the cathedral represent many different communities and constituencies. Recent scholarship on the anthropology of religious pilgrimage similarly insists on the heterogeneity of the experience, recognizing that 'pilgrimage is above all an arena for competing religious and secular discourses', an arena in which differences are both resolved and contested.[9]

Eco seems to countenance the possibility of cultural difference, when he admits the secular possibility of walking *or* praying in the medieval cathedral. I read this as an acknowledgement that as historians and medievalists, we use these medieval sites in ways that often resemble a kind of scholarly tourism as much as a spiritual or devotional ritual. For many of us, especially those living in countries with no medieval history, walking in cathedrals involves considerable time and expense in travel: it is an activity that closely resembles tourism. There must also be substantial and important differences amongst us, according to whether we share the same faith or creed as the church's community. Medievalists are not always exclusively either scholars, tourists, or pilgrims, but far from lessening or diluting our responses, I suggest that this mixed experience offers instructive shifts in our own subject position as we stroll through these sites with notebook in hand, and/or with family in tow.

In the context of such diversity, it is clear that the concept of 'authenticity' is deeply problematic. Medieval scholars are more than conscious

---

[9] John Eade and Michael J. Sallnow, 'Introduction', *Contesting the Sacred: The Anthropology of Christian Pilgrimage* (London and New York, 1991), 3.

of this, of course: all our training as historicists bids us be wary of the post-medieval accretions, revisions, and reforms of medieval artefacts, to reject them as spurious or, at best, to consign them to the field of reception studies or the still uncertain discipline of medievalism studies. This process is more straightforward when we are dealing with medieval texts, however, even when we read a medieval manuscript with, for example, sixteenth-century annotations in nineteenth-century binding in a twentieth-century library. While the manuscript remains the preserve of the specialists who are its material and intellectual custodians, medieval churches belong to a much broader, more diverse community. Entering these buildings demands a more complex cultural and social identity than does entering the specialized, élite spaces of the manuscript reading-room; they have a much more dramatic and immediate effect on the subjectivity of the visitor, in ways that are both intellectual and embodied.[10] To invoke Bourdieu's terminology, the cathedral, assigned with a special privilege in historical, cultural, religious, and tourist practice, receives a more emphatic and more general kind of cultural consecration than the texts which are the usual domain of scholars.

In this essay I seek to make some distinctions between the various ways in which medieval English religious sites are mediated for a range of visitors, while they still affirm a distinctive sense of national heritage. My examples, all from the Anglican tradition, range from medieval cathedrals and buildings in which we can still walk or pray in their original location (cathedrals and churches such as Canterbury Cathedral and Westminster Abbey), to specially constructed museums which foreground their archaeological or topographical claims to the medieval 'real' (for example, the Canterbury Tales Visitor Attraction in Canterbury), or sites whose religious orientation has been more or less displaced onto a more general notion of heritage or royal tourism, such as St George's Chapel at Windsor Castle, home of the Order of the Garter. It is a central assumption of this essay, which concludes with some examples of post-modernist medievalism, that the easy and customary distinction we so often draw between 'medieval' and 'medievalist' is brought into question by these examples. Authenticity is a far more mixed category than it first appears,

---

[10] Jill Mann discusses the 'dialogic' possibilities for the modern atheist medievalist reading medieval Christian texts, in her Presidential Address to the New Chaucer Society, 'Chaucer and Atheism', *Studies in the Age of Chaucer*, 17 (1995), 5–19. The subject formation I am considering here is more mixed and less stable than that of the atheist *tout court*, but Mann's essay opens up some intriguing possibilities for a more sustained study of the embodied and social politics of scholarly medievalism.

while the forms of alterity—spiritual, cultural, historical—offered by such sites are also highly variable.

These debates are familiar in the field of tourism studies, where it is recognized that the desire for 'authentic' and 'special' experience, no matter how heavily mediated, or contradictory, propels the visitor's attention.[11] Dell Upton develops an important critique of the modern intellectual's 'loyalty to modernity's concept of authenticity', which we might apply to medieval studies, and its insistence on its own difference from medievalism. He comments:

As architects, planners, historians, anthropologists, and preservationists [*and I would add, medievalists*], we are part of the mechanism that manufactures heritage. As relatively prosperous, privileged people, we are consumers of tradition. As postmodern intellectuals, we understand that authenticity is an elusive, perhaps non-existent quality. [my emphasis] . . .

To reconcile our emotional investment in authenticity with our intellectual scepticism, we commonly locate authenticity in the realm of *identity*, defined by *difference* and validated by *culture*. *Tradition* is evidence of the continuity of identity through time. [original emphasis][12]

This understanding of tradition lies behind comments like Eco's and a myriad similar assumptions about the possibility of recuperating an authentic medieval experience, through the visitation of medieval sites, the reading of medieval manuscripts, or walking through medieval cathedrals. This appeal to the authentic as much forms part of scholarly discourse as it drives the tourist experience, though the scholar is typically more of a purist about the distinction between the medieval and the post- or quasi-medieval. I argue, however, that in the case of medieval tourist sites, with their variable mix of continuous use and the effects of historical change, the distinction rapidly becomes blurred, with profound, and sometimes disturbing, effects on our hard-won scholarly identity.

As a consequence of these diverse interests in medieval religious sites, we can distinguish different kinds, or degrees, of investment amongst both visitors and custodians or guardians of their heritage. The work of Pierre Bourdieu offers the neatest formulations of the complexities here:

[11] For example, see Dean MacCannell, *The Tourist: A New Theory of the Leisure Class* (New York, 1976, 1989); and Alison J. McIntosh and Richard C. Prentice, 'Affirming Authenticity: Consuming Cultural Heritage', *Annals of Tourism Research*, 26.3 (1999), 589–612.
[12] Dell Upton, '"Authentic" Anxieties', in Nezar AlSayyad (ed.), *Consuming Tradition, Manufacturing Heritage: Global Norms and Urban Forms in the Age of Tourism* (London, 2001), 298–306: 300.

we can distinguish different kinds and degrees of cultural capital being negotiated and distributed, while also thinking about the ways in which academics, historians, and the clergy bring 'distinction' on themselves, through their response to, or management of these sites.

The Canterbury Tales

The Canterbury Tales Visitor Attraction in Canterbury is the most specialized of all the sites I discuss in this paper, since the whole museum is dedicated to the realization of selected Tales; that is, the narrative and contextual frame of just one medieval text. This specialization alone demands a detailed reading, but because the Canterbury show thematizes the activities of medieval and medievalist tourism and pilgrimage to a sacred site, it is a particularly fitting starting-point.

The Canterbury Tales[13] is housed in what was formerly the parish church of St Margaret in the city of Canterbury, though the building was not used as a church after suffering extensive bomb damage in World War II. In 1987 it was purchased by Heritage Projects (the company that also designed the Yorvik Centre at York), who established the current exhibition. It is a deconsecrated site, but nevertheless one that celebrates and enacts a religious ritual, interpellating its visitors as virtual pilgrims to the Cathedral.

Visitors queue up in the street outside St Margaret's, and assemble into small groups, who walk together through a series of chambers, first clustering around a life-size model of Chaucer at the Tabard Inn, who warms his hands by the fire, while a voice audible through one's hand-held speaker sets the scene for the visit. The voice is that of an old man looking back in solitude: Chaucer tells us how the Host organized the pilgrims into a story-telling competition. The retrospective nature of the scene constructs history unambiguously as a form of nostalgia, and thus eases its visitors into a comfortable state of familiarity with the presentation of history as personal, authentic memory. The visitors then walk through a vividly realized street scene, representing Borough High Street, Southwark. They make their own pilgrimage, as it were, though various darkened passages and chambers, with lights and sound springing to action when the group is assembled in each chamber to hear a tale *en route*. The

---

[13] Unless otherwise specified, I use this phrase here to refer to the Visitor Attraction, not Chaucer's poem.

timing of each group's stay in each chamber is carefully monitored: doors open invitingly onto the next scene, while the Host's voice also encourages them on.

The Host briefly outlines the characters and appearance of the five pilgrims whose tales are told—Knight, Miller, Nun's Priest, Wife of Bath, and Pardoner—while the tales themselves are performed in varying ways. Stained-glass windows, lit up and darkened in sequence, illuminate the *Knight's Tale*; and a rowdy series of life-size wooden or plaster figures moves dynamically, with a rowdy clatter, in and out of windows for the *Miller's Tale*; while the *Pardoner's Tale* display makes dramatic use of lighting to heighten the cavernous cheeks of the Pardoner and the haunting face of the Old Man. The narratives are wonderfully condensed, though, as we might expect, this condensation comes at the cost of most of their distinctive literary and rhetorical qualities. The medieval specialist or student wanting to hear Chaucerian English will be sadly disappointed. Textual subtlety gives way to narrative plot and visual pleasure in these retellings.

After the last tale, the visitors pass through the Westgate Towers of Canterbury and into another street scene. Strolling through the Market Place at Canterbury, we see fishmongers, souvenir sellers, and so forth, and are invited to marvel at a piece of crude dentistry being performed as we pass: here the 'medieval' clearly signifies the pre-modern and the pre-technological. All the street scenes and the tableaux themselves are finished to a high degree of verisimilitude; they have clearly been made with great attention to detail, and cannot easily be faulted on the grounds of historical accuracy. The plastic artefacts of clothing, building, and daily life are more easily translated for immediate consumption than texts of Middle English. When visitors reach the high point of the pilgrimage, the Cathedral itself is suggested by another marvellous piece of condensation: visitors stand in front of a model of the famous effigy of Edward the Black Prince, interred in the Cathedral, and look beyond that to a 'reconstruction' of the Shrine of St Thomas à Becket (the original was destroyed in the Reformation), both guarded by a blue-lit image of the saint himself.

As the commentary makes clear, we are but a stone's throw from the Cathedral, on the other side of the High Street, while our pilgrimage from Southwark to Canterbury, to the shrine of St Thomas, has imitated the pilgrimage made by so many others, framed by the other distinctive aspect of tourism: consumerism. Emerging into the area of the bookshop, gift shop, and café, we are asked to choose, by placing a bead counter in a clear perspex tube, which tale we enjoyed the most, bringing a kind of closure to the competition that Chaucer was unable to do. For the record, the day I visited, the *Wife of Bath's Tale* was the clear winner.

The Canterbury Tales Attraction depends heavily on a sense of place, and a condensed virtual 'pilgrimage' through its darkened chambers and streetscapes, towards its own holy of holies, the Cathedral and the shrine of St Thomas. It successfully mediates the potential contradiction between pilgrimage as a spiritual journey and tourism as a secular, spectacular, and commercial concern.

The text of the *Official Guide* plays an important role in re-enforcing the mutual imbrication of pilgrimage and tourism, articulating a subtle relationship between the two, in ways that allow the reader a choice of positions with which to identify. Initially, the *Guide* readily embraces the more generalized, secular sense of 'pilgrimage':

After the death of Canterbury's most famous archbishop, Thomas Becket, the city began to attract visitors who came on a journey of public penance. For those unable to travel as far as Jerusalem or Rome a pilgrimage to the shrine of a great saint might, they believed, effect a cure or miracle, or bestow virtue upon the penitent. . . .

To visit the splendid cathedral, wander through historic streets, to shop and sightsee is to follow in the footsteps of countless visitors.[14]

The spiritual dimension of pilgrimage is firmly identified, yet isolated and distanced as an anthropological curiosity ('pilgrimage might, they believed, effect a cure . . . '), while the *Guide* also invites its readers to embrace the idea of historical continuity around the more secular and attractive tourist activities of sightseeing and shopping, of walking through 'the splendid cathedral', presented here primarily as a spectacle, rather than a holy place. Yet the *Guide* also describes the Pilgrim's Way, and includes pictures of modern backpackers walking with staffs, heading towards Canterbury, and attending a candlelit service in the Cathedral. Such images allow secular tourists a means of acknowledging the seriousness with which some 'others' still treat the idea of pilgrimage.

Nevertheless, the text reassures those who are not making a religious pilgrimage that there are other reasons for coming to Canterbury: it certainly avoids the assumption that we are all simple tourists, interested in spectacle alone. Michael Harkin, among others, stresses that most

---

[14] *The Canterbury Tales Official Guide* (Canterbury, n.d.), 3.

cultural tourists resist such an identification.[15] Any anxiety of this kind is gently assuaged by the *Guide*:

> . . . as Chaucer wryly observed, people then—as now—came to Canterbury for many different reasons. They came as an expression of faith or simply to 'get away from it all'.[16]

The modern visitor is interpellated as one who is seeking knowledge, while also wanting to identify in very particular and restricted ways with medieval customs. Again, this consolatory strategy allows visitors to transcend their own modernity, with its habitual scepticism.[17] The pressure of such anxiety is eased by the *Guide*'s assimilation of modern sensibilities into an accessible medieval world-view. This comment about Chaucer is given very little supporting evidence, but it does appeal to a familiar image of the poet—making a 'wry observation' that is little more than a generalization. The historical dimension is introduced, only to be immediately collapsed in an easy, anachronistic universalism: 'getting away from it all'.

In a later discussion of pilgrimage, the *Guide* once more treads this delicate line between embracing continuity with the medieval past and acknowledging the modern, more secular interests of its visitors. As a tourist attraction built around a specific medieval spiritual practice, it claims a second-order level of consecration, in Bourdieu's terms, to reinforce its own cultural centrality and heritage value, without alienating those who do not actually share the beliefs commemorated in the Cathedral.[18] It does so by holding together the potential contradiction between the diversity of people's needs and the apparently universal character of pilgrimage. Again, the *Guide* comments:

> the character of pilgrimage has changed over time. Where piety may have been the motivating force to begin with, in medieval times it provided a means of escape from the restrictions of feudal society. Pilgrimages became holidays and pilgrims became tourists, eager to satisfy a desire for travel and new experiences.[19]

---

[15] Michael Harkin, 'Modernist Anthropology and Tourism of the Authentic', *Annals of Tourism Research*, 22.3 (1995), 650–70: 653.

[16] *Canterbury Tales Official Guide*, 3.

[17] Harkin comments that 'an anxiety about authenticity pervades the tourism experience, and reflects the perceived inauthenticity of modern life' ('Modernist Anthropology', 653).

[18] I borrow the term 'consecration' from Pierre Bourdieu, but it is doubly appropriate here for its sense of the added layer of religious or spiritual significance. See especially his 'The Market of Symbolic Goods', *Poetics*, 14 (1985), 13–44.

[19] *Canterbury Tales Official Guide*, 7.

It is a very familiar, even prototypically modernist construction of feudal-ism as a set of constraints from which the 'natural' urge is to escape. In an-other neat collapse of historical distinctions, the commentary naturalizes, even praises, the 'desire for travel and new experiences' with which the modern tourist easily identifies. But the impulse towards diversity, sanc-tioned earlier by no less an authority than Chaucer himself, is closed down, in the final comment in this section. 'Noblemen and common folk, they came from many different backgrounds with but one aim— "To be a pilgrim".' This last quote is particularly fascinating: it is pre-sented here as a reprise from the fuller quotation from Sir Steven Runciman, ' "The desire to be a pilgrim is deeply rooted in human nature" '; but it surely evokes for many readers John Bunyan's famous hymn, whose stirring lyrics have echoed through countless British and Commonwealth school assemblies.

The tour guide and the voiced commentary at the show itself cover all bases. Simultaneously conscious of the historical difference between then and now, they also allow the visitor to identify with all or part of their rep-resentation of medieval tourism and pilgrimage. They naturalize the very idea of pilgrimage as tourism, and the idea of consumerism associated with such sites, giving it a long and honourable history. In the Canterbury Tales' insistence on the importance of place, these commentaries also jus-tify the importance of the show's location in Canterbury.

Yet the show also undermines its own dependence on place. Its struc-turing ideology, after all, is predicated on the idea of a pilgrimage: it com-mences by imaginatively transporting its visitors back to Southwark, and so disrupts—by means of the deliberate defamiliarization produced by the black-outs—any immediate sense of location. Similarly, while the show is located in a medieval church, the visitors' experience of the build-ing *qua* church is limited to the wait outside the walls, themselves faced with flints in the nineteenth century, 'giving it a characteristically Victo-rian appearance'.[20] Once inside, there is no sense of the building as a sa-cred space; its original architecture and topography are completely overlain and overrun by the exigencies of the dramatic performance and the necessities of the black-out, to transport us back into the past, and to fourteenth-century Southwark and Canterbury. In the *Guide's* schema-tized map of the site, we see the split levels of the Tales themselves, and the 'route' followed up and down and round about the building, while the Norman bell-tower is renamed 'The Control Tower', with an image of a

---

[20] Ibid. 13.

technician seated before a computer terminal controlling the lighting and puppetry below.

As a representation of Chaucer's texts, there is no doubt that the show is dramatically thin: the Chaucerian expecting a nuanced reading of the interplay between irony and allegory would be bitterly disappointed. While the retellings are not dramatically 'untrue' to the spirit of Chaucer's text, the stories are stripped of much, though not all, of their philosophical depth and rhetorical colour. The poet himself appears as a snuffling old man warming himself by the fire, and I, at least, was relieved when his wheezy old voice was displaced by the more lively conversation of the Host and the dramatic characters of the pilgrims. The professional medievalist's confidence is not inspired, though, by the brochure, which I read as I waited for my group's turn to enter, with its staggering misquotation of Chaucer:

> 'From every shires ende
> of Engelond to Canterbury they wende,
> the hooly blisful martir for to seke,
> That hen hath holpen that they were seeke. [*sic*]

It would be naïve to expect a sophisticated post-colonial or queer Chaucer, of course, and perhaps unreasonable to expect to hear Chaucer's own words in the retelling, but it is not unreasonable to expect an accurately quoted text. The Attraction's chief mission, though, is one of popular entertainment: if it is organized around a literary figure from high culture, that figure is heavily mediated by his eighteenth-century reputation as a comic poet of human frailty and sexual cheer. It came as no surprise, searching the various British tourist sites for references to the Attraction, to find the pilgrims described as an 'unforgettably rumbustious' band. But this image is just one of many: the signifier 'Chaucer' can be pressed into the service of a number of agendas and cultural associations. A page from the Outdoor Britain site lists Chaucer first in their 'Be Inspired' section, with a side link: 'Are you a fan of Chaucer? Then why not get out and enjoy the wonders of the countryside that inspired him? The North Downs Way National Trail follows for a part the route that the pilgrims may have taken.'[21]

This picks up on the very familiar idea of Chaucer as a national poet of nature, landscape, and Englishness. It also licenses readerly passions and

---

[21] <http://www.visitbritain.com/uk/outdoorbritain/get_inspired/poets_authors/chaucer. htm., accessed 3 Jan. 2003.

welcomes visitors, by virtue of their knowledge and love of Chaucer, to claim their cultural heritage. The flattening effect of the World Wide Web is evident here: another link on this page, to 'Very British Activities', or 'Quirky Events', offers these options: 'Experience the beauty of Britain's countryside by snorkelling through a bog, or chasing cheese down a hill.' These sites are crucial for the cultural bridge of transition they offer to international tourists. Where Chaucer's text mentions pilgrims coming merely 'From every shires ende of Engelond', tourism sites like the Canterbury Tales Attraction also need to attract international visitors. This one delicately negotiates the appeal of the familiar with information for the less familiar, or those less strongly identified with Britain's cultural heritage. Mention of the 'quirky' activities of bog snorkelling or cheese chasing taps into the familiar trope of the eccentric English, reassuring for anyone in danger of feeling awed by Britain's cultural heritage or suffering the agonies of cultural cringe.

Returning to the question of pilgrimage, however, The Canterbury Tales is a perfect site for cultural tourism, as it offers the ready-made possibility of historical otherness combined with the easy entertainments of bawdy or moralizing narrative. We can pay homage to Chaucer from a modernist perspective, while also participating in a genuinely medieval activity. We need look no further than the anonymous *The Tale of Beryn* for a fifteenth-century account of Canterbury pilgrims, touring the Cathedral and staring up at its stained-glass windows, and collecting souvenirs. The Canterbury Tales show thematizes and authorizes a very similar notion of cultural tourism around the theme of pilgrimage to a medieval cathedral, while also tapping into a well-recognized cultural icon: the image of Geoffrey Chaucer.

'Recovering the Calm': Tourist Management

Cathedrals and churches are far from silent, passive monuments, to be consumed by either the tourist or the scholarly gaze. Nor do they bear much relationship to the modern interpretative museum, where visitors are encouraged to make their own narratives. Medieval churches that are still in use as places of worship are governed by a range of constraints that are given very practical, material form by the chapters, colleges, or parishes that maintain them. Larger churches have developed elaborate programmes and plans to direct the movement of tourist traffic, to sequester various parts of the church from the more casual visitor, and to regulate the flow of visitors, especially at service times. Tea-rooms, souvenir stalls, bookshops, and gift shops are similarly subject to careful management plans. More subtly, too, the demeanour of the attendants, and the many notices and signs, all work to mediate the tourist visit.

In his discussion of tourism and ritual, Michael Harkin comments:

> tourism is, rather, precisely a desacralization, not merely in the most obvious sense of the tourist tramping through Gothic cathedrals, but rather in the project as a whole, the object of which is precisely to appropriate alterity. Ritual constitutes an irreducible otherness, tourism negates otherness altogether.[22]

Harkin invokes the easy target of the tourist 'tramping through Gothic cathedrals' to exemplify his first, most 'obvious' sense of desacralization, but this is radically to simplify the visitors' experience of such places, and to assume a misleadingly homogeneous tourist identity. As the *Canterbury Tales Guide* makes quite clear, not all tourism negates otherness absolutely. There is a whole series of varied negotiations that cultural tourists and modern scholars, both Christian and non-Christian, make for themselves in such sites, while 'otherness' is also a much less absolute quality for many visitors. Historical knowledge or curiosity still renders these sacred sites of deep cultural, and sometimes emotional interest—even if visitors do not all come to worship—while even the least interested visitor simply does walk and talk and behave differently in such places, either under the influence of the general atmosphere or admonished by guides or parents.

As Eco suggests, walking or praying in the naves of medieval cathedrals can imply an experience closely resembling a medieval one; it seems possible here to construct a fantasy of medieval presence, of aesthetic, spiritual, or cultural continuity. Everything we know about the phenomenology of built space tells us that to walk the naves of medieval cathedrals must be a distinctive experience. The very scale and design of their arches and buttresses, their symbolic orientation and topography, the visible and tangible signs of their history, all produce a powerful impact on the visitor. But of course, such an experience will always be a mixed one. Most cathedrals are themselves architectural and social accretions, and most bear signs of radical or minor rebuilding, reconstruction, the vicissitudes of war, or of religious reform—especially in England—and changes in fashion. They are hung with the flags of past wars and the trophies of Empire, so they play an important role in the way a nation

---

[22] Harkin, 'Modernist Anthropology', 655.

imagines itself as a community of shared interests; they feature statuary and monuments from later centuries; as well as appeals for famine relief and other signs of use by the modern church community. The music heard there is rarely medieval, and sometimes features women's voices, for example, while the English prayers offered up bear little relation to those of medieval Catholicism. For the tourist, and for the medieval scholar, these signs of modernity are strictly controlled and framed by the overall significance of the cathedral as a site of pilgrimage and heritage, but they do, all the same, need to be negotiated in order to produce the symbolic import of the visit.

Sometimes the negotiations are quite complex. Lincoln Cathedral offers a radical rereading of one of its famous medieval monuments. Next to the shrine of Little Saint Hugh, a notice-board reads:

Trumped up stories of 'ritual murders' of Christian boys by Jewish communities were common throughout Europe during the Middle Ages and even much later. These fictions cost many innocent Jews their lives. Lincoln had its own legend, and the alleged victim was buried in the Cathedral in the year 1255.

Such stories do not redound to the credit of Christendom, and so we pray:
Lord, forgive us what we have been,
amend what we are,
and direct what we shall be.

The Cathedral's recognition that the Church's Christian legacy is a mixed one, and that the patterns and practices of Christian belief are mutable, not only reminds us that we are 'walking' in a modern institution whose history is in fact a history of change, but makes the important concession that change is value-laden. Such a notice 'teaches' the visitor something about medieval anti-Semitism, and about the Church's willingness to correct its past; it is a powerful reminder that the Cathedral is not simply a place of tourist visitation or even simply scholarly research, that it actively reaches out to the visitor to invite their involvement. However, the 'we' here is problematic. Is the speech-act 'and so we pray' constative (*when we pray, this is what we say*)? Or does it have performative force (*Let us pray*)? It is a most productive ambiguity, forcing the issue for the medieval scholar. What is it we want the past to teach us, and how? If the Church itself has already developed its own internal critique of its past, what role is left to the scholar or even the tourist interested in medieval history? How can he or she recover an 'authentic' sense of medieval anti-Semitism when the tomb is so clearly marked as a lesson from the past, speaking to present concerns in ways which are profoundly ahistorical, but which take for granted the idea that history can indeed 'teach' us things about ourselves?[23]

Even if we confine ourselves to the search for architectural or archaeological authenticity, the medieval monuments in such sites are rarely offered in a pure, unmediated form.[24] Sometimes it is the exigencies of conservation and preservation that moderate our access to medieval artefacts, even when they survive in their original sites. In Canterbury Cathedral, the Black Prince's tomb is placed in the Trinity Chapel, while his achievements—his helm and crest, surcoat, shield, gauntlets, and his scabbard—hang above his tomb. But these are replicas. Interestingly, however, they are neither as shabby and worn in appearance as the originals, preserved in a glass case below the tomb, in the crypt, nor as bright in colour as if they were brand new: the replicas simulate age and antiquity, but are far more legible as heraldic icons than the real items.

Because they are governed not simply by curators, but by chapters and parishes, medieval cathedrals have a complex mission, when it comes to balancing the needs of tourists, or visitors interested in heritage or history, with the needs of those who come to worship. In the cities of London, York, and Canterbury, where there are so many visitors, cathedrals, churches, and abbeys must develop elaborate plans by which to direct the traffic, control crowds and noise, and encourage various behavioural patterns and responses in their visitors.

One of the most problematic examples of medieval tourism of this kind is Westminster Abbey. It is one of the most famous tourist sights, and one of the most public places in London; it is deeply entrenched in the national consciousness as the site of coronations, royal weddings, and funerals; it remains an important site for commemoration of many kinds, and also for scholarly research. It is also the most extensively 'managed' of medieval religious sites; its crowded chapels and naves force the visitor to confront the potential contradiction between tourism and pilgrimage.

Like most such buildings, the Abbey's administration is torn between the rival impulses to attract visitors while also protecting the Church's life of prayer. It does this by establishing a hierarchical order of places open to the public at various times, as a means of regulating the paths of its visitors, and keeping some parts closed to tourists. Most notably, the shrine

---

[23] My thanks to Elizabeth Allen for helping me formulate these questions.

[24] In Tony Bennett's formulation, it is 'a truism . . . whose implications are significant', that 'the past, as it is materially embodied in museums and heritage sites, is inescapably a product of the present which organizes it' (*The Birth of the Museum: History, Theory, Politics* (London, 1995), 129).

of Edward the Confessor is sequestered away from the tourist gaze completely. According to John Field, author of *A Historical Guide to Westminster Abbey*, it 'remains, appropriately, a mystery apart, unvisited, but glimpsed between other royal tombs'.[25]

The history of many of the Abbey's other medieval artefacts is a mixed one. The rival tombs of Elizabeth I and Mary Queen of Scots attract more attention than the more humble tombs of the Plantagenets, for example, while the Coronation Chair is now displayed with a gaping hole where the Stone of Scone lay until its removal to Edinburgh Castle in 1996, whence it will return to the Abbey only for coronations. The stone's abduction by Ian Hamilton and others in 1950 is now part of the Abbey's history, while viewers of the Scottish television series 'Hamish MacBeth' will also experience a double *frisson* of modernity and familiarity when they recall the Stone's role in the series' mystical concluding episode.

As Field remarks: 'The Abbey cannot survive without the visitors who threaten to wear it out.'[26] He describes the programme put in place in 1997 by the Dean and Chapter, called 'Recovering the Calm', as a means of controlling the tourist-led chaos that threatened the tranquillity of the Abbey. Field attempts to make concessions to the 'up to three million visitors a year, the vast majority of whom do not attend a service and are not practising Christians', but in fact, his tone is somewhat condescending as he describes the reforms.[27] After 1997, visitors must pay to enter the Abbey, he says, but they are 'calmed' by the 'psychologically shrewd' preliminaries of their visit and their 'high quality ticket and brochure bearing the gilded image of Edward the Confessor from the Litlyngton Missal', and the fact of being channelled at a slower pace into the Abbey. Moreover, 'Many visitors are calmed further by the handsets they carry, like blessed one-way mobile phones, as intent as if they are listening to God direct.'[28]

A similar tone is evident in William Swatos's account of the management of visitors to services such as Evensong in St Paul's Cathedral. Many visitors want to be more than casual sightseers and wish to take part in the service, but are not familiar with the elaborate conventions of Anglican worship. Accordingly, the printed order of service contains directions for when to stand, sit, or kneel. Swatos attempts to examine the 'interplay' between 'various levels of pilgrimage and tourism' in various London

---

[25] John Field, *Kingdom Power and Glory: A Historical Guide to Westminster Abbey* (1996; 2nd edn. London, 1999), 150.
[26] Ibid. 149.   [27] Ibid. 148.   [28] Ibid. 150.

churches, but in fact his rhetoric is more comfortable distributing a hierarchy of those who are more and less familiar with the practices of the church:

Virtually all of the participants follow the printed directions regarding standing and sitting, but the majority will not kneel, notwithstanding the kneeling pads (which some attendees use instead as back supports)—though perhaps the most curious posture, seen on rare occasions, is those in the crossing who kneel facing into their chairs, rather than toward the altar.

Such comments not only reveal the perspective of the custodians of medieval churches and their sense that tourist or visitor behaviour can and should be regulated or modified; Field and Swatos also betray the superior understanding of the insider, comfortably demonstrating their own familiarity with Anglican rituals and the 'proper' understanding of its monuments, assumed to be well beyond the majority of visitors. A more interesting question might be the interrogation of this refusal, or unwillingness, to kneel, to adopt such a very unmodern bodily gesture: we can read this, perhaps, as an embodied marker of the limits to the modern empathy with the medieval.[29]

Restricted Access

While the official discourse of most large English churches is more welcoming to a range of visitors, there is an important subset of smaller churches and private chapels, in the care of the monarchy or the aristocracy, where the possibilities for the visitor are much more limited. One of the most dramatic cases in point is St George's Chapel at Windsor Castle, the home of the Order of the Garter. Once a year, in June, the annual procession takes place from the Castle to the Chapel: it is one of the highlights of the year for the substantial enterprise of royal tourism. Membership of the Order is still limited to the Queen, the Prince of Wales, and twenty-four Knights Companion and a small number of Stranger (i.e. non-English) Knights; so entry to the Chapel on this day is restricted to the thousand or so guests of the Order. However, the grounds of the Castle are crowded with visitors, who come, not to worship, but to

---

[29]   In this example, Swatos is writing of St Paul's Cathedral, not a medieval building at all, but his observations about the behaviour of visitors are applicable to most cathedrals, whatever their architecture.

watch the elaborate procession of those who do enter the chapel, according to an elaborate hierarchy of members of the royal household, the military knights of Windsor, the Officers of Arms, the Knights and Ladies of the Garter, other members of the royal family, the Officers of the Order, including Black Rod, and other officials. It is a colourful procession, dominated by the deep blue velvet robes, with gold and red trimmings, and the distinctive white ostrich feathers on the caps of the Companions. This is not a completely open event: tickets for the day must be requested from the College of Arms, and the crowds are predominantly English fans of the royal family, the self-styled 'real Royalists'.[30] In her important study of these royal-watchers, Anne Rowbottom describes their activities as a kind of 'civil religion'.

After the procession has passed, a picnic atmosphere develops amongst the crowds waiting on the grass. The service is broadcast over the grounds, but it is almost impossible to catch more than a faint murmur of voices and muted singing. The crowds wait, however, to witness the return to the Castle, though the Companions do not walk, but make the uphill journey in cars or carriages.

Like many royal rituals, the annual procession at Windsor does not represent any long medieval history. In its current form, the procession dates only from 1948. Nor has the Chapel itself, first established in 1475 (superseding an older chapel built by Henry III), enjoyed continuous use. When the body of Charles I was brought there for burial in 1649, 'no-one remained who belonged to St George's, and the Chapel was "so altered and transformed" by the pulling down of all its familiar landmarks that it was impossible to find the royal vault until an aged poor knight appeared to point it out'.[31]

Nevertheless, the Chapel, like the Order itself, and like many institutions of the English monarchy, offers a subtle mediation between the twinned appeals to continuity (affirming heritage values) and to modernity (affirming contemporary relevance). The guidebook to the Chapel, first published in 1933 but revised in 1992, comments:

The Most Noble Order of the Garter, founded six centuries ago and prayerfully supported through the years by the College of St George, reminds us of the aims and ideals of those far off days of chivalry, which are in their essence in no way

---

[30] Anne Rowbottom, '"The Real Royalists": Folk Performance and Civil Religion at Royal Visits', *Folklore*, 109 (1998), 77–88: 85.
[31] A. K. B. Evans, 'St George's Chapel, Windsor, 1348–1975', *History Today*, 25.5 (1975), 360.

inappropriate to modern times, and which should be, by present generations, by no means forgotten.[32]

'Present generations', of course, is deceptively inclusive and modern: membership of the Order is not open to anyone not already a peer.

It is easy to forget that many important medieval monuments are not so publicly accessible as those in the great cathedrals. Like manuscripts, many are held in private collections, or form part of private chapels, or are chapels in the royal residences with restricted public access. During the course of some research into the Order of the Garter, I visited the church of Stanton Harcourt, in Oxfordshire, which contains one of two surviving fifteenth-century effigies of women wearing their insignia around the forearm or upper arm, instead of around the left calf, as male Companions do.[33] As a parish church, St Michael's was open to visitors, but the tombs of Margaret Byron and her husband Sir Robert Harcourt were firmly locked away, with other family tombs, behind an iron grille. Once I had been directed towards the village, to the front door of the lady of the manor, the Hon. Mrs Gascoigne, I had to explain why I wanted to photograph her family's tomb. Deeply conscious of my jeans and Australian accent, and never having met a member of the English nobility before, I nervously explained what I wanted to see and why. She was at first reluctant—'It's private, you see', she explained—and there were one or two races at Ascot which she needed to watch first. However, once she joined me at the church and unlocked the grille, she was all courtesy and helpfulness, even encouraging me to climb up and lean over Sir Robert so that I could inspect the garter draped above the left elbow of Lady Margaret.

This episode, and my visit to Windsor, made a huge impression on me, reminding me that in spite of Britain's magnificent public institutions, its libraries and cathedrals, the ruling élite still governs and maintains many of its medieval religious resources very firmly in private hands. If we are scholars, if we are lower or middle class, and perhaps especially if we are foreigners, we do not 'own' this heritage in the same way as we can enter a cathedral, though our recognition of its significance is crucial. I related my adventures to my New Zealand colleague Kim Phillips, who commented astutely, 'Yes, it's not *for* you', she said, 'but they need you all the same.'

---

[32] Peter J. Begent, *The Romance of St George's Chapel, Windsor Castle* (1st edn. by H. W. Blackburne, 15th edn. 1933; rev. Peter J. Begent, Windsor: Friends of St George's Chapel, 1992), 14.

[33] The other effigy is part of the beautiful double tomb of Alice Chaucer, Duchess of Suffolk, at St Mary's Church, Ewelme, also in Oxfordshire.

Post-modern Medievalism

In the examples considered so far, I have distinguished between different kinds of visitors, institutions, and kinds and degrees of management and custodianship of medieval churches, cathedrals, and chapels. In this final section, I want to compound the complex act of walking in cathedrals by introducing the troubling perspectives of post-modernism. At the risk of solipsism, my concern here is principally with academic subjects: medievalists walking through cathedrals. At every level—architectural, historical, and conceptual—we do not enter the same Gothic cathedrals as Coleridge did. We observe our own responses just as he did; but we are more likely to observe the contradictions in our own desires, and our own histories, as we approach the sacred things of the medieval past, just as we are conscious of the mixed histories of the buildings through which we walk. Our experiences, then, are strategic and hybrid, rather than naturalized, or given.[34] Despite the easy appeal of my epigraph from Umberto Eco, there is little straightforward cultural continuity in the experience of walking through medieval cathedrals, perhaps especially for medievalists, so well trained to distinguish what is authentically medieval from its post-medieval accretions or imitations. In all likelihood, it is easier for non-specialists to experience or imagine a form of continuity with the medieval past.

This essay concludes with two examples which give material or cinematic form to the dialectic of post-modern medievalism. The obvious architectural example of hybridity is the cultural translation displayed in the Cloisters Museum in Fort Tryon Park, part of the Metropolitan Museum of Art in New York. The cloisters of Saint-Guilhem, St-Michel de Cuxa, Bonnefont, and Trie were 'collected' by George Grey before 1914, and were bought by the Museum, with funds donated by John D. Rockefeller, Jr, in 1925. Rockefeller also presented to the City the land on which the Cloisters Museum stands, overlooking the Hudson River in Upper Manhattan, while also reserving the land around the Museum to protect its views and vistas from development.

The Cloisters Museum presents a very privileged form of cultural tourism. In these very selective reconstructions, the curators have

---

[34] I borrow the formulations of Dell Upton, who proposes a strategic—even hybrid—understanding of concepts such as 'the authentic' and its relation to ideas of identity, heritage, and tradition: 'Individuals routinely shift from one cultural position to another, adopt one identity or another, as occasion demands. Sites likewise seem to take on varying colourations according to the angle from which one views them' ('"Authentic" Anxieties', 300).

stripped the stones of all post-medieval traces, planted gardens, and piped appropriate music through strategically placed speakers. The mixture of the technological and the 'real' encourages visitors to project themselves into the imagined past of these medieval spaces, whether that past is primarily spiritual or historical. What is on offer is a very generalized and open 'alterity': it is the otherness of the medieval, the European, and the religious, in whatever mix appeals to the visitor, but firmly lifted out of the urban routines of Manhattan. Jean Baudrillard describes the Cloisters as 'an artificial mosaic of all cultures', commenting that the proposed 'repatriation' of the cloister of St-Michel de Cuxa, in the name of authenticity, would, rather, be a 'total simulation'.[35]

As Baudrillard remarks, no one is 'fooled' by the Cloisters.[36] Visitors are fully conscious of their artificiality, and are implicitly invited to marvel not only at the spectacle of the site, but at the phenomenon of translation. There is even a second-order degree of nostalgia for a period when such grandiloquent gestures of cultural appropriation were naturalized as a form of social philanthropy, and when a city like New York seemed to need its own set of medieval European buildings. The Cloisters is a very privileged, even an élite museum. Not only is it somewhat difficult of access, well off the main city grid of Manhattan, but its very specialization, and the relative purity of its exhibit, attract a very distinctive kind of visitor, one who already feels at home, we must suspect, in the nave of a cathedral or in the 'cloistered' spaces of medieval studies.[37]

There are a number of ways in which we can use the Cloisters example to read back through the examples I have considered in this essay. First, we can use it to interrogate and challenge the privilege customarily accorded to the link between authenticity and place, or continuous use. The extremely artificial 'use' made of these medieval artefacts permits a rare architectural purity to emerge, even as it strips away the idea of continuous religious community. Second, the Cloisters reminds us that all medieval objects have a reception history which also often involves a history of *translatio*—that is, of cultural movement, whether this is movement across space or time, in the transformation from me-

---

[35] Jean Baudrillard, 'The Precession of Simulacra', in *Simulations*, trans. Paul Foss, Paul Patton, and Philip Beitchman (New York, 1983), 21–2.

[36] Ibid. 22.

[37] Bonnie Young, *A Walk Through the Cloisters*, with photographs by Malcolm Varon (New York, 1979).

dieval Catholic to post-Reformation Anglican ritual, the movement of a predominantly spiritual to a predominantly secular society, or the transition from a privileged aristocratic class to a professional caste of medievalists.

My final example condenses many of these concerns, in a way that is typical of the cinematic medium. Brian Helgeland's post-modern medieval romance, *A Knight's Tale* celebrates the possibilities of play with anachronism and authenticity, particularly in its sound-track, its costume, and its founding premiss, that despite the repeated official insistence on class hierarchy and nobility through birth, a man who is 'noble' at heart can still 'change his stars'. It is a film about 'passing'—as a jousting knight, an aristocrat, a courtly lover; and it is deeply concerned with the importance of class for reading embodied forms of behaviour, especially gesture and language.

Most interesting for my purposes, *A Knight's Tale* also features a number of love scenes set in cathedrals. When the heroine, Jocelyn, and her maid enter Notre Dame in Paris, for example, they pause at the font and cross themselves with holy water. When 'Ulrich von Lichtenstein' (in reality, a humble English thatcher's son named William) enters the cathedral three steps behind them, he too stops and wets his hands, but in order to wash them and to smooth back his hair before pursuing his lady. It is an interesting scene, in that it affirms William's status as an outsider by virtue of his birth (the actor, Heath Ledger, after all, is also an Australian) while also 'showing' us how to behave; how, precisely, to 'walk or pray in the naves of the cathedral'. This scene is also the locus for one of the film's quasi-feminist moments, in one of many instances that invite the modern viewer's empathy. When the lovers begin to quarrel, an officious priest turns up to bid Jocelyn to be quiet, and she retorts loudly, 'Do not shoosh me and spare him!'

Helgeland interpellates his audience as very knowing: we do not need to be medieval historians or scholars to tell the difference between medieval and modern in this film, though if we have read Chaucer's *Canterbury Tales*, or know that there really was an Ulrich von Lichtenstein, we will certainly experience the familiar joys of scholarly expertise.[38] At the same time the film reassures us that the difference between medieval and modern, between 'real' and 'fake', does not really matter: it is just a romantic comedy, after all. This disjunction is played out at a thematic

---

[38] Maurice Keen, *Chivalry* (New Haven and London, 1984), 92–3.

level, too. When the Black Prince formally recognizes Sir Ulrich as a knight, he announces that his 'personal historians' have discovered that William 'truly' is of noble birth. There is a real question in the film as to whether Sir William's new 'patents of nobility' are any more real than those forged for him by Chaucer, but again, the question of textual authenticity takes second place to the question of narrative closure and ideological resolution. The patents, like Chaucer's forgeries, are not dissimilar to modern manuscript facsimiles, whether they are designed, like the Ellesmere facsimile, to protect the original and serve the purposes of scholars, or like the commercial facsimiles produced by Moleiro editions, to conjure up the texture, colours, and 'smells' of the originals.

Many medievalists—and I count myself amongst them—still wish to make a meaningful theoretical and practical distinction between the original and the facsimile, between, say, the Ellesmere manuscript in the Huntington Library and its recent facsimile edition.[39] But this does not mean that facsimiles do not play an important role in medieval scholarship. Which would be the more useful practical guide to medieval textuality? A single leaf of a medieval manuscript, ripped from its original context, sold separately and framed behind glass: the single leaf as fetish for the lost medieval? Or a complete facsimile, produced on a modern press, but presenting a medieval text in its entirety?

Because it is such an embodied and socialized experience, because it has such powerful, if contradictory, historical and dehistoricized effects, walking through cathedrals is a far more complex act than scrutinizing medieval documents. This is not to deny the undoubted *frisson* of holding the manuscript of a beloved poem in our hands for the first time, or to diminish the difficulties of gaining access to some of the more remote or forbidding libraries. One of the chief differences, however, is that when we walk, we walk in such mixed company, so that whether we pray or not, whether we feel we are making a cultural pilgrimage or engaging in 'pure' scholarly research, our experience of the visit is necessarily mediated both by pragmatic policies and by cultural contexts that are beyond our control, that are not really directed at us. It is only rarely that these policies and contexts reflect our professional identity back to us in any familiar way (when we are taken into the cathedral library, for example, or shown around by a guide who recognizes our expertise). Far

---

[39] Nevertheless, it is still possible to see how some of the structures and systems that reify the manuscript start to contaminate the treatment of the copy. The Rare Books librarian in my university library, for example, uses white cotton gloves to handle our copy of the facsimile, as a measure of its rarity and value.

from regretting this impurity, though, I suggest that it is indicative of the more general post-modern condition in which we conduct all our research. Whether we like it or not, there is no 'pure' medieval; there is only medievalism.[40]

University of Melbourne

[40] My thanks to Helen Hickey for research assistance; to Valerie Krips and Kim Phillips for valuable discussion; and to Elizabeth Allen and Tom Prendergast for their astute comments on an earlier draft of this essay.

Framing the Father: Chaucer and Virginia Woolf

Steve Ellis

WOOLF's writing on Chaucer may seem at first sight an occasional and even superficial affair, represented by only one critical piece of any length, the essay on 'The Pastons and Chaucer' that opens *The Common Reader* (1925). This essay indeed shows a curiously limited engagement with Chaucer, the reasons for which I shall trace below; even so, it anticipates in several of its positions a much more complex response that Woolf explores at the very end of her life, in the writing of her final novel *Between the Acts* (1941) and in the critical work she was concurrently pursuing. Here Chaucer becomes the focus for a series of ambivalences that recur throughout Woolf's writing concerning ideas of English nationhood, the relation between the writer and the community, the relation between a canonical literary tradition and writing of more marginal status, and the relation between continuity and historical change. Chaucer is, so to speak, at a point of intersection where these lines of enquiry cross, an enquiry substantially pursued in various drafts of Woolf's late writings that have been published only comparatively recently. I would stress that Woolf's engagement with such issues results in an appraisal of Chaucer that remains generalized and sketchy, and students of Chaucer are unlikely to gain new insight into his work by reading what Woolf has to say about him. This present essay speaks, rather, to students of modern medievalism in extending arguments I have conducted elsewhere into twentieth-century responses to a Chaucerian heritage that is both acknowledged and yet effaced, and Woolf's later thinking about Chaucer presents this duality in a particularly marked form.[1] If the 'Father of

---

[1] See Steve Ellis, *Chaucer at Large: The Poet in the Modern Imagination* (Minneapolis and London, 2000), 66–71, 80–97. For other work on Chaucer and Woolf see Stephanie Trigg, *Congenial Souls: Reading Chaucer from Medieval to Postmodern* (Minneapolis and London, 2002), 186–90; John Ganim, 'Chaucer and Free Love', in Robert M. Stein and Sandra Pierson Prior (eds.), *Reading Medieval Culture: Essays in Honor of Robert W. Hanning on his 65th Birthday* (Notre Dame, Ind., forthcoming).

English Poetry' is ultimately cut down to size in Woolf, some of the ambivalence towards her own father which she explored in her late memoir
A Sketch of the Past (1939–40) extends to Chaucer too, and, as we shall
see, though far less 'pro-medieval' than many of her modernist contemporaries, she ends up concerning herself with Chaucer rather more.[2]

In essence one might summarize Woolf's response to Chaucer as profoundly diachronic; that is, his interest for her lies in where he fits into
(dis)continuities of the literary tradition and nationhood that constantly
engrossed her. In the posthumously published essay 'Reading', written in
1919, Woolf talks about the 'immeasurable avenue' of the English tradition, on which, looking back,

> I could see Keats and Pope . . . and then Dryden and Sir Thomas Browne—hosts
> of them merging in the mass of Shakespeare, behind whom, if one peered long
> enough, some shapes of men in pilgrims' dress emerged, Chaucer perhaps, and
> again—who was it? some uncouth poet scarcely able to syllable his words; and so
> they died away.[3]

If this is one of Woolf's earliest references to Chaucer, those that feature
in her writing towards the end of her life again set him within a sequential
context that she intended to pursue in a critical work provisionally entitled 'Reading at Random', or 'Turning the Page', in which she would 'read
from one end of lit. including biog; & range at will, consecutively'.[4] 'The
Pastons and Chaucer' essay that opens *The Common Reader* also slots
Chaucer into chronological sequence; one of the minority of essays in the
volume that did not have a previous independent existence, it emphasizes
how far Woolf's interest in Chaucer is as a point of origin, both for that
which survives and that which is superseded. If in 'The Pastons and
Chaucer' the latter is emphasized, in Woolf's later work there is a greater
nostalgia for an ongoing Chaucerian presence, though in either case
Chaucer's being made to inaugurate the Woolfian 'ranging at will' con-
textualizes his work in some unusual and significant ways.

---

[2] Virginia Woolf, *A Sketch of the Past*, in *Moments of Being*, ed. Jeanne Schulkind, rev. edn.
(London, 1985), 61–159: 108.
[3] Woolf, 'Reading', in *The Essays of Virginia Woolf*, vol. iii: *1919–1924*, ed. Andrew McNeillie
(London, 1988), 141–61: 142.
[4] *The Diary of Virginia Woolf*, vol. v: *1936–41*, ed. Anne Olivier Bell and Andrew McNeillie
(London, 1984), 318. This project is also contemplated in a diary entry of 13 Jan. 1932, where
Woolf plans 'to go through English literature, like a string through cheese, or rather like some
industrious insect, eating its way from book to book, from Chaucer to Lawrence' (*The Diary
of Virginia Woolf*, vol. iv: *1931–35*, ed. Anne Olivier Bell and Andrew McNeillie (London, 1982),
63).

The extract from 'Reading' above, in which if one 'peers' long enough one may 'perhaps' make Chaucer out behind the massive figure of Shakespeare, suggests that in 1919 Chaucer was an obscure and barely apprehended figure for Woolf, and indeed there is no reason to believe that the reading of him she documents from July 1922 onwards, with 'The Pastons and Chaucer' in mind, is not her first sustained encounter with his work.[5] The results of that encounter, as displayed in *The Common Reader*, are, as I have argued elsewhere, hardly progressive, giving us a simplified and unsophisticated figure based solely on the *Canterbury Tales* who seems to step out of the critical ambience of writers of several generations earlier, notably James Russell Lowell, Woolf's godfather.[6] Chaucer's gift is essentially for narrative: to make us wish 'to learn the end of the story'.[7] With this in mind he will lay no stumbling-blocks or distractions in our path in the shape of complex characterization, moods, or atmospheres; his world is always 'gay and picturesque' (p. 28), eschewing the mysterious and contemplative, his eyes fixed on the 'ordinary things' and 'ordinary people' (p. 32) on the road before him:

Eating, drinking, and fine weather, the May, cocks and hens, millers, old peasant women, flowers—there is a special stimulus in seeing all these common things so arranged that they affect us as poetry affects us, and are yet bright, sober, precise as we see them out of doors. (p. 33)

This investment in 'the life that was being lived at the moment before his eyes', what Woolf goes on to describe as 'the common facts of this very moment of Tuesday, the sixteenth day of April, 1387' (p. 30), earns Chaucer the right to be called, if not the 'Father of English Poetry' (a tag Woolf never in fact uses), then at any rate a progenitor of the novel, which also, at least in its modern form, typically presents 'ordinary intercourse' outside of any moralizing scheme (p. 32). Chaucer's language too is relatively 'ordinary and quiet' and unmetaphorical (p. 33), a fact explained by his linguistic context, as provided by the Paston letters, which is 'matter of fact . . . far better fitted for narrative than for analysis . . . very stiff

[5] *The Diary of Virginia Woolf*, vol. ii: *1920–24*, ed. Anne Olivier Bell and Andrew McNeillie (London, 1978), 185. In a letter of 13 June 1910 written from Canterbury to Saxon Sydney-Turner she notes, 'I have tried, but cant [*sic*] persist' in connection with 'addressing' herself to Chaucer (*The Flight of the Mind: The Letters of Virginia Woolf*, vol. i: *1888–1912*, ed. Nigel Nicolson and Joanne Trautmann (London, 1975), 426).
[6] See Ellis, *Chaucer at Large*, 68; James Russell Lowell, 'Chaucer', in *My Study Windows*, introd. Richard Garnett (London, n.d.), 205–62.
[7] *The Common Reader*, in *The Essays of Virginia Woolf*, vol. iv: *1925–1928*, ed. Andrew McNeillie (London, 1994), [17]-242: 27.

material to put on the lips of men and women accosting each other face
to face': 'in short, it is easy to see, from the Paston letters, why Chaucer
wrote not *Lear* or *Romeo and Juliet*, but the *Canterbury Tales*' (p. 35).

The Common Reader therefore begins with the picture of an exceedingly common writer, his material and style provided by the everyday
things he sees and hears about him, enforced by a 'simple faithfulness to
his own conceptions' (p. 29), and although Woolf at the very end of her
account notes that Chaucer was 'witty, intellectual, French' (p. 33), there
is no illustration of these characteristics in the body of her essay. It is as if
in constructing his work Chaucer had never read a book, had never considered the complexities of human interaction and motivation, had no
philosophical interests, and had not learned to manipulate the 'stiffness'
of his linguistic material through an innovative and prolonged attention
to metrics. He simply went out into the streets and fields and recorded
what he saw. Woolf's essay is typical of many general estimates of Chaucer
in being based solely on the *Canterbury Tales*, as noted above, and there is
no indication that she read *Troilus and Criseyde*, for example, until several
years later, as we shall see; perhaps if she had, she might have felt less sure
about the simplicity of Chaucer's characterization of 'young women' (pp.
28–9). In May 1923, when the Chaucer chapter was already finished,
Woolf admitted to not 'feel[ing] inclined' to read *Troilus and Criseyde* as a
way of exploring the question of 'what happened between Chaucer
and Shakespeare?' (*Diary*, ii. 242). It is remarkable however that the *Tales*
themselves are not enough to allay the ideas of the innocent and the
rudimentary which form the foundations of Woolf's essay.

Such puzzles are partly answered when we see that Chaucer occupies
an incidental place in *The Common Reader*, and indeed in the essay 'The
Pastons and Chaucer' itself, the focus of which is on the first- rather than
the second-named; Chaucer is a pretext not only for establishing the beginning of the journey, which will lead to a much greater literary sophistication, but also for establishing the figure of the common reader
himself, given that the account of Chaucer is framed in the essay by
Woolf's evocation of Sir John Paston's reading of Chaucer, for here the
journey of reading begins too—a new activity of the more private, less
practical self, which baffles members of the previous generation like John
Paston's mother. Reading is an act of compensation for the 'rough, cheer-
less, and disappointing' business of daily life: 'there, on the hard chair in
the comfortless room with the wind lifting the carpet and the smoke
stinging his eyes, [Paston] would sit reading Chaucer, wasting his time,
dreaming' (p. 26). This enigmatic activity of reading is part of what makes

Paston 'one of those ambiguous characters who haunt the boundary line where one age merges in another and are not able to inherit either' (p. 33); ambiguous, that is, in Woolf's re-creation of him from the evidence of the Paston letters.

There are several explanations, therefore, for Woolf's practice of inserting a curiously limited and simplified picture of Chaucer into an account of Sir John Paston. Chaucer is used as a foil for modern supplementation in Woolf's novelistic evocation of the character of Paston, a character far more sophisticated than anything in Chaucer himself, and also as a foil for a new sense of the private self, linked with reading, that emerges more clearly if any sense of Chaucer himself as reader is suppressed, even though the dramatization of the poet as solitary reader is a feature of Chaucer's own work in pre-*Tales* poems like the 'Book of the Duchess' and the 'Parliament of Fowls'. The 'common reader' is empowered above the canonical poet, who is deprived of any literary and intellectual context and even, as we have seen, of any linguistic context beyond that provided by the Pastons. Indeed, after 'The Pastons and Chaucer' we hear far less about the history of reading in *The Common Reader*, with the essays becoming appraisals of the qualities of various authors from Woolf's own point of view; but the first essay has done its job of exemplifying the importance of the 'common reader' in his right 'as Dr. Johnson maintained [to] some say in the final distribution of poetical honours' (p. 19). It is hardly necessary to remark that the fiction of John Paston's immersion in the *Canterbury Tales* is entirely Woolf's own; although the Paston letters do contain an inventory of 'Englysshe Bokes' in the Paston library, this mentions among Chaucer's works solely the 'Parliament of Fowls', the 'Legend of Good Women,' and, ironically, 'a Boke of Troylus'.[8]

Woolf's acquaintance with the Paston family, through their letters, went back a good deal further than that with Chaucer; Gairdner's edition of the letters had been part of what prompted her to write, as early as 1906, 'The Journal of Mistress Joan Martyn', an account of the discovery of a fictional manuscript diary kept in 'the year of our Lord 1480', which details like the *Letters* late-medieval life in a Norfolk family.[9] Joan Martyn, as that family's only literate member, is passionately addicted to reading as well as writing, though on this occasion Lydgate is referred to as her

---

[8]   *The Paston Letters: A.D. 1422–1509*, ed. James Gairdner, 6 vols. (London and Exeter, 1904), vi. 65–6.

[9]   Woolf, 'The Journal of Mistress Joan Martyn', in *The Complete Shorter Fiction of Virginia Woolf*, ed. Susan Dick (London, 1985), 33–62: 41.

reading matter, to the exclusion of Chaucer (pp. 46–7). When Woolf later began planning the opening chapter of *The Common Reader*, the starting-point, as indicated by the earliest references to this in her diary, is significant: 'its [*sic*] my evening with the Pastons. Tonight my reading begins' (*Diary*, ii. 156). The decision to switch from the fiction of a female reader of Lydgate, in the person of Joan Martyn, to a male Paston as a reader of Chaucer, may reflect the long-standing tradition of Chaucer as what G. K. Chesterton called a 'a clubbable fellow or a man's man', an instance of the tradition of Chaucer's male congeniality recently explored in detail in Trigg's *Congenial Souls*.[10] It is also, of course, a carry-over from the brief preface to Woolf's volume, in which, following Dr Johnson, the common reader is relentlessly described as a 'he' (p. 19). Woolf's volume thereafter starts to question traditional accounts of literary history in ways described below, particularly in its mixing of genres, some of which, like domestic letters, afforded one of the few opportunities for women to write.[11]

The Common Reader, then, as a historical survey of (largely) English writing, begins by prioritizing the (male) reader, and then proceeds to the 'orthodox' starting-place with Chaucer, though the treatment of him as literary forebear is anything but orthodox. Chaucer is not invested as the 'Father', nor are we to hear the canonical commonplaces of filial veneration towards him—in other words, we do not then pass in Woolf's history to Spenser. Nor do we pass to Shakespeare, to find his creations anticipated by the *dramatis personae* of Chaucer, as in the famous 'roadside drama' formulation of Kittredge; indeed, to return to 'The Pastons and Chaucer', Woolf is remarkably silent on any part played in the 'gay and picturesque appearance of the medieval world' by the more conspicuous and characterful pilgrims like the Wife of Bath, or Miller, or the Host.[12] Chaucer's characters lack variation and individuality; thus his female figures 'are parts, one feels, of the same personage . . . as she goes in and out of the *Canterbury Tales* bearing different names' (p. 29), a formulation that anticipates Woolf's use of the pilgrims in *Between the Acts* to signify a recurring, stable, and undifferentiated English identity through the ages, discussed below. In *The Common Reader* Woolf's deliberately non-canonical route will take us in the later chapters on English literature by way of prose writers from Hakluyt to Sir Thomas Browne, minor Elizabethan dramatists, the Duchess of Newcastle, Evelyn and Defoe.

---

[10]   G. K. Chesterton, *Chaucer* (London, 1932), 205.
[11]   See Woolf, 'Dorothy Osborne's Letters', in *Essays*, iv. 553–9: 554.
[12]   George Lyman Kittredge, *Chaucer and his Poetry* (Cambridge, Mass., 1915), 154–5.

This eclectic selection will take us to the end of the seventeenth century, and is notable for the way in which, although chronology is observed, the avenue traversed takes us through many different genres, suggesting that a comparative consideration of, for example, poetry, travel-writing, letters, diaries, and so forth is possible. In the opening chapter itself, Chaucer is forced to acknowledge his contiguity and kinship with the more everyday genre of the domestic letter.

This consecutive treatment linked with the multi-genred 'ranging at will' is also part of the scheme for the later *Reading at Random*, as noted above, and represents, as suggested, a subversive and anti-canonical approach to literary history. Stephanie Trigg has remarked on the practice of filleting 'The Pastons and Chaucer' essay for the section on Chaucer alone and reprinting this in author-based critical anthologies, a practice which mitigates the challenging and innovatory qualities of the piece (*Congenial Souls*, 189); but in turn, considering the essay as a whole outside the scheme of *The Common Reader* and, indeed, outside a set of recurring Woolfian preoccupations discussed below, limits our apprehension of what Woolf is doing with or to Chaucer. To read on in *The Common Reader* is to realize that even the restricted merits established for Chaucer in the opening chapter become more severely qualified, and that the Middle Ages generally are indeed only to be 'peered' at.

In her writing Woolf repeatedly celebrates the Renaissance in terms of its drama, its acquaintance with the Greek classics, which give us 'the originals ... of the human species,' where Chaucer gives us merely the 'varieties',[13] the writing of mystery, fantasy, and adventure consequent on seafaring and exploration, and just as significantly that literature of inward exploration in which 'the mind steals off to muse in solitude; to think, not to act; to comment, not to share; to explore its own darkness, not the bright lit-up surfaces of others'.[14] This writing of interiority, practised by Donne, Montaigne, and Sir Thomas Browne, emphasizes the limitations inherent in the 'brightness' or gaiety of Chaucer's outdoor picture. Indeed, throughout Woolf's work the ability to conjure up both the lights and the shadows of one's subject is a key component of the writer's craft, as in her tribute to Henry James's memoirs, full of 'the mellow light which swims over the past ... the shadow in which the detail of so many

---

[13] Woolf, 'On Not Knowing Greek', in *The Common Reader*, 38–53: 42.

[14] Woolf, 'Notes on an Elizabethan Play', in *The Common Reader*, 62–70, 69. Alice Fox's book is compelling confirmation of Woolf's work as a whole 'testifying', in Fox's words, 'to her pleasure in the English Renaissance more than in any other period' (*Virginia Woolf and the Literature of the English Renaissance* (Oxford, 1990), 19).

things can be discerned which the glare of day flattens out, the depth, the richness, the calm, the humour of the whole pageant'.[15] By the side of this, the Chaucerian pageant, 'bright', 'precise', 'out of doors', is crude indeed, and partly explained by the rudeness and harshness of the medieval world which Chaucer sought to compensate in his writing, as John Paston in his reading (p. 33). Especially after reading the Renaissance chapters of *The Common Reader*, Chaucer's work seems indeed a place of infancy, brightly coloured like a child's picture-book, a refuge of innocence located on the farther side of a decisive historical shift. Doubtless here Woolf's account is silently indebted to that whole strain of Victorian–Edwardian infantilization of Chaucer which was so prevalent in her own youth.[16]

Woolf is indeed unusual among many of the major writers of the earlier twentieth century in being able to resist any infatuation with the Middle Ages, the literature of which had for her, as we have seen, a great deal to compensate. Elsewhere, as a civilization of order, unity, orthodoxy, and aesthetic and intellectual clarity—the latter demonstrated by what Ezra Pound called the 'medieval clean line'—the period was a cultural refuge for many of Woolf's contemporaries, including Joyce and T. S. Eliot.[17] For Woolf, the term 'medieval' is practically one of abuse, signalling deprivation and discomfort, as in the description of the Pastons' household above. In a letter to Ethel Smyth of 1940, 'medieval' is synonymous with losing one's electricity, cooking over a fire, and remaining unwashed;[18] the diary of Woolf's trip to France in May 1937 includes a description of the 'sordidly medieval' art of Najac, along with her pronouncement: 'no place for human beings to live in—the middle ages' (*Diary*, v. 88). Apart from Chaucer, her interest in medieval literature is confined to one other writer, Dante, whom she read intermittently throughout her life and whom she seems to see, on one occasion, as occupying a curiously ahistorical continuum of literature in which his 'surpassing' quality 'makes all writing unnecessary'.[19] And in spite of being a

---

[15] Woolf, 'The Old Order', in *The Essays of Virginia Woolf*, vol. ii: *1912–1918*, ed. Andrew McNeillie (London, 1987), 167–76: 168.

[16] See Ellis, *Chaucer at Large*, 46–57; David Matthews, 'Infantilizing the Father: Chaucer Translations and Moral Regulation', *Studies in the Age of Chaucer*, 22 (2000), 93–114.

[17] Ezra Pound, 'Cavalcanti', in *Literary Essays of Ezra Pound*, ed. T. S. Eliot (London, 1960), 149–200: 150.

[18] *Leave the Letters Till We're Dead: The Letters of Virginia Woolf*, vol. vi: *1936–1941*, ed. Nigel Nicolson and Joanne Trautmann (London, 1980), 381; compare her use of the phrase 'mediaeval gloom' in a letter to Dorothy Bussy of Nov. 1939, p. 367.

[19] *The Diary of Virginia Woolf*, vol. iii: *1925–30*, ed. Anne Olivier Bell and Andrew McNeillie (London, 1980), 313.

voracious reader of history, she found 'the dreary middle ages', at least in Michelet's *Histoire de France*, something 'I cannot get on with', and only the later volume 'tolerable'.[20]

It seems likely that Woolf's anti-medievalism was confirmed by the august status which the Middle Ages enjoyed in the period of (male) high modernism, particularly in the patriarchal pieties invoked by Eliot: 'at Dante's time thought was orderly and strong and beautiful . . . the thought behind [Dante's poetry] is the thought of a man as great and lovely as Dante himself: St. Thomas'.[21] Woolf's interest in the everyday documentation of personal experience, the record of 'the common facts' of life itself, finds as we have seen some sustenance in Chaucer ('The Pastons and Chaucer', p. 30), but generally one peers into the medieval gloom in a vain search for the personal record, especially the record of women's lives.[22] Towards the end of the fifteenth century and the 'boundary line where one age merges in another' which John Paston straddles, the knell of the Middle Ages has sounded, emphasized for Woolf by the crucial invention of printing, as we shall see. On the farther side of this boundary is alien and dimly perceived territory, which Woolf shows no inclination to explore. Thus *Orlando*, published in 1928, begins no earlier than the Elizabethan age, when Knole enters the possession of the Sackville family, even though the bulk of the house dates from the mid-fifteenth century. In the third chapter of *A Room of One's Own* (1929) Woolf begins her reconstruction of the suppressed line of female writing again in the Elizabethan age; it may be possible for her to hypothesize a Judith Shakespeare, but surely not a Judith Chaucer.[23]

Alongside these historical preferences, however, Woolf did continue to read Chaucer himself. Thus in 1928 she finally read *Troilus and Criseyde*, as she informs Vita Sackville-West in a letter of 29 December:

I have finished Troilus and Cressida (by Chaucer) and see now that long poems are the only things I want to read—Next Spenser; then Daniel; then Drayton, and so on, down one long road after another, to Cowper . . . to Crabbe; and then?

[20] *The Diary of Virginia Woolf*, vol. i: *1915–19*, introd. Quentin Bell, ed. Anne Olivier Bell (London, 1977), 23, 31, 34.

[21] T. S. Eliot, 'Shakespeare and the Stoicism of Seneca', in *Selected Essays*, 3rd edn. (London, 1951), 126–40: 136.

[22] Although Woolf knew and occasionally socialized with Eileen Power, I have been unable to find evidence so far that the latter's well-known *Medieval People* (1924) was read by Woolf; certainly, its attempt to 'personify' the medieval past seems to have had no appeal to her. See *Medieval People*, 10th edn. (London, 1963), pp. vii–viii.

[23] Woolf, *A Room of One's Own*, in *A Room of One's Own, Three Guineas*, ed. and introd. Morag Shiach (Oxford, 1992), 1–149: 53, 60–2.

Again, in reading Chaucer she has half an eye on where he leads to, and her estimate of him—Tolstoy is 'not a patch on Chaucer!'[24]—again shows how, for all her interest in literature as a chronology, comparative pronouncements are possible that overleap historical context. When she began preparing for *Reading at Random* in the late 1930s, Woolf noted in her diary how much she was 'enjoying' Chaucer; this, together with her new enthusiasm for *Troilus*, might lead us to consider how far the response to Chaucer at the end of her life differs from that in *The Common Reader* (*Diary*, v. 209, 217). We shall indeed find, I shall argue, not only a more complex response to Chaucer, but one that paradoxically reflects some attraction towards the depersonalized, 'anonymous' culture that Chaucer supposedly represents. Here Woolf's belated 'medievalism' makes rather more of Chaucer than, for example, does Eliot, who, with his insistence on the European context of English literature, tends to see Chaucer as little more than a pale reflex of Dante.[25] Eliot's response to the London Blitz in 'Little Gidding' famously takes the form of a homage to canto XV of the *Inferno*; on 13 January 1941, Woolf took time off from revising *Between the Acts* to visit a bomb-damaged London, and recorded in a letter her 'passion for that great city . . . its [*sic*] what, in some odd corner of my dreaming mind, represents Chaucer, Shakespeare, Dickens. Its [*sic*] my only patriotism' (*Letters*, vi. 460; see also *Diary*, v. 353).

A draft of the opening chapter of *Reading at Random*, entitled 'Anon', and a fragment of the second chapter, 'The Reader', are all that survive of the project, dealing with the transition from the Middle Ages to the Renaissance and, more specifically, as Brenda R. Silver notes in the introduction to her edition, with the contrast between 'the communal aspects of early literature' and the 'isolation of the individual writer who emerged' in the later period.[26] This distinction between a medieval literature which, if not always anonymous, nevertheless acts as a mouthpiece for collective tales and traditions and the presentation of a writer's own interiority and individuality is enforced for Woolf by the invention of printing at the end of the fifteenth century: 'the first blow has been aimed at

---

[24] *A Change of Perspective: The Letters of Virginia Woolf*, vol. iii: *1923–1928*, ed. Nigel Nicolson and Joanne Trautmann (London, 1977), 569–70.

[25] See his review of R. K. Root's edition of *Troilus and Criseyde*, 'Chaucer's *Troilus*', *Times Literary Supplement*, 19 Aug. 1926, p. 547.

[26] Brenda R. Silver (ed.), ' "Anon" and "The Reader": Virginia Woolf's Last Essays', *Twentieth Century Literature*, 25 (1979), 356–441: 360.

Anon when the authors [*sic*] name is attached to the book. The individual emerges. His name is Holingshed; his name is also Harrison' ('Anon', p. 385). The book that gives the writer a 'separate existence' also 'brought into being a little group of readers' (p. 389), and here Woolf assigns the birth of the reader proper to a later date than in 'The Pastons and Chaucer': namely, the end of the sixteenth century, by which time private reading, with a wide range of native, European, and classical texts to choose from, is a much more sophisticated activity. And again unlike 'The Pastons and Chaucer', here Spenser, and Spenser's response to Chaucer, is an important focus for Woolf.

Spenser is indeed for Woolf the first modern artist, 'aware of his art as Chaucer was not . . . no longer a wandering voice, but the voice of a man practising an art, asking for recognition, and bitterly conscious of his re- lation [to] the world, of the worlds [*sic*] scorn' (p. 391). Chaucer is seen here as part of the tradition of minstrelsy, and although Woolf acknowl- edges Spenser's veneration of Chaucer, quoting the *Fairie Queene*'s fa- mous homage to the 'well of English undefiled' (IV. ii. 32), she considers this an act of piety *faute de mieux*, the idea of a Chaucerian 'golden age' being Spenser's refuge from and defence against the tremendous and incessant explosion of literature going on around and within him. Chaucer's simplicity—indeed, his 'crudity'—'served as an antidote to [Spenser's] own facility'. In this attraction of opposites, the 'sensuous, sin- uous, dallying' imagination of the later writer is drawn to the 'clear sharp definite' qualities of the *Canterbury Tales*, with its 'real' men and women (pp. 390–1). Thus far, it might seem that we have little progression from *The Common Reader*.

If with the invention of printing 'the individual emerges', the press also 'brought the past into existence', and the Elizabethan writer's conscious- ness of that past. While establishing the native literary tradition, it also showed the impoverishment of that tradition, the 'lack of intellectual ancestry', a pedigree that 'only reached back to Chaucer, to Langland to Wycliffe', and one that writers like Harrison find it difficult to enthuse about (pp. 385–6), or that writers like Spenser enthuse about on escapist or self-deluding grounds. The writer emerges in the sixteenth century into a world of isolation, cut off from the anonymous collective, cut off from any ancestry, though establishing contact with the emerging band of readers. In some notes that Woolf made for *Reading at Random* she ponders discussing the situation of the Elizabethan writer 'who had no literary past; only read classics in translation'. This note is followed immediately by another note in question form: 'Did Shakespeare read

Chaucer?' (p. 378). The question, hardly difficult of answer, is in fact never treated in her discussion; perhaps this is because Woolf had no real interest in it, and no conviction that Shakespeare's reading of Chaucer would have been of any use to him.[27]

In contrast to *The Common Reader*, there is no sustained writing on Chaucer in *Reading at Random*, but what there is is congruent with the positions in the earlier work. In the later discussion, however, Chaucer is largely subsumed within the figure of 'Anon': 'during the silent centuries before the book was printed his was the only voice that was to be heard in England' ('Anon', 383). Anon/Chaucer is a 'common voice singing out of doors' (p. 382), partly because the medieval indoors was again such an inhospitable place, as Woolf noted in an early draft: 'they were out of door songs, because there was no comfort indoors, little light, and no books'. When Anon speaks to us via the vehicle of 'crude early dramas', these works, like Chaucer's, 'have the power to make us ask . . . the childs [*sic*] question: what comes next?' The association of the medieval artist with the child is also carried over from 'The Pastons' essay:

that babbling, child like, story telling singer, that gossip at the farm yard door, that innocent eyed, naked, alternately lustful, obscene and devout singer, who was now and again a great artist died [with the advent of printing]. And with him died the part of his song that the audience sang.[28]

Yet in some ways, as may already be apparent, *Reading at Random* is an elegy for Anon. Although

the play has outgrown the uncovered theatre where the sun beats and the rain pours. That theatre must be replaced by the theatre of the brain. The playwright is replaced by the man who writes a book. The audience is replaced by the reader. Anon is dead,

yet he is 'not yet dead in ourselves. We can still become anonymous' (p. 398). In a draft Woolf notes how 'anonymity is a great possession . . . Nor is anon dead in ourselves' (p. 424). These ideas develop from *A Room of One's Own*, where anonymity represents a quality that 'runs in [the] blood' of women writers through centuries of effacement, and contrasts

---

[27]   See E. Talbot Donaldson, *The Swan at the Well: Shakespeare Reading Chaucer* (New Haven and London, 1985), for ample evidence of Shakespeare's reading Chaucer 'with understanding and great care' (p. 4).

[28]   The previous three quotations are taken from various early drafts of 'Anon', provided in Silver's edition (pp. 403, 424, 404).

with the anxious clamouring of male writers about 'the health of their fame' (p. 65).

It is clear, then, that the major difference between 'The Pastons and Chaucer' and *Reading at Random* is not in any changed estimate of Chaucer (in spite of the 'intervention' of Woolf's having read *Troilus and Criseyde*) but a new emphasis on, and nostalgia for, a culture of anonymity and collectivity within which Chaucer is made to function. In Woolf's final novel, *Between the Acts*, written contemporaneously with *Reading at Random*, the open-air pageant and village-community audience Woolf creates as the focus of the novel resurrect 'the uncovered theatre where the sun beats and the rain pours'. At the same time, Woolf's response to Anon does not preclude or annul her fascination with Renaissance individuality, nor her commitment to the private intimacies of reading and to the 'author' as such. This ambivalence is manifest in Woolf's writing not a pageant-play itself (though she was asked to write one by the local Womens' Institute in Rodmell[29]) but a novel that incorporates one; moreover a tragicomic novel that is both elegiac and satirical towards the communal pageant form at its heart.

In the face of World War II, *Between the Acts*, published in July 1941, a few months after Woolf's death, suggests an England of continuity and recurrence, where the village families go back centuries, and a sense of historical and communal kinship can help appease fragmentation and isolation: there were never such people as the Victorians, muses Mrs Swithin, 'only you and me and William dressed differently'.[30] The pageant, a chronological series of events from different periods of England's social and literary history, incorporates at the outset a scene of 'England in the time of Chaucer', as Mrs Swithin describes it, with 'Canterbury pilgrims . . . passing in and out between the trees' that form the backdrop to the grass terrace where the pageant takes place (p. 50). The pilgrims, dressed in 'shirts made of sacking' (p. 48), are not individualized; nor does 'the time of Chaucer' depict anything beyond anonymous rituals of worship and rural labour; singing in unison chants and ditties, the pilgrims embody generations of such labour, and reappear to thread together the later scenes.[31] As members of the cast from whom protagonists for these later

---

[29] See her letter to Margaret Llewelyn Davies of 6 Apr. 1940 (*Letters*, vi: 391).

[30] Woolf, *Between the Acts* (London, 1990), 108.

[31] A similarly Spartan view comes into Woolf's mind on a trip to Greece in 1932: 'How strange the patiently amenable flat land is, set with biblical trees, grazed by long woolled sheep, & not a house to be seen. This is England in the time of Chaucer' (*Diary*, iv: 92).

scenes are taken, they also bear out the vicar's closing words of communal exhortation in giving thanks for the pageant: 'we act different parts; but are the same' (p. 119). Here 'Chaucer', as in *Reading at Random*, seems to be swallowed up by Anon.

However, another Chaucer is present in *Between the Acts*, or at least was present in the novel's early draft, and this time set within an author-ial, rather than an anonymous, context. The first part of the novel takes place inside Pointz Hall, in the grounds of which the pageant is staged, a location which indeed gave it its original working title; there, in a scene set in the library, we have a meditation on Chaucer in book form as the 'great originator' of the institution of reading: 'there was the whole of literature here; from Chaucer . . . to the latest bright-jacketed nursling which . . . had sprung on Smith's Railway bookstall only last Wednesday'.[32] Here Woolf offers Chaucer as a source of solace in written form not to a 'timeless' village audience which has come to hear and see but to individual readers in a 'harassed' modern age imaginatively en-gaging with the printed word: 'This is my England. This is visible to me; I am padding along the road; I am the Clerk; I am the Nun; I am the Knight' (p. 49). The identification posited here again emphasizes conti-nuity and recurrence, though this time of a more individualized kind than that represented by the pilgrims of the pageant, and this com-muning with the past via the book is a more solitary and private act: 'in the course of three centuries, several dozens of people had opened that very copy of the Canterbury Tales in the bookcase opposite the window' (p. 50).

Woolf did not include this substantial Chaucer episode in the much-altered later draft; she may have felt that its discussion of, for example, the language difficulties in Chaucer (p. 49) made it too much of an excursus (indeed, a piece of literary criticism) in a novel characterized by deftness and concision. But its removal should not imply that in the final version of *Between the Acts* Woolf is prioritizing the oral over the written, the pageant over the library, or the communal over the private. Some critics have argued that the novel does indeed lament the gap between writer and community that could be closed by a return to oral performance and the revival of Anon,[33] but this must be seen as coexisting not only with Woolf's enduring commitment to her beloved activities of writing and

---

[32] *Pointz Hall: The Earlier and Later Typescripts of* Between the Acts, ed. Mitchell A. Leaska (New York, 1983), 48–9.

[33] See, e.g., Lyndall Gordon, *Virginia Woolf: A Writer's Life* (Oxford, 1984), 268.

reading,[34] but also with a pervasive irony directed at the pageant, its audience, and its interpreters throughout the novel itself; thus the inconvenience of open-air conditions, in which 'not a word [of the pilgrims] reached the audience' is repeatedly stressed (p. 48). *Between the Acts* is not, one might repeat, a pageant-play, but a novel 'framing' one.

In Woolf's later writing, Chaucer takes on a number of different roles, roles that indeed represent a series of irreconcilable identifications in Woolf that are present throughout her work. He signals a perished idea of the communal, of the writer fully integrated within his community; yet he is also an 'author' created retrospectively by the invention of printing, the *Canterbury Tales* being one of the first books off Caxton's press, and avidly appreciated as such in *Reading at Random* in the scene of Lady Anne Clifford in the seventeenth century poring over 'excellent Chaucer's book' (p. 427). Throughout the centuries he has allowed those reading him in the library at Pointz Hall to nourish their imaginations and sense of identity on what is still seen by Woolf as a fairly unsophisticated, if potent, writing, still taking readers into the realms of the ordinary and the visible, and gripping them by the prospect of what happened next (*Pointz Hall*, 49). This division between the communal and the solitary, between outdoor stage and library, is one of several antitheses played out in *Between the Acts*, and if the pageant and its players are hardly idealized by Woolf, neither are the solitary protagonists of the audience in their private worlds of alienation, each thinking 'I'm damnably unhappy' (p. 109). Moreover, if the pageant represents in microcosm an English literary tradition founded by Chaucer that is Woolf's 'only patriotism' (see above, p. 44), Woolf's sense of the provisionality and contingency of nationhood is demonstrated throughout the novel in the vast temporal, natural, and geographical contexts she introduces that render 'Englishness' so (tragi) comical and precarious.[35] The contrast between community and exclusion, more particularly the writer's exclusion, is a constant in

---

[34] See, e.g., Woolf's claim that the fact 'we have loved reading' is the sole reason for the progression out of the primitive to civilization, and the erection of 'some sort of shelter and society on the waste of the world' ('How Should One Read a Book?', in *Essays*, iv: 388–400: 399).

[35] See, e.g., Gillian Beer, 'The Island and the Aeroplane: The Case of Virginia Woolf', in Homi Bhabha (ed.), *Nation and Narration* (London, 1990), 265–90. A prevailing critical consensus that tends to efface Woolf's sense of 'Englishness' has lately been ably contested by Joshua D. Esty, 'Amnesia in the Fields: Late Modernism, Late Imperialism, and the English Pageant-Play', *ELH*, 69 (2002), 245–76. This present essay concurs with what Esty calls Woolf's 'troubled half-love for England' (p. 262) and the way that *Between the Acts* 'shuttles between recuperative ideas of national heritage and fundamental wariness about any kind of collective ethos' (p. 257).

Woolf, and frequently raises specific issues of nationality, as in a telling diary entry of 1928, where Woolf records watching a village wedding at Rodmell:

I felt this is the heart of England—this wedding in the country: history I felt; Cromwell; The Osbornes; Dorothy's shepherdesses singing: of all of whom Mr & Mrs Jarrad seem more the descendants than I am: as if they represented the unconscious breathing of England & L[eonard] & I, leaning over the wall, were detached, unconnected. I suppose our thinking is the cause of this. We dont [sic] belong to any 'class'; we thinkers: might as well be French or German. Yet I am English in some way. (*Diary*, iii. 197–8)

Here Woolf, excluded from 'the heart of England', yet remains English 'in some way', and it is significant that the national tradition perpetuated in the villagers includes a reference to Dorothy Osborne (1627–95), whose *Letters* Woolf was currently reviewing. In that review, Woolf notes that 'women letter writers were the true forerunners of the women novelists', but in the transcript they leave us of common things—'a record of life seen from the chimney corner day in and day out'—they remain part of a collective experience and tradition that is sundered once the writer becomes an 'author' (*Essays*, iv. 554).

The last sentence of 'The Pastons and Chaucer' celebrates the 'plain-faced Pastons indefatigably accumulating wealth, treading out the roads of Norfolk, and persisting with an obstinate courage which does them in-finite credit in furnishing the bareness of England' (p. 35), just as Woolf's expanded essay on Dorothy Osborne, published in *The Second Common Reader* of 1932, salutes the growth in letter writing in the seventeenth century as the means whereby the 'bare landscape' of an earlier literary tradition 'that has neither letter-writers nor biographers' is planted and furnished.[36] The opening essay in the first *Common Reader* thus signifi-cantly ends not on Chaucer's contribution to the literary tradition, but in a typically Woolfian tribute to the cultural continuity established by gen-erations of the obscure. English civilization, and more specifically its great ancestral houses (including metaphorically the 'vast building' of literature itself, see below), are the result of the 'anonymous work of creation' and the 'labours of . . . vanished hands', as *Orlando* puts it,[37] and although the terms 'obscurity' and 'anonymity' might be particularly 'watchwords . . .

---

[36] Woolf, 'Dorothy Osborne's "Letters"', in *The Second Common Reader* (New York, 1932), 59–67: 59–60.
[37] Woolf, *Orlando: A Biography* (Harmondsworth, 1942), 75.

of the latter half of her career', in the words of Lyndall Gordon (*Virginia Woolf,* 259), they represent values Woolf clung to from her earliest writing, as in her 1907 review of the *Memoirs* of Lady Fanshawe:

> Nor would it be hard for a stranger . . . to perceive a family history running alongside of all seasons of English life, inconspicuously, as a murmured accompaniment. So set humming, the whole land seems to swim in a pleasant kind of harmony, in which no age is more present than another, and all are of the one piece.[38]

In writing English literary history Woolf repeatedly pays tribute to the diarists and letter- and memoir-writers who constitute 'The Lives of the Obscure', to quote one of the chapter headings from *The Common Reader* (p. 118), and this attention to the lower slopes of literature is a remarkably consistent metaphor in her sense of that tradition as an organic landscape.[39] 'A student of letters is so much in the habit of striding through the centuries from one pinnacle of accomplishment to the next that he forgets all the hubbub that once surged round the base,' she notes in an early review, and the idea that a history exclusively concerned with great figures and events 'lacks an eye' is a constant insistence long before it is enshrined in feminist terms in *A Room of One's Own.*[40]

Woolf's response to that first 'pinnacle of accomplishment', 'Father' Chaucer, therefore has the effect of cutting him down to size, whether this be to immerse him in the hubbub of the Pastons around his base, or to contextualize him within Anon, or to present his pilgrims as representing obscure continuity rather than 'larger-than-life' personality. Where Chaucer is granted 'authorial' status, as in the library scene of *Pointz Hall,* someone has been careful to again introduce the Paston letters alongside him—'The Paston letters did very well side by side with Chaucer'—as a reminder of his inescapable origins (*Pointz Hall,* 50). The 'Canterbury pilgrims' in *Between the Acts,* anonymous and recurring, are thus made to represent, to continue the musical terminology from the review quoted above, the *continuo* of English history, 'in which no age is more present than another, and all are of the one piece'. Huge changes did occur at the Renaissance, and yet, 'save that self consciousness had not yet raised its mirror, the men and women are ourselves' ('Anon', 384). In spite of the

---

[38] 'Lady Fanshawe's Memoirs', in *The Essays of Virginia Woolf,* vol. i: *1904–1912,* ed. Andrew McNeillie (London, 1986), 143–7: 144.

[39] Woolf, 'Dorothy Osborne's "Letters"', 59.

[40] Woolf, 'Thomas Hood', in *Essays,* i. 159–64, 159; ' "Modes and Manners of the Nineteenth Century"', in *Essays,* i. 330–5: 331.

moderns being 'sharply cut off from our predecessors' (*Essays*, iv. 238) in a similarly dramatic way, in part occasioned by World War I, as discussed in the final chapter of *The Common Reader*, 'How It Strikes a Contemporary', we are assured that literature

has lasted long, has undergone many changes, and it is only a short sight and a parochial mind that will exaggerate the importance of these squalls, however they may agitate the little boats now tossing out at sea. The storm and the drenching are on the surface; continuity and calm are in the depths. (*Essays*, iv. 241)

Here also is the vision of the importance of the obscure in literary terms, of contemporary writers who are 'engaged upon some vast building, which being built by common effort, the separate workmen may well remain anonymous' (p. 241). In the original, pre-*Common Reader* version of 'How It Strikes a Contemporary', published in the *Times Literary Supplement* in April 1923, the final part of the above quotation is given thus: 'the sight of her [i.e. 'truth'] will convince us that she is always the same, from Chaucer even to Mr Conrad. The difference is on the surface; the continuity in the depths.'[41] It may seem strange that when we reach *The Common Reader*, whose survey indeed begins and ends with Chaucer and Conrad respectively, Woolf effaces these framing names in 'How It Strikes a Contemporary'; but once again this is to remind us that the true history of literature is one of collective, rather than individual, endeavour, and that despite all the changes there is an underlying unity where historical and individual difference are not.

University of Birmingham

---

[41] 'How It Strikes a Contemporary', in *Essays*, iii: 353–60: 359.

William Worcester Writes a History of his Reading

Daniel Wakelin

In A. S. Byatt's recent novel *The Biographer's Tale*, the eager graduate student Phineas G. Nanson is writing a biography of the deceased biographer Scholes Destry-Scholes. One day, he is excited to discover the rough papers of his elusive subject. From Destry-Scholes's own notes concerning other authors, Nanson struggles to reconstruct Destry-Scholes's life and, during the long hours of immersion, like many graduate students, he develops a personal fascination with his subject:

> I found my self, ludicrously, reacting as if Destry-Scholes had put together the three faded blue carbons under the hanging folders in the Lincoln University archive, in order to baffle and intrigue me, me personally, Phineas G. Nanson. All this writing was a conundrum bequeathed by him to me.
>
> I wasn't born, when he drowned, if he did drown. . . .
>
> A drowned, or possibly drowned, biographer, in 1965, could have had no conceivable reader in mind for this limp cache of unbegun and unended stories.[1]

In this passage, Nanson idly imagines that the inscrutable archive might have been left deliberately to aid the production of a future biography. A. S. Byatt is, of course, poking gentle fun at literary scholars, as she has elsewhere. Yet Nanson's naïvety here lies not in this supposedly ludicrous suggestion, but in his own incredulity at it: why could one biographer not have envisaged a future biographer as a 'conceivable reader' of his notes? Even if he did not await Nanson in particular, nevertheless, why should Destry-Scholes not have dreamt that someone would chart his life as he had charted the lives of others?

When I began to read the notebooks and marginalia of the fifteenth-century scholar William Worcester (1415–*c*.1483), I found myself reacting just as apparently 'ludicrously' as Nanson. When I traced the circulation

---

[1] A. S. Byatt, *The Biographer's Tale* (2000; repr. London, 2001), 97–8.

of books in Worcester's milieu and analysed his own responses, scribbled in their margins and in his voluminous notebooks, intending to write a history of his reading, it seemed as if Worcester had left his notebooks with such future scholarship in mind. It was possible to describe Worcester's books and reading, within the framework of those larger topics of the history of the book and the history of reading, often fanfared as comparatively new developments in research, because Worcester himself had imagined future enquiries into such subjects.[2] First, Worcester's intermittent tendency to describe, in some rudimentary way, the books that he had seen or acquired adumbrates the long-standing interest among medievalists, certainly, in the history of the book or in the histories of particular manuscript books. Secondly, Worcester's documentation of his encounters with these books charts his own intellectual biography through a history of his reading. Besides tracing the books Worcester used or the life story he tells, it is also possible to ask how and why he, like some of his contemporaries, left records which facilitate potential historical enquiry into his books and reading.

This essay begins, then, with description: Worcester is an obscure figure, and his notebooks remain, except for one, little known, left in scattered manuscript collections. However, his practices of historical record are not as unusual as they may at first seem, but, I will finally argue, have implications for our wider understanding of the records used by all historians of manuscript culture. Worcester's notebooks remind us that we can write the history of the book or the history of reading only because of some sort of story-teller's or historian's practice by those who left the records we employ. Such recognition could of course warn us of the biases and shaping structures of such records. As one advocate of the history of reading admitted, 'the documents rarely show readers at work', and, moreover, 'the documents are texts themselves, which also require interpretation'.[3] However, this observation need not entail epistemological despair. We can, in practice, still look carefully *through* 'documents' like Worcester's: but we can also look directly *at* them; we have the option of adding to the historical study of reading the 'interpretation' of its written texts. The traditional definition of a 'work' open to literary examination has often excluded ephemeral or functional writings, even if produced by

---

[2] For these developments, see Guglielmo Cavallo and Roger Chartier (eds.), *A History of Reading in the West*, trans. Lydia G. Cochrane (Cambridge, 1999), 1–5, and Leah Price, 'The Tangible Page', *London Review of Books*, 31 Oct. 2002, pp. 36–9.
[3] Roger Darnton, 'History of Reading', in Peter Burke (ed.), *New Perspectives on Historical Writing* (Cambridge, 1991), 140–67: 142.

a famous author.[4] Yet Worcester's rough notebooks and annotations certainly deserve the fair consideration accorded to more polished texts. Besides providing information about other books and works, these short snippets of writing are themselves a 'conundrum' bequeathed to our curiosity, as they raise various intriguing questions: who is the 'conceivable reader', what the conceivable purpose, of such documents?

Worcester's Biography and Books

According to his own records, William Worcester was born in Bristol in 1415. In the late 1430s he studied at Hart Hall in the University of Oxford and, perhaps while still at Oxford, and certainly soon after leaving, he was employed by Sir John Fastolf of Caister Castle, Norfolk (*c.*1380–1459), a formidable war veteran, landowner, and occasional political counsellor to his aristocratic superiors. After Fastolf's death, Worcester was one of his executors and fought against many grasping contemporaries to preserve his master's inheritance as he wished. He had served his master with devotion as a secretary and adviser: he not only wrote Fastolf's correspondence, administered his properties, and made legal enquiries for him, but also copied astrological tables, composed political memoranda, treatises, and translations, and may have offered medical advice. The literary by-products of this diligence were revisions to Stephen Scrope's *The Dicts and Sayings of the Philosophers*, a translation of Cicero's *De Senectute*, a prose political treatise known as *The Boke of Noblesse*, an account of Fastolf's military career, and a genealogical survey of Norfolk families (the latter two now lost). Beyond Worcester's share in the correspondence of the Paston family, his Norfolk neighbours, three manuscripts partly in his hand contain his personal or collaborative compositions.[5]

However, here I want to focus not on these finished works but on Worcester's notebooks, marginalia, and *ex libris* inscriptions. These notes

---

[4] On which, see Michel Foucault, 'What Is an Author?', in Paul Rabinow (ed.), *The Foucault Reader* (1984; repr. Harmondsworth, 1991), 101–20: 103–4, 107–8.

[5] The essential biography is K. B. McFarlane, 'William Worcester: A Preliminary Survey', printed in his *England in the Fifteenth Century: Collected Essays*, ed. G. L. Harriss (London, 1981), 199–224, supplemented by Colin Richmond, *The Paston Family in the Fifteenth Century: Fastolf's Will* (Cambridge, 1996), 53–106. For valuable contexts, see Jeremy Catto, 'Masters, Patrons and the Careers of Graduates in Fifteenth-Century England', in Anne Curry and Elizabeth Matthew (eds.), *Concepts of Service in the Later Middle Ages* (Woodbridge, 2000), 52–63, and Jonathan Hughes, 'Stephen Scrope and the Circle of Sir John Fastolf: Moral and Intellectual Outlooks', in Christopher Harper-Bill and Ruth Harvey (eds.), *Medieval Knighthood*, iv (Woodbridge, 1992), 109–46.

can be identified by his atrocious handwriting, with its jagged and ir-
regularly sized anglicana letter forms and its disjointed flow.[6] Worcester's
scholarship and research for Fastolf's and his own pleasure generated
seven extant notebooks and produced copying, marginalia, or ownership
inscriptions in at least thirteen others (listed in Appendix 1 below). His
marginalia engage with authors from pseudo-Seneca and Pliny to
Chaucer and the anonymous *Gesta Henrici Quinti*, in a manner often
scholarly and sometimes polemical. Yet across a catholic range of
materials, Worcester identifies himself as the annotator, or sometimes as
the owner, and he often places and dates his encounter with the text in
question. 'An annotator has his scruples too,' as Wallace Stevens put it.[7]
Why does he exercise this intriguing precision?

Richer still in their detail are Worcester's notebooks, which all contain
both materials in his hand and materials annotated by him. Each notebook has a perceptible, but never exclusive, focus (listed below). (I give
each an abbreviation for future parenthetical references.[8]) They are:

Ca   Cambridge, Corpus Christi College, MS 210: topography
Ad   London, British Library, MS Additional 28208: estate records
Ju   London, British Library, MS Cotton Julius F. vii: classicism and
     history
Ro   London, British Library, MS Royal 13. C. i: classicism and history
Sl   London, British Library, MS Sloane 4: medicine
Ar   London, College of Arms, MS Arundel 48: history and warfare
La   Oxford, Bodleian Library, MS Laud misc. 674: astronomy

Four of the notebooks (Ca, Ad, Ju, and Sl) share an unusual elongated
format, roughly 110 millimetres by 300 millimetres, and are apparently
constructed from individual sheets folded lengthways, portable in a
long pocket or holster. Worcester filled these leaves with notes while

---

[6] Illustrated by Jean F. Preston and Laetitia Yeandle, *English Handwriting 1400–1650: An
Introductory Manual* (Binghampton, NY, 1992), 18–21.

[7] 'The Comedian as the Letter C', in Wallace Stevens, *Harmonium* (1923; repr. London,
2001), 37.

[8] I have silently expanded Worcester's abbreviations; the triangular brackets ⟨ and ⟩ mark gaps
or lost text; slashes \ and / mark later interlinear additions. I have translated word for word to preserve his long-winded tone. I cite manuscript Ca with page-numbers from the printed edition in
William Worcestre (*sic*), *Itineraries*, ed. John H. Harvey (Oxford, 1969). Harvey edits this topographical notebook as a continuous text in chronological order of writing, rather than as roughly
scribbled and now misbound. The reconstruction is sound and helpfully tidy, but must not mislead the unwary reader to think that this notebook was composed as a finished work. William
Worcestre (*sic*), *The Topography of Medieval Bristol*, ed. Frances Neale, Bristol Record Society
Publications, 51 (Bristol, 2000), prints sections omitted by Harvey.

travelling and reading, and then he or someone else roughly gathered them into small quires to make a sturdier volume.[9] This process renders Worcester's notebooks haphazard, discontinuous, and their contents heterogeneous. However, if one wishes to chart Worcester's intellectual biography, each notebook can be mentally disbound and reassembled in chronological order, because, despite the muddled binding process, Worcester often appends to his notes or books a brief 'inscription' (as I shall call them) which describes with great care the origins and dates of his use of each text.

Worcester Writes the Histories of Books

Worcester's 'inscriptions' are, first, striking for their number. Although it is sometimes hard to differentiate the individual texts which Worcester read, it seems that he took notes from, annotated, or owned at least 223 particular works or volumes. (Of that total, eleven notes sound suspiciously like oral cures or reminiscences, given their ascription to barbers, his hostess in London, and so on, especially on Sl fo. 56^v.) Of these 223 occasions on which Worcester recorded his access to a text, in some 103 cases he provided details of the place in which he found the text, or details of its current or previous owner: that is, Worcester specified the origins or provenances of 46 per cent of the texts to which he had access. Moreover, and more strikingly, Worcester then also provided the date upon which he read, acquired, or occasionally relinquished some fifty-eight of the texts: that is, he dated 26 per cent of his recorded reading. Beyond some early astronomical tables, and two French books read in 1450 and 1453, most of his dated notes were apparently written between 1460 and 1480, perhaps because he had greater leisure for study after the death of Fastolf, his master. Worcester's effort to report the social context, place, or date of nearly half of his textual encounters constitutes a strikingly large archive for the fifteenth century. Of course, there are also extant books which Worcester mentioned in his notebooks but did not annotate, and vice versa; *The Boke of Noblesse* reveals his crafty use of other works nowhere attested in his documented library. Worcester did not record every encounter with a text. However, that lack of complete knowledge confirms that anyone who traces Worcester's books now must rely heavily upon his own auto-biographical record.

---

[9]   McFarlane, 'William Worcester', 221 n. 129.

Moreover, not only is the volume of Worcester's extant note-making rare, but so too is the detail. That detail is best illustrated through an egregious example, the comments attached to Worcester's transcription of some Latin verses allegedly by John Somerset, former royal physician and political fixer (d. by 1455).[10] Somerset gave numerous books to Cambridge University Library and to individual college libraries in Cambridge, including some from the estate of Humphrey, Duke of Gloucester; he also fought for the university at court. Yet Somerset's Latin verse *Querimonia*, or complaint, accuses Cambridge of ingratitude for these kindnesses.[11] Worcester's copy of the text concludes:

Explicit Epistula contra ingratitudinem scripta in Vniuersitate Cantebrigie per W. Wyrcestre 19 die mensis Septembris anno christi 1471 copiam cuius habui de magistro Rugshaw Collegij sancti petri. (Ju fo. 201ᵛ)

Here finishes the letter against ingratitude, written in the University of Cambridge by William Worcester, the nineteenth day of the month of September the year of our Lord 1471; of which I had a copy from Master Rowkshaw of Peterhouse.

And then Worcester added a title in a different ink, squashed uncomfortably above the text itself:

Querimonia magistri Johannis Somerset phisici domini henrici Regis sexti de Ingratitudine vniuersitatis Cantebrigie et specialis [*sic*] contra suppremos socios Collegij Regis suo medio cicius fundati c⟨opia⟩ istius Epistule scripta fuit de manu magistri ⟨gap⟩ Barber Collegij sancti michelis. (Ju fo. 201ʳ)

The *Querimonia* of Master John Somerset, doctor to the lord King Henry VI, concerning the ingratitude of the University of Cambridge; and especially against the greatest fellows of King's College, founded more quickly thanks to him. The c⟨opy⟩ of this letter was written in the hand of Master ⟨gap⟩ Barber of Michaelhouse.

These lines capture three topics which recur throughout Worcester's notes, marginalia, and ownership inscriptions: (i) palaeography and the provenance of books; (ii) the history of scholarship and of universities; (iii) Worcester's own access to texts.

---

[10] On Somerset's career, see A. B. Emden, *A Biographical Register of the University of Cambridge to 1500* (Cambridge, 1963), 540–1, and recently David Rundle, 'Two Unnoticed Manuscripts from the Collection of Humfrey, Duke of Gloucester', *Bodleian Library Record*, 16 (1998), 211–24, 299–313: 306–10.

[11] Thomas Hearne (ed.), *Thomæ de Elmham Vita et Gesta Henrici Quinti Anglorum Regis* (Oxford, 1727), 347–50, prints his *Querimonia*.

Worcester's palaeographical interest recurs throughout his notebooks. Some vaguely visual descriptions of texts might, at a stretch, make it easier to find them again: for example, written in 'a paper book in large quires' owned by one Master Davy of London or in the margin of an agricultural text 'in the style of the notes of ⟨the hand⟩ of an Italian' ('de papiro in magno quaterno', Ju fo. 48ᵛ; 'per modum notulorum de ma⟨nu⟩ vnius Italici', Sl fo. 9ʳ). However, these details are less helpful as finding-aids than title, owner, and location, and they expand into palaeographical and codicological analysis. Most frequently, of course, Worcester simply notes an *antiquus* book or hand (Ju fos. 43ʳ, 64ʳ, 116ʳ; Ar fo. 209ʳ; Ca p. 271), but even this common designation is rationalized and deliberate: an ancient hand, he explains, is one which belongs to 'as it seems, previous years' ('quasi annos preteritos', Ju fo. 114ʳ). Besides age, Worcester notes the quality of handwriting, or the origins of books either vaguely *alieni-genus* or foreign, or more precisely 'in a Roman hand written like that found in papal bulls' (Ju fo. 113ʳ; Ca p. 86; Sl fo. 60ʳ). His more striking inscriptions bring into focus the embryonic historical interest in other, more banal, and conventional references to 'ancient' books.

Moreover, like the best codicologists today, Worcester's interest in books extends to a human interest in their makers and users. Worcester names at least forty-four people and twenty-eight institutions from which he acquired books or access to books: for example, he writes a 'memoran-dum' that he has spoken with Andrew Barvale, a Cambridge friar, about chronicles (Sl fo. 57ʳ). Such familiar references to Worcester's friends and associates might suggest that the original 'conceivable reader' of these inscriptions was Worcester himself. In a manuscript culture with a patchy supply of each individual text, observations on the owners and resting-places of books would be useful for the future borrowing, copying, and acquisition of texts (and, as shown below, Worcester often returned to his earlier notes).[12] However, in many cases he gives too much information about the sources of his texts. He documents not only the owners of books when he last saw them, but often the previous owners too or, in the case of institutional books, donors. For example, in October 1464 he takes notes from a flyleaf of Guy de Chauliac's *Chirurgia* donated to St Paul's Cathedral, London, by John Somerset, and seven years later from Somerset's copy of Piero dei' Crescenzi's *Ruralium commodorum*

---

[12] Ralph Hanna III, *Pursuing History: Middle English Manuscripts and their Texts* (Stanford, Calif., 1996), 8–9, begins to address this issue.

donated to Cambridge University Library (Sl fos. 56ʳ, 6ᵛ).[13] Worcester is also, like the best codicologists, willing to express scholarly doubt about a book's provenance: for example, one martyrology comes from 'an abbey in Lincolnshire, as I believe, Peterborough', and another 'I believe' from Bayonne or Bordeaux ('abbathie Comitatus lincolnie vt credo peter-burgh', 'vt credo'). Such comments cannot be useful finding-aids: by Worcester's own day these respective manuscripts rested securely, he notes, in the choir of the Cambridge Augustinians and with William Hunt of Sheen (Ju fo. 64ʳ; Ca p. 268). Rather, each inscription's fussy 'as I believe' worries about discovering and preserving snippets of historical fact.

What is the point of this information? What 'conceivable reader' might Worcester have had in mind for his 'cache of unbegun and unended stories' about the Peterborough martyrology, or about Somerset's *Querimonia*, Rowkshaw, and himself? A twenty-first-century historian of Cambridge, of manuscript circulation, or of Worcester's own life might find these inscriptions of use. Yet, in recording this information, Worcester appears to share those academic concerns; the records which one might now plunder for information about fifteenth-century intellectual history were never innocent of a historian's interest. As was clear in the first example, of Somerset's *Querimonia*, these reports cannot always be finding-aids: he is unlikely to be able to spot Master Barber's handwriting from afar among other documents. Moreover, he does not need to recognize Barber's handwriting in order to find these verses, because Master Rowkshaw owns Barber's transcription now and, anyway, Worcester has made his own copy. These notes can only serve future knowledge of the past transmission of Somerset's *Querimonia*. Worcester's comments on the history of particular texts or books express a historical curiosity as otiose as twenty-first-century palaeographical and textual criticism.

Yet Worcester's records can be clarified not only by comparison with today's research, but by comparing the practice of other scholars with whom he had dealings in life. Such comparisons importantly remind us that although Worcester's note-making habits are distinctive in their volume and specificity, they are not unique. His inscription concerning Somerset's *Querimonia* also reveals one possible influence upon Worcester's historical record: institutional memory in fifteenth-century universities. For example, other books donated by Somerset to college libraries and to St Paul's Cathedral, London, contained lengthy

---

[13] For further records of this lost book, see Peter D. Clarke (ed.), *The University and College Libraries of Cambridge*, Corpus of Medieval Library Catalogues (London, 2002), no. UC3.21.

autobiographical notes explaining their provenance.[14] Master Rowkshaw, who provided the aforementioned *Querimonia* 'in the hand of Master ⟨gap⟩ Barber', remarked elsewhere on the handwriting of a document: his inscription upon an inventory of Roger Marchall's books donated to Peterhouse, Cambridge, observed that the list was written in Marchall's hand; as bursar of that college, he seems to have overseen Marchall's donation.[15] Somerset and Rowkshaw show that the exercise of historical memory was part of archival practice in such institutional libraries: a note of a book's donation, especially in the donor's own hand, had legal value. Moreover, many institutional libraries were organized by donor, given that most libraries grew sporadically through random bequests.[16] Roger Lovatt's insightful introduction to catalogues of Cambridge libraries warns that most 'catalogues' were the baldest bursarial inventories, with an eye on the book as property. However, he also observes that many college bursars and administrators fulfilled such roles only briefly within longer careers as scholars and sometimes bibliophiles: their financial and legal records occasionally shade into historical reports. Indeed, the most striking catalogue, from Corpus Christi College, Cambridge, in 1368, describes the quiring, illuminations, and even the handwriting of books with a sophistication far outstripping that of William Worcester.[17] Worcester ostentatiously recorded the collegiate affiliations of fourteen books and their owners.[18] Did his

[14] For example, on 4 May 1448 Somerset, 'doctor of liberal arts and of the art of preserving human life', donated what is now MS 137 to Pembroke College, Cambridge, 'by which college I was educated as a child' ('Arcium liberalium at a\r\tis conseruatiue vite humane doctor', 'qua alumnus educatus sum', fo. 389ᵛ). See also Cambridge, Gonville and Caius College, MS 183/216, p. 2; Cambridge, Peterhouse, MS 231, fo. 1ᵛ; N. R. Ker, *Medieval Manuscripts in British Libraries*, 5 vols. (Oxford, 1969–2003), i. 242–3 (London, St Paul's Cathedral, MS 3).

[15] Clarke (ed.), *University and College Libraries*, 532. On Rowkshaw, see Emden, *Biographical Register of the University of Cambridge*, 493, and Roger Lovatt, 'Two Collegiate Loan-Chests in Late Medieval Cambridge', in Patrick Zutshi (ed.), *Medieval Cambridge: Essays on the Pre-Reformation University*, The History of the University of Cambridge: Texts and Studies, 2 (Woodbridge, 1993), 129–65: 141–2, 151.

[16] See N. R. Ker, *Medieval Libraries of Great Britain: A List of Surviving Books*, 2nd edn. (London, 1964), pp. xviii, xx; Richard Sharpe, 'Accession, Classification, Location: Shelfmarks in Medieval Libraries', *Scriptorium*, 50 (1996), 279–87: 283–4. This useful special issue of *Scriptorium* focuses upon manuscript record-keeping and archival practice.

[17] Roger Lovatt, 'Introduction', in Clarke (ed.), *University and College Libraries*, pp. xxix–xcii: pp. xl–xli, lix–lxiii. Compare also the Corpus Christi College catalogue (pp. 168–84).

[18] For example: Master John Wylley of Michaelhouse, Cambridge (Ju fos. 59ʳ, 64ᵛ); John Hall of Gonville Hall, Cambridge (Ju fo. 47ʳ, Ca p. 346); John Free of Balliol College, Oxford (Oxford, Balliol College, MS 124, fo. 1ʳ); Plato's *Timaeus* and a Psalter in Hebrew at Peterhouse, Cambridge (Ju fos. 59ʳ, 121ʳ–2ᵛ), both attested in the fifteenth-century inventory (Clarke (ed.), *University and College Libraries*, no. UC48.164, now lost; no. UC48.73, now lost; and no. UC48.74, now London, Lambeth Palace Library, MS 435).

university connections introduce to him precedents for his historical inscriptions in their intermittent habits of historical memory?
Worcester's history of books begins to look a little more like record-
keeping, and vice versa.

Of course, a fifteenth-century donor to the charitable, religious colleges of his day could have sought historical remembrance alongside or
after divine recognition. So Worcester also notes the connections of
twenty-seven of his books or companions in learning to ecclesiastical
institutions or parishes (as in his aforementioned visits to Cambridge's
Augustinians and to St Paul's, London). Yet Worcester is notably silent
on the piety which presumably motivated many book donations.
Even when, in 1473, he gives a *Liber de sacramentis ecclesiae* to Bishop
William Waynflete, in memory of Sir John Fastolf, there is no request
for prayers, but an inscription that informs Waynflete that his cathedral
at Winchester 'once before the time of the consecration was called
the temple of Dagon in the era of the pagan people' ('olim ante tempus
consecracionis dicte Ecclesie Templum dagon vocabatur tempore
paganorum gencium').[19] Godly hope for the afterlife, even Christian
decorum, makes room for scholarly posing and historical curiosity.
Could Worcester's self-conscious documenting of the history of books
and scholarship reflect contemporary humanist interest in antiquity
and history? After all, he also exchanged with Waynflete a manuscript of
Boccaccio and his own rendering of Cicero's *De Senectute*,[20] and many
of Worcester's remarks upon his texts and books flag their connections
with Italian and Italianate humanist scholars.[21] Worcester records the
transmission of texts, as did Italian classical scholars from Petrarch to
Pontano, and aggrandizes the advancement of learning with the keen
sense of historical recovery and self-importance sometimes ascribed to
them.[22]

---

[19] Oxford, Magdalen College, MS lat. 26, fo. ii^v. Richmond, *Fastolf's Will*, 213–22, 255–6,
describes the wrangling between Waynflete and Worcester over Fastolf's will.

[20] See Ca pp. 252–5 and Oxford, Magdalen College, MS lat. 198, fo. ii^v.

[21] Oxford, Balliol College, MS 124, fos. 1^r, 242^v; Oxford, New College, MS 162, fo. ii^v; Ca
pp. 274–7; Ju fos. 67^r–8^v, 93^r–6^v, 105^r–11^v, 118^r. Daniel Wakelin, 'Vernacular Humanism
in England, *c.*1440–1485' (PhD. thesis, Cambridge, 2002), 6–7 and 157–205, further traces
Worcester's humanism.

[22] On self-presentation, see accounts such as Lisa Jardine, *Erasmus, Man of Letters: The Construction of Charisma in Print* (Princeton, NJ, 1993), 4, 58, and Anthony Grafton, 'Is the History
of Reading a Marginal Enterprise? Guillaume Budé and his Books', *Papers of the Bibliographical
Society of America*, 91 (1997), 139–57: 155–6.

Worcester Writes a History of his own Reading

William Worcester is not interested only in other scholars, however; ultimately, his *ex libris* inscriptions and notebooks offer a historical record of
his own achievements too. As Walter Benjamin observed, a catalogue of
the books one has acquired (or in Worcester's case, read) is also an orderly
record of one's own life, into which those books have come.[23] So, in that
first example, the colophon to Somerset's *Querimonia*, Worcester dated
and located his transcription to 19 September 1471 in the University of
Cambridge: he remembers his own past scholarship. These details cannot
help him to find the text again or to make any legal claim. Instead, he
himself has become part of the broader history of the scholarship of his
acquaintances towards which his notes tend. It has been suggested that
the book-plates of monk Thomas Hyngham of Norfolk, perhaps the
Hyngham known to Worcester (Ca p. 238, Ju fo. 208ʳ), conjure a 'faint
literarité' for the owner, simply by including Hyngham's name alongside
a literary text copied for personal interest.[24] Sheer contiguity in any
inscription in any book suggests some connection between the owner and
the revered author. In Walter Burley's fourteenth-century *Super Aristotelis
problemata*, Worcester wrote:

Explicit abbreuiacio libri problematum Aristotilis secundum ordinem alphabeti
laborata per Walterum Burley \doctor in theologia/ vniuersitatis Oxoniensis
et pertinet iste liber Willelmo Worcestre nato de Bristollia Wigorniensis
diocesis.[25]

Here ends *The Abbreviation of the Book of Problems* arranged in alphabetical
order by Walter Burley, \doctor of theology/ in the University of Oxford. And
this book belongs to William Worcester, born in Bristol in the diocese of
Worcester.

Worcester lets any future reader know some biographical facts not only
about Burley but also about himself, and places himself alongside this

---

[23] Walter Benjamin, 'Unpacking My Library', in his *Illuminations*, ed. Hannah Arendt, trans.
Harry Zorn (1968; repr. London, 1999), 61–9: 61–3.

[24] Richard Beadle, 'Monk Thomas Hyngham's Hand in the Macro Manuscript', in Richard
Beadle and A. J. Piper (eds.), *New Science Out of Old Books: Studies in Manuscripts and Early
Printed Books in Honour of A. I. Doyle* (Aldershot, 1995), 315–41: 331, 333 n. 4.

[25] Oxford, Magdalen College, MS 65, fo. 58ᵛ. Worcester perhaps learnt of Burley's university
career from a catalogue of writers which he copied elsewhere (Ju fo. 38ᵛ). Another flyleaf inscription, in French and not in Worcester's hand, clarifies the book's legal status: 'The book belongs
to William Worcester, sometime called Botoner, of Bristol; by witness of Nicholas Nesand'
('Ce liure appartient a Guillaume Worcester autrement dit Botoner de Bristoll Teste Nicolao
Nesande', fo. iiiᵛ).

scholar of the past. In his notebooks, Worcester sometimes explicitly describes his activity as a man of letters: he read classical histories in a French book owned by Sir John Fastolf in Paris in November and December 1453 (Ro fo. 143^r), and transcribed material 'from diverse chronicles in the city of London in order to please Nicholas Ancrage, prior of St Leonard's near the city of Norwich in the county of Norfolk, around the year of our Lord 1465' ('de diuersis cronicis in ciuitate londiniarum ad complacenciam dompni Nicholi Ancrage priori sancti leonardi prope ciuitatem Norwici in patria norffolchia circa anno christi 1465', Ju fo. 169^r). He dates even his collections of notes with solemnity and provides details of his own biography. Who was his 'conceivable reader' for such excessive detail? The implied reader must be someone looking back on Worcester's world from a historical or geographical distance and therefore needing to be told these facts. There would be an amusing hubris in such an expectation, were this essay not now answering his implicit call for future recognition.

Might Worcester have conceived of himself as the future reader and beneficiary of these records? Did he expect that the future need to recall the transmission of Somerset's *Querimonia* or his research in London for Nicholas Ancrage would be part of some forthcoming work of his own? If so, he could be simply an exemplary scholar, recording in which books he obtained his references, even down to folio numbers (for example, Ju fos. 124^r–8^r), thanking their owners, and acknowledging the occasions and limitations of his enquiries. Such habits of reference are applauded among scholars today; however, an examination of Worcester's extant complete writings, *The Boke of Noblesse* and the translation of *De Senectute*, reveals that he was often coy and sometimes dishonest about his sources.[26] We might, alternatively, wonder whether he intended to write some autobiographical account of his studies, just as he narrated the now lost *Gesta* of Sir John Fastolf. Is that why he tried to remember his past reading? Such speculation about his intentions is unverifiable, and leads us needlessly away from the notes themselves. Even if the creation of autobiography were unconscious or unwitting, simply by recording his scholarly progress Worcester created historical sources.

Moreover, as it happens, Worcester's creation of historical records appears deliberate and distinctive. Even the simplest inscriptions in his notebooks betray a historian's perspective, a sense that his reading might be worth remembering. This perspective is most evident in Worcester's

---

[26] Wakelin, 'Vernacular Humanism', 166–7, 193–4, identifies some of Worcester's hidden sources.

dates: as mentioned, Worcester often describes not only from whom he obtained texts, but when he read them; he gives a date for some 26 per cent of his known textual encounters. Of those fifty-eight dated notes or books, for twenty-four he gave the year alone, for fifteen the year and the month, and for nineteen the exact date. Worcester's habit is unusual: dated manuscripts by English scribes are infamously rare, although commoner among Italian humanists.[27] A survey of donor inscriptions and notes of ownership recorded in N. R. Ker's *Medieval Libraries* and its *Supplement*, a sizeable sample, if more ecclesiastical, than Worcester's reading materials, found only 381 dates in a list of donors nearly 140 pages long, a measure of the practice's rarity. Worcester may be among the pioneers in a developing fervour for dating: a closer look at Ker's lists finds an average of one per year for the first half of the fifteenth century (fifty-five dates); but this rate nearly doubles in the second half of the century (101 dates), and increases again between 1500 and the Reformation (153 dates).[28] For some months, Worcester's notebooks track his reading almost week by week.[29] His classical and historical notebook (Ju), in particular, narrates his reading only slightly less thoroughly than the so-called *Itineraries* notebook (Ca) traces his travels around southern England in 1478–80.

The barest date added to a manuscript, I suggest, constitutes a form of historical record. For, even more sharply than the provenances in Worcester's inscriptions, the dates are clearly surplus to any utilitarian requirements. So what inspires them? Worcester's cultivation of astronomy and calendrical science may have sharpened his temporal awareness: his earliest dates appear in astronomical tables copied on 4 March 1438 (La fos. 12^r, 42A^r), and calendars and almanacs remained for centuries a favoured site of the personal or familial archive.[30] However, just as his notes on other scholars and their books resemble some proprietorial marks in

---

[27] P. R. Robinson, *Dated and Datable Manuscripts c.737–1600 in Cambridge Libraries*, 2 vols. (Cambridge, 1988), i. 5, 9–11, gives details.

[28] Figures compiled from Ker, *Medieval Libraries*, 225–325, and A. G. Watson, *Supplement to the Second Edition* (London, 1987), 75–114.

[29] For example, in 1471 he moved from London on 7 Aug. (Ju fo. 105^r), to Canterbury by 16 Aug. (Ju fo. 123^r), to Cambridge by the end of the month (Ju fos. 121^r–2^v), to Norwich by 6 Sept. (Ju fo. 113^v), and back to Cambridge by 19 Sept. (Ju fo. 201^r).

[30] See, e.g., William H. Sherman, *John Dee: The Politics of Reading and Writing in the English Renaissance* (Amherst, Mass., 1995), 25, and Roger E. Stoddard, *Marks in Books* (Cambridge, Mass., 1985), no. 57. Worcester added personal details to an almanac known as 'The Chronicle of John Somer, OFM', ed. Jeremy Catto and Linne Mooney, in *Camden Miscellany XXXIV: Chronology, Conquest and Conflict in Medieval England*, Camden Society, 5th ser., 10 (Cambridge, 1997), 197–285: 214.

institutional books, so his concern with placing and dating his references and discoveries may also develop from his research into law and its cousin, genealogy. K. B. McFarlane long ago proposed that Worcester's wider antiquarian studies may have sprung from his duties tracing titles and descents for the lands acquired by Sir John Fastolf.[31] A legalistic mind-set could explain Worcester's precise histories of the books he had seen: many manuscripts in institutional or communal ownership had complex legal status as property, chained by entailments, usufruct, and reversions; *ex libris* and *ex dono* marks could serve to jog future legal memory (or even to jog the memory of thieving borrowers).[32] However, legal memory shades imperceptibly into historical memory, and Worcester's inscriptions cross that boundary. The places and owners he documents are often what literary critics call 'overdetermined': there is simply too much being said to allow only a utilitarian, legal interpretation. Moreover, even if such great detail would offer ideal, exemplary clarification in a public, legal document, why would Worcester exemplify that detail in his private marginalia and notebooks? Why should they require the content and carefulness of a paralegal text like an *ex libris*? The memorial function of legal record may influence Worcester, but from it he creates a private, literary history.

This suggestion perhaps sounds as if it stretches what one can say about such slight marks. However, the historian's impulse is clearer if we return to other elements of Worcester's inscriptions. First, although only a third of his dates give the exact day, when he gives only the month and year, he often leaves a space in the middle of the added inscription before the month. For example, he copied a list of famous men in London 'the ⟨gap⟩ day of September the year of our Lord 1469' and a list of saints compiled 'by the labour of Master William Clyff, the ⟨gap⟩ day of April, in London, the year of our Lord 1472' ('london' ⟨gap⟩ die mensis Septembris Anno christi 1469', 'de quodam labore magistri Willelmi Clyff ⟨gap⟩ die Aprilis london' Anno christi 1471', Ju fos. 42ᵛ, 57ʳ). The impulse to leave a precise report was strong enough for Worcester to leave a gap so that he might return to his notebooks on later occasions in order to complete the exact date as elsewhere. Had Worcester added the exact date in such cases, those dates would have been additions made by him as, strictly speaking, a

---

[31] K. B. McFarlane, 'The Investment of Sir John Fastolf's Profits of War', printed in his *England in the Fifteenth Century: Collected Essays*, ed. G. L. Harriss (London, 1981), 175–97: 194.

[32] Wendy Scase, 'Reginald Pecock, John Carpenter and John Colop's "Common-Profit" Books: Aspects of Book Ownership and Circulation in Fifteenth-Century London', *Medium Ævum*, 61 (1992), 261–74, records some such inscriptions.

historian: that is, as someone who records and clarifies details about events which are already in the past at the moment at which he writes. Yet, of course, the plan to compose a retrospective chronology of his studies is visible because, as here, he often failed to complete its gaps. Moreover, his initial failure to recall the dates of his reading suggests, finally, that Worcester may have added the inscription and its vaguer month and year late enough after the reading itself for him to have forgotten its exact date. His autobiographical inscriptions were not a spontaneous outpouring of marginalia, but reading recollected in tranquillity.

A closer glance at the manuscripts confirms this suspicion. At least fifty-five of those 103 inscriptions describing his reading are entirely later additions to his notes themselves. (This figure counts only the headings in his notebooks and omits *ex libris* and *ex dono* marks, which were necessarily added to finished texts.) Some thirty-seven of these added inscriptions tidy up his collection of classicizing and historical notes (Ju). These added records are in Worcester's hand, but are revealed to be supplements by a different coloured ink, by a cramped position above or alongside the scholarly notes themselves, or usually by both features. Some inscriptions also use a retrospective Latin past or 'perfect' tense: beside a medical recipe appears '1466 scripsi' or 'I wrote' (Sl fo. 26'). Therefore, brief and bare as their facts are, half of Worcester's identifications of the books he read and of the occasions on which he read them were in fact identifications added sometime after the textual encounter. Worcester's inscriptions, which one could use to compile a history of his reading, were originally themselves a historian's writings: they recorded his reading as a past event.

Writing and Reading

To identify Worcester as a historian for this reason may seem to overstate a case. We cannot know how much later he added these inscriptions in different ink; and the other half of his inscriptions seem contemporary with the scholarly notes they describe. However, this sane warning about dubbing Worcester's delayed inscriptions a 'history of reading' must also, dialectically, define all records of reading as immediately historical. As a physical process, to read and to write at the very same moment would be a difficult task: marginalia are necessarily records of one's thoughts written after one has, even if only momentarily, interrupted one's reading (that is, stopped actually running one's eyes over the text): as Eugene R.

Kintgen has observed, marginalia are 'products of reading rather than the process that led to those products'.[33] The *ex libris*, catalogue, marginalium, and notebook are all records of the use of books in what was already the past when those archives were composed. It seems fair to admit that the very possibility of historical research into Worcester's intellectual biography is predicated upon his own retrospective activity as a historical writer. As a consequence too, we need not then feel obliged to rewrite exactly those old histories: we ourselves have the liberty of readers to reinterpret those records.

Nevertheless, the time-lag in Worcester's inscriptions need not prompt global distrust of their historian's witness; a more cunning palaeographical and codicological analysis of watermarks, other extant records, and so on allows us to verify Worcester's account in many cases. The archaeologist of the material text perhaps has a greater, or at least a different, security of knowledge than the historian. Although some scholars have favoured more discursive or material sources than marginalia for the history of reading, H. J. Jackson's masterful, pragmatic overview of the subject warns that marginalia are the best evidence we have, if used with caution.[34] Rejecting the 'counsel of despair' of those who would ignore such evidence, Anthony Grafton concedes that the marginalia of sixteenth-century scholars were indeed 'a more formal, and later, reaction' to the texts they studied, but that we could study this more formal discourse of annotation in its own right.[35] Accordingly, many people have observed the communal and, by extension, political character of fifteenth-, sixteenth-, and seventeenth-century scholarship: readers such as Guillaume Budé, John Dee, and Gabriel Harvey preserved their readings for the future use of others.[36] A mnemonic utility may also dictate the explicit efforts at temporal record by Worcester; indeed, he explains that he gave some books or notes to other learned friends (for example, Ju fo. 169^r, Ca pp. 262, 312). Moreover, within such communal scholarship, the

---

[33] Eugene R. Kintgen, *Reading in Tudor England* (Pittsburgh, 1996), 214.

[34] H. J. Jackson, *Marginalia: Readers Writing in Books* (New Haven, 2001), 252–6. For various recent doubts about the usefulness of marginalia and notes, see William H. Sherman, 'What Did Renaissance Readers Write in their Books?', in Jennifer Andersen and Elisabeth Sauer (eds.), *Books and Readers in Early Modern England: Material Studies* (Philadelphia, 2002), 119–37: 130, and Randall Ingram, '*Lego Ego*: Reading Seventeenth-Century Books of Epigrams', in the same collection, 160–76: 160–1.

[35] Grafton, 'Is the History of Reading a Marginal Enterprise?', 155.

[36] Paul Saenger and Michael Heinlen, 'Incunable Description and its Implication for the Analysis of Fifteenth-Century Reading Habits', in Sandra Hindman (ed.), *Printing the Written Word: The Social History of Books circa 1450–1520* (Ithaca, NY, 1991), 225–58: 250.

biographical record of one's personal involvement can earn 'cultural capital', and thereby social or economic rewards.[37] Given that Worcester had once earned his living as Sir John Fastolf's household clerk, the careerist benefits of cultural capital may also perhaps explain his own concern to trace his scholarly progress.

However, within this communal, political, and economic space, Worcester's notes also carve out the private pathways of autobiography. Maurice Blanchot suggested that as the writer surrenders himself to the self-annihilation of literary creation, to the posterity and universality of art, he often begins his diary, dating and recording even his most mundane actions, in a rearguard preservation of selfhood.[38] William Worcester, as he participates in the communal scholarship of fifteenth-century England, similarly preserves a fragile historical record of his own self. The history of reading often focuses upon the community, whether 'interpretive', 'textual', or 'imagined';[39] Worcester, however, steps forward to assert his own role as one of the individuals of whom such communities are constituted and by whom they are recorded. Yet, although Worcester's practice is unusual for the fifteenth century in bulk and in explicitness, its extremity only highlights the self-aggrandizement and self-memorialization implicit in the more fleeting, spare, or scattered marks of reading or book use by others such as the amateur bibliographers Thomas Swalwell of Durham, Clement of Canterbury, or the librarians of Rochester and Chichester.[40] Was other people's record-keeping, or were other, more familiar forms of scribal activity, an autobiographical and historical written discourse?

Two scholars of the history of reading have introduced their subject by speaking of the 'fundamental distinction' between writing and reading:[41] this distinction perhaps seemed essential as the history of reading flourished in the space created by scepticism concerning the author's role in literary culture. However, Worcester's example suggests that the so-called history of reading could be redescribed as the history of previous people's

---

[37] Grafton, 'Is the History of Reading a Marginal Enterprise?', 155–6; Sherman, *John Dee*, 88–9.

[38] Maurice Blanchot, 'The Essential Solitude', in his *The Gaze of Orpheus and Other Literary Essays*, trans. Lydia Davis (Barrytown, NY, 1981), 63–77: 71–2.

[39] For the background and bibliography of this focus, see Jocelyn Wogan-Browne, 'Analytical Survey 5: "Reading is Good Prayer": Recent Research on Female Reading Communities', *New Medieval Literatures*, v (2002), 229–97: 230.

[40] On whom, see Ker, *Medieval Libraries*, pp. xxvii, 160, 243, 248, and Watson, *Supplement*, 97.

[41] Cavallo and Chartier (eds.), *History of Reading*, 1.

writings about reading. Such a reconceptualization might allow a *rapprochement* between the history of reading and the concerns of literary criticism: both in fact untease people's practices of representation and self-presentation in texts, whether those texts are brief *ex libris* notes or fuller fictions and autobiographies. In her recent book *The Anthology and the Rise of the Novel*, Leah Price brings the history of reading into rewarding dialogue again with literary criticism. Price explains that she has not analysed how novels were technically anthologized, in order to learn how they were read by contemporaries; rather, her method of 'close reading' made it more rewarding to study the prefaces, notes, and commentaries of such anthologies, 'where the editor becomes a writer'.[42] It is when the past reader becomes a writer that the historian of reading can herself actually begin to read.

But what happens to the past reader if we too become readers, of his writings? In *The Biographer's Tale*, Phineas G. Nanson worries that his study of Scholes Destry-Scholes will become confused if he concedes that Destry-Scholes shaped the archive of his intellectual life deliberately for some 'conceivable reader':

> It has been dinned into me that objectivity is an exploded and deconstructed notion. But subjectivity—the meeting of two hypothetical subjects, in this case Scholes Destry-Scholes and myself—is just as suspect, since it can't be looked at objectively.[43]

Nanson worried that to move from history to personal engagement, or to criticism, was a suspiciously solipsistic move. However, to reconceive the history of the book and the history of reading as a study of certain written discourses treats the past reader-writer with fair recognition. The very possibility of narrating a history of a book or of a particular reader rests upon the historical records and foresight of the people whose textual encounters we study. We may think that the scribblers of marginalia, of *ex libris* or *ex dono* marks, or even of catalogues 'could have had no conceivable reader in mind' for their rough jottings: but in fact we, like Nanson, should recognize that it is we who read history in those marks, and yet we can do so because they wrote that history first.

Christ's College, Cambridge

---

[42] Leah Price, *The Anthology and the Rise of the Novel from Richardson to George Eliot* (Cambridge, 2000), 11–2. See also Ingram, '*Lego Ego*', 160–2, 172–4, for a similar approach, which has informed this study of Worcester.
[43] Byatt, *Biographer's Tale*, 98.

Appendix: Books Containing Worcester's Hand

This list excludes correspondence and other loose documents by Worcester or in his hand, some in Norman Davis (ed.), *Paston Letters and Papers of the Fifteenth Century*, 2 vols. (Oxford, 1971–6), and others to appear in a third volume, edited by Richard Beadle and Colin Richmond, forthcoming from the Early English Text Society in 2005. I must thank Dr Beadle and Prof. L. Mooney for assistance in tracing Worcester's books. Items in this list marked with an asterisk do not contain his name, but his hand alone.

I. His own works

* Cambridge, Emmanuel College, MS I. 2. 10 (Scrope's *Dicts*, revised by Worcester)
* London, British Library, MS Royal 18. B. xxii (*The Boke of Noblesse*)
* London, Lambeth Palace, MS 506 (historical 'codicil' to *The Boke of Noblesse*)

II. Notebooks

Cambridge, Corpus Christi College, MS 210 (topography: *Itineraries*)
London, British Library, MS Additional 28208 (estate records)
London, British Library, MS Cotton Julius F. vii (classicism and history)
London, British Library, MS Royal 13. C. i (classicism and history)
London, British Library, MS Sloane 4 (medicine)
London, College of Arms, MS Arundel 48 (history)
Oxford, Bodleian Library, MS Laud misc. 674 (astronomy)

III. Annotations or ownership notes

* Cambridge, Pembroke College, MS 215 (Chaucer, *Boece*)
Cambridge, University Library, MS Additional 7870 (French treatises on cardinal virtues)
London, British Library, MS Cotton Julius E. iv (4) (*Gesta Henrici Quinti*)
* London, College of Arms, MS M. 9 (Fastolf's chronicle)
Oxford, Balliol College, MS 124 (classical geography and history)
Oxford, Bodleian Library, MS Auct. F. 3. 25 (Greek literature)
* Oxford, Magdalen College, MS lat. 8 (Isidore of Seville)
Oxford, Magdalen College, MS lat. 26 (*Liber de sacramentis ecclesiae*)
Oxford, Magdalen College, MS lat. 65 (Walter Burley, *Aristotelis problemata*)
Oxford, Magdalen College, MS lat. 166 (Cassiodorus, *Variae*)
Oxford, Magdalen College, MS lat. 198 (Boccaccio, *De casibus virorum illustrium*)
* Oxford, Magdalen College, MS lat. 206 (part ii: Nonius Marcellus)
Oxford, New College, MS 162 (Arnoldus de Villanova, *De Febribus*)

Vernacular Philosophy and the Making of Orthodoxy in the Fifteenth Century

Mishtooni Bose

I

STUDENTS of the early Christian Church have long been aware that, as one has put it, 'orthodoxy is *constructed*, in the processes of both theological and political conflict'.[1] This perspective can usefully be brought to bear on later phases of Christian thought. The Wycliffite controversies have served to focus scholarly attention on the processes whereby religious 'orthodoxy' has evolved diachronically and dynamically through interaction with specific political, social, and cultural circumstances. Studies of the controversies, particularly in the broader context of medieval European heresy, have gradually called into question the adequacy of modern taxonomy used to describe such cultural phenomena, and the extent to which the terms 'orthodoxy', 'heresy', and, in this particular instance, 'Lollardy' can usefully function as distinct historiographical categories that do justice to complex and heterogeneous manifestations of late-medieval religion.[2] In line with this desire to revise the historiographical framework in which we seek to understand the impact

This is a revised version of papers given at the 36th International Congress on Medieval Studies at Kalamazoo, Michigan, and to the Medieval Graduate Seminar in the Faculty of English, University of Cambridge. I am grateful to Miri Rubin, James Simpson, and the participants on both occasions for encouragement and stimulating discussion; and particularly to Rita Copeland for asking me about 'vernacular philosophy'. Further work on the article was supported by the University of Southampton, the British Academy, the Arts and Humanities Research Board, and Clare Hall, Cambridge.

[1] Rowan Williams (ed.), *The Making of Orthodoxy: Essays in Honour of Henry Chadwick* (Cambridge, 1989), p. ix.

[2] The following is a representative sample of articles that explore this issue from a variety of perspectives: J. A. F. Thomson, 'Orthodox Religion and the Origins of Lollardy', *History*, 74 (1989), 39–55; R. N. Swanson, 'Literacy, Heresy, History and Orthodoxy: Perspectives and Permutations for the Later Middle Ages', in Peter Biller and Anne Hudson (eds.), *Heresy and Literacy, 1000–1530* (Cambridge, 1994), 279–93; Andrew Larsen, 'Are all Lollards Lollards?', in Fiona Somerset, Jill C. Havens, and Derrick G. Pitard (eds.), *Lollards and their Influence in Late Medieval England* (Woodbridge, 2003), 59–72.

of Wycliffism, it has recently been suggested that English culture during the late fourteenth and fifteenth centuries was in fact marked by a preoccupation with 'anti-heresy'.[3] This perspective re-emphasizes the agency of contemporary ecclesiastical legislators, rather than that of their often shadowy quarry, in shaping the cultural and intellectual atmosphere of this period. It also recalls us to a perspective on the same period best represented by Michael Wilks's observation that 'as [Lollardy] became less dangerous, so it was the more severely persecuted'.[4]

Although Wilks's comment was originally intended to describe the 'ecclesiastical censure' brought to bear on suspected heretics during the fifteenth century, it is an equally apt reflection on the literary dimensions of the controversies; and, in particular, on the fact that the years that saw the failure of the Oldcastle rebellion, the executions of Jan Hus and Jerome of Prague at the Council of Constance, and the subsequent exhumation and burning of Wyclif's bones inaugurated a period during which, as original Wycliffite writings themselves became more scarce, avowed 'orthodoxy' was as much in dialogue with itself as it was with Wycliffite positions, whether real or imagined.[5] This period, in which Lollardy entered its 'underground' phase, is the setting of the present article. I will trace here the contrasting intellectual trajectories of two monumental bodies of anti-Wycliffite writing produced at this time: Thomas Netter's *Doctrinale Antiquitatum Fidei* (c.1421–30) and the writings of Reginald Pecock (1440s–50s), of which six vernacular works are extant.[6] The radical disjunction between the argumentative strategies used by Netter and Pecock brings sharply into focus the unresolved concerns among the avowedly orthodox over the kinds of learning (*clergie*) that it was appropriate, or even possible, to 'translate' into the extramural world. In exploring this disjunction, I will show how developments in

---

[3] Ian Forrest, 'Ecclesiastical Justice and the Detection of Heresy in England, 1380–1430' (D.Phil. thesis, Oxford, 2003), 1–17.

[4] Michael Wilks, 'Royal Priesthood: The Origins of Lollardy' (1978), repr. in *idem, Wyclif: Political Ideas and Practice*, selected and introduced by Anne Hudson (Oxford, 2000), 101–16: 113.

[5] For a vivid and detailed evocation of the contested character of religious orthodoxy in mid-fifteenth-century England, see R. M. Ball, 'The Opponents of Bishop Pecok', *Journal of Ecclesiastical History*, 48 (1997), 230–62.

[6] On the 'underground' phase of Lollardy, see J. A. F. Thomson, *The Later Lollards, 1414–1520* (Oxford, 1965); Anne Hudson, *The Premature Reformation: Wycliffite Texts and Lollard History* (Oxford, 1988), 446–56 (with an important distinction between the production of new works and the copying of existing ones (p. 453)). The term itself comes from Malcolm Lambert, *Medieval Heresy: Popular Movements from the Gregorian Reform to the Reformation*, 3rd edn. (Oxford, 2002), 288–305: 288.

intellectual life in fifteenth-century England affected, and exposed, the constructed and contingent character of its religious 'orthodoxy'.[7]

Recent work on the dissemination of bodies of knowledge (*clergie*) beyond the universities and into the vernaculars, on the nature of Lancastrian religious culture, and on the scope and content of post-Wycliffite theology, has laid the foundations of a critical narrative that might make sense of the intellectual discontinuity between Netter and Pecock.[8] The narrative presented here, however, both complements and complicates established readings of this period. In focusing on Pecock, for example, it draws attention to one of the two most stubborn, substantial, and egregious exceptions to Nicholas Watson's influential interpretation of Lancastrian religious culture, the other exception being the *Boke* of Margery Kempe (Watson significantly separates Pecock and the *Boke* from 'hagiographic poets such as Capgrave, Bokenham and Lydgate'[9]). It might reasonably be argued that the *Boke*'s devotional and hagiographical generic markings reflect an overwhelmingly different religious *mentalité* from that manifested in Pecock's works. Nevertheless, if we view the *Boke* as a text that fundamentally expresses and transmits clerical, and specifically episcopal, priorities, its relationship to Pecock's vernacular experiments begins to seem more substantial.[10] It is rewarding to reflect on possible connections between these bodies of writing (and not merely because Pecock, the eager purveyor of *skiles* to the spiritually ambitious laity, would have made a provocative and ambiguous character in the *Boke*; one can only view with irony the fact that accidents of time and space mean

[7]   On the necessity for further study of intellectual life in England during this period, and its relation to broader European currents of thought, see Kantik Ghosh, *The Wycliffite Heresy* (Cambridge, 2001), 213–14, 216. A seminal study is N. D. Hurnard, 'Studies in Intellectual Life in England from the Middle of the Fifteenth Century till the Time of Colet' (D.Phil. thesis, Oxford, 1935). A rich characterization of the variety and eclecticism of English theology during this period is given in Jeremy Catto, 'Theology after Wycliffism', in J. I. Catto and Ralph Evans (eds.), *The History of the University of Oxford*, vol. ii: *Late Medieval Oxford* (Oxford, 1992), 263–80.

[8]   Fiona Somerset, *Clerical Discourse and Lay Audience in Late Medieval England* (Cambridge, 1998); Nicholas Watson, 'Censorship and Cultural Change in Late-Medieval England: Vernacular Theology, the Oxford Translation Debate, and Arundel's Constitutions of 1409', *Speculum*, 70 (1995), 822–64; Catto, 'Theology After Wycliffism'; Ghosh, *Wycliffite Heresy*; Katherine Walsh, 'Die englische Universität nach Wyclif: Von geistiger Kreativität zur Beamtenausbildung?', in Alexander Patschovsky and Horste Rabe (eds.), *Die Universität in Alteuropa* (Constance, 1994), 85–110.

[9]   Watson, 'Censorship', 833.

[10]   A persuasive reading of the *Boke* as 'an affirmation of the authority of the episcopacy', written 'by men, for men, and about men', is offered in Sarah Rees Jones, ' "*A peler of Holy Cherch*": Margery Kempe and the Bishops', in Jocelyn Wogan-Browne *et al.* (eds.), *Medieval Women: Texts and Contexts in Late Medieval Britain: Essays for Felicity Riddy* (Turnhout, 2000), 377–391: 390–1.

that it is not he, but the hostile Netter, who features in its pages). Both explore strategies for the brokering of relationships between laity and clergy in the post-Arundelian world, and thus suggest that in the interstices of Watson's narrative lie the possibilities of alternative mappings of the period, readings that emphasize the variety of intellectual resources and argumentative stances still available to its religious writers.[11] In uncovering specific academic contexts for Pecock's experimentation with vernacular orthodoxy, I will offer one such alternative narrative.

Studies of the intellectual dimensions and context of the Wycliffite controversies have shown that they self-consciously advanced the translation and transformation of academic currents of thought in the extramural world.[12] I will suggest here the usefulness of comparative perspectives in enabling us to interpret the intellectual cultures that arose in their aftermath. One comparatively unexplored aspect of Lancastrian culture is the extent to which England's 'curiously intimate as well as adversarial contact' with France during the Hundred Years War provoked any awareness among English readers of what was being achieved in contemporary French vernacular theology.[13] During precisely the same period in which Archbishop Arundel's *Constitutions* were seeking to prohibit the theological scope of literary materials proffered to readers of English, Jean Gerson, an ardent 'anti-heretic' himself, was experimenting prolifically with pastoral, polemical, and allegorical literature in both Latin and French, providing a provocative reminder of the many ways in which academic theology could attune itself to the extramural world, and to the spiritual needs of 'simples gens'. The literary experiments of theologians such as Gerson or Jean Germain, whose anti-Islamic and other avowedly orthodox writings are roughly contemporary with those of Pecock, provide a rich context in which to reassess his own bid for vernacular authority.[14] For the purposes of the present essay, however, the

---

[11]   Forrest, 'Ecclesiastical Justice' (e.g. p. 99) offers important criticisms of Watson's treatment and assessment of the significance of Arundel's legislation, and must be taken into account in future discussions of this period.

[12]   Somerset *et al.* (eds.), *Lollards and Their Influence*; Ghosh, *Wycliffite Heresy*; Somerset, *Clerical Discourse*.

[13]   Susan Crane, 'Anglo-Norman Cultures in England', in David Wallace (ed.), *The Cambridge History of Medieval English Literature* (Cambridge, 1999), 35–60: 52.

[14]   Mark Stephen Burrows, *Jean Gerson and* De Consolatione Theologiae *(1418): The Consolation of a Biblical and Reforming Theology for a Disordered Age*, Beiträge zur historischen Theologie, 70 (Tübingen, 1986); François Berriot, 'La *Tapisserie crestienne* manuscrite de Jean Germain, fresque sociale et culturelle (1457)' and 'L'Islam dans le *Débat* manuscrit de Jean Germain (1450)', both reprinted in *Spiritualités, Hétérodoxies et Imaginaires: Études sur le Moyen Âge et la Renaissance* (Saint-Etienne, 1994), 65–80 and 173–85.

principal comparative field is Scotland, and in particular the substantial vernacular writings of the Gerson-inspired theologian John Ireland.[15] J. A. W. Bennett has rightly pointed out that 'as a philosophical writer in the vernacular [Ireland] stands next to Hilton, Usk and Pecock', and it is surprising that this brief comparison has never been taken further.[16] In exploring some of the philosophical and rhetorical resources that Pecock and Ireland mobilized in order to make their theologies intelligible to lay audiences, I will show here that intellectual developments that might seem to have been generated solely within the matrix of the Wycliffite controversies were also being manifested in apparently independent cultural milieux.

This brings us to the definition and the implications of the term 'vernacular philosophy'. Coined for the purposes of the present discussion, the phrase obviously recalls 'vernacular theology', a term used productively in recent, influential discussions of late-medieval religious writing as a way of acknowledging the revisionary, transformative energies of the European vernaculars and the variety of ways in which they provided a forum for the transmission, exploration, criticism, and transformation of material that had originated in academic, monastic, or other learned settings.[17] Thus, for Bernard McGinn, the expression of religious discourse in the vernaculars resulted not in 'simple translation' but in 'remarkable new configurations' for the 'representation of mystical experience'.[18] Nicholas Watson uses the phrase specifically to denote a process that goes beyond 'mere' translation, involving a distinctive and often heterodox intervention in the development and dissemination of religious doctrine.

[15] John Ireland, *The Meroure of Wyssdome*, ed. C. Macpherson, F. Quinn, and C. MacDonald, Scottish Text Society, (Edinburgh, 3 vols. 1926–90). References to this work will give volume and page numbers.

[16] J. A. W. Bennett, ' "Those Scotch Copies of Chaucer" ', *Review of English Studies*, 32 (1981), 294–6: 296. Brother Bonaventure Miner rejects the notion that a substantial parallel can be drawn between Ireland and Pecock, but his characterization of Ireland's work as 'a thoughtful summary of Christian doctrine independent of any particular external challenge except the general one of improving the tone of Scottish society as a whole' underplays the rhetoric of confrontation with heresy that informs the structure of the *Meroure* and, I would argue, its emphasis on the importance of natural reason: 'The Popular Theology of John Ireland', *Innes Review*, 13 (1962), 130–46: 131.

[17] Bernard McGinn, 'Introduction: Meister Eckhart and the Beguines in the Context of Vernacular Theology', in Bernard McGinn (ed.), *Meister Eckhart and the Beguine Mystics: Hadewijch of Brabant, Mechtild of Magdeburg, and Marguerite Porete* (New York, 1994), 1–14. The current critical understanding of 'vernacular theology' is briefly appraised in Renate Blumenfeld-Kosinski, Duncan Robertson, and Nancy Bradley Warren (eds.), *The Vernacular Spirit: Essays on Medieval Religious Literature* (Basingstoke and New York, 2000), 2–3.

[18] Bernard McGinn, *The Flowering of Mysticism: Men and Women in the New Mysticism (1200–1350)* (New York, 1998), 19.

In such cases, far from being merely derivative of those in Latin, vernacular works 'generate their own systems'.[19]

With such a semantically rich term as 'vernacular theology' readily to hand, it might be asked what need there might be for the separate consideration of 'vernacular philosophy'. Clearly, the term could be used heuristically as a means of detecting equally transformative encounters between academic philosophy and the medieval vernaculars, and much work remains to be done in this area.[20] The justification for its use here, however, arises from the closest affinity between Pecock's and Ireland's vernacular experiments: namely, their shared emphasis on the importance of appeals to natural reason in the presentation of theological arguments. The prominence of 'doom of resoun' in Pecock, and of 'natural ressone' in Ireland, arises from their recognition that the writing of theology in the vernacular necessitates the restructuring of the *clergie* offered to a lay readership, and thus provides an opportunity to mould that readership in ways not attempted by the writers of devotional literature or hagiography. Both Pecock and Ireland use this opportunity to construct notably *philosophical* theologies, and thus to shape their lay audiences as fit consumers of a particular kind of dense and demanding *clergie*. In each case, the vernacularization of theology is accompanied by a renewed emphasis on its rationally defensible qualities to the extent that *resoun/ ressone* becomes the hallmark of these episodes in cultural translation. While wishing to harness the general conception of a transformative encounter between learned subject-matter and the vernacular, therefore, I am concerned here with a particular species of transformation that is quite at odds (most markedly so in Pecock's case) with the contemporary spread of the devotional, visionary, pastoral, and poetic literature that has hitherto provided fruitful contexts for discussion of 'vernacular theology'. In both of the cases to be considered here, albeit in different ways, the singularity of the final achievement is brought about by a renewed emphasis on the logical and philosophical dimensions of theology. Pecock's sense of the distinctiveness of his philosophical orientation is announced in the 'introductorie' to his earliest surviving work, *The Reule of Cristen Religioun*, in which the embodied 'treuþis of universal philosophie', combin-

---

[19] Nicholas Watson, 'Visions of Inclusion: Universal Salvation and Vernacular Theology in Pre-Reformation England', *Journal of Medieval and Early Modern Studies*, 27 (1997), 145–87: 146.

[20] Fiona Somerset's brief but suggestive comments on the translation of scientific texts in the late Middle Ages provide one starting-point for such an enquiry (*Clerical Discourse*, 11–12).

ing 'law of kynde' (nature) and 'lawe of feiþ', urge the author to restore
them to their rightful place at the heart of the work undertaken by the
'sones of God', the intellectual élite.[21] While his selection and adaptation
of philosophical resources for his vernacular experiments set them apart
(as Watson recognized) from the theological literature produced by his
contemporaries, I will also suggest that his involvement in this process is
one route by which he is connected, by analogy with Ireland's later experimentation, to broader currents and tendencies in northern European
thought during the fifteenth century. Singular though Pecock may appear
when viewed solely in the context of English theology, comparison between his methods of argumentation and Ireland's appeals to 'natural
ressone' shows how their impulses towards the reform and renewal of theological method were provoked and governed specifically by the rhetorical exigencies of addressing lay audiences in their respective vernaculars.
The result is two presentations of theology that construct a nexus between intramural and extramural worlds on emphatically philosophical,
rather than affective, grounds, and do not shield their readers from questions that continued to preoccupy professional theologians. Both broach
the delicate balancing act involved in preserving clerical authority while
turning lay readers into extramural 'schoolmen'. In 'translating' their
theologies, Pecock and Ireland reveal more fully to their readers, and in
genuinely disinterested ways that go beyond the rigid mentalities con-
jured up by the polarities of 'orthodoxy' and 'heresy', the intellectual
creativity of the academic cultures in which these theologies had
taken shape. Examination of their works thus takes us beyond both the
Wycliffite controversies themselves and the questions that have recently
exercised modern scholars concerning their complex contributions to the
dissemination of *clergie*.[22] Our critical narrative, which begins with the
discontinuity between Netter and Pecock, will move into different
territory, generating fresh questions about this phase in late-medieval
intellectual life.

[21] Pecock, *The Reule of Cristen Religioun*, ed. W. C. Greet, EETS os 171 (Oxford, 1927),
31–6.
[22] The terms in which Somerset discusses the problematic 'translation' of *clergie* during
the late fourteenth and early fifteenth centuries are useful for the interpretation of Pecock's
and Ireland's own cultural translations (see esp. *Clerical Discourse*, 3–16). Both could be said
to have produced late variations on 'extraclergial' writing, and Somerset's comments about
the surplus information provided in the texts she considers are particularly pertinent here
(p. 14).

II

In *The Repressor of Over-Much Blaming of the Clergy* (*c*.1449) Pecock comes closest to engaging in the hand-to-hand combat with Wycliffite arguments that had characterized Netter's method throughout the *Doctrinale*.[23] Nevertheless, these texts take their readers on markedly different journeys. Never the dutiful younger sibling of the *Doctrinale*, the later vernacular work is rather more like its dark twin, mapping out an intellectual world ostentatiously estranged from that evoked by Netter. In many respects, this should not surprise us. Recent critical attention to the considerable creative resources of theology in the vernacular certainly helps us to hear more clearly the mingled accents of revision, experimentation, and subversion at work in Pecock's prologue. In particular, his use of a quotation from St Paul that had also featured significantly in the prefatory material of Netter's *Doctrinale* provides us with the opportunity precisely to measure the difference between their respective intellectual orientations, and thus to trace the process whereby, in Watson's terms, Pecock 'generated' his own 'system'.

The text in question is Paul's injunction in 2 Tim. 4: 2: 'argue, obsecra, impreca in omni patientia et doctrina' ('reprove, entreat, exhort in all patience and doctrine'). In Netter's text, this injunction is woven into a network of biblical and patristic quotations that together constitute an elaborate humility topos, as when, in the prologue to Book I, he directs the injunction at himself. This is complemented by the active disavowal of his own authorial agency as further articulated through the words of Christ in John 7: 16: 'mea doctrina non est mea, sed ejus qui misit me' ('my doctrine is not mine, but that of him who sent me'). He thus invites his readers to believe that a ready separation can be made between the work's doctrine and its rhetoric, its demonstrations and its persuasions. By explicitly disowning his purposeful and motivated creativity, Netter instead claims for his text the role of the conduit through which an undiluted, uninflected 'concors Patrum' may flow.[24]

---

[23] Pecock, *The Repressor of Over-Much Blaming of the Clergy*, ed. Churchill Babington, 2 vols. (London, 1860); Netter, *Doctrinale Antiquitatum Fidei Ecclesiae Catholicae*, ed. B. Blanciotti, 3 vols. (Venice, 1757–9; repr. Farnborough, 1967). References to both works will give volume and page numbers.

[24] For discussion of Netter's investment in the distinction between 'text' and 'interpretation', see Ghosh, *Wycliffite Heresy*, 174–208. I explore the problematic relationship between Netter's intentions and his execution in 'Netter as Critic and Practitioner of Rhetoric: The *Doctrinale* as Disputation', in a forthcoming volume of essays on Netter, edited by Richard Copsey, O.Carm.

Whereas Paul's injunction had been only one of many quotations in Netter's preface, Pecock's prologue is structured as an extended commentary on this text, beginning with his own translation: 'Undirnyme thou, b013eche thou, and blame thou, in al pacience and doctrine.' This brings to the fore the necessary relationship between translation and transformation, since the necessity of translating the injunction for the benefit of his readers calls forth some creative exegesis from Pecock. In inviting his reader to ponder the meaning of Paul's words, he focuses specifically on the extent of the critical licence that the apostle was permitting to members of the early church. Roaming through the semantic field of the imperative 'undirnyme', he dwells in particular on the related English terms 'correpcioun' and 'correccioun', which denote distinct but related modes of criticism, the former more moderate than the latter.[25] In telling Timothy to 'undirnyme', he argues, Paul was advising his bishop merely to 'corrept', rather than to 'correct'; all the more should an unlearned person, who may be insufficiently learned to furnish examples in support of his anticlerical criticisms, desist from the harsher 'correccioun'. The crucial differences between acceptable and unacceptable criticism of the clergy should not, he insists, be blurred by the closeness of the lexemes that respectively represent them.

In enjoining 'correpcioun' on his reader, Pecock binds himself by the same terms. Saying that he will 'preie, speke and write in al pacience and doctrine', he adapts the Pauline injunction to authorize what he intends as the emollient rhetorical tenor of the ensuing work. It is here that he comes closest to resembling Netter, who had similarly used Paul's words to authorize and restrain the polemical stance of the *Doctrinale*. But Pecock was explicitly attempting to focus and direct the critical energies of lay people, and to provide a clerically authored primer in 'correpcioun'. By the end of his short prologue, he readily concedes that there are transgressions 'for whiche the clergy is worthi to be blamed in brotherly & nei3bourly correpcioun', and which he would 'not be aboute to excuse neither defende'.[26] The journey on which he takes his reader, therefore, swerves decisively away from the agenda and cultural world of the *Doctrinale*, and the distance between the cultural environments that produced these two texts can be precisely measured by the transformation of the exegetical freight that Paul's injunction carries as it passes from Netter's text to that of Pecock.

---

[25] Pecock, *Repressor*, i. 1.   [26] Ibid. i. 4.

III

Both Netter and Pecock represented their anti-heretical writings as breaks with a contaminated past, although there are considerable differences between the cultures that they identify as being in need of reformation. When introducing his literary monument, Netter reached for another Pauline topos, presenting himself as the 'wise master builder' (or more precisely the renovator) of a 'city' of orthodox Christendom under constant attack and badly in need of repair. He stated that he wished to rebuild 'murum in circuitu Civitatis, veterem scilicet professionem, et doctrinam Sanctorum Patrum' ('the wall surrounding the city, namely the ancient profession and doctrine of the holy Fathers').[27] Once again, a comparative perspective proves instructive. It is unlikely that Netter would have known or cared that he shared his city-building topos, and its revisionist energies, with Christine de Pizan. Pecock, however, dramatically recalls *Le Livre de la Cité des Dames* with his strikingly similar evocation in the *Reule*, of the 'annunciation' by the 'treuþis of . . . philosophie', who identify themselves as daughters of God.[28] They have been exiled not by an onslaught of heresies, but, less specifically, by 'oolde rehercellis, strange stories, fablis of poetis, newe invenciouns', which have beguiled the attention of clerks, or 'sones of god'. The terms of Pecock's criticism in the 'introductorie' to the *Reule* range from general disillusionment at the apparently diffuse, trivial, and worldly nature of a broadly conceived 'orthodox' culture to a more sharply focused critique of particular, and possibly heretical, transgressions based on misunderstandings of the semantic range of the term 'scripture'. Nevertheless, the 'introductorie' puts a clear distance between Pecock's position and that which he imputes to other clerks, allowing him to advance his distinctive views regarding the particular kinds of *clergie* appropriate to 'popular' orthodox discourse. Like the prologue to the *Repressor*, this scene invites the reader to follow Pecock on a markedly different path from that followed by Netter (and later, by Pecock's assiduous critic, Thomas Gascoigne) and to explore the possibility of alternative directions and sources of argumentation for

---

[27] Netter, *Doctrinale*, i. 25. On medieval uses of the master-builder trope, see Mary Carruthers, *The Craft of Thought: Meditation, Rhetoric, and the Making of Images, 400–1200* (Cambridge, 1998), 16–21.

[28] Pecock, *Reule*, 32. I discuss the parallels between Pecock and Christine further in 'The Annunciation to Pecock: Clerical *Imitatio* in the Fifteenth Century', *Notes and Queries*, 47 (2000), 172–6. The tradition of the Boethian 'inventive vision', to which both Christine and Pecock are indebted, is discussed by Carruthers, *Craft of Thought*, 173–6.

orthodoxy. Pecock thus used his entry into vernacularity not merely to 'translate' theology, but actively to criticize and reform it.

The marginal place that Pecock affords to patristic arguments contrasts markedly with Netter's copious citations from the Fathers. Having established himself as an artisan who has come to renovate the city of orthodoxy, Netter had described his particular selection of building materials in self-consciously disarming terms: 'Alii supervestiant . . . scholastico carmine rationum ordines . . . Mihi nihil aliud vacat, nisi lapides simplices Scripturarum, cum coemento veteris expositionis Sanctorum Patrum adjungere' ('Let others dress themselves . . . with the sequence of arguments in a scholastic song . . . My only task is to bind the simple stones of the Scriptures with the cement of the ancient expositions of the holy Fathers').[29] It has recently been argued that Netter can be viewed as Wyclif's 'hermeneutic confrère'.[30] By restricting himself to using only the patristic and other *auctoritates* acknowledged and used by Wyclif, he certainly runs the risk of making it seem as if Wyclif had done his thinking for him, carving out a canon of texts in which the truth of doctrine had been incorruptibly preserved. In fairness to Netter, however, it should be pointed out that there are precedents for this rhetorical manœuvre in earlier controversies, as when Occam in his *Dialogus* chose 'the terrain of his adversary', principally the *Decretum* and *Decretals*, in his polemic against the heretical pope John XXII.[31] Certainly, Netter presented his argumentative tactic as a deliberate rhetorical choice, rather than as a decision that had largely been made for him. This becomes clear in his aggressive characterization of Wyclif as a Goliath to Netter's David, challenging the whole of 'Israel'—that is, a clearly demarcated 'orthodoxy'—to single combat.[32] Just as David eventually cut off Goliath's head with his own sword, so Netter saw himself as destroying Wyclif from within the very argumentative frame of reference that his opponent had established.[33]

In his deployment of the David and Goliath imagery, Netter was self-consciously recycling the rhetoric of the twelfth-century Eucharistic controversies, taking up the stance of a latter-day Lanfranc against a new

---

[29] Netter, *Doctrinale*, i. 25.

[30] Ghosh, *Wycliffite Heresy*, 174–208.

[31] Jean-Philippe Genet, 'Les Auteurs politiques et leur maniement des sources en Angleterre à la fin du moyen âge', in Monique Ornato and Nicole Pons (eds.), *Pratiques de la Culture Ecrite en France au XVe Siècle: Actes du Colloque International du CNRS Paris, 16–18 Mai 1992* (Louvain-La-Neuve, 1995), 345–59: 347–9.

[32] Netter, *Doctrinale*, i. 7, referring to i Sam. 17: 8. David beheads Goliath with his own sword in v. 51.

[33] Netter reprises the David and Goliath imagery in *Doctrinale*, i. 808.

Berengar.[34] If he is caught in a rhetorical web, therefore, it is a denser one than that spun solely by Wyclif. In a single paragraph in the *Repressor*, however, Pecock moves beyond such controversial rhetoric altogether, invalidating the use of patristic quotations in anti-heretical argument and using exactly the same scriptural *locus* as that used by Netter with which to do so. He imagines an opponent who would counter his own arguments with material drawn from 'summe writingis of oolde and holy Doctouris', even if such writings contradicted that opponent's own views:

Not for that he admyttith, receueth, and allowith the writingis of tho Doctouris, for thane he schulde smyte him silf with his owne stroke; but for that he knowith me admytte and allowe the writingis of Doctouris, therefore he makith aʒens me this assaut, in pretending as thouʒ he wole do to me as Dauid did to Golie in smiting of of Golies heed with his owne swerd.[35]

What Pecock invalidates here is not merely the use of patristic authorities in such a context, but the rhetorical manœuvres that the citation of *auctoritates* permits and the stalemate in which they trap those who use them (the sense of hermeneutic 'deadlock' to which Ghosh refers is surely communicated by Pecock here[36]). His dismissal of the imagined challenge in this passage takes matters much further than Netter had envisaged, and we may view with irony the fact that this is achieved through his appropriation of precisely the same topos as that used by his illustrious predecessor. Pecock was convinced that his opponent would be using the arguments of the Fathers in bad faith, and he used this as an excuse for not buttressing his own arguments with patristic quotations: it is as if they have been drained of their rhetorical energies by constant use in controversy, and have thus become the devalued currency of anti-heretical argumentation. In essence, Pecock is simply acknowledging here that authority has a 'wax nose', but his exploration of the problems that this posed for anti-heretical argumentation is by no means glib.[37] His exposure of the limitations of a patristically grounded orthodoxy led him to search for a radically different theological method. In the quest for this new foundation, he turned away not only from an imaginary hereti-

---

[34] See, e.g., *Liber de Corpore et Sanguine Domini, Patrologia Latina*, ed. J. P. Migne (Paris 1841–) 150, col. 412. I am grateful to Ian Levy for a copy of his unpublished paper 'Forcing the Heretic out of the Tradition', in which he points out Lanfranc's use of this imagery.

[35] Pecock, *Repressor*, i. 71.

[36] Ghosh, *Wycliffite Heresy*, 212.

[37] On this topos, see P. von Moos, 'Das argumentative Exemplum und die "wächse Nase" der Autorität im Mittelalter', in W. J. Aerts and M. Gosman (eds.), *Exemplum et Similitudo: Alexander the Great and Other Heroes as Points of Reference in Medieval Literature* (Groningen, 1988), 55–84.

cal opponent but also, more controversially, from a prestigious anti-Wycliffite predecessor.

IV

In the epistle to Martin V with which he begins Book I of the *Doctrinale*—a book in which he would mount a detailed and adept critique of Wyclif's logic and metaphysics—Netter declares that his work is not a scholastic game but a work of faith ('non scholasticus ludus est, sed fidei series'). With this rhetoric, as with his disavowal of 'scholastic song' in the quotation given above, Netter contributes to the reification of 'scholasticism' as a distinct, coherent phenomenon, and his characterization of Wyclif as an obfuscating schoolman is an important dimension of such rhetoric. His authorial self-definition and his intentions for the *Doctrinale* are thus bound up with a tension in his attitudes towards the language of scholastic 'sublimitates'. Throughout the *Doctrinale*, the lines between critical analysis and polemic are repeatedly blurred, so that Netter's absorbed engagement in logic is framed by a rhetoric of disengagement not only from Wyclif's own logical 'subtleties' but more generally from these aspects of professional, academic discourse. In re-creating the heated controversies of a recent academic past, Netter memorializes them, installing the patristic orientation of the *Doctrinale* as their replacement.

Although he never mentions Netter, the evolution of Pecock's 'vernacular philosophy' can be understood as a direct and hostile reaction to the attitudes embedded, and embodied, in Netter's anti-scholastic rhetoric. In *The Folewer to the Donet*, he ruefully evoked what he saw as the sterility of contemporary intellectual life in a sour little vignette:

[Y] haue wiste wiþin þese vj yeeris passed þat it haþ be seid of hem which helden hem clerkis: 'fy in resoun, fy in argumentis.' And summe oþire wolden lauȝe and calle 'sophym', whanne it was alleggid þat a trouþ was prouyd by sillogisme, which is þe strengist argument forto proue that may be.[38]

Pecock insisted that faith could not be understood except 'bi argument, which is a sillogisme; or bi sum other reducible into a sillogisme', and that teaching could not take place 'without such seid agument being in the undirstonding of the leerner, whilis he it leernith'.[39] The centrality of the

---

[38] Pecock, *The Folewer to the Donet*, ed. E. V. Hitchcock. EETS os 164 (London, 1924), 10.
[39] Pecock, *The Book of Faith*, ed. J. L. Morison (Glasgow, 1909), 126.

syllogism in his thought, and in particular his view that lay people possessed the innate ability to syllogize, are the most important and distinctive characteristics of his work, and the originality or otherwise of this aspect of his work has until now proved difficult to assess. Although he does not attribute this central aspect of his thought to any particular theologian or theological 'school', it will be shown here that it is possible to reconstruct a rich discursive context for his ideas on this subject. In distancing himself from methodological solutions of the kind that had been offered by Netter, Pecock turned pointedly back to logic and natural philosophy in his search for a means to reinvigorate and reinvent theology in the particular vernacular setting that he planned for it.

Pecock's broader intellectual affiliations come into focus in the eighth chapter of the *Folewer*. Here, the 'son', who is one of the interlocutors in the book's pedagogical dialogue, suggests that animals 'maken trewe proposicions in summe of her inward wittis, and arguen and prouen in sensible þingis'.[40] He further ventures the argument that animals possess rational powers analogous to those of men in that they are capable of learning new things on the basis of what they hold as established knowledge. This, he explains, is the kind of rudimentary reasoning exhibited by greyhounds when they alter their course to anticipate and thus cut off a hare's escape route across a field, rather than simply following their prey round it.[41] In the father's response, Pecock immediately distances himself from established thinking on this matter.[42] Acknowledging that authoritative academic opinion holds that 'no beest may in his wittes make discurse', he nevertheless admits that he cannot see why this might not be possible, and is clearly tempted by the theory that 'beestis mowe and kunnen forme proposicions, argue and proue and gete knowyng to hem bi argument of verri silogisme and of induccioun about þo þingis whiche þei mowe bi her outward and inward wittis perceyue'. He concedes that beasts may not reason as perfectly as men, just as some beasts are more capable of reasoning than others, but he maintains that it is easier to hold

---

[40] Pecock, *Folewer*, 35.
[41] Ibid. 35–6.
[42] On this theme in classical thought, see Richard Sorabji, *Animal Minds and Human Morals: The Origins of the Western Debate* (London, 1993), 12–16, 78–98. Sorabji discusses disagreements between Aristotle and other thinkers concerning the extent to which animals are capable of rationality. Philo of Alexandria considers the argument that a hound in pursuit of its prey makes use of 'the fifth complex indemonstrable syllogism' in Abraham Terian, *Philonis Alexandrini* De Animalibus: *The Armenian Text with an Introduction, Translation, and Commentary* (Chico, Calif., 1981), 237 (text), 156–7 (commentary, in which Terian points out the Chrysippean provenance of this argument). I am grateful to Sarah Pearce for sharing her expertise regarding Philo.

the view that beasts are capable of some rational thought than that they are not, the latter conclusion 'comonli holden and writen in summe bookis of philosophie'. He ends with the caveat that this is not his settled opinion, however, and he distinguishes his arguments here from 'myne oþire synguler opynyons', in which he has more confidence. In response to the son's request, the father points out that a dog that has been beaten for taking meat from a table can be taught not to repeat its actions. In order to avoid being beaten again, the dog needs in effect to reason syllo-gistically, associating the taking of meat with the punishment to be avoided. Pecock argues that although the dog is not able in this case to rea-son demonstratively, the conclusion reached is sufficient to alter the dog's behaviour. This enables him to make an important analogy between the elementary reasoning of beasts and *illiterati*: 'þilke silogismes be maad hastili and quycli, as they ben oft made swiftly and quycli in men, þou3 þei be not lettrid and not enformyd in craftial logik, but endewid oonli with natural and usual logik, which neuerþeles is þe same with craftial logik, so þat y take þis name "craftial" here largely for al þat is founden and formyd expresseli bi mannys witt and bisinesse.'[43]

Pecock presents this aspect of his thought as purely original, and his modern editors tacitly endorse this view. In what follows, he draws atten-tion to the potentially transgressive elements of his thinking. In his role as the exemplary sceptic, the 'son' presses the 'father' on this issue, pointing out that 'summe men wolen wondre here upon þis'. The father's answer is robust and revealing:

[M]any wolen wondir if y schulde putte so greet wijsdom in lay peple þat þo sim-plyst of hem han and maken silogismes, and þat þe simplyst persoon of kunnyng þat is, may not knowe eny trouþ of þo trouþis whiche ben not open to ech re-soun, but if he þerupon have a silogisme, and þat he may not leerne eny þing of þe new wiþout þat he haue þerupon a silogisme in his undirstondying . . . Also, sone, if y schulde seie þat þe lay people han in her undirstondyng naturali þe same logik whiche clerkis han craftily or doctrinali, many men wolen wonder herupon, and hit [*sic*] if þis be wel considered, it wole be founde for trewe.[44]

'Wondering', the father concludes, is no basis on which to undermine truth. In his final words on this subject, he points out that some clerks agree with him as to the extent of the knowledge acquired by beasts, but that they see this knowledge as the product of 'natural instinct or . . . natural prickyng or stiryng', whereas he insists on its being the fruit of a rudimentary form of syllogizing.

[43] Pecock, *Folewer*, 37.   [44] Ibid. 37–8.

Pecock then moves to a brief discussion of optical theory, in order to conclude his discussion of the inward and outward 'wits'. This topic might initially seem to have no bearing on the subject of 'doom of resoun', but, as will shortly be seen, it is absolutely germane to Pecock's thought on that issue, and points us towards a possible source for his fundamental ideas. He explains how 'the wirchyng of spiritis' renders the objects of sight visible, carrying them into 'þe comune witt and into þe ymaginacioun', and thereby offering a model of the way in which the other senses convey information to the mind. The chapter concludes with a paragraph that explains how sight is achieved, and it is here that Pecock's precise debts to academic traditions become clearer. He understands sight to be achieved in three ways: directly, 'bi riȝt beemes goyng from þe obiect into þe iȝe seyng', by refraction ('bi broken beemes'), and by reflection ('bi reboundid beemes'). This reveals him to subscribe to the long-established theory of intromission, which held that sight is achieved by the multiplication of species ('spiritis' in Pecock) from external objects to the eye, and thus into the mind. It is Pecock's familiarity with the theory of intromission that enables us to locate more precisely the tap-root of his thinking not merely about optical theory, but also about the innate syllogistic powers of the laity.

The suggestive juxtaposition in the *Folewer* between a discussion of the rational powers of 'parfite notable beestis' and one concerning optics leads us first to a treatise that discusses psychological aspects of visual perception. As Chaucer attests in the *Squire's Tale* (l. 232), the *auctoritates* in the field of optical theory included 'Alocen, and Vitulon'. Although they post-date the period in which Pecock took his BA by some twenty years, the Oxford statutes of 1431 permitted students to substitute the study of 'Alicen' or the Polish philosopher Witelo on perspective for the first six books of Euclid's geometry.[45] 'Alicen' (otherwise known in the Middle Ages as 'Alhacen' and referred to as such here), is the Arab philosopher Ibn Al-Haytham, author of a treatise on optics, the Latin title of which was variously given as *Perspectiva*, or *De aspectibus*.[46] Passages from *De*

---

[45] *Statuta Antiqua Universitatis Oxoniensis*, ed. Strickland Gibson (Oxford, 1931), pp. xciv, 234. 28–30; J. D. North, 'Natural Philosophy in Late Medieval Oxford', in Catto and Evans (eds.), *History of the University of Oxford*, 64–102: 97.

[46] Katherine H. Tachau, *Vision and Certitude in the Age of Ockham: Optics, Epistemology and the Foundations of Semantics 1250–1345* (Leiden, 1988); on Alhacen's writings on optics and this work in particular, see *The Optics of Ibn Al-Haytham, Books I–III: On Direct Vision*, trans. A. I. Sabra, 2 vols. (London, 1989), i. pp. xxxii–xxxiii, liii–lxxiii. The text and translation given below are from *Alhacen's Theory of Visual Perception: A Critical Edition, with English Translation and Commentary, of the First Three Books of Alhacen's* De aspectibus, *the Medieval Latin Version of Ibn*

aspectibus provide one substantial, authoritative, academic context for Pecock's own belief that the laity are capable of syllogistic thought.

In Book II, Alhacen draws an extended comparison between the manner in which perception occurs and the way in which individuals judge the conclusion of an argument. In each case, he points out, the process takes place in an instant, effectively before it makes itself felt as 'discourse' (and here we may remember Pecock's observation that 'natural' syllogisms occur 'swiftly and quycli' in the minds of the unlearned):

Sillogismi ergo quorum propositiones sunt universales et manifeste comprehenduntur in tempore insensibili . . . Et secundum hunc modum erit comprehensio virtutis distinctive ad plures intentiones que comprehenduntur ratione in tempore insensibili sine indigentia argumentationis iterande.

Therefore, syllogisms whose premises are universal and obvious are grasped in an imperceptible amount of time . . . In this way the faculty of discrimination will grasp numerous deductions that are reached by means of judgment in an imperceptible amount of time without having to go through the steps of argumentation.[47]

It follows from this that knowledge of the precise technical terms by which such discourse is subsequently represented is unnecessary for all human beings who perceive and judge. This may be seen from the fact that children and unlearned individuals exercise the ability to form rational judgements, even when uninstructed in the formal workings of the syllogism:

[P]uer, quando ei demonstrantur duo ex eodem genere, sicut duo poma, et fuerit unum pulcrius alio, accipiet pulcrius et dimittet alterum . . . electio pulcrioris non est nisi per propositionem universalem dicentem quod est pulcrius est melius, et quod est melius est dignius ad eligendum. Ipse ergo utitur hac propositione, et non percipit quod utitur ea . . . Et cum puer arguit et nescit quid est argumentum, anima ergo humana est nata ad arguendum sine difficultate et labore, et non percipit homo apud comprehensionem rei quod sit huiusmodi quod sit per argumentum.

[W]hen two things of the same kind, such as two fruits, are shown to a child, and when one is more attractive than the other, he will accept the more attractive one and reject the other . . . the choice of the more attractive is based entirely upon a major premise that asserts that what is more attractive is better, and what is better is more worthy of being chosen. The child therefore uses this premise, but he does

---

al-Haytham's Kitab al-Manazir, ed. and trans. A. Mark Smith, 2 vols. (Philadelphia, 2001). References are to volume and page number.

⁴⁷ *Alhacen's Theory of Perception*, i. 107, ii. 435.

not perceive that he is using it . . . [S]ince the child does deduce yet has no idea
what a deduction is, it follows that the human soul is inherently apt to engage in
deduction without difficulty or effort, yet when a man perceives that something
is of such-and-such a kind, he does not perceive that he achieves this perception
through deduction.[48]

Whether or not Alhacen is the single source of Pecock's theories concerning the accessibility of 'doom of resoun' by the lay intellect, his writings present one authoritative means by which such views could have
been transmitted to Pecock. He is not, however, the only possible source
for Pecock's views on this subject. Roger Bacon's mid-thirteenth-century
exploration of the 'innateness' of logic and grammar had led him to discuss the close relationship between naturally endowed and professionally
acquired modes of reasoning and in the process to assemble a rich cluster
of texts in which Alhacen's observations on the cognitive powers of children are considered together with similar views taken from Aristotle,
Boethius, and Avicenna:

De logica enim non est vis tanta, quia scimus eam per naturam, licet vocabula
logicae in lingua, qua utimur, quaerimus per doctrinam. Sed ipsam scientiam
habent homines ex natura, sicut docet author Perspectivae in secundo libro, et
Boetius hoc docet in primo libro super Topica M. Tullii, et inferius in eodem
commentario. Et Aristoteles dicit quod idiotae syllogizant.[49]

Logic is not a very powerful art, because we know it naturally, even though we acquire through teaching the logical terminology that we use. Men possess this science naturally, as the author of the *Perspective* teaches in book two; and Boethius
teaches this in his first book on Cicero's *Topics*, and later in the same commentary.
Aristotle, too, says that the uninstructed syllogize.

Bacon goes on to observe that people discourse rationally, commanding
notions of causality and offering supporting reasons in discussions, none
of which could take place without argumentation. Furthermore, he argues, all men respond to falsity by denying it, and to fallacies by saying
that they do not follow them 'because of such and such a cause' ('propter
talem vel talem causam'), unwittingly using what amounts to technical
terminology. This leads Bacon to his conclusion:

Unde licet laici non habeant vocabula logicae quibus clerici utuntur, tamen
habent suos modos solvendi omne argumentum falsum. Et ideo vocabula sola

[48] *Alhacen's Theory of Perception*, i. 108–9; ii. 436–7.
[49] Roger Bacon, *Opus tertium*, in *Opera quaedam hactenus inedita*, ed. J. S. Brewer (London,
1859), 102.

logicorum deficiunt laicis, non ipsa scientia logicae . . . Et Avicenna dicit, in log-ica sua, quod rusticus Arabicus scit grammaticam per naturam; quod oportet, si logicam sciamus per naturam, quae posterior est. Vocabula enim grammaticae et logicae discimus; sed naturaliter scimus componere orationes ex dictionibus, et argumenta ex propositionibus. Et hoc docet grammatica, et logica.[50]

Thus, although laymen do not have at their command the logical terms that clerks use, nevertheless, they have their own ways of solving every false argument. Thus, the laity only lack the logicians' terms, rather than the understanding of logic itself . . . And Avicenna says, in his writing on logic, that an Arab peasant naturally knows grammar, which must follow if we naturally know logic, which builds on grammar. We learn the technical terms of grammar and logic, but we naturally know how to compose speeches from words and arguments from propositions. This is what grammar and logic teach.

What is most distinctive about this conclusion, and seems to anticipate Pecock's own engagement with this subject, is its emphasis on the close-ness between clerical and lay mental worlds. In his conclusion, Bacon im-plicitly acknowledges that a clerk was once a layman who has since been initiated into the world of *clergie* by having been exposed to *doctrina*, and having acquired the requisite *vocabula* through which to represent and understand the operations of his mind. He lays bare the extent to which access to *clergie* is a matter of professionalization and acculturation.

It is hard to resist seeing parallels between Pecock and Bacon, two creative, transgressive thinkers engaged in the criticism and reformation of theological method and renegotiating its relationship with the arts of discourse. Whether or not Pecock was familiar with Bacon's particular exploration of this topic, however, the sources that Bacon cites in support of his observations about the 'natural logic' of the laity independently form a more precise and substantial academic context for Pecock's own theories concerning 'doom of resoun' than has hitherto been recognized. In particular, Bacon's reference to *idiotae* points to the medieval transla-tions of *De sophisticis elenchis*, and hence to a widely accessible and likely forebear of Pecock's own arguments. Aristotle had argued that even those who are ignorant of a particular art possess rudimentary access to its prin-ciples, and he indicated the consequences of this possibility for dialectic in particular:

[O]mnes etiam idiotae [ydiote] quodam modo utuntur dialectica et temptativa; nam omnes [quidem] usque ad [ali]quid conantur diiudicare pronunciantes. Haec [Hec] autem sunt communia; nam ea nichil minus sciunt ipsi, quamvis

---

[50] Ibid. 103–4.

videantur valde extra dicere. Arguunt ergo omnes; nam sine arte participant id de quo artificialiter dialectica est [est dyalectica], et [qui] arte syllogistica temptativus dialecticus.[51]

[E]verybody, including even amateurs, makes use in a way of dialectic and the practice of examining; for all undertake to some extent a test of those who profess to know things. What serve them here are the general principles; for they know these themselves just as well as the scientist, even if in what they say they seem to go wildly astray. All, then, are engaged in refutation, for they take a hand as amateurs in the same task with which dialectic is concerned professionally; and he is a dialectician who examines by the help of a theory of deduction.[52]

Bacon's reference to Avicenna's *Logic* is to a passage very much in the spirit of *De sophisticis elenchis*, in which Avicenna ponders at length the relationship between what common sense and *doctrinae* respectively teach us about logic, grammar, and music. Avicenna points out that, just as divine inspiration can serve as a 'short cut' to the understanding of a body of knowledge, so the common sense of the Arab peasant, who lacks formal teaching, can lead him to an understanding of Arabic comparable to that of those who are taught it: 'Hac autem doctrina eget homo qui acquirit scientiam considerando & cogitando; nisi fuerit homo diuinitus inspiratus; cuius comparatio ad considerantes est sicut comparatio rustici arabici ad discentes arabicum' ('Unless he is divinely inspired, a man who acquires knowledge by consideration and reflection lacks this teaching; and the comparison of an inspired man to those who proceed by such reflection is like the comparison of an Arab peasant to those who learn Arabic').[53] Avicenna's consideration of the cognitive powers of an Arab peasant thus brings us back to Alhacen's views on the same subject.

These passages from Aristotle, Avicenna, Alhacen, and Boethius have a shared emphasis on the innate expertise of *idiotae*, *rustici*, who are naturally in possession of the tools that academics use. This network of authorities thus brings us closer to understanding more precisely the nature

---

[51] *Aristoteles Latinus*, ed. G. Verbeke, vi. 1–3. *De Sophisticis Elenchis: Translatio Boethii, Fragmenta Translationis Iacobi et Recensio Guillermi de Moerbeke*, ed. Bernard G. Dod (Leiden and Brussels, 1975). I have given the text as it appears in the *Translatio Boethii*, which dates from before 520 (pp. 26–7); text in brackets shows variants in the *Recensio Guillelmi* (de Moerbeke), produced *c*.1269 (p. 89).

[52] *On Sophistical Refutations* (172^a20–172^a35), trans. W. A. Pickard-Cambridge, in *The Complete Works of Aristotle: The Revised Oxford Translation*, ed. Jonathan Barnes, 2 vols. (Princeton, 1984), i. 292 (slightly emended).

[53] *Logyca*, in *Avicenne perhypatetici philosophi ac medicorum facile primi opera in lucem redacta: ac nuper quantum ars niti potuit per canonicos emendata* (1508, repr. Frankfurt, 1961), 3.

of Pecock's originality: namely, his perception that such a tradition of thought could be made the basis of a self-sufficient 'vernacular philosophy' distinct from an orthodoxy grounded in patristics. By enacting this philosophical turn in a vernacular setting, he dramatically changed the value of its cultural currency.

V

Fifteenth-century Scotland, customarily understood as a place of largely unruffled orthodoxy, can appear a distinctly enigmatic place to modern scholars more accustomed to tracing the course of the Wycliffite controversies and the sequence of ecclesiastical legislation that they generated in England.[54] Thus, while it is perfectly clear why Pecock's writings seem to have invited the hostile attention that they eventually received, it is still difficult to understand precisely what risks, if any, the theologian and diplomat John Ireland (*c.*1440–95) was running by writing his theological treatise *The Meroure of Wyssdome* in what he called 'ynglis toung'. Coming from a different cultural setting from Pecock, and being of a different generation, Ireland also seems, by virtue of his education and experience, to be a rather less provincial figure.[55] Having served as confessor to James III, he partly intended his treatise, a theological *summa* completed in 1490, to procure further employment for him with the young James IV. His authorial self-fashioning lacks the candour and self-revelation, and still less the defensiveness, of Pecock's prologues; there is in his writing no garrulity comparable to that with which Pecock makes late-medieval English culture, from its urban rituals to its ecclesiastical gossips, vividly

---

[54] In 'The State of Late Medieval and Early Modern Scottish History', Steve Boardman and Michael Lynch call for 'a proper assessment of the fifteenth-century Church, its triumphs and failings; and of the nature of popular piety, patronage, devotion and dissent' (in Terry Brotherstone and David Ditchburn (eds.), *Freedom and Authority: Scotland c.1050–c.1650* (East Linton, 2000), 44–59: 50). David Ditchburn considers the evidence for Lollardy, Hussitism, and Catharism in Scotland, but concludes that 'the impact of all three heresies on Scotland was . . . minimal' ('The Religious Bonds', in *Scotland and Europe: The Medieval Kingdom and its Contacts with Christendom, c.1215–1545* (East Linton, 2001), 39–40). I am grateful to Eila Williamson for these references and for advice concerning the present state of research into late-medieval religious life in Scotland.

[55] J. H. Burns, 'John Ireland: Theology and Public Affairs in the Late Fifteenth Century', *Innes Review*, 41 (1990), 151–81. Ireland produced many other works, some of which are no longer extant. Books III and IV of his commentary on the *Sentences* of Peter Lombard survive as Aberdeen University Library MS 264, but they await detailed examination (see Burns's appendix for a full list).

present. Nevertheless, despite the marked differences between the cultural milieux of these two writers and the independence of their projects from each other, consideration of Ireland's vernacular experimentation gives us access to a broader critical context in which to place Pecock's translations and transgressions than that provided solely by the Wycliffite controversies. Indeed, it is these writers' very separateness from one another that makes the similarity between their intellectual trajectories more significant, expressing as they do, and in such substantial prose works, the close relationship between the desire to renew the intellectual resources of theology and to adapt it to the needs of what Ireland called 'lawde pepil'. When Ireland announces that he will 'proced be ressoune naturall, that I sall causs thi naturall wyt and ressoune to conforme it to the faithe and the artikilis of it' (i. 16), it is impossible not to sense an affinity between these two intellectual temperaments.[56]

The most significant period in Ireland's life for the purposes of the present argument is the fifteen years in which he taught in the Faculty of Arts at Paris, during which period his own studies 'moved from arts to theology'.[57] During his later years at the arts faculty, he protested unsuccessfully against the royal decree of 1471, which banned the teaching of nominalist texts, and which was not revoked until 1481. *Circa* 1477, he began teaching in the theology faculty, and the impact of Ireland's long career in Paris is inevitably imprinted on the *Meroure*, in which he was able to use the nominalist texts that had previously been proscribed. Ireland's thought did not, therefore, develop in an environment free from intellectual constraints, and the traces of circumspection that they bear cannot but urge us to discover more about the particular implications of his having chosen to write theology in the vernacular. The treatise 'Of Penance and Confession', which appears in the Asloan Manuscript and which has been attributed to him, suggests a potentially hostile context for his vernacular project. In a passage whose concerns will seem very familiar to a reader of Pecock, Ireland considers 'þe gret synnis regand be Ignorans and defalt of doctrine in þe peple' and attributes this state of affairs to 'faltis and negligence of kirkmen prelatis and oþer'.[58] He explains that he has been asked to write by 'my masteris and frendis', but also observes that there is potential resistance to his dissemination of theology 'in þis toung and langage', since 'some personis appruf nocht þe translacoun of

[56] Ireland, *Meroure*, i. 16.
[57] Burns, 'John Ireland', 152.
[58] *The Asloan Manuscript*, ed. W. A. Craigie, Scottish Text Society (Edinburgh and London, 1923), i. 2.

haly writ in ynglis toung'. This is not in itself unreasonable, he explains 'ffor þe werray letter, beand [*being*] translatit without þe hie devyne and hevinlie mynd [*meaning*] þat It contenis In It, delarit be þe haly gast, The sone of god, Ihesu, þe kirk and haly doctouris, as þe apostle sayis, quhilis [*often*] soundis evill *Quia littera occidit spiritus autem viuificat* ['For the letter kills, but the spirit gives life']'.[59] Such formulaic warnings against the perils of translation naturally give rise to curiosity as to whether or not they played a more pointed role in Ireland's cultural milieu than current scholarship suggests. Nevertheless, he was confident that he could communicate in the vernacular 'þe writ declarit efter þe mynd and spirituale significacoun of It, with þe mynd of þe gast The kirk and profound doctouris'. In the *Meroure*, however, he is careful to point out that 'it pertenis to þe kyrk of rome and the paip/to expone [*expound*] & declar the faith', and that the pope's authority should be referred to when a general council of the Church is not in session. He adds that 'a maister and professour in theologie may expone the haly writt and delar the artiklis of the faith to þe pepil *doctrinaliter*' ('in the manner of a teacher'), but nevertheless invites the 'correccioun' of his writings, submitting them to the judgement of the arbiters of orthodoxy. The submission of his writings to 'correccioun' is one sign of Ireland's continuous preoccupation with the challenges posed by heretics and infidels. Throughout the *Meroure*, moreover, he puts natural reason at the disposal of a theology specifically tailored to confront these challenges. He was aware of the availability of contemporary heretical literature in both English and Scots vernaculars (the latter now lost to us), but he also addresses ancient heresies and the arguments of the Jews, to whom he sought to demonstrate the compatibility of the truths of faith with the processes of natural reason.[60] Thus, although Ireland does not broach the searching questions raised by Pecock in the *Repressor* concerning the adequacy of *auctoritates* in theological disputation, many passages in his work bear direct comparison with Pecock's emphasis on the validity of natural reason as a fundamental instrument in the making of orthodoxy, and one that complemented the use of 'autoriteis' in theological discussion. It is significant that he affirms his belief in the necessity and profit of expounding the Creed and articles of the faith 'in all maner possible and conuenient'.[61] This pragmatism leads to Book III,

---

[59] Ibid. i. 4; punctuation mine. Ireland is quoting 2 Cor. 3: 6. For Arundel's comparable moulding of Jerome's observations concerning the translation of the Scriptures, see Rita Copeland, *Pedagogy, Intellectuals and Dissent in the Later Middle Ages: Lollardy and Ideas of Learning* (Cambridge, 2001), 201–4, also 119–23.

[60] Ireland, *Meroure*, ii. 50–1.   [61] Ibid. ii. 51.

the manuscript title of which (*Liber de fide domini Ihesu*) indicates its thematic and methodological affinities with Pecock's own *Book of Faith*. Here, Ireland initiates his lay readers into an appreciation of the explicitly argumentative structures of religious doctrine, as understood by academic theologians: 'in the hali doctrine of ihesu and the faith þar is sum proposiciouns þat procedis as þat þat ar of the dictamen of resson naturale . . . And uthir proposiciouns ar proper and principally pertenand to þe faith and thir ar the artiklis of þe faith. And uthir proposiciouns are folowand as conclusiouns and correleris þat may be deducit of þe artiklis of þe faith'.[62]

Ireland's preoccupation with 'infidelis/as paganis iowis machometistis sarracenis ydolatryis and herretikis' is at its most explicit and sustained in the Book IV, in which he sets himself the task of showing 'be naturale ressoune' that the articles of faith are 'richt ressonable'.[63] He invites his readers to consider the situation that would obtain if neither scripture nor revelation had been granted to them. It is at this point that Ireland revisits and 'translates' the justification of explicitly argumentative theology that dates from the period in which it was first becoming established as an academic discipline. Having adduced the authority of St Augustine to show that it is by 'persuasiouns and naturall ressons' that faith is 'acquired, nurtured, defended and strengthened' ('gignitur, nutritur, defenditur et roboratur'), he locates a further source justifying the use of 'natural and probable ressouns' in the form of the first chapter of William of Auxerre's *Summa Aurea*. I have argued elsewhere that Pecock's justification of his own obtrusive use of the syllogism replicates, in a vernacular setting, defences of argumentative theology that date from the twelfth and thirteenth centuries.[64] In the beginning of Book IV of the *Meroure*, Ireland similarly replays the kind of defence of rational argument in theological discourse that had once been a regular feature in prologues to commentaries on the first book of Peter Lombard's *Sentences*. His reference to the *Summa Aurea* makes it explicit that he was continuing the processes of professional self-definition in which the theologians of William's generation had been so robustly engaged. Throughout the rest of Book IV, he systematically shows how examples from a range of authors from

[62]   Ireland, *Meroure*, ii. 16.
[63]   Ibid. ii. 81.
[64]   Mishtooni Bose, 'Two Phases of Scholastic Self-Consciousness: Reflections on Method in Aquinas and Pecock', in Paul Van Geest, Harm Goris, and Carlo Leget (eds.), *Aquinas as Authority* (Leuven, 2002), 87–107: 90.

Aristotle to Ovid can be used to make intelligible the rational (as distinct from 'rationalistic') character of faith.

For both Pecock and Ireland, therefore, the challenge of translating theology not merely into vernacular languages but also into vernacular arenas carried with it the obligation to retrace the processes of legitimation that had accompanied its emergence as a discipline. What is striking is the fact that they both insist on drawing the attention of their lay readers to this process, instructing them not only in the articles of faith but also in the history of theology. The result is that in the works of both men we find a rich intellectual surplus, a constant infusing of the pedagogical matter in hand with the desire to explore and contextualize ideas for their own sake. Ireland does comparatively little to shield his intended audience from the academic context that his vernacular works mediate, and in his references to that context he is careful to construct it as the source of 'ressonis', as when, at the beginning of the treatise on penance, he takes care to identify 'sanct augustyn and . . . a clerk þat studyit in paris callit scotus subtilis' as the sources of his arguments. His pedagogical note in the *Meroure* that 'oftymes the sentens of a conclusioune is schawin and manifest in the probacioune of it, for sal dois all doctouris that writis bukis' recalls Pecock's synopsis of the essentials of logic for the critical layperson in the *Repressor*.[65] Ireland's raiding of academic theology is equally pointed towards the provision of an informal but demanding education in the workings of logic and rhetoric and, no less than Pecock, he constructs the projected audiences of his vernacular works as 'lay scholastics' in need of explicitly intellectual, rather than predominantly devotional, exercise.

VI

Pecock's writing was grounded in a strong reaction against the tenor of contemporary academic theology, the 'introductorie' to the *Reule* articulating and dramatizing his disaffection from the institutions and methods that were supposed to combat heresy. I have suggested that the vernacular experimentation with which he sought to address this situation is based

---

[65] Ireland *Meroure*, i. 16; Pecock, *Repressor*, i. 9. I discuss the example from Pecock in 'Reginald Pecock's Vernacular Voice', in Somerset *et al.* (eds.), *Lollards and their Influence*, 217–36: 234.

on views of human reasoning that would have been readily accessible to him at Oxford. Ireland does not identify a single textual source for his own appeals to natural reason, but, as we have seen, his constant references to the utility and necessity of both the faculty of 'ressoune' and the finesse of particular 'ressons' identifies the *Meroure of Wyssdome*, and in particular Book IV, as being directly descended from the theological *summas* through which the professional lineaments of the discipline, and in particular its explicitly argumentative dimensions, were first charted. His alertness to the situation of his theological discourse at the hinge between demonstration and persuasion, Aristotelian logic and Ciceronian rhetoric, shows him reaching instinctively, comprehensively, and unapologetically for the *artes* when crafting the argumentative framework of his vernacular texts. Behind these two vernacular experiments, these two interventions in literary and intellectual history, therefore, lie discrete episodes from parallel institutional histories, vividly bringing to the fore the shifts in the delicate relationships between theology and the arts during the course of the fifteenth century. Both men identify their respective brands of intellectual revisionism with the quest for a theological discourse appropriate to the laity, and hopefully construct their projected lay audiences as consumers of authoritative discourses very different from those represented in devotional literature. For these writers, the appeal to natural reason is the chief distinguishing characteristic of extramural theology, and the instrument of its radical and substantial difference from both academic *clergie* and vernacular devotion. In the writing of these clerical architects, therefore, natural reason is the foundation-stone and distinguishing characteristic of 'vernacular philosophy'.

It is convenient to describe the kinds of institutional and intellectual plate tectonics that one can sense in these texts in terms of emerging tensions between 'scholasticism' and 'humanism'. This certainly helps to make Pecock and Ireland (as distant from each other as they can appear to be from better-known intellectual revisionists such as Gerson and Erasmus) more readily intelligible to us than they might otherwise be. But we must also acknowledge the equally important fact that their tantalizing affinities are balanced by the ineluctable discontinuity between them. As Netter had been rendered invisible in Pecock's vernacular work, so Pecock in turn was invisible to Ireland, and to a later 'anti-heretic', Thomas More. Such discontinuities contribute to the fragmented aspects of intellectual life in late-medieval England and its enigmatic relations with other cultural milieux. I have sought to suggest that the interventions of Pecock and Ireland could function as important components of a critical narrative that broadens the concerns of 'Wycliffite studies' by exposing them to the challenges of a comparative setting. Exploration of these vernacular projects equally reminds us that arguments, methods, and experiments sometimes live and die with particular individuals.

Christ Church, Oxford

'Fals flesch': Food and the Embodied Piety of Margery Kempe

Melissa Raine

ONE OF the most conspicuous ways in which the heightened religious experience of Margery Kempe is communicated to those around her is through the violation of certain norms of everyday bodily regulation: Margery weeps, howls, all but collapses in her contemplative ecstasies. The sheer inability to regulate her own physicality signifies piety in these instances. Yet this lack of regulation is, perhaps ironically, also a highly conformist gesture, as these losses of self-control signify Margery's participation in a tradition of female affective piety. However, it is not only the flamboyant physicality of Margery's piety that demonstrates the ambiguity of notions of control and its loss, and of conformity as distinct from singularity or individuality: other, more everyday forms of self-regulation are also intrinsic to communicating Margery's exceptional spiritual experiences to her audiences. In particular, Margery's network of popular support is also negotiated, or made apparent to others, through practices involving food.[1]

The importance of the social aspects of food and feeding have been hinted at but not pursued in recent criticism. Lynn Staley, for example, argues that whereas fasting in the lives of other religious women is used to suggest their 'otherworldliness', 'Kempe uses food as a signifier of both Margery's private and public communities'.[2] As Staley points out, Kempe's food rules are formulated in private conversations with Jesus, demonstrating 'Margery's allegiance to a community of the spirit

---

[1] The concept of a negotiable self is taken from Susan Crane, *The Performance of Self: Ritual, Clothing, and Identity during the Hundred Years War* (Philadelphia, 2002). Crane's ' "negotiable self" or "self in circulation" ' is distinct from 'modern individuality, which resides in private thoughts and feelings' (p. 20); rather, 'what is "individual" is most of all what one can put into circulation' (p. 20). For passing affirmations of Margery's piety expressed through food, see the successful meals shared with a lady of Norwich (148 ll. 2–23), and with the monks of an undisclosed location (25 l. 28–26 l. 6).

[2] Lynn Staley, *Margery Kempe's Dissenting Fictions* (University Park, Pa., 1994), 50–1.

by describing her adherence to a private rule for living'.[3] But Staley also acknowledges that the food practices in the *Book* seem more vivid and coherent when connected with Margery's circulation within contemporary society: 'of even more interest is Kempe's use of food to indicate the nature of the contemporary English community, which thrusts Margery from its midst because her eating practices are different'.[4] While I agree with Staley's suggestion that the dynamic relationship between food and community conveys far more complexity within *The Book* than the mysteries associated with fasting and the eucharist, I do not always share her interpretation of specific episodes, as discussed below.

Sarah Beckwith's study of embodiment focuses on eucharistic consumption, describing Margery's imitation of the suffering body of Christ as 'a form of mimesis of Christ which makes of her body a text, and a form of internalized devotion that makes her written text itself the resource of sacramentality. Such an exchange can only operate through the symbol of Christ's body, which is both body and word.'[5] Many of Margery's food practices are not strictly part of her *imitatio Christi*, and are not addressed by Beckwith; nevertheless, Margery's relationship with food beyond her eucharist consumption demonstrates important variations on the text–body relationship that Beckwith associates with Margery's mimesis of Christ.[6]

This essay provides a more extended analysis of Margery Kempe's food practices, adding new dimensions to the discussions found in recent criticism. More broadly, it contributes to the ongoing debate concerning the relationships between food, the female body, and religious practices in medieval Europe associated with the work of Caroline Walker Bynum

---

[3]   Lynn Staley, *Margery Kempe's Dissenting Fictions*, 51.

[4]   Ibid.

[5]   Sarah Beckwith, 'The Uses of Corpus Christi and *The Book of Margery Kempe*', in *Christ's Body: Identity, Culture and Society in Late Medieval Writings* (London, 1993), 78–111: 93. Karma Lochrie, *Margery Kempe and Translations of the Flesh* (Philadelphia, 1991), takes the 'repression of the female body' (p. 2) as the starting-point for her study of the body in the *Book*; however, Lochrie does not discuss the interaction of the spiritual and social dimensions of the text, or refer to food and eating in the *Book*.

[6]   David Aers focuses on the presence of mercantile values in Margery's piety, noting that in a pre-capitalist society, 'her class fostered restless drives to acquire money *enabling power over consumption*' ('The Making of Margery Kempe', in *Community, Gender and Individual Identity: English Writing, 1360–1430* (London, 1988), 73–116: 78, my emphasis). Aers does not elaborate on the forms of consumption that he has in mind, but, as I will discuss, the highly symbolic role of food in medieval culture exemplifies his contention that Margery 'indicates the personal and psychological drives within her class and community', as her food practices express both spiritual and social preoccupations (p. 76).

and others. These broader implications will be addressed in the last section of the essay.

Margery Kempe had available to her a considerable array of dynamic devotional food practices. The idea of a meal—especially, although not exclusively, the sharing of bread—seems to have been an essential component of Christianity from the early church onwards, and the sharing of food was a vibrant aspect of medieval religious devotion, one that permeated the daily life of the whole population.[7] The year was punctuated by changes to diet dictated by religious observance, and food formed part of myriad feasts, festivals, and other commemorations.[8] On a day-to-day basis, doles might be provided by institutions and greater households, and leftover food distributed through the alms dish.[9] The danger of gluttony was a force to be reckoned with at every meal, for those fortunate enough to have access to plentiful food.[10] The religious significance of food did not always express straightforward adherence to orthodoxy: quasi-religious rituals such as guild fraternity dinners suggested a potentially rivalrous relationship with the eucharist, and therefore with clerical authority.[11] Local variations of food-based practices did not always harmonize with official doctrine.[12] Eating and abstaining from eating were

[7] For Judaic and other food practices in the Gospels, as well as early Church practices, see Gillian Feeley-Harnik, *The Lord's Table: The Meaning of Food in Early Judaism and Christianity* (Washington, 1981, 1994); Marcus J. Borg, *Conflict, Holiness and Politics in the Teachings of Jesus* (New York, 1984), chs. 4 and 5; J. D. Crossan, *The Historical Jesus: The Life of a Mediterranean Jewish Peasant* (Edinburgh, 1991), 360–1; Richard H. Hiers and Charles A. Kennedy, 'The Bread and Fish Eucharist in the Gospels and Early Christian Art', *Perspectives in Religious Studies*, 3 (1976), 20–47. Andrew Boorde combines biblical traditions with medical traditions (where Galenic medicine was transmitted to the West via Muslim learning) in his mistrust of pork (*Andrew Boorde's Introduction and Dyetary, with Banres in the Defence of the Berde*, ed. F. J. Furnivall, Early English Text Society, ES 10 (Millwood, 1870, 1981), 272).

[8] See Ronald Hutton, *The Stations of the Sun: A History of the Ritual Year in Britain* (Oxford, 1996).

[9] Maria Moisà, 'The Giving of Leftovers in Medieval England', *Food and Foodways*, 9.2 (2001), 81–94. For a discussion of doles, see Barbara Harvey, *Living and Dying in England, 1100–1540* (Oxford, 1993), 23–33.

[10] For a discussion of gluttony, see Hugh Magennis, *Anglo-Saxon Appetites: Food and Drink and their Consumption in Old English and Related Literature* (Portland, Ore., 1999), 92–4.

[11] Gervase Rosser, 'Going to the Fraternity Feast: Commensality and Social Relations in Late Medieval England', *Journal of British Studies*, 33 (1994), 430–46: 434. The infrequency of communion amongst the general population could be compensated for by the distribution of the eulogia; see Miri Rubin, *Corpus Christi: The Eucharist in Late Medieval Culture* (Cambridge, 1991), 73–4; T. F. Tentler, *Sin and Confession on the Eve of the Reformation* (Princeton, 1977), 79–80.

[12] For instance, in the late fourteenth century, the Bishop of Lincoln objects to the blessing of bacon and eggs in the parish church of Nettleham, arguing that 'the chosen people were forbidden in the Old Testament to eat [swine's flesh] because it was impure' (Dorothy L. Owen, 'Bacon and Eggs: Bishop Buckingham and Superstition in Lincolnshire', *Studies in Church History*, 8 (1972), 141–2: 142).

powerfully expressive activities, capable of articulating highly nuanced versions of religious devotion. Complementing the complex significance of religious food practices, the symbolic meanings of particular food-stuffs, the manner of preparation, presentation, and service, and the modes in which food was consumed, participated powerfully in the world of social distinction.[13] This essay discusses Margery Kempe's extensive use of the richly symbolic dynamics of food in the negotiation of her spiritual authority.

Margery Kempe: The Madwoman in the Pantry?

After a short discussion of her former, secular self and her descent into madness, the story of the converted Margery begins with her first vision of Christ, which causes her to recover from this period of mental instabil-ity.[14] Following the vision, the text recounts what is both Margery's first act of sanity and the beginning of her spiritual enlightenment:

> And a-noon þe creatur was stabelyd in hir wyttys & in hir reson as wel as euyr sche was be-forn, and preyd hir husband . . . þat sche mygth haue þe keys of þe botery to takyn hir mete and drynke as sche had don beforn. Hyr maydens & hir kepars cownseld hym he xulde delyuyr hir no keys, for þei seyd sche wold but ȝeue awey swech good as þer was, for sche wyst not what she seyd as þei wende [*imagined*]. Neuyr-þe lesse, hir husband, euyr hauyng tendyrnes & compassyon of hir, co-mawndyd þei xulde delyuyr to hyr þe keyys. And sche toke hyr mete & drynke as hir bodyly strength wold seruyn hir & knew hir frendys & hir meny [*household*] & all oþer þat cam to hir to se how owyr Lord Ihesu Cryst had wrowt hys grace in hir. (8 l. 25–9 l. 1)[15]

Thus Margery's first meeting with Christ prompts her to eat, and the world's (including the reader's) first witnessing of the blessed Margery is

---

[13] On the symbolism of food preparation and service, see Bruno Laurioux, 'Table et hiérar-chie sociale à la fin du moyen âge', in Carole Lambert (ed.), *Du Manuscrit à la table: Essais sur la cuisine au moyen âge et répertoire des manuscrits médiévaux contenant des recettes culinaires* (Montreal, 1992), 87–108; Jean-Louis Flandrin, 'Structure des menus français et anglais aux XIVᵉ et XVᵉ siècles', in Lambert (ed.), *Du Manuscrit à la table*, 173–92. The formalities of food service and seating arrangements amongst the upper classes are detailed in *John Russell's Book of Nurture*, in F. J. Furnivall (ed.), *The Babees Book: Early English Meals and Manners*, Early English Text Society, os 32 (London, 1868), 186–7.

[14] Margery's failed brewing and milling ventures are presented as aspects of her pre-conversion sinfulness (for a discussion, see Staley, *Margery Kempe's Dissenting Fictions*, 48).

[15] Sanford Brown Meech and Hope Emily Allen (eds.), *The Book of Margery Kempe: The Text from the Unique MS owned by Colonel W. Butler-Bowdon* (London, 1940). All quotations are from this edition.

to watch her having an ordinary meal. In order to understand how this event contributes to Margery's spiritual authority at this crucial point in its development, it is necessary to consider why she was denied access to the household food supplies by other household members.[16] It is not difficult to infer that Margery told her servants of her vision; after all, their reason for blocking her access to the buttery is that 'sche wyst not what sche seyd': they do not believe that Margery's sanity has been restored to her. (Similarly, the claim that all who observed her eating saw how Christ had 'wrowt hys grace in hir' suggests that Margery's audience had been told of her encounter with Christ in order to reach such a conclusion.) Margery's maidens and keepers seem to be responding to an unspoken connection between Margery's claims of personal contact with Christ, and the act of giving away 'swech good as þer was'.

The drama of this episode affords us a glimpse into some nuances in the reception of models of female piety during this period. As Bynum points out, tales of religious women flouting the authority of their husbands and households through covert charitable food distribution circulated widely in medieval Europe, and there is reason to think that the maidens and keepers might be interpreting Margery's request as a move in this direction. Baskets of food that devout women take from their family stores to give to the poor are miraculously turned into baskets of roses when the theft is discovered by a member of the household; this trope is associated with Elizabeth of Hungary, Florence of Beaulieu, Rose of Viterbo, Elizabeth of Portugal, and Margaret of Fontana.[17] An elaborate triptych of the late fifteenth century shows Godelieve of Ghistelle taking a basket of food from her parents' home, which turns into wood shavings when a servant confronts her; no details of any such food thefts are recounted in her eleventh-century life.[18] The accretion of this episode to the

---

[16] Although the buttery is usually a storage room for alcohol, this passage suggests either that other comestibles may also have been stored there in this household, or that the beverages locked away were considered to be essential components of the normal meal; on the importance of ale to the diet, see Christopher Dyer, *Standards of Living in the Later Middle Ages: Social Change in England c.1200–1520* (Cambridge, 1989), 57–8.

[17] Caroline Walker Bynum, *Holy Feast and Holy Fast: The Religious Significance of Food to Medieval Women* (Berkeley, 1987), 135–6.

[18] My thanks to Jacqueline Murray for providing me with her unpublished translation of the Godelieve legend. It is now available in Jacqueline Murray, 'An Unhappy Marriage: Godelieve of Ghistelle', in *Love, Marriage, and Family in the Middle Ages: A Reader* (Peterborough, 2001), 349–59. See also Renée Nip, 'The Canonization of Godelieve of Gistel', *Hagiographica: Rivista di agiografia e biografia della società internazionale per lo studio del Medio Evo Latino*, 2 (1995), 145–55; *idem*, 'Godelieve of Gistel and Ida of Boulogne', in Anneke B. Mulder-Bakker (ed.), *Sanctity and Motherhood: Essays on Holy Mothers in the Middle Ages* (New York, 1995), 191–223;

Godelieve legend, as well as its presence in so many other lives of holy women, suggests the enduring popularity of this convention throughout medieval Europe.[19] Such tales were supposed to exemplify exceptional piety, but the possibility of Margery giving away 'swech good as þer was' is interpreted by her maidens and keepers as the ravings of a mentally incompetent woman.

If such tales are obliquely alluded to in the servants' and keepers' fears, then Margery is rejecting a food practice which signals a version of pious female behaviour that is rebellious towards familial and secular authority, and interpreted by those around her with scepticism (treated as insanity) and hostility. Margery chooses instead to express her spiritual encounter to the world through the simple, orderly consumption of a meal, in which her experience of Christ is communicated through her obedience to everyday domestic conventions. It is instructive to watch how such a banal activity is transformed, in Margery's hands, virtually into a religious ritual, as eating food is presented by Margery to her observers as concrete proof of her bond with Christ.

The value of food in this episode resides not only in its ability to nourish Margery and allow her to begin her new vocation 'as hir bodyly strength wold seruyn hir': eating is represented here, and repeatedly in *The Book*, as a *visible* activity. In this case, the table is transformed into a stage upon which Margery's sanity is displayed for anyone who will come and look: a first, important step in having herself taken seriously as a religious figure. She opts for an *available* version of piety; as a result of Christ's intervention, Margery in this episode is someone with whom a meal can be shared, not someone whose behaviour is remote, like that of an ascetic, or furtive, like that of some holy women who pilfer from their families. For all of Margery's supposedly outrageous and individualistic behaviour, her first Christ-inspired act is one of utter social conformity.

Georges Duby, 'The Matron and the Mismarried Woman,' in *idem* (ed.), *Love and Marriage in the Middle Ages*, trans. Jane Dunnett (Chicago, 1988), 36–55. The triptych is reproduced in Maryan W. Ainsworth and Keith Christiansen, *From Van Eyck to Bruegel: Early Netherlandish Painting in the Metropolitan Museum of Art* (New York, 1998), 126–7.

[19] The triptych itself is an example of the 'increasing numbers of individuals . . . desirous of portraits, altarpieces, and other types of devotional works' who turned to the painters of Bruges from the mid- to late fifteenth century to paint popular compositions, resulting eventually in 'a mass market for painting' (Jean C. Wilson, *Painting in Bruges at the Close of the Middle Ages: Studies in Society and Visual Culture* (University Park, Pa., 1998), 189–90). A small indication that Godelieve's story had reached England can be found in the *Canterbury Tales*, where the Host's wife's name is Goodelief; see *The Riverside Chaucer*, ed. Larry D. Benson (Boston, 1987), 240 l. 1894.

Fasting, Abstinence, and the Eucharist

This first unassuming and conformist religious food practice of Margery's career seems to contrast starkly with her various acts of food deprivation and her consumption of the eucharist, which unequivocally proclaim Margery's singularity. However, there are marked parallels between these food practices and the episode discussed above: fasting, abstention, and eucharistic consumption also provide visual evidence for potential supporters of Margery's individual experience.

Abstinence and fasting were amongst the most fundamental rituals of medieval Christianity; Bossy refers to fasting as 'a domestic observance, one of the few domestic rites which medieval Catholicism possessed', an observation that underscores the importance of fasting in everyday life, in all reaches of medieval society.[20] From Ash Wednesday to Holy Saturday, and during the rest of the year on Fridays, meat was strictly forbidden, as were 'white meats' (all animal-derived foods, but especially milk, butter, cheese, and eggs).[21] In more pious households, meat was also prohibited before and during Advent,[22] as well as on Wednesdays and Saturdays (except under special circumstances, such as illness). Some orders, such as the Carthusians, abstained from meat entirely, and Nicholas Love, prior of the Carthusian Priory of Mountgrace, pointedly describes Jesus as maintaining the same regime in the highly popular *Mirror of the Blessed Life of Jesus Christ*, a text that heavily influenced Margery.[23] Abstinence from meat was thus a potent expression of religious obedience; therefore, Christ's request that Margery take this abstinence to a greater extreme than is required of the general population is highly charged symbolically, representing the adoption of a bodily practice strongly associated with monastic life, or with ascetic techniques designed to cultivate contemplative experience.[24] Margery's abstinence identifies her with the practices of

[20]   John Bossy, *Christianity in the West, 1400–1700* (Oxford, 1987), 51.

[21]   The strictness of this period of abstinence was possibly being eroded in parts of Europe, including the south of England, from the early fifteenth century (Bossy, *Christianity*, 51). This is supported by Dyer's observation that eggs frequently accompanied fish (*Standards of Living*, 63).

[22]   See Harvey, *Living and Dying*, 92.

[23]   *Nicholas Love's* Mirror of the Blessed Life of Jesus Christ: *A Critical Edition based on Cambridge University Library Additional MSS 6578 and 6686*, ed. Michael G. Sargent (New York, 1992), 149. Love explains that the only time Jesus ate meat was at the Last Supper, 'more for mistery þan for bodily fode' (p. 149 ll. 35–6). The Carthusian rule demanded abstention from meat, although fish could be consumed if given to the monks (p. xxi). One of the annotations in the *Book*, believed by Meech to be the work of a monk at Mountgrace, is 'fleysse' (p. 161) in response to Christ asking Margery to eat meat (*The Book*, p. xxxvi).

[24]   Richard Rolle's *Incendium Amoris*, a text known to Margery, declares that 'a man who gives up this world completely, and attends closely to reading, prayer, meditation, watchings, and

religious orders, but, as a member of the lay population, this practice also individualizes her.

Christ formally demands the incorporation of a two-part food practice into her piety in the form of abstaining from meat and substituting Christ's flesh on a weekly basis:

þu must forsake þat þow louyst best in þis world, & þat is etyng of flesch. And in-stede of þat flesch þow schalt etyn my flesch & my blod, þat is þe very body of Crist in þe Sacrament of þe Awter. Thys is my wyl, dowtyr, þat þou receyue my body euery Sonday, and I schal flowe so mych grace in þe þat alle þe world xal meruelyn þerof. þou xalt ben etyn & knawyn of þe pepul of þe world as any raton [*rat*] knawyth þe stokfysch. (17 ll. 9–17)

The discomfort of abstinence does not seem, in any direct way, to enhance Margery's spiritual enlightenment; the only reference made here to any actual *experience* of Margery's is that she is partial to eating meat, 'þat þow louyst best in þis world'.[25] Nor does Margery need to abstain as a penance: before asking her to give up meat, Christ assures Margery that 'I ... forʒefe þe þi synnes to þe vtterest poynt ... And I grawnt þe contrysyon in-to þi lyues ende' (16 ll. 34–5–17 ll. 2–3). This remission implies liberation for Margery from the penitential associations of the act and the season (the Friday before Advent is, as Hope Emily Allen points out, a time of penance). As Allen makes clear in her note on this line, this forgiveness is reiterated many times in the *Book*, and yet Margery continues to participate in activities that will absolve her.[26]

It is important not to mistake Margery's abstinence from meat as merely an *absence*, a symbolic and literal denial of bodily lusts and worldly

---

fastings, will gain purity of mind and conscience, to such an extent that he would like to die through his supernal joy, for he longs to depart and to be with Christ' (*The Fire of Love; Translated [from the Latin] into Modern English with an Introduction by Clifton Wolters* (Harmondsworth, 1972), 121).

[25] The closest that the *Book* comes to locating fasting as isolated from the world is when it mentions Margery's intention to consume bread and water with an anchoress on Our Lady's Eve (119 ll. 19–24).

[26] There is considerable mistrust of the act of fasting in the *Book*. Margery admits to abusing the penitential benefits of fasting in her pre-conversion life, using it to avoid the sacramental powers of confession (6 l. 32–7 l. 8); Christ tells Margery that he values being able to speak directly to her soul far more than he values fasting and other ascetic practices (89 ll. 19–27). Beckwith sees Christ's downplaying of fasting in this episode as part of a larger struggle about clerical authority versus Margery's self-authorizing piety, which often takes its cues directly from Christ, thus circumventing clerical authority ('Uses of Corpus Christi', 91–2). But when put together with other discussions of fasting, as well as the very fact that Christ brings it up himself numerous times, a more general ambivalence about its merits is apparent throughout the *Book*.

orientation; it is also a positive step towards a readily recognizable pious identity, because Margery's refusal to eat meat would have been easily perceived at the medieval table (indeed, the pilgrims *en route* to Jerusalem specifically objected to it, 61 ll. 16–18), where most dishes were communal, and where meat was a highly prized component of a meal. While her eucharist consumption was visible at the altar, her abstinence from meat was demonstrated at the many tables at which we are told Margery dined.

The social *visibility* of Margery's fasting and abstaining is an implicit feature of Margery's exchange of her Friday fasts for sexual abstinence:

Anoþer tyme, as þis creatur prayd to God þat sche myt leuyn [*live*] chast be leue of hir husbond, Cryst seyd to hir mende, 'þow must fastyn þe Fryday boþen fro mete & drynke, and þow schalt haue þi desyr er Whitsonday, for I schal sodeynly sle þin husbonde.' (21 ll. 8–12)

When the married couple finally negotiate a resolution to their grievances, the transaction is reinforced by the added condition that Margery pay her husband's debts as well:

'Sere, yf it lyke ȝow, ȝe schal grawnt me my desyr, & ȝe schal haue ȝowr desyr. Grawntyth me þat ȝe schal not komyn in my bed, & I grawnt ȝow to qwyte ȝowr dettys er I go to Ierusalem. & makyth my body fre to God so þat ȝe neuyr make no chalengyng in me to askyn no dett of matrimony aftyr þis day whyl ȝe leuyn, & I schal etyn & drynkyn on þe Fryday at ȝowr byddyng.' Than seyd hir husbond a-ȝen to hir, 'As fre mot ȝowr body ben to God as it hath ben to me.' (25 ll. 4–13)

Beckwith has described this transaction as 'John Kempe's trade of his conjugal debts for the repayment of his financial debts. . . . It indicates the interaction of earthly and heavenly social roles at the most concrete material level—the exchange of hard cash. Kempe literally buys the right of her own body back from her husband.'[27] Beckwith's silence on the food component of this transaction implies that financial matters form a more significant bargaining chip than Margery's food practices. But if John Kempe was *only* interested in the money, why was it necessary for Margery to give up this fast at all? Bynum surmises that he was 'obviously ashamed of her queer penitential clothes and food practices', implying

---

[27] Beckwith, 'Use of Corpus Christi', 86. Aers does not refer to the food aspect of this transaction in his discussion of the episode, 'The Making of Margery Kempe', 95–6. Thomas J. Heffernan, in *Sacred Biography: Saints and their Biographers in the Middle Ages* (Oxford, 1988), argues that 'she convinces her husband that if he attempts to sleep with her, God (who has revealed this to her) will kill him' (p. 187), making no mention of the fasting or payment of debts.

that Margery's religious persona is bemusing to John.[28] However, the 'obviousness' of this shame is not clearly communicated, if it is present at all, in this episode. Margery's personal conversion represented something of a political victory for the powerful religious sections of Lynn over the burgesses; thus, her Friday fasts represent her obedience not only to Christ, but her alignment with the adversaries of John Kempe and his peers.[29] John's compensation for his renunciation of sex—by having Margery as a table companion on Fridays—seems to reside in the symbolic restoration of his authority over his own household; Margery agrees, after all, to eat at 'ȝowr byddyng'.

The other component of Margery's pact with Christ, the frequent consumption of the eucharist, could be described as the apex of her spiritual food practices: eating Christ's flesh and blood overwhelms her on many occasions. Nevertheless, as with her fasts, Margery's eucharist consumption does not clearly evoke an interiorized spiritual experience.[30] For instance, when Margery receives the eucharist in Jerusalem, it provides the same benefit to her as to any other pilgrim, '*for in þis place is plenyr remyssyon*' (72 ll. 20–1, my emphasis).[31] Despite numerous personal assurances from Christ that she is absolved of all sin, a preoccupation with penance displaces other more contemplative forms of experience. Even Christ privileges the communication of her singularity to the general populace as the primary benefit of Margery's eucharist consumption. By likening her body to food—' "þou xalt ben etyn & knawyn of þe pepul of þe world as any raton knawyth þe stokfysch" '—Christ displaces the emphasis from Margery's experience of her relationship with him, to her relationship with the public.[32]

---

[28] Bynum, *Holy Feast and Holy Fast*, 221.

[29] Beckwith, 'Use of Corpus Christi', 98–101.

[30] Ibid. 95. Margery's only unusual experience eating the eucharist occurs when she sees it flutter once as a portent (47 ll. 14–24).

[31] Christ promises that she will never find herself in purgatory (16 l. 36). Aers discusses Margery's repeated need to purchase pardons ('The Making of Margery Kempe', 78–80). See also 20 ll. 10–18; 72 ll. 15–21.

[32] Despite the antagonistic connotations of this image, for Staley, 'where *knawyn* implies Margery's figurative dismemberment by the world, *etyn* connotes her nurture of the world. Similarly, Margery is at once rejected by her world and an active means of joining the fragmented sections of the social body' (p. 100). This conflation of the acts of eating and nurture, implies, in an argument reminiscent of Bynum's work, that the violent and destructive metaphor of a rat gnawing on stockfish is related to the maternal act of feeding a child with the mother's milk, the goodness of her own body. Considering that the town of Lynn derived considerable wealth from trade in stockfish, it is difficult to see this image of vermin violating (a higher) order, stealing supplies, and disrupting organization to satisfy their appetites as anything but contemptuous, indicating that humanity is actually undeserving of Margery because it is destructive and self-serving.

Charity, Hospitality, and Commensality

More than her fasts and abstinences, the religious and social associations of giving and receiving food demonstrate the complicated negotiations made by Margery Kempe as a lay woman aspiring to a career in piety. Almsgiving in medieval England was sometimes presented as an act of self-interest for the rich:

yn þe day of dome pore men schull be domes-men wyth Cryst, and dome þe ryche. For all þe woo þat pore men hauen, hit ys by þe ryche men; and þogh þay haue moche wrong, þat may not gete amendes, tyll þay come to þat dome; and þer þay schall haue all hor one lust of hom. . . . Wherfor, syrs, for Goddys loue, whyll ȝe byn here, makyth amendes for your mysdedys, and makyþe hom your frendes þat schall be our domes-men, and tryst ȝe not to hom þat schall com aftyr you, lest ȝe ben deseyuet, and dredyth þe payne of hell þat schall last wythouten any ende.[33]

In this formulation, the poor are endowed with tremendous moral power over the consciences of the rich, in lieu of any *actual* power over their own fates. Margery Kempe makes great use of the idealization of poverty, from the perspective of the materially comfortable, as a holy state of existence.

Margery also echoes popular sentiments about the distinction between the deserving and the undeserving poor in her objections to the raising of funds for a charming but needy stranger by a priest (her first *amanuensis*).[34] She insists that alms would be better directed towards 'many powyr

---

Assimilating Margery's consumed flesh to an implicitly feminized act of 'nurture' seems tenuous, given the extremely negative overtones of the image. There is a reference to the literal nourishing of vermin on the body of Thomas Becket in John Mirk's sermon 47; see *Mirk's Festial: A Collection of Homilies*, ed. Theodor Erbe, Early English Text Society, ES 96 (London, 1905), 197 ll. 20–4. Margery also sees herself as being gnawed at by hostile people (154 ll. 23–4). A similar image is used by her potential lover in order to reject her advances (15 ll. 27–8).

[33] *Mirk's* Festial, ed. Erbe, 4 l. 33–5 l. 11.

[34] See Miri Rubin, *Charity and Community in Medieval Cambridge* (Cambridge, 1987), 293, for a discussion of distinctions between recipients of charity. See also Harvey for a preference at Westminster Abbey, from the mid-fourteenth century, for giving alms to the 'established local poor, the respectable poor with addresses' (*Living and Dying*, 31). This distinction is also discussed by David Aers, '*Piers Plowman* and Problems in the Perception of Property: A Culture in Transition', *Leeds Studies in English*, 14 (1983), 5–25, especially in relation to the distinction by Richard Fitzralph between those who beg by necessity and those who do not (p. 9). See also Aaron Jenkins Perry (ed.), *Trevisa's Dialogus inter Militem et Clericum Sermon by FitzRalph and þe Bygynnyng of þe World*, Early English Text Society, OS 167 (London, 1925), 88 ll. 3–18. This formulation is taken up by the Lollard William Taylor; see Anne Hudson (ed.), *Two Wycliffite Texts: The Sermon of William Taylor 1406, the Testimony of William Thorpe 1407*, Early English Text Society, OS 301 (Oxford, 1993), p. 100, notes to ll. 451–9. Another distinction between the deserving and the undeserving poor can be found in Arthur Brandeis (ed.), *Jacob's Well, An Englisht*

neybowrys wheche þei *knewyn wel a-now*', who 'hadyn gret nede to ben holpyn & relevyd, & it was mor almes to helpyn *hem* þat þei *knewyn wel for wel dysposyd folke & her owyn neybowrys* þan oþer *strawngerys wheche þei knew not,* for many spekyn & schewyn ful fayr owtward to þe sygth of þe pepyl, God knowyth what þei arn in her sowlys' (56 ll. 19–25, my emphasis). Margery believes that her community is vulnerable to exploitation by interlopers whom we would be inclined to call 'con-men'; therefore, it is preferable to help only those whose circumstances are known personally to the donors. The opinions expressed here identify Margery with the *givers*, not the *recipients*, of charity, and thus, as some-one in a position of privilege.

Felicity Heal points out that in medieval usage, 'the canonists em-ployed the term "hospitality" interchangeably to refer to the care of strangers and the general support of the local poor'.[35] Although food given at one's own table in a convivial social setting can thus be seen, like almsgiving, as a morally correct act, in *The Book of Margery Kempe* these activities are in fact clearly distinguished from each other. the *Book*'s de-scription of a meal taken by Margery Kempe with the Bishop of Lincoln illustrates this lucidly:

Anoþer day þis creatur cam to mete at þe request of þe Bysshop. And sche saw hym ȝeuyn [*give*] wyth hys handys, er he set hym to mete, to xiij powyr men xiij pens & xiij lovys wyth oþer mete. & so he ded euery day. þis creatur was steryd to hy deuocyon wyth þis sygth & ȝaf God preysyng & worshepyng þat he ȝaf þe Bysshop grace to don þes good dedys wyth plentyuows wepyng, in so mych þat alle þe Bysshopys meny wer gretly merveylyng what hyr eyled. And sythen sche was set to mete [*seated at the meal*] wyth many worthy clerkys & prestys & swyers [*squires*] of þe Byshoppys, and þe Bysshop hym-self sent hir ful gentylly of hys owyn mees [*portion of food*]. (34 l. 26–35 l. 2)

By giving alms with his own hands, the bishop demonstrates both that he is not repulsed by poverty and also that he takes his charitable obligations seriously, as feeding the poor was usually carried out by lesser household members, who were therefore in a position to purloin the foodstuffs.[36] By seating Margery amongst the gentle ranks of his household, and showing

---

Treatise on the Cleansing of Man's Conscience Part 1, Early English Text Society, os 115 (London, 1900), 310 ll. 13–19.

[35] Felicity Heal, 'The Idea of Hospitality in Early Modern England', *Past and Present*, 102 (1984), 66–93: 76 n. 43.

[36] *Bishop Grosseteste's Household Statutes*, in Furnivall (ed.), *Babees Book*, refers specifically to this activity, stating that the head of household must make sure his (or her) alms, in the form of food, go directly to the poor, and are not purloined by untrustworthy household members (p. 329).

her the great courtesy of sharing food with her from his own mess, the bishop reinforces her social worth and validates her piety at the same time. Christ warns Margery that public almsgiving is rife with the potential for hypocrisy (205 ll. 28–33), but because Margery's tears and sobs occur only during spiritually powerful moments, they guarantee for the reader the absence of hypocrisy in the bishop's behaviour.[37] By validating the scene before her, Margery, approving as she does of the seating and eating arrangements for herself, the gift of bread to the indigent, and the bishop's personal contact with the poor, signals her tacit approval of the form and function of charity during the period.

Margery's meditations on Mary are marked by charitable acts of food provision. For Mary, Margery begs (19 ll. 13–18), cooks a caudle (195 ll. 7–8),[38] fasts (162 ll. 11–13), and carries foodstuffs (discussed below); Mary, in turn, ordains food for Margery (93 ll. 15–17), and implores Margery to eat and keep herself healthy (162 ll. 13–17). In contrast to the food practices associated with Christ (which tend to be asocial, in theory at least), which Margery undertakes as commanded, with Mary, Margery often takes the initiative, and the acts themselves are usually somewhat domestic in nature. Or rather, Margery *appears* to take the initiative, since these activities are laid out as appropriate modes of behaviour in other texts, most notably Love's *Mirror*. Love's Mary gives away human food to the poor (20 ll. 41–3), as well as feeding the holy family on simple, homely foods; 'we mowe þenke how þei þre eten to gedire euery day at one litel borde, not preciouse & delicates metes bot symple & sobre as was onely nedeful to sustenance of þe' (64 ll. 42–4).[39] Love also details Mary's role in procuring wine at the wedding feast at Cana (82 ll. 3–26). Mary is

---

[37] Beckwith describes Margery's tears and cries as 'legitimizing symptoms of her compassion with Christ and the stages of her becoming Christ . . . [and] also simultaneously the signs of a rampantly competitive and quantified display' ('Uses of Corpus Christi', 88).

[38] Love suggests that the devoted feed the grieving Mary, as Allen notes (the *Book*, 335–6). Staley includes Margery's making of a caudle for Mary as an example of her allegiance to her spiritual community; however, all the other practices that Staley lists in this category are acts of abstinence in one form or another. Terence Scully refers to a French recipe for a caudle in 'The Sickdish in Early French Recipe Collections', in Sheila Campbell, Bert Hall, and David Klausner (eds.), *Health, Disease and Healing in Medieval Culture* (New York, 1992), 132–40; it is included amongst recipes for the sick, and made of egg yolks & wine (p. 133). The *Middle English Dictionary* distinguishes between two kinds of caudle, one of which is a restorative food.

[39] When angels come to Christ at the end of his temptation in the desert and ask 'Oure worþi lorde ʒe haue longe fastode, & it is now ʒour tyme to ete what is ʒour wille þat we ordeyn for ʒow?', Christ replies, 'Goþe to my dere modere, & what maner of mete she haþe redy bringeþ to me, for þer is none bodily mete so lykyng [*pleasing*] to me as þat is of hir dihhtyng [*arranging*] . . . & so of þat symple mete þat she hade ordeynet to hir self & Joseph þe angeles tokene with a lofe & a towel, & oþer necessaryes, & brouhten to Jesu, & perantere [*perhaps*] þerwiþ a fewe smale fishes þat oure lady hade ordeynet þen, as god wolde' (76 ll. 31–44).

presented as a model feeder whose example is at once imperative but impossible to follow, whose capacities for feeding seem to be amplified by her son. Margery emulates Mary, and Mary, Love emphasizes, provides food.

But Margery does not draw exclusively on Love for her meditations on the Virgin. Love admonishes those who glamorize Mary, insisting instead upon her lowly social status and her poverty:

Now take hede how þat blessed lady qwene of heuen & of erþe goþ alone with hire spouse & þat not vp on hors bot on fote. She ledeþ not with hire many knyhtes & barones nor þe grete companye of boure maidenes & damyseles, bot soþely þere goþ with hire a wele better companye, & þat is Pouert, Mekenes, & honest Shamefastnes, ʒei & þe plente [*abundance*] of alle vertues, & þe best of alle þat is oure lorde god is with hire. She haþ a grete & wirchipful company, bot not of þe vanyte & þe pompe of þe world. (30 ll. 26–34)

Despite her heavy reliance on the *Mirror*, Margery resorts to precisely the version of Mary against which Love rails. In her first meditation on Mary, Margery carries a container of *pyment* (spiced, sweetened wine) and spices to Elisabeth: 'þan went sche forth wyth owyr Lady wyth Iosep, beryng wyth hir a potel [*2-quart container*] of pyment & spycys þerto' (18 ll. 33–5). This choice of activity seems lowly, but Margery's chosen foodstuffs tell us much concerning what is envisaged here. Sweetened wines were a fashionable luxury item during the early fifteenth century, and spices were also expensive and highly desirable.[40] As part of her entourage, she bears the sign of Mary's largesse, the wine and spices, widely associated with hospitality, honourable behaviour, and the highest standards of living. In this scenario, Margery is a member of a model aristocratic household, and her subordination here is in fact social advancement. In this instance, Mary, contrary to Love's insistence, is not a lowly woman, but most decidedly a lady.

Margery's devotion to Mary is described in *Holy Feast and Holy Fast* as unusual amongst holy women (p. 269). Bynum explains it as 'less a reverence for a "representative woman" than a reverence for body, for the bearer and conduit of the Incarnation' (p. 269), pointing out that Margery and Ida of Louvain 'sometimes identified with Mary as she

---

[40] On sweet wines, see Dyer, *Standards of Living*, 62, and Kate Mertes, *The English Noble Household 1250–1600: Good Governance and Politic Rule* (Oxford, 1988), 110. Household records also demonstrate that the practice of giving luxurious foodstuffs to each other was widespread amongst the wealthy; see Jennifer C. Ward, *English Noblewomen in the Later Middle Ages* (London, 1992), 105.

suckled Jesus or received visions of taking the Christ child to their breasts' (p. 270).[41] But Bynum makes no reference to the social and communal food-related activities that form bonds between Mary and Margery. To claim that Mary is conflated with her breast milk and reduced to a 'conduit', no matter how venerable, is inadequate for assessing the extent of Margery's relationship with Mary, particularly where food is involved.

Margery's attitudes towards poverty prove to be extremely sensitive to context. Aware of the considerable symbolic capital of holiness that poverty yields, Margery taps into the spiritually rich vein of indigence by giving all her money away in Rome. In an environment where her sacrifice is recognized and rewarded, she uses the charitable distribution of food by others to usurp the role of the poor in the obligation upon the wealthy to give away superfluous goods to those in need, and begs cheerfully for her own food on the limited number of days when she is not invited to sit at someone's table (84 ll. 20–4; or indeed, sent away with a hamper to tide her over, as by her beloved Lady Florentine 93 ll. 33–7). This period of Margery's version of poverty is notable for the lack of discomfort she suffers: money, good food, and wine flow quickly and abundantly in her direction, as indeed Christ promises they will. But, we find, there are the poor, and then there are the poor. Particularly infatuated with poverty after receiving a cup of wine from an impoverished young mother suckling an infant boy, she declares herself a 'partynyr wyth hem [the poor] in meryte' (94 l. 24). But why 'partner'? Why is she not simply one *of* them? At the bishop's dinner, the men rounded up for the distribution of alms were clearly in a different social category from those seated at his boards. It is noteworthy, then, that even when Margery divests herself of her money in Rome, others often share their *table* with her. Presumably, there are aspects of Margery's self-presentation, and perhaps a network of recommendations, that help her to avoid the humiliating line-up she so approved of at the bishop's meal.

Margery does not, in this narrative, offer hospitality in her home. She begins her religious career by publicly rejecting the opportunity to give her own household's food to the poor. Nevertheless, Margery engages in charitable feeding not as the head of an affluent household, but by begging on behalf of others. Her vision of the newly delivered Mary aside, her

---

[41] Margery is told, 'Dowtyr, he sowkyn euyn on Crystys brest' (18 l. 2) by an anchorite, a conventional image of eucharistic piety promoted in Cistercian writings (Beckwith, 'Uses of Corpus Christi', 86); Margery does not describe herself in this way.

first worldly act of charitable feeding occurs when she begs for a poor, old woman in Rome (85 ll. 33–6), not by her own volition, but by order of her confessor:

Than þe good preste hir confessowr bad [*asked*] hir be vertu of obediens & also in party of penawns þat sche xulde seruyn an hold woman þat was a poure creatur in Rome. & sche dede so sex wekys. Sche seruyd hir as sche wolde a don owyr Lady. & sche had no bed to lyn in ne no clothys to be cured [*covered*] wyth saf hir own mentyl. & þan was sche ful of vermyn & suffryd gret peyn þerwyth. Also sche fet hom watyr & stykkys in hir nekke for þe poure woman and beggyd mete and wyn bothyn for hir. And, whan þe pour womans wyn was sowr, þis creatur hir-self drank þat sowr wyn & ȝaf þe powr woman good wyn þat sche had bowt for hir owyn selfe. (85 l. 33–86 l. 7)

As Staley observes, this pact seems most significant to Margery for the bond it provides between herself and the priest: 'bound by their love of Christ, they contract a new society';[42] he endures ill will on her behalf, and the service she gives the old woman betokens her obedience to him. Margery confirms her sense of her own high social status by agreeing to 'seruyn' this lowly poor woman 'as sche wolde a don owyr lady' (85 ll. 35–6), an almost parodic choice of words, a luxurious dabbling in the idea of poverty as a token of how far she will bend (on a temporary basis) to show her obedience to the priest. Margery's service of the old woman can indeed be compared with the service that she provides for Mary in her meditations, particularly with her role as a kind of lady-in-waiting, the situation where the verb 'seruyn' would be most appropriate. Whereas Margery carried pyment and spices to Elisabeth as part of Mary's *familia*, by consuming the old woman's sour wine and magnanimously giving her the wine she had bought for herself, the reader is not permitted to forget that in truth, she retains superior economic and social powers.[43]

Somewhat paradoxically, Margery's willing embrace of poverty shields her from its true misery. However, this is not the case when she is forced into an insecure position, rather than adopting it of her own volition. Margery's romantic brushes with poverty in Rome contrast strongly with her later trip to Prussia, where she makes no attempt to disguise her disgust at the company of the poor that she is obliged to keep after being abused and abandoned by various fellow-travellers, a situation

---

[42] Staley, *Margery Kempe's Dissenting Fictions*, 112.

[43] Clarissa Atkinson, *Mystic and Pilgrim: The Book and the World of Margery Kempe* (Oxford, 1983), sees Margery as a loving daughter-in-law (p. 83), but, as I have argued, the relationship is also more formal. For a discussion of the 'feudal submission' shown to Mary by Elizabeth of Hungary, see Sarah McNamer, *The Two Middle English Translations of the Revelations of St. Elizabeth of Hungary* (Heidelberg, 1996), 104.

in which she prefers to buy food rather than beg with her destitute companions:

So sche was receyuyd in-to a cumpany of powr folke, &, whan þei comyn to any towne, sche bowte hir mete & hir felaschep went on beggyng . . . Nede compellyd hir to abyden hem & prolongen hir jurne & ben at meche mor cost þan sche xulde ellys a ben . . . Sche kept forth hir felaschep wyth gret angwisch & disese. (237 ll. 17–29)

Far from finding this an occasion to exercise charity (or to imitate Christ's poverty, for that matter), she resents the poor and refuses the symbolically communal act of procuring her food with them. Considering the attachment to commensality with kindred spirits that Margery displays elsewhere, it is important to note here that she does not accuse them of lacking piety; they are merely poor and dirty. She reaffirms her superior social status by buying food (and complaining of their dirtiness). Margery likes to beg when it is a matter of *choice*, and prefers, in her fantasies, to beg for Mary rather than to be forced into genuine association with the genuinely poor.

During meals consumed with her fellow pilgrims *en route* to Jerusalem, where Margery has paid her own way and has plenty of gold in reserve, she turns to the ideal of commensality itself to achieve singularity. Far from the standard set by her meal with Master Aleyn—'þer was a dyner of gret joy & gladnes, meche more gostly þan bodily, for it was sawcyd & sawryd [*made savoury*] wyth talys of Holy Scriptur' (170 ll. 21–3)—the *Book* suggests that Margery's pilgrimage companions practise a debased, secular version of commensality. Because the pilgrims wish to punish Margery for her refusal to eat meat and drink wine, and her insistence on talking of Christ at the table, behaviours which disturb their version of commensality, they effectively demote her social standing by forcing her to sit in the place reserved for the lowest rank of participant in the meal; 'þei madyn hir to syttyn at þe tabelys ende be-nethyn alle oþer þat sche durst ful euyl spekyn a word' (62 ll. 19–20). But Margery's vindication comes through the same system; outsiders to this group encountered during the journey manage to see Margery's virtue despite the hierarchical slight, and demonstrate their approval of her by feeding her from their own messes, as did the Bishop of Lincoln:[44]

not-wythstondyng al her malyce, sche was had in more worshep þan þei wher-þat-euyr þei comyn. & þe good man of þe hows þer þei wer hostyellyd, þow sche

---

[44] See also 63 ll. 1–64 l. 13, where a doctor of divinity comes to Margery's defence at the dinner table.

sat lowest at þe tablys ende, wold al-wey cheryn [*encourage*] hir be-for hem alle as he cowde & myth & sent hir of hys owyn mees of swech seruyse as he had, & þat greuyd hir felawshep ful euyl. (62 ll. 23–7)

Margery does not abandon the hierarchical model of the table, but rather is reincorporated into the group through a shared meal within a meal. The significance attributed by Margery to the politics of table practices signals her acceptance of, and dependence upon, some of the profound injustices in the medieval social order that are represented in the microcosm of the table.

Appetite/Gluttony/Hypocrisy

Just as the public aspect of Margery's contact with Christ began with a meal in which she demonstrated self-control and an adherence to everyday conventions, her last engagement with the secular world takes place at a meal where, once again, Margery's bodily regulation is the key issue in the public perception of her vocation.[45] However, far from seeing the episode as 'masterly', as Staley does,[46] I see authorial control at this point in the text as weak indeed, as it grapples with a particularly persistent accusation against Margery of a failure in bodily regulation.

Whilst travelling anonymously through London on her way home from Aachen, Margery is confronted with a slanderous proverbial refrain uttered at mealtimes far and wide, at her expense, and with which she is personally humiliated as she dines anonymously at 'a worschepful wedows hows in London' (244 l. 11):

Sum on person er ellys mo personys, deceyuyd be her gostly enmy, contriuyd þis tale not long aftyr þe conuersyon of þe sayd creatur, seying þat sche, sittyng at þe mete on a fisch-day at a good mannys tabyl, seruyd wyth diuers of fyschys as reed heryng & good pyke & sweche oþer, þus sche xulde a seyd, as þei reportyd, 'A, þu fals flesch, þu woldist now etyn reed herying, but þu xalt not han þi wille.' & þerwiyth sche sett a-wey þe reed herying & ete þe good pike. & swech oþer þus sche xuld a seyd, as þei seydyn, & þus it sprong in-to a maner of prouerbe a-ȝen hir þat summe seydyn, 'fals flesch, þu xalt ete non heryng.' (243 l. 34–244 l. 7)

---

[45] The final chapter is dominated by interactions within the sacralized space of Sheen, and then with Margery's confessor on her return to Lynn, making the episode that I am about to discuss her last true encounter with secular society.

[46] Staley, *Margery Kempe's Dissenting Fictions*, 55.

Margery, as she stands accused, supposedly refuses the lowly red herring (associated with Lenten privation) under the pretence of disciplining her fleshly cravings, ironically 'punishing' her flesh by taking instead the highly desirable pike, which often forms the centre-piece of fish-day feasts.[47] Margery is guilty here of gluttony for craving the richer food-stuff,[48] but the sin is immediately subsumed by the proverbial utterance to which it leads, strongly suggesting that the delight taken in the circulation of this verbal fragment of the original episode derives from the exposure of hypocrisy. The focus of the episode is therefore displaced from the purported lapse in bodily regulation on to the power of language, in the form of gossip, over reputation and authority.

Margery and the amanuensis stridently deny any basis in reality for this refrain:

þer was neuyr man ne woman þat euyr myth preuyn þat sche seyd swech wordys, but euyr þei madyn oþer lyars her autorys, seying in excusyng of hem-self þat oþer men telde hem so. On þis maner wer þes fals wordys fowndyn [devised] þorw þe Deuelys suggestyon. (243 ll. 30–4)

Words in themselves are not evil: it is the lack of (reputable) authorities, and the absence of Christian love that is the problem. But apart from these admittedly serious deficiencies, what the authors identify is remark-ably similar to the informal means through which Margery's reputation has been established. The very means of negotiation that Margery has em-ployed are being turned against her, discrediting her displays of bodily regulation and overwhelming her claims to spiritual authority. This pre-sents a harsh irony, and a considerable hurdle for the *Book* itself to over-come; Margery is represented as having worked assiduously to establish a reputation for piety, having made it her business to commune with peo-ple searching for spiritual aid, in many cases accepting their food and proclaiming the ardour of her devotions through her abstinences at the tables of the pious. The fame that is implicitly craved within the *Book*, the desire for the name of Margery Kempe to be uttered no less than proverbially, far and wide, is grotesquely realized when Margery is

---

[47] See C. M. Woolgar, *The Great Household in Late Medieval England* (New Haven, 1999), 118–20, on the importance of red herring (the smoked version of the fish) to the English diet, and on the relative status of dried and fresh fish. Pike, as a freshwater fish, was far more expensive to procure; as Woolgar explains, the construction and maintenance of ponds for breeding freshwa-ter fish was a large expense for the greater households, as was the purchase of such fish from spe-cialized fishmongers (p. 122).

[48] For gluttony as it concerns the quality, as well as quantity, of food, see Magennis, *Anglo-Saxon Appetites*, 92–4.

finally brought face to face with this sly ridiculing of her religious identity, which has apparently dogged her since the early days of her conversion.

The irrepressible Margery of the text immediately launches into a form of damage control as she attempts to assimilate this bad publicity to the kinds of public contempt that she had often faced before this, countering hostility with irreproachable sanctity. Her moral authority is regained through a shift which is at once discursive and performative. Confronted to her face with this disrespectful refrain, she defends herself with this 'rebuke' to her fellow diners:

'Lo, serys,' sche seyd, 'ȝe awt to seyn no wers þa ȝe knowyn & ȝet not so euyl as ȝe knowyn. Neuyr-þe-lesse her ȝe seyn wers þan ȝe knowyn, God forȝeue it ȝow, for I am þat same persone to whom þes wordys ben arectyd [*imputed*], whech oftyntyme suffir gret schame & repref & am not gylty in þis mater, God I take to record.' What þei beheldyn hir not meuyd in þis mater, no-thyng repreuyng hem, desiryng thorw þe spirit of charite her correcyon, þei wer rebukyd of her owyn honeste, obeyng hem to a-seeth [*amends*] makyng. (244 l. 34–245 l. 6)

The conspicuousness of Margery's body as it refrains from eating certain items offers her no assistance here; if anything, her bodily performance at the table is now a liability, as it would inevitably serve as a reminder to those familiar with this accusation of hypocrisy. Margery's change of tactic involves a shift to a different mode of bodily regulation; that she is 'not meuyd' suggests a mildness of delivery that implies that she has all but removed herself personally from involvement in the incident, and speaks only as a kind of channel for Christian morality. This neutrality of delivery conveys such complete bodily control that the result is a denial of embodiedness, just the dissociation required from a body accused of betraying her.

However, this disembodied Margery Kempe is not sustained by the text. After this rebuke is made, Margery 'spak boldly & mytily wher-so sche cam in London a-geyn swearars, bannars [*cursers*], lyars & swech oþer viciows pepil, a-geyn þe pompws aray boþin of men & of women. Sche sparyd hem not, sche flateryd hem not, neiþyr for her ȝiftys, ne for her [*their*] mete, ne for her drynke' (245 ll. 7–13). This sounds remarkably like a series of sermons, and the implied forcefulness of Margery's delivery represents a dramatic shift from the mild persona of the previous rebuke. The accusation against Margery of hypocrisy, based on an incident that occurred a long time ago, has already been firmly refuted several times over. Nevertheless, the text continues to deny that Margery flatters people in exchange for food and drink in her current circumstances. It seems as though the numerous earlier refutations have not dispelled the charge completely; rather, more discourse on the topic of bodily regulation is produced, apparently in the hope of burying the accusation under the substance of as many denials as possible. Rather than successfully resolving the problem, the repeated denials seem, if anything, to imbue the slander with considerable power.

Margery's last encounter with an ungrateful secular world features an event that turns upon a purported loss of self-control, giving considerable prominence to the relationship between Margery's bodily regulation and her exceptional piety. The episode reveals the true Achilles' heel of this method of seeking a popular base for Margery's spiritual authority; her heavy reliance on reputation is established not only through her more extravagant pious behaviours, but also through accessibility, mobility, and the public orientation of her holiness, including the support won at meals shared at many tables, where the evidence of her bodily regulation for Christ's sake could be displayed. The near breakdown of that system here clearly demonstrates its limitations.

While it is impossible to know whether or not the words attributed to Margery in the 'herring episode' were ever spoken, and if so, under what circumstances, it is nevertheless difficult to imagine anyone but an uncharacteristically irreverent Margery—that is, atypical of the textual Margery—uttering those words. The considerable difference between this unauthorized representation of Margery Kempe and the Margery endorsed by the *Book* alerts us to the complexities of composing an authoritative text amid competing judgements of Margery's piety. The almost compulsive denial of Margery's guilt in the herring matter suggests that it was a troubling incident for the authors to relate. Its placement so close to the end of the narrative gives the episode such prominence that it seems reasonable to ask whether the *Book* itself might have had a specific relationship with this slander. The almost organic circulation of gossip contrasts strikingly with the rather fragile process of authorization that is the project of the historical Margery Kempe and her amanuensis, whose repeated condemnation of this gossip seems to confirm, rather than to dissipate, the potential of the rumour to undermine the authority of their own text. The *Book* itself could thus be seen as an attempt to shore up the clerical authority that would offer some protection from the vagaries of popular support by recasting Margery Kempe in firmly hagiographical (and thus, textual) conventions. Without such support, the authority of Margery's body for the purpose of establishing her piety is condemned to instability. *The Book* itself may have served as a potential replacement for the literal dependence upon Margery's embodiedness for communicating her spiritual authority to her supporters.

Conclusion

I have attempted to identify the importance of food-related activities for the negotiation of Margery Kempe's spiritual identity. These negotiations rely on the communal nature of eating, where the hierarchized rules of conduct in play at the medieval table constantly demonstrate social standing through seating and serving arrangements, and through inclusion and exclusion. I have referred to specific differences in my interpretation of some episodes from those offered by Caroline Walker Bynum in *Holy Feast and Holy Fast*; I wish now to draw out more fully the underlying premises concerning gender and food that inform our respective projects.

None of the critiques of *Holy Feast and Holy Fast* has dealt extensively with food *per se* in this widely influential text. Kathleen Biddick's forceful reassessment of *Holy Feast and Holy Fast* focuses on representations of history and gender, having very little to say about food.[49] For David Aers, who argues that eucharistic devotion is less the fulfilment of natural feminine impulses than the interpellation of women as good daughters of orthodoxy that upholds the interests of a powerful clerical hierarchy, Bynum's argument that women were empowered by their religious food practices is unconvincing.[50] However, while his discussion of food offers some important corrections to Bynum's arguments, it is limited to food production. Nicholas Watson addresses the very success of *Holy Feast and Holy Fast*, arguing that, despite its shortcomings, its most important legacy is the prominent role of empathy within it. Thus, Watson presents a case for greater acknowledgement of affect—specifically, for desire of the past—amongst medievalists.[51] Watson identifies an important and hitherto unacknowledged aspect of the success of *Holy Feast and Holy Fast*, but he does not consider the relationship between the empathy that

[49] Kathleen Biddick, 'Genders, Bodies, Borders: Technologies of the Visible', *Speculum*, 68 (1993), 389–418.
[50] David Aers, 'The Humanity of Christ: Reflections on Orthodox Late Medieval Representations', in David Aers and Lynn Staley, *The Powers of the Holy: Religion, Politics and Gender in Late Medieval English Culture* (University Park, Pa., 1996), 15–42, esp. 28–39. On food production, see pp. 31–4.
[51] Nicholas Watson, 'Desire for the Past', *Studies in the Age of Chaucer*, 21 (1999), 51–97.

he identifies and the version of embodiment that is put forward in *Holy Feast and Holy Fast* through its singular treatment of food.

In *Holy Feast and Holy Fast*, the fullest discussion of the roles of *food* and *eating* in medieval culture are found in the first four pages. In this short space, Bynum moves quickly from very general observations about food, to the eucharist as *the* quintessential medieval food; to eat is a 'powerful verb. It meant to consume, to assimilate, to become God' (p. 3). Thus, the meaning of eating has been circumscribed and hierarchized right at the outset of *Holy Feast and Holy Fast*, with the eucharist placed at the pinnacle of this hierarchy. It is declared to be both the ultimate edible substance and the ultimate act of eating, neatly subsuming the business of everyday living to religious devotion. Work on the eucharist since the publication of *Holy Feast and Holy Fast* challenges this idealized view of eucharistic devotion in medieval Europe.[52] But more significant for the purposes of this discussion is the conflation of the meaning of eating with the meaning of the eucharist, through which Bynum implicitly removes from consideration many of the explicitly religious aspects of food consumption that have been addressed in this essay.

Bynum regards the correlation between women's relationship with the eucharist and their secular role as food providers as a natural extension of the biological fact of lactation: 'women's bodies, in the acts of lactation and giving birth, were analogous both to ordinary food and to the body of Christ, as it died on the cross and gave birth to salvation' (p. 30). Thus, the 'distinctive spiritualities' of the religious women studied by Bynum are said to form 'a threefold pattern' of fasting, feeding, and eating (p. 186), through which they express desire for closeness to Christ. These *exceptional* and exceptionally pious women express themselves through these food practices because of the innate sense, shared by *all* women, of themselves as feeders, as controllers of the giving of food.[53] This universal association of women with 'feeding'—'to prepare food is to control food . . . food is not merely *a* resource that women control; it is *the* resource that women control—both for themselves and for others' (p. 191)—is modelled on the nuclear family, where a mother breast-feeds her own children and prepares family meals in the kitchen of a private domestic dwelling. However, as Gail Kern Paster has pointed out in relation

[52] See Rubin, *Corpus Christi*; Beckwith, 'Uses of Corpus Christi', 78–111; Stephen Justice, 'The Idiom of Rural Politics', in *Writing and Rebellion: England in 1381* (Berkeley, 1994), 140–92.

[53] Roger Chartier discusses the shortcomings of cultural divisions based on gender in *The Order of Books: Readers, Authors and Libraries in Europe between the Fourteenth and Eighteenth Centuries*, trans. Lydia G. Cochrane (Stanford, Calif., 1994), 7.

to the early modern period (although her observation is also relevant to the Middle Ages):

it is clear that material differences in infant-feeding practices between early modern culture and our own are evidence of fundamental changes in understanding of the female body and its products. . . . For us, suckling a baby is an intimate bodily act between two persons related by blood. . . . Mother's milk has been removed from the sphere of commodity exchange, excluded from its former 'natural' place within the system of other commodifiable foods.[54]

Furthermore, sociological work shows that even where food preparation *is* clearly the responsibility of women (and Bynum argues that it is 'a fact cross-culturally that food is particularly a woman-controlled resource', p. 189), it is particularly misleading to claim that it automatically gives women 'control';[55] on the contrary, such responsibility can create situations where women must please men, where an unsatisfactory meal can challenge masculine authority in patriarchal families, sometimes resulting in violence.[56] There is no reason to assume that medieval food preparation created fewer complexities for people than is the case now; as Aers points out, the activity of food preparation in the Middle Ages 'existed within networks of power, chains of command, and financial resources dominated by men'.[57]

For Bynum, the self-starvation, the feeding of others, and the eating of the apparently inedible are not, 'at the deepest level, masochism or dualism but, rather, efforts to gain power and give meaning' (p. 208). This state of affairs stands in stark contrast to that facing modern women, as it is laid out in the Epilogue of *Holy Feast and Holy Fast*: 'modern attention to the topic "women and food" appears to be very much more one-sided than medieval practice and symbolism' (p. 298). The Epilogue is, I argue, the *raison d'être* of Bynum's study. It offers a form of empowerment to modern women: 'if their images and values cannot become our answers,

---

[54] Gail Kern Paster, *The Body Embarrassed: Drama and the Disciplines of Shame in Early Modern England* (Ithaca, NY, 1993), 231–2. While 'nurture' and its cognates can refer to the specifically feminine activity of breast-feeding, it is more commonly used in Middle English to denote the teaching of the art, and the condition, of dutiful and courteous conduct, attainments which are shown to be a mixture of refinement and practical skills, taught primarily to boys by men. This concept of nurture is typified by *John Russell's Book of Nurture*.

[55] See Marjorie DeVault, *Feeding the Family: The Social Organization of Caring as Gendered Work*, ed. Catharine R. Stimpson (Chicago, 1991).

[56] See Nickie Charles and Marion Kerr, *Women, Food and Families* (Manchester, 1988); William Alex McIntosh and Mary Zey, 'Women as Gatekeepers of Food Consumption: A Sociological Critique', *Food and Foodways*, 3.4 (1989), 317–32.

[57] Aers, 'Humanity of Christ', 30.

they can nonetheless teach us that we need richer images and values. Perhaps also they can point the direction in which we should search' (p. 302).
Throughout the Epilogue, Bynum emphasizes the *absence* of the medieval meanings that she found in her study of *piety* from the practices of
a modern secularized world;[58] food manipulation is transformed from a
source of self-liberation, where women cultivate 'closeness to God' (p.
298), to the material for self-imprisonment, where 'refusal to eat' is associated 'with the question of control' (p. 298). Identification with Christ is
the key to changing what seem to be the same practices from negative into
positive. Bynum's generalizations about food and women's relationship
with it are intended to expose the bedrock of the female body beneath the
topography of historical change; even when women held little collective
or individual power, they were still able to express their devotion to Christ
forcefully. They used their bodies, the most reliable resource that they
had, and still do have. Bynum's project is one of *building links* between
women through the concept of worship; it relies not on detailing historically specific interactions of gender, culture, and food, but rather on their
suppression. In other words, *Holy Feast and Holy Fast* reads more coher-
ently as a theological treatise than as an argument about history.

Holy Feast and Holy Fast makes the point that powerful aspects of embodied experience had previously been overlooked in scholarship, and its
attention to this subject perhaps contributes to its enduring popularity, or
at least this suggestion should be considered alongside Watson's argument
for empathy. However, Bynum's methodology does not, in the end, assist
with the negotiations involved in understanding the nature of embodied
experience in the Middle Ages through the limited access provided by
textuality. Indeed, Bynum's assessment of *The Book of Margery Kempe*
constrains and distorts the meanings associated with Margery Kempe's
religious food practices. That Margery Kempe is female is inextricable
from the form of her piety; without the possibility of participating legitimately within the institutional structure of the Church, she negotiates a
range of behaviours acceptably performed by women, participating in a
paradoxical dance of conformity and singularity. Her experiences of
childbirth and her sexuality inform her piety, as do the social limitations
imposed upon women. But her physical femininity does not define her
pious food practices in accordance with Bynum's model. The intimate
bonds that Margery forms with Christ are not enhanced by her eucharist
consumption or her abstinences; these practices are more useful for

---

[58] See also Bynum, *Holy Feast and Holy Fast*, 299–300.

demonstrating their purported intimacy to others. Her acts of charitable feeding suggest her to be a tourist amongst the poor, rather than demonstrating the enactment of any innate desire to feed. Many of the food practices favoured by Margery, from receiving food as alms to sharing tables with other devout people, do not distinguish sharply between the sexes, and perhaps even assist Margery by de-emphasizing gender. Eating, as an obligatory bodily practice, provides an important point of reference for how embodied selves are imagined and experienced, and Margery's embodied relationship with food consistently reveals her to be preoccupied with the recognition of her own standing. However, while Margery's food practices are based on communally shared presuppositions about social status, gender, and forms of devotion, they do not represent a formulaic acting out of convention. Rather, they demonstrate the active negotiation of expectations governing social and spiritual behaviour in late medieval England from a highly motivated and individual perspective.

University of Melbourne

Urban Utterances: Merchants, Artisans, and the Alphabet in Caxton's Dialogues in French and English

Lisa H. Cooper

THE FRENCH–ENGLISH phrasebook that William Caxton printed at Westminster sometime between the years 1480 and 1483 begins by selling itself.[1] First advertising its wares—its words—as 'prouffytable lernynge', it next spreads out a sample of them 'all by ordre' (1 ll. 2–3) before the reader in a table of contents that is seventy-five lines long. It then affirms its utility and instructional expediency, asserting that from this 'ryght good lernyng' one can 'lerne / shortly frenssh and englyssh' (3 ll. 14–16). Finally, it discredits its competitors in the literary market-place, even while acknowledging that such competition does in fact exist. Although

My research for this essay was funded in part by the Medieval Academy and the Richard III Society; I am grateful to both organizations for their support. I presented an earlier and much compressed version of my argument at the April 2002 meeting of the Medieval Academy in New York, and thank my very responsive audience there for their queries and comments. I owe a special debt to Heather Blurton, who insisted on the alphabet, and to Jean Howard, who pointed me to the work of Patricia Crain. I further owe a great many thanks to Christopher Baswell, Andrea B. Denny-Brown, Mary Agnes Edsall, Robert W. Hanning, Marlene Villalobos Hennessy, Seth Lerer, Douglas Pfeiffer, Nicole R. Rice, Robert Stein, and Paul Strohm for their scrupulously attentive readings of earlier drafts.

[1] A. W. Pollard and G. R. Redgrave (eds.), *Short-Title Catalogue*, 2 vols., rev. edn. (London, 1976, 1986) (STC) #24865. All English citations will be from Henry Bradley (ed.), *Dialogues in French and English by William Caxton*, Early English Text Society, ES 79 (London, 1900), with page and line numbers (which run 1–40 on each page) given in text and notes. Bradley's edition, although the most accessible, contains a serious number of errors. I have used as a silent corrective the less widely available but more accurate edition of Jean Gessler (ed.), *Le Livre des Mestiers de Bruges et ses dérivés: quatres anciens manuels de conversation* (Bruges, 1931). I also follow Gessler's use of lower case (instead of Caxton's own capitals) at the beginning of lines, his corrections of misprints in Caxton's edition, his modernization of 'v' and 'w', and his punctuation. For a facsimile of Caxton's book, see J. C. T. Oates and L. C. Harmer (eds.), *Vocabulary in French and English: A Facsimile of Caxton's Edition c.1480* (Cambridge, 1964). On the four surviving copies and one fragment see Oates and Harmer (eds.), *Vocabulary*, p. v, and Seymour de Ricci, *A Census of Caxtons* (Oxford, 1909), #97, 100–1. For a primarily linguistic analysis of the text see Werner Hüllen, *English Dictionaries 800–1700: The Topical Tradition* (Oxford, 1999), 95–102.

'that which can not be founden / declared in this / shall be founde
somwhere els', still the book's potential owner may 'knowe for trouthe /
that in the lynes of this auctor / been moo wordes and resouns / comprised, and of answers, / than in many othir bookes' (3 ll. 28–35).

One goal of this essay is to demonstrate just how fitting a beginning
this is for a text meant to impart a set of lessons in the mercantile arts: its
opening sally neatly serves both as a sales pitch and as a sample of what
precisely is being sold. But first a brief word on the book's textual history
is in order, because what Caxton was selling in the *Dialogues* both was and
was not a brand-new product, in ways that have important consequences
for reading it. Caxton's 'ryght good lernyng' was in fact only the latest,
and then not the last, incarnation of a French–Flemish vocabulary first
written in Bruges around 1340 by a master for his pupils. This school-text
appears to have quickly become popular beyond that master's school-
room and beyond Bruges: an altered and abridged version, in which the
original Flemish half is replaced by the closely related but still noticeably
different Dutch dialect of the period, circulated from at least 1377 to
1420.[2] This second version was not, however, the one from which Caxton
was to print his later book; he used a manuscript that, while it has not sur-
vived, clearly contained a third, much longer text. Finally, almost twenty
years after Caxton printed the *Dialogues*, Roland Vanden Dorpe printed
another French–Dutch version at Anvers before his death in *c.*1501. This
fourth version closely resembles Caxton's, but several significant discrepancies reveal that the Anvers printer worked not from the English book,
as might otherwise be expected, but rather from yet another manuscript.[3]

---

[2] This version is the *Gesprächbüchlein*; see n. 3 below. On the 'related dialects' of the Low
Countries (including Flemish and Dutch), see Laura Wright, 'Trade between England and
the Low Countries: Evidence from Historical Linguistics', in Caroline Barron and Nigel Saul
(eds.), *England and the Low Countries* (New York, 1995), 169–79: 170.

[3] Gessler's *Le Livre des Mestiers* includes editions of all the derivatives of the text, each with
separate pagination: (I) the earliest surviving manuscript of the lost fourteenth-century proto-
type (an earlier edition of which is H. Michelant (ed.), *Le Livre des Mestiers: Dialogues français-
flamands composés au XIVe siècle par un maître d'école de la ville de Bruges* (Paris, 1875)); (II) the
Gesprächbüchlein of *c.*1377, from a manuscript of *c.*1420; (III) Caxton's *Dialogues*; and (IV)
Vanden Dorpe's *Vocabulair en roman et flameng* of *c.*1501. Citations of versions other than
Caxton's will be by part (I, II, IV) and page number in Gessler's edition. For a brief history of each
text, see Gessler's thorough Introduction; on the relationship of the Caxton and Vanden Dorpe
editions in particular see pp. 44–8 and the useful diagram showing the filiation of all four texts at
p. 47. See also K. J. Riemens, *Étude sur le texte français du 'Livre des Mestiers', livre scolaire français-
flamand du XIVe siècle* (Paris, 1924), 27–8. Riemens argues for a date between 1370 and 1385 for
the manuscript on which Caxton's translation was based (pp. 22–3).

It is this last situation in particular—two books nearly identical in content but in different languages, derived from a source produced over 100 years earlier, and printed independently of one another within twenty years—that suggests both the general availability of different versions of the vocabulary on the Continent during the later fifteenth century and some kind of demand for that availability to be extended in print. This was the demand that Caxton probably hoped to encourage and upon which he hoped to capitalize across the Channel. The former mercer may even have been responding to an already existing demand for the vocabulary among his friends and acquaintances; as Anne F. Sutton notes, the last step of apprenticeship for an English merchant-adventurer was often a trip abroad to practise trading skills and other languages, particularly French and Dutch.[4] Although much of the *Dialogues'* history is unknown—including when and where Caxton acquired the manuscript from which he worked and who translated its Flemish into English—what is certain is that the existence of three other closely related vocabularies makes any attempt at interpretation of this one work something of a vexed enterprise from the outset.[5] For example, much of what I shall argue below about the book's implicit and explicit narratives of mercantile fantasy, fulfilment, and frustration is almost equally applicable to the near-contemporary Anvers edition. It is, however, to the English text that I shall refer, and to the ramifications of the book's English context that I shall pay particular attention.

[4] Anne F. Sutton, 'Caxton was a Mercer: His Social Milieu and Friends', in Nicholas Rogers (ed.), *England in the Fifteenth Century: Proceedings of the 1992 Harlaxton Symposium* (Stamford, 1994), 118–48: 122.

[5] Caxton is thought to have acquired the manuscript sometime during his extended sojourn in Bruges c.1446–76 (broken by return trips to England and stints in Ghent and Cologne), and perhaps particularly in 1462–70 when he served as governor of the Company of Merchant Adventurers there. For overviews of his career, see among many other studies the biographies of N. F. Blake, *Caxton and his World* (London, 1969), and George D. Painter, *William Caxton: A Quincentenary Biography of England's First Printer* (London, 1976). Whether Caxton himself translated the vocabulary has been a matter of some debate because of its many irregularities and errors. On these see Oates and Harmer (eds.), *Vocabulary*, pp. xi–xxix; Hüllen, *English Dictionaries*, 94–5; and N. F. Blake, 'The *Vocabulary in French and English* Printed by William Caxton', *English Language Notes*, 3.1 (1965), 7–15. Blake suggests that the translation was done by a mercer well before Caxton acquired it; his argument is based in part on that of Philip Grierson, 'The Dates of the "Livre des Mestiers" and its Derivatives', *Revue Belge de Philologie et d'Histoire*, 35 (1957), 778–83, who dates the English translation eventually printed by Caxton to 1465–6 on the basis of its monetary references. Another uncertainty is the precise date of Caxton's imprint; William Blades assigns it to 1483 (*The Biography and Typography of William Caxton* (London, 1882), 262); E. G. Duff, however, dates it to 1480 (*Fifteenth-Century English Books* (London, 1917), 48–9).

Therefore, I want first to note that in that English context, the *Dialogues*' opening claim to lexical abundance is, at least at first glance, something of an exaggeration. One exactly contemporary vocabulary, the English–Latin *Catholicon Anglicum* (1483), contains almost 8,000 entries, far more than appear in Caxton's relatively short book; an earlier English–Latin word-list, the *Promptorium parvulorum* (1440), a version of which was to be printed by Richard Pynson in 1499, contains some 12,000.[6] It must be conceded, however, that of *French*–English vocabularies, Caxton's was certainly longer than the few that had preceded it; it was also, of course, the very first to be printed.[7] If these considerations recuperate the first half of the book's opening boast, its claim to contain 'moo wordes' than others of its kind, the title *Dialogues* (with which it was provided by its first editor, for Caxton left the vocabulary without either title-page or preface) at least partially recuperates the second half of the assertion. For the *Dialogues* does something with words that most medieval vocabularies do not: of the many word-lists produced in medieval England, Caxton's is one of the first since the late tenth century to contextualize much of its linguistic information in 'resouns' (that is, questions)[8] and 'answers'—or, that is, in conversation.[9]

[6] The Pynson edition of the *Promptorium* is STC #20434; another edition was printed in 1510/11 by Caxton's successor, Wynkyn de Worde (STC #20436). On the *Promptorium* and *Catholicon Anglicum*, including information on manuscripts and printed editions, see DeWitt T. Starnes, *Renaissance Dictionaries: English–Latin and Latin–English* (Austin, Tex., 1954), 3–23, and Gabriele Stein, *The English Dictionary before Cawdrey* (Tübingen, 1985), 91–120.

[7] The earliest French, or rather, *Anglo-Norman*-English vocabulary is a thirteenth-century versified manual on estate management; see William Rothwell (ed.), *Gautier de Bibbesworth: Le tretiz*, Anglo-Norman Text Society, Plain Texts Series, 6 (London, 1990). On the history of French-language instruction in England see William Kibbee, *For to Speke Frenche Trewely: The French Language in England, 1000–1600: Its Status, Description and Instruction*, Amsterdam Studies in the Theory and History of Linguistic Science, Series III (Amsterdam, 1991); see also Hüllen, *English Dictionaries*, 89–93. On the challenges which Caxton and other printers faced as they introduced printed texts into a manuscript market, see A. S. G. Edwards and Carol M. Meale, 'The Marketing of Printed Books in Late Medieval England', *The Library*, ser. vi, 15 (1993), 95–124.

[8] Here 'resouns' translates the French 'raysons', which in this period could refer to language, words, and, somewhat more specifically, enquiries; it could even mean a record of account, which is very interesting given the book's subject as a whole. See 'raison' in Frédéric Godefroy, *Dictionnaire de l'ancienne langue française*, 10 vols. (1889; repr. New York, 1961), vi. 567–9.

[9] It is not, however, quite the first to do so. The French–English *Manière de Langage*, which survives in three different versions (1396, 1399, and 1415), is also in dialogue form. See Hüllen, *English Dictionaries*, 92–3, and bibliography. The earliest surviving dialogic vocabulary produced in England is the Latin school-book known as Aelfric's *Colloquy*; for an edition see G. N. Garmonsway (ed.), *Aelfric's Colloquy*, 2nd rev. edn. (Exeter, 1991). On the history of the colloquy form, which developed from the Latin debate tradition, see G. N. Garmonsway, 'The Development of the Colloquy', in Peter Clemoes (ed.), *The Anglo-Saxons: Studies in Some Aspects of their History and Culture Presented to Bruce Dickins* (London, 1959), 248–61.

But here again we need to hesitate, since 'conversation' does not adequately describe the character of almost half the book.[10] In fact, the last
twenty-one of forty-nine black-letter pages present not dialogues, but
rather brief *statements* about no fewer than 116 people. These are introduced alphabetically by their first names, a curious point to which I will
return, and seventy-four of them are workers—craftspeople, tradesmen,
and labourers.[11] When the Flemish schoolmaster called his first version of
the text the 'Livre des Mestiers' (Book of Crafts, or Trades) (I, 51), it was
clearly this artisanal grouping that he had in mind; his title, at least,
overtly acknowledges the book's attention to the nature and purpose of
professional occupation.[12]

Ultimately, however, the craft most at stake in the *Dialogues* (as I will,
though somewhat unhappily, continue to refer to it for the sake of convenience) is not the *mestier* of any artisan, but rather the social skill and
commercial fluency of the bourgeois citizen whom it instructs in manners, dress, and, above all, speech.[13] In this regard, the *Dialogues* resembles
the many other conduct manuals that flooded the bookstalls of London
and other European cities in the later Middle Ages. As several recent
studies have shown, such works were eagerly purchased by members of
the upwardly mobile mercantile class, those well-to-do urban residents
whose 'vested interest in commercial activity and self-enhancement',

---

[10] On the obvious inadequacy of Bradley's choice of title and the equally obvious reasons for
that choice see also Hüllen, *English Dictionaries*, 102.

[11] Ibid. 133. I disagree with Hüllen's categories here; he finds that twenty-eight of the names
are connected to a journey and staying at an inn, and that the remaining eighty-eight involve the
arts and crafts. I, however, find no specific reference to an inn except in a later section that gives
no names (49 l. 5–50 l. 24). In the alphabetized section I count forty-two servants, friends,
acquaintances, women and their relatives (for whom no profession is mentioned), one saint,
and one squire; the remaining seventy-four are all connected to an occupation. Hüllen also
claims that all of these entries are 'typical dialogues', but in fact very few of them seem dialogic,
and no dialogue markers appear in Caxton's imprint.

[12] By the thirteenth century the word *mestier*, which derives from the Latin *ministerium*
(divine service), referred to any kind of paid labour or professional service; in the fourteenth
century it was particularly connected to artisanal labour and the guilds in particular. See Paul
Robert, *Dictionnaire historique de la langue française*, 2 vols. (Paris, 1993), ii. 1235b–1236a; see also
Adolf Tobler and Erhard Lommatzsch, *Altfranzösisches Wörterbuch*, 10 vols. (Stuttgart, 1925–),
v. 1689–1703. The author of the *Livre des Mestiers* might well have known of the collection of Paris
guild statutes and regulations of 1268, the *Livre de Métiers* of Étienne Boileau; see Bernard
Mahieu, ' "Le livre des Métiers" d'Étienne Boileau', in *Le Siècle de Saint Louis* (Paris, 1970),
64–74, and for an edition see G.-B. Depping (ed.), *Réglemens sur les arts et métiers de Paris*, 2 vols.
(Paris, 1837).

[13] On the representation of artisans and their labour in medieval vocabularies before the
Dialogues, see my ' "These Crafty Men": Figuring the Artisan in Late Medieval England'
(Ph.D. thesis, Columbia University, 2003), 18–52.

writes Claire Sponsler, made them avid consumers of behavioural guides.[14] William Caxton, as is well known, capitalized on the popularity of such books throughout his printing career. *The Game and Playe of the Chesse* (c.1474 and c.1483), *Stans Puer ad Mensam* (c.1477), *The Boke of Curtesye* (c.1477), *The Morale Proverbes of Cristyne* (1478), *The Curial* (c.1484), *The Knyght of the Toure* (1484), *The Book of Good Manners* (1487), and *The Ryall Book* (c.1488) constitute only his most obvious imprints of this sort; as Mark Addison Amos has convincingly argued, Caxton's entire corpus might well be read as a set of primers in the social codes of the gentry.[15]

But whereas most conduct manuals train their readers to emulate the manners and mores of nobility (proffering, as Amos puts it, 'aristocratic modes of conduct as a field for the self-transformation of the professional elite'[16]), the *Dialogues*' social and ethical curriculum is far more flexible than its counterparts in the genre. My analysis of this curriculum in the following pages is in three parts. First, I show that while the book provides something of a template for social advancement for the aspiring bourgeois, it also validates mercantile activity as something worth undertaking for its own sake. As a courtesy manual and shopping list for the affluent householder, the *Dialogues* certainly inculcates a taste for the finer things in life, including not only polite speech and fine clothes, rich food and a well-furnished home, but also particular markers of gentle status: doublets and suits of armour, painted shields, country homes. But as an instructional manual for the travelling merchant, it also whole-heartedly embraces the culture of the market, a culture not of luxurious leisure but rather of bargaining and borrowing, of commercial alliances and enmities, of joys and sorrows accumulated primarily in the margins of profit and loss. Amos observes that all the texts that Caxton printed participate to some degree in the formation of 'an urban ideology that, even as it adopts noble dress and manners, is fully permeated by tensions and paradigms of identity that are specifically mercantile.'[17] The *Dialogues*,

---

[14]   Claire Sponsler, 'Eating Lessons: Lydgate's "Dietary" and Consumer Conduct', in Kathleen Ashley and Robert L. A. Clark (eds.), *Medieval Conduct*, Medieval Cultures, 29 (Minneapolis, 2000), 1–22: 4. For an overview of conduct literature, see the introduction by Ashley and Clark (eds.), *Medieval Conduct*, pp. ix–xx, and Jonathan Nicholls, *The Matter of Courtesy: Medieval Courtesy Books and the Gawain-Poet* (Woodbridge, 1985).

[15]   Mark Addison Amos, 'William Caxton's Corpus and the Forging of London's Urban Self' (Ph.D. thesis, Duke University, 1994).

[16]   Mark Addison Amos, ' "For Manners Make Man": Bourdieu, de Certeau, and the Common Appropriation of Noble Manners', in Ashley and Clark (eds.), *Medieval Conduct*, 23–48: 34.

[17]   Amos, 'William Caxton's Corpus', p. ii.

however, is not simply 'permeated' by mercantilism: commerce in all its guises, from production to consumption, is its explicit subject, while the means to successful exchange is its explicit lesson. By urging its readers into the market and quite literally prompting them to transact, the *Dialogues* validates merchant culture even as it also holds out the promise of gentrification—or at least its trappings—to those who desire it.[18] Unlike a courtesy manual, that is, the *Dialogues* is suited less to helping its readers act more like gentry than it is to helping them act more like merchants.

The identity to which the *Dialogues* urges its audience to aspire is one configured entirely through transactions that are in equal measure discursive, material, and social: the capable merchant-consumers into whom it promises to transform its readers will blithely and simultaneously exchange English for French, money for goods, capital for status, and luxuriate in the multiple possibilities which the market offers for doing so. In the next section, however, I show that perhaps the most important lesson the vocabulary teaches about the market is not about exchange at all. For acting like a merchant, this book suggests, means learning how to speak *to* and *about* artisans with authority rather than engaging in dialogue *with* them. In the artisanal alphabet that takes up almost half the book, I argue, the *Dialogues* responds on the linguistic level to what merchants in the manufacturing towns of late-medieval England saw as a fairly acute economic and social problem. As Heather Swanson has shown with particular reference to the city of York, medieval merchants continually sought ways to draw firm boundaries between themselves and master craftsmen, who usually traded in the goods that they and their lesser associates made and who were sometimes as wealthy as the merchants themselves. In fact, a very wide spectrum of medieval society encompassed those who sold and purchased for resale, and the categories of 'merchant' and 'artisan' were almost always to some degree artificial designations; that of 'artisan', in particular, was frequently imposed from above by merchant oligarchs seeking to protect a jealously guarded trading monopoly.[19] In other words, whereas today's consumer engages in

---

[18] D. Vance Smith, *Arts of Possession: The Middle English Household Imaginary*, Medieval Cultures, 33 (Minneapolis, 2003), has recently challenged the prevailing view that all English medieval merchants sought to join the ranks of the aristocracy. He demonstrates from surviving records that it was in fact the other way around, for gentry often also operated as merchants, while merchants studiously avoided being classed as knights (pp. 21–36).

[19] Heather Swanson, *Medieval Artisans: An Urban Class in Late Medieval England* (Oxford, 1989), 2–8 and *passim*. See also James Farr, *Artisans in Europe 1300–1914* (Cambridge, 2000), 2–3; and Christopher Dyer, *Standards of Living in the Later Middle Ages: Social Change in England c.1200–1520* (Cambridge, 1989), 24. An excellent historical overview of merchant culture across

what Grant McCracken calls 'an ongoing enterprise of self-creation' that he identifies with the act of purchase,[20] medieval merchants created themselves, in part, by enacting laws and levelling fines (as well as, as I have already mentioned, emulating the social codes of a higher class). The merchant-consumer imagined by the *Dialogues* must do something else: he must learn to speak—*before* he buys—in a way that will tie him advantageously to the craft community even while it separates him from its members. The alphabet, I suggest, is the mechanism the book offers by which to achieve both objectives at once. In her intriguing study of early American primers, Patricia Crain argues that 'alphabetization in a market-driven culture indelibly links acts of reading to acts of acquisition, conjoining subjectivity and consumption'.[21] This observation, as we will see, applies equally well to the medieval *Dialogues*, which encourages its reader to recite an 'a.b.c.' that is both a prelude to purchase and a guide to the formation of a particularly mercantile subjectivity.

By emulating the speech of the persona whom I will interchangeably call the narrator or speaker, the reader of the *Dialogues* learns how to position himself both outside, above, and also, paradoxically, at the very centre of an extensive manufacturing community.[22] The book encourages him to think of himself as the hub of a market he can control by organiz-

Europe is Peter Spufford, *Power and Profit: The Merchant in Medieval Europe* (London, 2002). The standard study of the same subject for England alone has long been Sylvia L. Thrupp, *The Merchant Class of Medieval London, 1300–1500* (Ann Arbor, 1948); but now see Jenny Kermode, *Medieval Merchants: York, Beverley and Hull in the Later Middle Ages* (Cambridge, 1998). On merchants in medieval English literature, see Roger A. Ladd, 'Merchants, Mercantile Satire, and Problems of Estate in Late Medieval English Literature'. (Ph.D. thesis, University of Wisconsin-Madison, 2000).

[20] Grant McCracken, *Culture and Consumption: New Approaches to the Symbolic Character of Consumer Goods and Activities* (Bloomington, Ind., 1988), 88; cited and discussed by Sponsler, 'Eating Lessons', 18.

[21] Patricia Crain, *The Story of A: The Alphabetization of America from* The New England Primer *to* The Scarlet Letter (Stanford, Calif., 2000), 9.

[22] Hüllen calls this the 'author-voice' of the work; however, he also notes that in teaching himself, the 'reader-learner' becomes a 'speaker-learner' (*English Dictionaries*, 97 and 102). I should note that I will refer to this narrator, as well as to the reader who is meant to imagine himself in that narrator's place, by the masculine singular pronoun throughout. I do this not only because the speaker is signalled as male throughout the text—called 'Syre', for example (11 l. 8)—but also because he speaks in the artisanal alphabet from a male perspective, something I will discuss further below. This does not, of course, obviate the possibility of the book's use by women, who often worked with their husbands or on their own in a wide variety of trades and in small-scale retail operations as well as (especially in London) in international trade, while widows frequently carried on their husbands' businesses. See Kay E. Lacey, 'Women and Work in Fourteenth and Fifteenth Century London', in Lindsey Charles and Lorna Duffin (eds.), *Women and Work in Pre-Industrial England* (London, 1985), 24–82: 52–4; Maryanne Kowaleski, 'Women's Work in a

ing and utilizing privileged knowledge about the artisans with whose
working methods, business practices, and private lives the book itself
offers to make him fully familiar. Yet the things the narrator of the *Dialogues* says about the craftspeople whom he attempts to contain and control within and through his alphabet reveal that he is himself still socially
and financially tied to the artisanal community of which he speaks. His
comments also reveal that many members of that community—who, it
turns out, are as engaged as he in acts of self-creation and self-promo-
tion—frequently resist his attempts to subordinate them to his wishes.
Constructing the mercantile self by imposing the hegemony of the letter
upon others turns out to be a more demanding task than it might first
have seemed. In the last section of this essay, I consider the way in which
the book's narrator ends his 'a.b.c.' by departing from the market-place
in some disgust, as if he has failed to find the self he was looking for
within it. I then suggest that Caxton's material transformation of the
Dialogues out of manuscript and into print further complicates the version of urban identity the book offers up for its readers' consumption,
eroding the barrier it has otherwise overtly attempted to erect between
what were, by the 1480s, the already long-overlapped estates of merchant
and artisan.

Prouffytable Lernynge': Greetings and Goods

Even in its original fourteenth-century context, and certainly by the late
fifteenth century, the *Dialogues*' images of merchants and artisans alike
would almost certainly have been perceived as highly nostalgic. The book
looks back to a less complicated commercial moment in which 'face-to-
face transactions between buyers and sellers', rather than large-scale transactions between 'merchant intermediaries', were as regular occurrences in
cities like London and Bruges as they remained in small towns.[23] Furthermore, through a narrator who is able to negotiate on a first-name
basis on both sides of the Channel, the *Dialogues* domesticates the foreign
city, making the international market appear an even more familiar

Market Town: Exeter in the Late Fourteenth Century', in Barbara A. Hanawalt (ed.), *Women
and Work in Pre-Industrial Europe* (Bloomington, Ind., 1986), 145–64: 146–8; and Kermode,
Medieval Merchants, 94–5.

[23] Rodney Hilton, 'Market Towns and Small Commodity Production', *Past and Present*, 109
(1985), 3–23: 21–2. See also Joel Kaye, *Economy and Nature in the Fourteenth Century: Money,
Market Exchange, and the Emergence of Scientific Thought* (Cambridge, 1998), 54.

place than it already was for many London merchants.[24] While Caroline Barron observes that fifteenth-century England 'was truly a part of northern Europe, bound by language, religion, and interdependent economies . . . into a single community and a common market',[25] the *Dialogues* of *c.*1483 tightens these ties that bound to a rather fantastic degree. Particularly in the context of this bilingual book, in which French and English 'utterances fac[e] each other as a sign of their assumed translatory equivalence',[26] what lies on the other side of the water, as on the other side of the page, becomes a comfortably reassuring reflection of a much simpler version of home.[27] For example, while at least seven goldsmiths were working in Bruges by 1394–96, sixty in neighbouring Ghent in 1400, and some 180 in London in 1477, this book names only one.[28] Of course, the very

[24]   De Certeau claims for street names in the modern world the same effect I am claiming here for personal names in the medieval city imagined by the *Dialogues*: 'proper names carve out pockets of hidden and familiar meanings. They "make sense"' (Michel de Certeau *The Practice of Everyday Life*, trans. Steven Rendall (Berkeley, 1988), 104).

[25]   Caroline Barron, 'England and the Low Countries, 1327–1477', in *England and the Low Countries*, 1–28: 1. In addition to this valuable collection of essays on the economic, political, and social connections between the two regions, see David Wallace, 'In Flaundres', *Studies in the Age of Chaucer* 19, (1997), 63–91.

[26]   Hüllen, *English Dictionaries*, 102.

[27]   This mirror, it must be admitted, reflects somewhat imperfectly. On the one hand, many of the names in the book have a distinctively Flemish ring, despite attempts made by the translator to modify them for English speech (cf. 'Firmin le tavernier' vs. 'Fremyn the taverner' (35 l. 17), suggesting either that Caxton did not find this important enough to change or that he expected the book to be used primarily by English merchants abroad. On the other hand, modifications made to the book in the sections listing towns and markets (18 ll. 25–40–19 ll. 1–10), bishops (23 ll. 6–20), and nobility (24 ll. 12–28) map a distinctly English geography including London, York, Bristol, Bath, Salisbury, Cambridge, Winchester, Chester, and Lincoln. These additions (which do not appear in the analogous section of Vanden Dorpe's edition) might have been meant to make an English-speaker feel at home while learning otherwise new words, but they might also have been imagined as potentially useful for French-speaking visitors to England. Perhaps the most that can be said is that Caxton probably hoped to sell the book to both. Interestingly, the facing-column format of the *Dialogues* was not repeated in later French–English texts that were clearly modelled upon it. In both *A lytell treatyse for to lerne Englysshe and Frensshe*, printed in 1497 by Wynkyn de Worde (STC #24866) and *A good boke to lerne frenche* (STC #24867), printed in 1500 by Richard Pynson, French words and phrases appear under, rather than across from, the corresponding English. For an edition of the de Worde text with the Pynson variants provided as notes, see Jean Gessler, *Deux Manuels de conversation* (Brussels, 1941).

[28]   For Bruges, although he cautions that the tally is incomplete, see Jean-Pierre Sosson, '"Metallurgies Urbaines" en Flandre et en Brabant au Moyen Âge: l'exemple des métiers du métal à Bruges, Bruxelles et Malines', in Paul Benoit and Denis Cailleaux (eds.), *Hommes et travail du métal dans les villes médiévales* (Paris, 1988), 163–72: 166, table 2. For Ghent, see David Nicholas, *The Metamorphosis of a Medieval City: Ghent in the Age of the Arteveldes, 1302–1390* (Lincoln, 1987), 272. For London, see Christopher Dyer, *Making a Living in the Middle Ages: The People of Britain 850–1520* (New Haven, 2002), 305.

existence of the *Dialogues*, much like that of Berlitz guides today, actually suggests exactly the opposite of what its idealizing fiction implies. For if foreign travel were as easy, exchanges as seamless, and craftspeople as compliant as this book wishes they were, there would presumably be but little need for the particular kind of instruction it proffers. Yet the work's table of contents urges its reader to leave home with confidence, equipped with 'the wordes that everyche / may lerne for to goo / fro one lande or toune to anothir' (2 l. 39–3 l. 1).

The remainder of the *Dialogues* explicitly imagines this confident reader, however, not as the travelling everyman its table of contents addresses, but rather as a hopeful entrepreneur. It constructs an audience interested not simply in exchanging England for France, but also in transferring English goods to French-speaking lands, and vice versa.[29] 'Who this booke shall wylle lerne', the narrator declares, 'may well entreprise or take on honde / marchandises fro one land to anothir' (3 l. 37–4 l. 1). The point, then, is not simply the achievement of a new language for the sake of social nicety. While this book, like other courtesy manuals, will teach 'how every man ought grete othir' (1 l. 7), it will also demonstrate 'the manere / for to learn rekene / by poundes, by shelynges, by pens' (3 ll. 5–8).[30] It will further explain how to exchange debt for profit, and here at the beginning intimates the importance of balancing the two: 'your receyte and your gyving oute / brynge it all in somme', the end of the opening table advises (3 ll. 9–11).

To this promise of ready instruction in the art of maintaining financial stability, the text adds a further enticement when it offers to sharpen its future owner's business acumen: an attentive reader not only will learn how to transport merchandise from one place to another, but also upon the completion of his studies will 'knowe many wares / which to hym shal be good to be bou3t / or solde for riche to become' (4 ll. 2–4). The reader is then encouraged to '[l]erne this book diligently, / for grete prouffyt lieth therin truly' (4 ll. 6–7). Many medieval works proudly proclaim the profit to be gained from their pages, and by this they usually mean the kind of social advantages that Pierre Bourdieu refers to as symbolic capital.[31]

---

[29] For background on the realities of such exchange, see Vanessa Harding, 'Cross-Channel Trade and Cultural Contacts: London and the Low Countries in the Later Fourteenth Century', in *England and the Low Countries*, 153–68.

[30] Or, in France, 'par livres, par soulz, par deniers' (3 ll. 5–8).

[31] For the multiple meanings of 'profit' in Middle English, including social and financial benefit, see *The Middle English Dictionary*, v, ed. Sherman M. Kuhn (Ann Arbor, 1983), 1366–70. On symbolic capital see Pierre Bourdieu, *Outline of a Theory of Practice*, trans. Richard Nice (Cambridge, 1977), 171–83, esp. 177–8; and *idem*, *The Logic of Practice*, trans. Richard Nice

Such, indeed, seems to be what the Flemish author of the first *Livre des Mestiers* meant by the 'mout grant / pourfit' that, he promises at the end of his book, will be the reward for having read it; after all, he immediately glosses such profit as the 'grant / honneur' that comes to the well-educated.[32] But in Caxton's later *Dialogues*, where the phrase appears at the work's beginning and is clearly intended as a selling point, 'grete prouffyt', like the 'prouffytable lernynge' promised earlier (1 l. 2), operates as a true *double entendre*. Anticipating Bourdieu's understanding of communication as an economic event by almost 500 years,[33] the book here collapses the distinction between material and symbolic capital, between being 'riche' (4 l. 4) and appearing 'good' (4 l. 3), and promises both at once to the reader who will avail himself of its linguistic capital before heading into the market-place (or rather, heading *back* into it following the mastery of this all-important initial purchase). Claire Sponsler's observation that the conduct books of this period 'sold themselves . . . by appealing to their purchasers' taste for didactic and educational reading material'[34] is thus literally true of the *Dialogues*, for the book's first lesson on the rewards of diligent study is also a lesson about the book itself: it, too, is a ware 'good to be bou3t'.[35]

(Stanford, Calif., 1990), 112–21, esp. 119–21. For a critique of Bourdieu's market metaphor that his use of the word 'profit' implies and that contradicts his own insistence that agents act in their own interests without any awareness that they do so, see Richard Jenkins, *Pierre Bourdieu* (London, 1992), 86–7.

    [32]   *Livre des Mestiers*, 51.
    [33]   'Linguistic exchange', Bourdieu observes, 'is also an economic exchange . . . between a producer [i.e. the speaker], endowed with a certain linguistic capital, and a consumer (or a market), and which is capable of procuring a certain material or symbolic profit' (*Language and Symbolic Power*, trans. Gino Raymond and Matthew Adamson (Cambridge, 1991), 66). Despite the distinction he draws here between the material and the symbolic, Bourdieu is generally attentive to the close relationship—and easy slippage—between economic and symbolic capital; see *Outline of a Theory of Practice*, 180–3, and *Logic of Practice*, 120–1. On the analogies between linguistic and economic exchange see also Marc Shell, *The Economy of Literature* (1978; repr. Baltimore, 1993).
    [34]   Sponsler, 'Eating Lessons', 4–5. The studious attention of the reader on which the *Dialogues* here insists resembles the work that, Sponsler argues, Lydgate's poem 'Dietary' urges upon its readers: 'labor and work are removed from the realms of material production and transported into the terrain of consumption, with the result that consumption becomes a form of work' (p. 14). As Sponsler makes clear, she is relying here on Michel de Certeau's definition of consumption as a form of production, on which see his *Practice of Everyday Life*, pp. xii–xiii.
    [35]   William Kuskin, in his 'Reading Caxton: Transformations in Capital, Authority, Print, and Persona in the Late Fifteenth Century', *New Medieval Literatures*, 3 (1999), 149–83, argues that the concept of 'capital offers a structure for reading Caxton that recognizes the essential doubling of textual and economic processes at work in his production process' (p. 151); it is precisely this kind of doubling that is operative here and, indeed, throughout the *Dialogues*.

The performance of mercantile identity that this book scripts for the enterprising reader, however, requires the accumulation of other wares that are 'good to be bou3t'. And it is to these items, following its initial section on salutation, that the *Dialogues* turns. Here the same narrator who has already positioned himself as a teacher of social grace ('Whan ye goo by the streetes, / and ye mete ony / that ye knowe . . . / be swyft and redy / hym or hem first to grete' (4 ll. 10–16)) and who will shortly become an instructor in domestic deportment ('Yf ye be maried . . . / so mayntene you pesibly' (9 ll. 15–18))[36] now establishes himself as a fount of practical advice regarding the acquisition and arrangement of 'thinges that ben used after the hous, / of which [one *my emendation*][37] may not be withoute' (6 ll. 18–20). But what begins as an image of 'well ordeyned' domestic space, whose 'chambres / loftes and garrettis' should be 'well wyndowed', and outfitted with beds, rugs, quilts, benches, chairs, and other furnishings (6 l. 23–7 l. 11), quickly turns into a shopping list that moves us out of the bourgeois home rather than further into it in celebration of both the variety and the convenience of the market that was often located just outside the merchant's front door.[38] Requisite 'pottes of earth', we are told, can be found 'in the potterye' (7 ll. 9–13), while elsewhere 'men fynd . . . all maneris' of bottles, platters 'of tyn', dishes, saucers, salvers, trenchers 'of tree and of erthe', and 'covercles of coppre, / of erthe and of yron' (7 ll. 26–36). Even while warning the prudent householder to lock up his valuables—his silver spoons in 'most sure kepyng' (8 l. 3), his jewels in a 'forcier / that they be not stolen' (8 ll. 21–2)—the narrator takes care to enumerate the several kinds of cups that might need securing in a 'whutche or cheste' (8 l. 20), including '[c]uppes of silver, / cuppes gylte, / couppes of goold, / cuppes with feet' (8 ll. 15–18).[39]

---

[36] This private behaviour has its public face; the reason for maintaining domestic harmony, the narrator adds, is so 'that your neyghbours saye not / of you othirwyse than well' (9 ll. 19–20).

[37] The use of 'me' as a translation of the French general pronoun 'on' is here and elsewhere in the text an error of the compositor or translator, although it is not noted by Oates and Harmer in their review of some of the *Dialogues'* English errors (*Dialogues*, pp. xvii–xxvii).

[38] Merchants' homes usually included a shop and warehouse space on the ground floor. That the domestic space of the medieval merchant was simultaneously part of the commercial space of the city may help explain the intertwining of house and market in this passage of the *Dialogues*. On both the construction and furnishing of merchant homes, see Thrupp, *Merchant Class*, 130–42; see also Margaret Wood, *The English Mediaeval House*, 1965 (London, 1994).

[39] On merchants' fondness for the display of such decorated cups, called 'mazers', see Thrupp, *Merchant Class*, 146. On craft specialization, the proliferation of manufactured goods, and the high levels of demand and consumption in England in the second half of the fourteenth and the fifteenth centuries, see Dyer, *Making a Living in the Middle Ages*, 296–7 and 320–7; Richard H. Britnell, *The Commercialisation of English Society, 1000–1500*, 2nd edn. (Manchester, 1996),

The speaker's evident anxiety over the security of commodities once they are brought home from the market is matched by an equal degree of interest in their production before they appear for sale within it. Having already turned our attention to the market-place from within the walls of the comfortably appointed household, the narrator next orders his servant, one 'Margret' (10 l. 7) out upon an actual shopping expedition. But the subsequent tale of Margret's adventures that this command anticipates is never told; the incipient narrative is foreclosed by a shopping list so long that even the fictional Margret protests—in an interruption that seems designed to acknowledge the peculiar form these instructions take—that her master has 'many mo named / than I wende to bye' (11 ll. 9–10). Lists of fowl, flesh, and fish gradually become a paean to material production, a celebratory dilation in which the phrase 'men make' operates like something of an incantatory refrain. '[O]f mylke and egges', for example, Margret (and, by extension, the reader) learns that 'men make flawnes', while of milk and flour, 'men make printed cakes' (12 ll. 33–6). From the grass in the meadows, 'men make heye' (13 l. 27), while from hides, 'men make lether' on the one hand and 'perchemyn, / in which men write' on the other (19 ll. 21–8). The narrator also notes that from spices 'be made confections', that a good sauce 'is made' from good powder (20 ll. 4–7), and that 'men make mustard' (20 l. 14). Even in a list of metals, some of the rawest of raw materials, the speaker slips from naming pure 'yron' to man-made 'steell, leed, tynne' as well as 'thinges silverid, / gyrdelis with nayles of silver', and from there to 'purses wrought *with* the nedle' (21 ll. 22–9).[40] Unlike Lydgate's extremely popular courtesy poem 'Dietary', whose instructions on eating and etiquette, notes Sponsler, 'teac[h] the reader how to be a good consumer who can safely negotiate the dangers of the world of plenitude',[41] the *Dialogues* here promotes rather than cautions against the production and consumption of a plethora of ready-made food and other wares.[42]

164–75; Dyer, *Standards of Living*, 205–10; and Swanson, *Medieval Artisans*, esp. 112–13 and 172–3.

[40] My emphasis. This focus may in part be explained by the book's origin in Bruges, a city famous not only as a centre for manufactured goods but also as a major market-place for raw materials. See Spufford, *Power and Profit*, 318–20.

[41] Sponsler, 'Eating Lessons', 5–7: 7. For an edition of 'Dietary' see Henry N. MacCracken (ed.), *The Minor Poems of John Lydgate*, 2 vols., Early English Text Society, ES 107 and OS 192 (Oxford, 1934), 702–7.

[42] The only exception is the passage, providing zoological vocabulary, in which the speaker warns Margret against buying a whole variety of fowls whose 'flessh shold greve' him because he is 'seeke', explains that men do not eat horse meat or the flesh of wild animals like wolves, elephants, and apes, and warns that anyone bitten by a poisonous snake will die without treatment (10 l. 33–11 l. 32).

Indeed, there is so much of this 'made' stuff that the narrator, a kind of epic poet of the market-place, turns more than once to the topos of inexpressibility to convey the sheer inexhaustibility of the commercial catalogue: 'Of thise thinges I am wery,' he complains, adding, 'I shall reste me' (22 ll. 12–13). Near the end of the book, however, he laments that there can in fact be no rest for the weary: 'Lordes, who wolde, / this boke shold never be ended, / for men may not so moche write / [one][43] shold fynde alway more' (50 ll. 25–8). He lays the blame for this dilemma not upon makers of goods, but rather on his 'parchemen', which is 'so meke: / hit suffreth on hit to write / whatsomever men wylle' (50 ll. 29–31).[44] Despite his complaint, the narrator-as-scribe clearly finds more pleasure than irritation in the potential infinitude of language and in his ability to pile up words upon the submissive page. His delight, in fact, anticipates that of the successful merchant who in using the book properly would presumably pile up goods, amass an infinite supply ('alway more') to meet a hopefully equally infinite demand, and so also attain infinite prosperity.

Writing at the turn of the century on the nature of greed and avarice, Georg Simmel argued that the 'strange coalescing, abstraction, and anticipation of ownership of property which constitutes the meaning of money is like aesthetic pleasure in permitting consciousness a free play, a portentous extension into an unresisting medium, and the incorporation of all possibilities without violation or deterioration by reality'.[45] In the *Dialogues*, just as the narrator finds pleasurable frustration in the 'unresisting medium' of his parchment, so too does he encode his readers' fantasies of profit in the 'portentous extension' enacted by the next (and last) section of the book.[46] This final segment, which has its own title—it is 'a littel book that men calle / the nombre' (50 ll. 33–4)[47]—lists the words for numbers in a sequence that progresses from 'one' to 'a myllyon' in the short space of fifteen lines (51 ll. 6–20). This rapidly exponential increase, which the narrator explains is 'thus alleway mountyng' (51 l. 21), is suggestive of the ever-expanding fortune presumably to be gained through

[43] Here again the compositor or translator has erred in translating the corresponding French pronoun 'on'.

[44] For an argument about submissive parchment as part of a larger medieval 'sexual poetics', see Caroline Dinshaw, *Chaucer's Sexual Poetics* (Madison, 1989), 9–10.

[45] Georg Simmel, *Philosophie des Geldes*, 2nd edn. (Leipzig, 1907), 351–4, 254–7; trans. in *On Individuality and Social Forms: Selected Writings*, ed. Donald N. Levine, trans. Roberta Ash (Chicago, 1971), 180; quoted in Shell, Economy of Literature, 8.

[46] This section is not, as Bradley suggests, Caxton's addition (*Dialogues*, p. xii), for it is also found in the Vanden Dorpe edition of 1501. See Gessler (ed.), *Le Livre des Mestiers*, 46.

[47] This reference makes one wonder if the writer is not incorporating another text already familiar to his audience into his own.

the shrewd accumulation and exchange of both 'alleway mountyng' goods and 'alway more' words.

Although the number of knowable words will always exceed the narrator's grasp, any number of available goods lies within the grasp of the consumer with the 'whereof' (7 l. 14) to buy them.[48] But in the world imagined by the *Dialogues*, which, as I have noted, personalizes to an extraordinary degree the small commodity production that still dominated the economy of northern Europe in the later Middle Ages, goods can be obtained only through direct dealings with the independent masters who make as well as sell them.[49] Therefore, just as the book tries to teach its reader to negotiate the difference between French and English, so too does it try to make good on its opening promise to teach the art of negotiation itself. In an extended lesson on how to 'bergayne / wullen cloth or othir marchandise' (14 ll. 28–9), a section embedded in the narrator's more general reflections upon the market, it becomes clear that actually obtaining goods can require a good deal more work than his exuberant catalogues might otherwise imply.

This most fully dialogic part of the work dramatizes a complete transaction between a male buyer and a female seller who together move from greeting through disagreement, discussion, eventual accord, payment, and courteous farewell (15 l. 2–19 l. 21).[50] Although the transaction ends successfully, the conversation is rife with tension, however courteous the verbal exchange may be on its surface. '[T]ake hede what I shall paye,' the speaker-as-buyer warns as he tries to drive a bargain (15 l. 14). To an asking price of seven shillings he responds that 'this is no suche cloth / of so moche money' (15 ll. 27–9), while the seller retorts that his offer of three shillings 'is evyll boden' (15 l. 35). Even after they compromise at five shillings (16 l. 6), the anxiety attendant upon the exchange of money for goods remains in evidence; the buyer first cautions the seller to 'mete [measure] well' (16 l. 29) as she cuts his cloth, and then, finding he has

[48] Hüllen incorrectly reads 'whereof' as referring to the furniture in the previous line (*English Dictionaries*, 98). But the French 'Se vous aves de quoy' clearly means 'if you have the funds'; Bradley, too, translates 'Yf ye have wherof' as 'if you can afford it' (*Dialogues*, 'List of English Words', 60).

[49] On small commodity production as the most common form of late-medieval market economy see Martha C. Howell, *Women, Production, and Patriarchy in Late Medieval Cities* (Chicago, 1986), 37–8.

[50] It is not at all surprising that the book's fullest dramatization of exchange involves cloth, since, as is well known, the cloth trade was central to the economy of northern Europe throughout the later Middle Ages. The scholarship on this topic is too vast to review here; for an overview see Spufford, *Power and Profit*, 232–55 and 326–32; and Kermode, *Medieval Merchants*, 170–5 and 202–6.

affronted her, protests against her insistence that the measurer be called in to prove her honesty (16 l. 35–17 l. 8). The seller, in turn, is compelled to ask if the variety of coinages with which her customer pays is 'good moneye' that she can 'gyve . . . oute' freely (17 ll. 36–7). Once each side's doubts have been put to rest, the two establish a theoretically lasting relationship through another kind of exchange, a mutually advantageous promise. Whereas the seller assures her customer future discounts of the 'halpeny or peny' (18 l. 9), the buyer assures her of his future business: 'it . . . is not / the last silver / that ye shal have of me' (18 ll. 18–20).

Michel de Certeau, who divides human practices into *strategies* (schemes and orders by which those in power maintain and promote their self-interest) and *tactics* (subterfuges by which those not in power manœvre their way around the strategies the powerful impose upon them), includes shopping in his list of necessarily tactical arts. Consumers, in his view, must employ 'ruses and surprises' in order to gain the upper hand and 'pu[t] one over the adversary on his own turf'.[51] But by codifying the improvisational tactics of the medieval shopper, the *Dialogues* in fact aims to eliminate utterly the need for surprise by ensuring (or at least pretending) that the book's reader will himself never be surprised in the market-place. The work's intent is precisely to empower the medieval consumer by lifting him out of the realm of tactics and into the realm of strategy, securing for him what de Certeau calls 'a certain independence with respect to the variability of circumstances'.[52] But in a world in which commodities have yet to be fully separated from the labouring hands—not to mention the labouring personalities—that produce them, just one script for the mercantile theatre will not suffice.[53] As the *Dialogues*' initial table of contents implies, the reader ought to buy this book in part because he will eventually have to deal not just with one seller but with many if he plans to acquire the wares or services not only of woolmongers but also

> of tayllours and upholdsters,
> of dyers and drapers,

---

[51] De Certeau, *Practice of Everyday Life*, 40. De Certeau's analysis of tactics here is deliberately ahistorical; he suggests that 'these practices [i.e. 'dwelling, moving about, speaking, reading, shopping, and cooking'] correspond to an ageless art,' and 'present . . . a sort of immemorial link' of human life to the natural world.

[52] Ibid. 36.

[53] As Bourdieu remarks, it is precisely this kind of attempted 'domination' that 'no longer needs to be exerted in a direct, personal way when it is entailed of possession of the means . . . of appropriating the mechanisms of the field of production' (*Outline of a Theory of Practice*, 183–4).

of bakers and shoomakers
of skriveners and bou[k]makers,
of mylnars and bochiers,
of fysshmongers and of lynwevers,
of ketelmakers and librariers,
of glovers and of maundemakers, *basket-makers*
of paintours and usuriers,
of tylers and thatchers,
of carpenters and hatmakers . . .

(2 ll. 18–27)

At the end of his famous and influential description of the body politic in the *Policraticus* (*c*.1159), John of Salisbury observes of the arts and crafts that 'there are so many of these occupations that the number of feet in the republic surpasses not only the eight-footed crab, but even the centipede; one cannot enumerate them on account of their large quantity'.[54] What John here identifies as a problem, the *Dialogues* takes as its subject-matter, for enumerating the 'large quantity' of crafts is precisely its goal. Already in this opening list the book offers its reader what de Certeau argues is another fundamental aspect of strategy: a 'place of power' that allows for '*panoptic practice*', an all-seeing point of view from which 'the eye can transform foreign forces into objects that can be observed and measured, and thus control and "include" them within its scope of vision'.[55] While one might argue that texts of all kinds provide their readers with such omniscience, the *Dialogues* is particularly invested in representing as an easily comprehended whole not only the market, but also the wider social world of which it is a part.

In its interest in social description, the vocabulary greatly resembles the estates literature to which it is clearly related, those medieval texts (including John of Salisbury's corporate fiction) which purport to give a full picture of the social hierarchy, usually while decrying its many ills.[56]

---

[54] 'Haec autem tot sunt ut res publica non octipedes cancros sed et centipedes pedum numerositate transcendat, et quidem prae multitudine numerari non possunt' (Clement C. J. Webb (ed.), *Iohannis Saresberiensis episcopi carnotensis policratici sive de nugis curialium et vestigiis philosophorum libri VIII*, 2 vols. (Oxford, 1909), ii. 6. 20, 59). The translation is from John of Salisbury, *Policraticus: Of the Frivolities of Courtiers and the Footprints of Philosophers*, ed. and trans. Cary J. Nederman (Cambridge, 1990), 126. On this image as it developed throughout the Middle Ages, see A. H. Chroust, 'The Corporate Idea and the Body Politic in the Middle Ages', *Review of Politics*, 9 (1947), 423–52, and the monumental study of Ernst H. Kantorowicz, *The King's Two Bodies: A Study in Medieval Political Theology* (Princeton, 1957).

[55] De Certeau, *Practice of Everyday Life*, 38 and 36.

[56] I take the term 'social description' from Helen Barr, whose recent work on estates literature and on literature as a social practice more generally I have found very useful (*Socioliterary*

While Jill Mann rightly cautions against assuming that all estates literature presents the members of society in descending order of rank, the *Dialogues* does in fact follow that fairly typical and conservative format, placing its artisans at the very bottom of the social scale that it first outlines in its table of contents and then returns to in somewhat greater detail in the section following shortly upon the wool-bargaining episode.[57] But in both sections, the book hurries through the titles of clergy and secular nobility (2 ll. 2–8; 22 l. 14–24 l. 39), giving short shrift to these eminent figures and hastily returning to the bountiful marketplace that we have already seen is its true concern.

And here we come to the most peculiar part of the *Dialogues*. For the narrator introduces his section on the 'craftes' (2 l. 10; 25 l. 23) *not* as a fitting end to his list of estates, but rather as a catch-all device. Observing apologetically that 'many wordes / shalle fall or may falle / which ben not playnly / here tofore wreton' (25 ll. 10–13), he declares that he will first remedy the defect by noting 'diverse maters / of all thynges', and then end his compendium with 'the names of men and of wymmen / after the order of a. b. c., / the names of craftes' (25 ll. 21–3). But in fact those 'diverse maters' are made fully subordinate to the 'a. b. c.' into which the book immediately launches and to which this essay now turns.

'The Order of A.B.C.': Alphabetized Artisans

At first the narrator's solution to his organizational dilemma seems entirely logical. Since antiquity, the alphabet had been recognized not only as a convenient schema for ordering a bewildering surplus of words but also as a useful mnemonic device. By the thirteenth century, alphabetization was a common textual practice, particularly evident in the ordering of glossaries and biblical concordances as well as of florilegia and exempla

---

Practice in Late Medieval England (Oxford, 2001), 3). For what remains the only survey of estates literature and its characteristics to date, see Ruth Mohl, *The Three Estates in Medieval and Renaissance Literature* (New York, 1933), 6–7 and *passim*. Where Mohl offers a fairly rigid definition of the works that fit into the category, Jill Mann, *Chaucer and Medieval Estates Satire: The Literature of Social Classes and the* General Prologue *to the* Canterbury Tales (Cambridge, 1973), takes a broader view, including in her scope 'any literary treatments of social classes which allow or encourage a generalised application' (p. 3). On the origin and development of the idea of societal 'orders' from which estates literature springs, see Georges Duby, *The Three Orders: Feudal Society Imagined*, trans. Arthur Goldhammer (Chicago, 1980). On the problem that artisans posed to the tripartite model of society and that model's gradual alteration to accommodate new social classes, see Jacques Le Goff, *Time, Work, & Culture in the Middle Ages*, trans. Arthur Goldhammer (Chicago, 1980), esp. 71–86 and 107–21.

[57] Mann, *Chaucer and Medieval Estates Satire*, 5–6, and appendix A, 203–6.

collections.[58] One of the most famous of such collections, the thirteenth-century *Alphabetum Narrationum*, even trumpets its alphabetization in its title.[59] So it is notable that the narrator of the *Dialogues* feels the need to introduce and explain his choice. In doing so, he not only creates an awkward transition to the last half of the book, but also highlights what is in fact the peculiarity of his decision.[60] For despite its regular use in many contexts, alphabetical ordering was not yet a commonplace for medieval vocabularies, which were also frequently ordered by topic. This was especially the case in England, where, as Werner Hüllen has shown, topical arrangement was a long-standing lexicographical tradition.[61] And we might observe that even in florilegia and exempla collections, alphabetization tends to operate in the service of topical arrangement: 'A' in the *Alphabetum Narrationum*, for example, groups together tales of abstinence (*abstinencia*), adultery (*adulterium*), amity (*amicitia*), and avarice (*avaritia*).[62]

As I have already indicated, the *Dialogues* itself is broadly topical in arrangement, proceeding in definite sections: salutations, household furnishings, victuals, buying wool, other goods, and the higher estates. But contrary to what we are led to expect from the topical tradition, from the book's own table of contents, and from the narrator's announcement before he begins his 'a. b. c.', what the *Dialogues* presents is not a list of alphabetized crafts, but rather a list of alphabetized *people*. Unlike the bulk of estates literature, which generalizes and stereotypes, the *Dialogues* thus specifies and personalizes (although not without, as will become clear, some stereotyping of its own).[63] No medieval Yellow Pages, this book

---

[58] See Lloyd W. Daly, *Contributions to a History of Alphabetization in Antiquity and the Middle Ages*, Collection Latomus, 90 (Brussels, 1967), 73–4. Despite its focus upon a much later culture, Crain's *Story of A* incorporates much historical and theoretical work on the subject of alphabetization.

[59] For a fifteenth-century English version see Mary Macleod Banks (ed.), *An Alphabet of Tales*, Early English Text Society, os 126 and 127 (London, 1904–5).

[60] Daly notes that Pliny makes a similarly awkward apologetic transition between Books 26 and 27 of his *Natural History* as he moves from classification to alphabetization (*Contributions*, 35–6).

[61] On the different functions of alphabetical and topical ordering see Hüllen, *English Dictionaries*, 11–15.

[62] Banks (ed.), *An Alphabet of Tales*, 16–20, 25–7, 37–45, and 64–6. See also Daly, *Contributions*, 63 and 74.

[63] Even as a mnemonic device, the *Dialogues*' 'a. b. c.' stands out among earlier and later exemplars of craft alphabets that survive from other cultures. An Egyptian school-book of the third-century BCE, e.g., lists the actual terms for craftsmen and traders in alphabetic order (Daly, *Contributions*, 40). So does an early American primer, *The Child's New Play Thing* (1750), which through phrases like 'B was a Butcher' and 'T was a Tinker' presents what Crain calls 'a republic

would be very difficult to use as an aid for finding particular kinds of craftspeople in a particular place; indeed, as a reference book for the travelling merchant operating in an unfamiliar city, its personal alphabet provides a rather bizarre, decidedly non-utilitarian form of commercial access. Just as strange as the *Dialogues'* alphabet in either an educational or commercial context is the fact that its ordering has been largely ignored by the few scholars who have studied the book. Hüllen, otherwise so sensitive to the difference between alphabetical and topical orders, accepts the *Livre des Mestiers'* editor Jean Gessler's remark that the names are clearly drawn from the real world of fourteenth-century Bruges—thus implying, without definitive evidence, that the names once corresponded to actual artisans of that city—and leaves it at that.[64]

In fact, this alphabetization by first name allows the *Dialogues*, at least initially, to remain topically ordered. The book groups together workers in the cloth trade, for example, under the letter 'C' (Cyprien the weaver, Colard the fuller, Conrad the shearer, Katherin (*sic*) the comber, Cecil the spinster, and Clarisse the napper (31 l. 39–33 l. 20)),[65] and makers of horse-trappings and armour (David the bridle-maker, Denis the furbisher, Damyan the armourer, and Donaas the doublet-maker) under the letter 'D' (33 ll. 21–40). However, after this early point the groupings become far more idiosyncratic, usually appearing in several sets of two or three under the rubric of a single letter—Fremyn the tavern-keeper, Frederik the wine-crier, and Fierin the baker, for example, fit together as members of the victualling trades, while Forcker the cordwainer and Ferraunt the hosier belong together as makers of foot-gear (35 l. 17–36 l. 4). Likewise, Laurence the mason logically follows Lambert the carpenter, while Logier, Lucian, and Lyon are a felter, a glover, and a purser (39 l. 39–41 l. 7). A suggestive association is implied by the proximity of Oberol the

---

of ABCs' as it inculcates the value of industry in its young readers (Crain, *Story of A*, 67–8: 68). Another primer studied by Crain, *The Uncle's Present* (1850), alphabetizes the cries of street vendors about their wares (*Story of A*, 80 and fig. 35).

[64] Hüllen, *English Dictionaries*, 94; quoting Gessler (ed.), *Le Livre des Mestiers*, introduction, 14. Bradley speculates, logically though without foundation, about the alteration of the names between the original *Livre des Mestiers* and Caxton's *Dialogues*, which he thinks could lead one to 'suspect that the names were those of actual tradesmen in Bruges, and that the alterations represent changes that had taken place between the earlier and later edition of the book' (*Dialogues*, p. viii).

[65] The exception, Colard the goldsmith, is to make a 'gyrdle' (31 l. 35), an item of clothing which does vaguely associate him with the cloth-workers who follow. The 'C' workers are in fact the first artisans we meet; 'A' and 'B' are all friends, acquaintances, and domestics (25–31), an order that replicates the book's earlier attention first to greeting acquaintances and furnishing the household before its shift to the market.

innkeeper to his fellow host of sorts, Onnour the prison-keeper (42 l. 38–43 l. 20); another is the juxtaposition of Quyntyne the dishonest toll-keeper with Queryne the dice-maker, who are, respectively, explicitly and implicitly involved in the making of illicit profit (44 ll. 29–40).[66] But for the most part the crafts under each letter have very little to do with one another. For example, it is not clear what links Guysebert the bow-maker, Gherard the miller, and Gervays the scrivener beyond the letter 'G' (36 l. 24–37 l. 30), or how, other than by their shared 'W', the work of Walter the paternoster-maker is related to that of William the brush-maker (46 ll. 1–9).

All the alphabetized workers, however, do have several important things in common. First, they are all active members of the community of the 'men [who] make', that group in whom the narrator has already ex-pressed intense interest. By fixing the artisans in place by their proper names rather than by the first letter of each craft, the *Dialogues* operates like many medieval library catalogues, which unlike vocabularies *were* routinely alphabetized by first name.[67] The book thus credits each artisan with the 'authorship' of his or her wares; it emphasizes the productive agency of craftspeople even as it also advertises the availability of their goods to the consumer. Here the author of the original *Livre des Mestiers* may well have been looking back to a particular model, a much older but very well known school-text: John of Garland's *Dictionarius* (*c*.1220).[68] This Latin vocabulary, which survives in over thirty manuscripts, repre-

[66] Perhaps ironically, or perhaps not, the narrator says only that Queryne sells his dice for 'redy money' and that they are 'good marchandyse' (44 ll. 39–40). The playing of dice, however, was consistently condemned by the clergy throughout the Middle Ages because of its connection to gambling. For example, in *The Game and Playe of the Chesse*, a translation of Jacobus de Cessolis's thirteenth-century exemplum collection *Libellus de moribus hominium et officiis nobilium ac popularium super ludo schacorum* that Caxton printed in 1474 (STC #4920) and again *c*.1483 (STC #4921), players of dice are linked with visitors of brothels as the 'worst of alle other' members of the polity (William E. A. Axon, *Caxton's Game and Playe of the Chesse, 1474: A Verbatim Reprint of the First Edition* (London, 1883), 151. On this work's own deep investment in the function of artisans within the social body see Cooper, ' "These Crafty Men," ' 292–311.

[67] This practice dates back to the library at Alexandria, and reappears again in twelfth-century Europe. See Daly, *Contributions*, 22 and 77–9.

[68] Most recently edited by Tony Hunt, *Teaching and Learning Latin in Thirteenth-Century England*, 3 vols. (Cambridge, 1991); for introduction and text, see i. 191–203 and for glosses see ii. 123–56. All references are to Hunt's edition by paragraph numbers. For the translation I have used, with some silent alteration, *The 'Dictionarius' of John de Garlande*, trans. Barbara Blatt Rubin (Lawrence, Kan., 1981). Rubin's translation is based on an edition of a different manu-script than is Hunt's (she uses that of Thomas Wright (ed.), *A Volume of Vocabularies* (London, 1857), 120–38), but the minor differences between the two manuscripts are of little consequence for my purposes here. For a very brief discussion of the *Dictionarius* see Hüllen, *English Dictionaries*, 85–6; for a more extended analysis see Cooper, ' "These Crafty Men" ', 40–6.

sents the city of Paris as a giant market-place through which its author strolls, naming the many 'res quas eundo per civitatem Parisius denotavi' ('things that I have observed in going through the city of Paris') (§8). Like the modern city-walker in whose ambulatory 'enunciation[s]' de Certeau is particularly interested, the thirteenth-century university master maps out a highly selective version of the urban landscape in both footsteps and words, a version that focuses almost entirely on the activity of artisans and the concomitant array of consumer goods.[69]

The *Dictionarius*, like the first part of Caxton's *Dialogues*, lists the items that should be '[i]n hospitio probi hominis' ('in the lodging of a worthy man') (§55). It also scrupulously enumerates the materials from which artisans craft their wares; John notes, to give just two of many possible examples, that hatters make headgear 'de feltro et de pennis pavonis et pillea de bombace' ('of felt or quilted material and from peacock feathers') (§20), and that brooch-makers make buckles 'de plumbo . . . et de stangno, ferro et cupro' ('of lead and of pewter, iron and copper') ((§22). At times John goes even farther than his Flemish successor in delineating the stages of craft process, as in his depiction of the leather-workers who 'secant corium cum ansorio atramentario denigratum et consuunt calciamenta cum subula et licino et seta porcina' ('after having darkened the tawed leather with a coloring matter, cut it with a razor or cobbler's knife, and put together the footwear with an awl and thread and pig bristles') (§25), and as in his equally detailed descriptions of the work of fullers, tanners, and weavers (§§50, 52, 66–7). Also like the later *Dialogues*, the *Dictionarius* acknowledges the role artisans play not only as makers but also as sellers in eager quest of financial gain. Among these John singles out the furbishers who 'cumulant denarios' ('accumulate money'), the skinners 'ditantur' ('made rich') by the skins they sell, the pastrycooks who aim 'quam plurimum lucrantur' ('to make as much money as possible'), and the apothecaries who prepare their concoctions 'causa lucri' ('for the sake of money') (§§17, 26, 34, 43).

While the narrator of the *Dictionarius* appears at first to be a detached observer of city life, by the end of his vocabulary John of Garland depicts himself as a fully engaged consumer who has hired artisans to make '[i]n aula mea . . . trapetas, solivas, lacunaria, tingna, lodia, trabes, latas, laquearia . . . columpnas' ('in my house . . . tables, sills, coffered ceilings, beams, louvres, cornices, panels, panelled ceilings . . . pillars') (§79). At this point, the Paris master truly begins to look like a direct ancestor of the

---

[69] See de Certeau, *Practice of Everyday Life*, 97–8.

often impatient narrator of the *Dialogues*, who understands many of the craftspeople he names in terms of their obligations to him.[70] And here it is worth nothing that another major late-medieval use of alphabetization by name was the maintenance of financial records of debt and payment, including not only government tax records but also mercantile account books.[71] As Luca Pacioli, author of the first theoretical codification of the already frequent practice of double entry bookkeeping, explained to merchants in his *Summa de Arithmetica Geometria et Proportionalita* (1494): 'you will enter all the debtors and creditors according to the letter with which they begin.'[72]

The narrator of the *Dialogues* makes no explicit reference to alphabetization of this kind, but it was a system with which a resident of Bruges, where branches of Italian companies using such methods of account had been present since the thirteenth century, might well have been familiar.[73] The narrator, however, does explicitly address the keeping of records of debt and credit in the concluding 'little book of the number' that I have already mentioned and that is to be used, he tells his reader, 'so may ye reteyne / the dettes that men owe you, / and the receyttes / that ye have re-

[70] My analysis of the text's artisanal personnel largely accords with Hüllen's delineation of four 'clearly distinguishable groups': namely, 'i) articles which simply speak of the activities of the person (craftsman) . . . ii) articles which add some special personal feature . . . and which betray a personal acquaintanceship . . . iii) articles which directly connect the person's activities with the speaker's business, and iv) articles which speak about persons as private individuals and in no other capacity' (*English Dictionaries*, 135–6).

[71] Daly, *Contributions*, 81–4; see also *The Dictionary of the Middle Ages*, ed. Joseph Strayer, 13 vols. (New York, 1982–9), i. 206–7. On debt as a form of 'socially recognized violence' that maintains 'relations of domination' in pre-capitalist societies see Bourdieu, *Outline of a Theory of Practice*, 191.

[72] *Distinctio nona, Tractatus XI De Scripturis*, fo. 201ᵛ; quoted and trans. in Daly, *Contributions*, 82. On Luca Pacioli and double entry bookkeeping as a signifying system see Mary Poovey, *A History of the Modern Fact: Problems of Knowledge in the Sciences of Wealth and Society* (Chicago, 1998), 37–9. On the history of double entry bookkeeping before Pacioli see Raymond de Roover, 'The Development of Accounting Prior to Luca Pacioli According to the Account Books of Medieval Merchants', in A. C. Littleton and B. S. Yamey (eds.), *Studies in the History of Accounting* (London, 1956), 114–74; repr. in *Business, Banking, and Economic Thought in Late Medieval and Early Modern Europe: Selected Studies of R. de Roover*, ed. Julius Kirchner (Chicago, 1974), 119–80. For the longer history of the practice see the essays in Basil S. Yamey (ed.), *Double Entry Bookkeeping in Western Europe, 1300 to 1800* (London, 2000).

[73] For the influence of Italian accounting practices upon bookkeeping in Bruges during the fourteenth century see De Roover, 'Development of Accounting', 163–5. See also De Roover's fuller study, *Money, Banking and Credit in Mediaeval Bruges: Italian Merchant Bankers, Lombards and Money-Changers*, Mediaeval Academy of America, 51 (Cambridge, 1948), esp. 211–15. It is worth noting that the *Livre des Mestiers* opens with an invocation of the Trinity, which was also traditional for the beginning of account books (I, 5; see De Roover, *Money, Banking and Credit*, 211); the same invocation appears in the *Dialogues* after the added table of contents (3 ll. 17–19).

ceyvyd / or that ye have payd' (50 l. 39–51 l. 3).[74] And whereas John of Garland's *Dictionarius* concentrates on artisanal profit, most of the *Dialogues'* craft alphabet reads like a record of artisanal debt, even though it may well be the speaker who is in debt for the goods he has commissioned. Colard the goldsmith, the narrator says, 'oweth me to make / my gyrdle' (31 ll. 34–5), while Cyprian the weaver 'hath promysed to weave / my cloth' (31 l. 40–32 l. 1). Denis the furbisher 'ought to furbysshe' the speaker's knife and sword (33. 26–31), while Elyas the dyer, he complains, 'tarieth so longe / my cloth to dye, / that I shall have harme of hym' (34 ll. 23–5).[75] The narrator makes a point of noting that the 'latthes' used by Lenard the thatcher in covering 'my little house' are 'nothyng worth' (40 ll. 32–3), is planning a complaint ('plete') against Jherome the barber (47 ll. 12–13), and finally is also furious that Josse the parchment-maker sold him a skin 'which nought was worth, / that I myght not write upon' (47 ll. 19–20). In only one case, in fact, do we see that the obligation is actually that of speaker to artisan: Katherin the comber 'was hiere [*sic*] right now for moneye', insisting that 'men shall paye her well' for her fine work (32 ll. 19–23).[76]

Although Chandra Mukerji notes that the line between consumer and capital goods in the later Middle Ages was a fungible one, the narrator frequently appears in the alphabetized section of the *Dialogues* to be speaking of goods meant for his own use rather than for resale to others.[77] The alphabet, however, implies that he will have the advantage either way, for rather than joining the members of the community of artisans to one another, it instead works to sever those relations and connect each artisan to the speaker of his or her name alone. Overall, in fact, it is striking just how few references the book makes to the craft guilds and religious

---

[74] He also extends this system of debit and credit to the reader's maintenance of spiritual economy, advising him that those who 'serveth our lord' and the rest of the heavenly host 'attendeth good reward' and that 'Yf ye owe / ony pylgremages, / so paye them hastely' (48 ll. 16–28 and 34–6). Indeed, late-medieval English merchants sometimes made testamentary bequests for pilgrimages to be undertaken on their behalf (Kermode, *Medieval Merchants*, 125–6).

[75] In Caxton's text, Elyas is referred to as a 'paynter', which word correctly translates the French 'pointurier' (which also appears in the Vanden Dorpe edition (Gessler (ed.), *Le Livre des Mestiers*, IV, 45)). However, the *Livre des Mestiers* has 'tainturier' (Gessler (ed.), *Le Livre des Mestiers*, I, 31), suggesting that at some point the text became corrupted. At any rate, Elyas is clearly a dyer and not a painter. See Godefroy, 'pointurier' and 'peinturier', in *Dictionnaire*, vi. 256 and 263, and 'tainturier', in *Dictionnaire*, vii. 628.

[76] Late medieval records reveal cases of craftsmen actively pressing for payment through legal means; for several examples see Christopher Dyer, 'The Consumer and the Market in the Later Middle Ages', *Economic History Review*, 2nd ser. 42.3 (1989), 305–27: 319.

[77] Chandra Mukerji, *From Graven Images: Patterns of Modern Materialism* (New York, 1983), 6.

confraternities that were such a fundamental part of medieval urban life in general and of Flemish urban life in particular: we learn only that the 'franchise' of shearers has established a going rate for the work of its members (32 ll. 15–17) and that Peter the wool-beater, who has not yet 'bought his franchyse', has been prohibited by the 'wardeyns of the craft' from practising his art (44 ll. 5–15).[78] The only other person who appears in a group is Kylian, who with 'his felaws' is not an artisan, but a saint 'in paradyse' (39 ll. 35–8). The absence of earthly artisanal association in the craft alphabet stands notably in contrast to the *Dialogues'* introductory table of contents, already mentioned above. There, like John of Garland's *Dictionarius*, the book lists artisans in groups by craft rather than as isolated individuals by name—they appear as 'goldsmythes, wevers, and fullers', 'cobelers and pursers', 'myntemakers and pybakers', and so on (2 l. 14; 2 l. 28; 2 l. 34).

This initial intimation of artisanal solidarity, however, has almost vanished by the book's second half. If alphabetic encyclopaedias, as Hüllen observes, reflect their culture 'the way in which a shattered looking-glass mirrors the surrounding world',[79] then so does the craft alphabet in the *Dialogues* provide a fragmented image of the communal artisanal culture that its chaotic introductory table in some sense more accurately depicts. In bringing what Crain calls the 'discipline and . . . arbitrary arrangement' of letters to bear on the craft community, the narrator, or so the book suggests, will be better able to divide and conquer it in his own self-interest.[80] Furthermore, some of his most telling references to artisanal labour done on his behalf are those that suggest his attempt to purchase

---

[78] On the complex guild structure of Ghent, e.g., see Nicholas, *Metamorphosis of a Medieval City*, 17–20 and *passim*. On the intensely associational culture of the later Middle Ages more generally see David Wallace, *Chaucerian Polity: Absolutist Lineages and Associational Forms in England and Italy* (Stanford, Calif., 1997), esp. 72–9 and 84–97; Gervase Rosser, 'Crafts, Guilds, and the Negotiation of Work in the Medieval Town', *Past and Present*, 154 (1997), 3–31; and Gervase Rosser, 'Workers' Associations in English Medieval Towns', in Pascale Lambrechts and Jean-Pierre Sosson (eds.), *Les Métiers au Moyen Âge: Aspects Economiques et Sociaux*, Publications de l'Institut d'Études Médiévales: Textes, Études, Congrès, 15 (Louvain-La-Neuve, 1994), 283–305. The only other kind of association the speaker acknowledges in the artisanal alphabet is the familial relation of men to women who are their daughters, wives, or sisters.

[79] Hüllen, *English Dictionaries*, 11.

[80] Crain, *Story of A*, 101. The narrator's ability to make use of the artisans' labour while effectively separating them from one another through alphabetization resembles what is for Marx one of the defining characteristics of a capitalist society: 'articles of utility', he writes, 'become commodities only because they are the products of the labour of private individuals who carry on their work independently of each other' (*Capital*, i, trans. Samuel Moore and Edward Aveling, repr. in Robert C. Tucker (ed.), *The Marx–Engels Reader*, 2nd edn. (New York, 1978), 321).

his way out of the mercantile class and into the aristocracy, a social translation for which craft labour must provide the props. The speaker is clearly working to accrue the trappings of higher status, including the plate armour he plans to buy from Damyan (33 ll. 35–7), the doublet and jacket he must pick up from Donaas (33 ll. 38–40), and the painted shield he has purchased from Harry, with whose work he is very 'plesid' (39 ll. 23–7). Sylvia Thrupp notes that in addition to purchasing such portable signs of nobility, successful London merchants frequently aspired to life in the countryside, away from the city streets in which they had risen to prosperity.[81] It is not surprising, then, to find that the narrator of the *Dialogues* has hired Lambert the carpenter to 'make [his] castell, / the nethercourt and a berne' (39 l. 39–40 l. 4), Rychard the carter to lay dung on his land, in his garden, and in his orchard (45 ll. 10–16), and Xpristrian (i.e. Christian) the collar-maker to make a collar for his two 'horses of the plowh' (46 l. 29).[82]

While all entries of this sort look like a set of personal receipts for particular goods and services, aristocratic in nature or not, other sections of the craft alphabet work as a more general but also highly subjective consumer's guide for the reader's use. While the names themselves may or may not have ever referred to historical workers, what matters most is not the particulars of each review, but rather that the reviews as a whole generate horizons of expectation for artisanal labour by exemplifying the kinds of things that *can* be said about it. Some craftsmen will deserve commendation for the quality of their wares: David the bridle-maker, the narrator informs his audience, is a 'good werkman' (33 l. 22), Logier the felter 'hath many a good hatte' (40 l. 38), Lyon the purser makes 'powches well wrought' (41 l. 7), and Nycholas the mustard-maker sells 'good mustarde' (42 l. 23). Others should receive approbation for their industry, especially if they resemble Forcker the cordwainer who puts 'more lether to werke / than thre othir' (35 ll. 35–9), or Eustace the tailor who 'resteth not

---

[81] On the purchase of shields by merchants, see Thrupp, *Merchant Class*, 249–55; on their purchase and management of country property, see ibid. 120–30, 144–6, and 279–87. Kermode, *Medieval Merchants*, 16–18 and 110–11, notes that of the Yorkshire merchants in her study, very few acquired the status of country gentlemen, although they often associated with these in society and gained connections to them through marriage; Smith, as I noted above, has argued that many merchants able to be officially recognized as gentry may have deliberately avoided the charge (*Arts of Possession*, 21–36). The merchant-narrator of the *Dialogues*, however, seems quite eager to embrace it.

[82] He also mentions that he has lent Reyner, a squire, his palfrey, steed, and spears for a tournament (45 ll. 25–32). The country residence of the speaker is another aspect of the *Dialogues* to which John of Garland's *Dictionarius* looks forward in its references to John's own garden, orchard, and woods (§§75–8).

/ nyght ne day' (34 ll. 1–12). Some, however, should be avoided, among whom Ferraunt the hosier stands out, for he

> maketh hosen so evyll shapen
> and so evyll sewed,
> that I shall counseille no man
> hosyn of hym to bye.
>
> (36 ll. 1–4)

Just as today's proverbial customer is always right, this narrator always has the last—indeed, virtually the only—word, so much so that readers of the *Dialogues* are as much consumers of his attitude toward artisans as they are of his language and inside knowledge of the workers whose products he buys and whose skill he admires or disdains. What many of the narrator's comments reveal, however, is that the artisans, like those observed many years earlier by John of Garland, are themselves adept players at the game of profitable exchange. It is precisely because the craftspeople already employ the very strategies the *Dialogues* works to teach its reader that their community requires this extended and somewhat anxious scrutiny. Maud the capper, for example, 'maynteneth her wisely' because she 'selleth dere' while sowing her caps 'with two semes' (42 ll. 17–20), a comment that does not quite reveal if she is to be respected for her industry or suspected for her haste. Fierin the baker is admired for keeping his and his customers' costs down; he 'byeth in tyme and at hour, / so that he hath not / of the dere chepe' (35 ll. 32–4). And there is also Valeryen the tawyer, who has 'moche avantage' because he sells the leather he has tawed himself (46 ll. 10–13). But the goal of the *Dialogues* is to reduce the 'avantage' that shrewd artisans like these might have over the reader. This the narrator does by either condemning the quality of their goods, as we have already seen, or by resorting to the strategy of the *ad hominem* attack.

As is well known, economic success in the later Middle Ages depended as much upon personal reputation as it did on skill.[83] The speaker's seemingly casual gossip therefore seems designed at least in part to defuse the potential threat of quick-witted craftsmen, for many of the artisanal portraits reveal a good deal more than what would meet the eye in the

---

[83] On the significance of personal reputation to the economic success of members of the crafts, see Gervase Rosser, 'Communities of Parish and Guild in the Late Middle Ages', in S. J. Wright (ed.), *Parish, Church and People: Local Studies in Lay Religion 1350–1750* (London, 1988), 29–55, esp. 37; and Rosser, 'Workers' Associations'.

market-place but that would be useful to know before entering it.[84]
Colard the fuller, for example, who can 'well full cloth', also has a quick
temper (he is 'moche dangerous' (32 ll. 9–12)), while Clarisse the napper
'can well her craft', but is overly fond of good living (she is 'moche
licorous' (32 ll. 12–20)). These personal insights go hand in hand with
other remarks that more closely resemble the familiar complaints of estates satire. Frederik the wine-crier must know the value of the wine he
advertises, the narrator wryly observes, because he 'drynketh grete
draughtes' of it (35 ll. 23–7). The speaker also mounts a mock defence of
Gherard the miller, who he claims 'steleth not, / but a lytyll of every sack'
of grain (36 ll. 33–4).[85] And the narrator's remarks upon the work of Johan
the usurer, who 'knoweth not the nombre / of the good that he hath / alle
evyll gadred togedyr' (39 ll. 30–2), and that of Randolf the changer, for
whose money 'folke put hem in peryll / to be dampned' (45 ll. 36–7), pay
only slightly anxious lip-service to similarly entrenched cultural tropes.
These remarks about troublesome temperaments, fraudulent practices,
and illicit gains are as intimate as they are stereotypical. But whether they
are read as privileged local information or as estates satire, they reinforce
the image of the foreign market as familiar place, the strange city as a
knowable and so manageable environment.

But the narrator's own relationship to the personalized world he
depicts reveals that whether one is at home or away, the market and the
artisans who populate it are less manageable than the *Dialogues'* fantasy of
the utterly familiar market-place would suggest. As I have already noted,
the speaker considers the majority of the craftspeople as figures who owe
him either product or service. Yet while this attitude consigns the artisans
to seemingly powerless positions of obligation, it also reveals the narrator's dependence upon them. Furthermore, his numerous remarks about
overdue or poorly done work make clear his frustration at the degree to

---

[84] The unpublished French poem *Le Regale du monde* also contains a detailed critique of artisans and merchants, with each description focused on deception under the rubric 'Dez deffautes
qui sont en tous mestiers'. One version, in a manuscript dated 1406 (Cambridge, Trinity Hall
MS 12 fos. 126ᵛ–134ᵛ), accompanies each condemnatory description with a detailed image of
each seller, his customer(s), and his wares. See Johnathan J. G. Alexander, '"The Butcher, the
Baker, the Candlestick Maker": Images of Urban Labor, Manufacture, and Shopkeeping from
the Middle Ages', in Curtis Perry (ed.), *Material Culture and Cultural Materialisms*, Arizona
Studies in the Middle Ages and Renaissance, 5 (Turnhout, 2001), 89–110: 95–8. Alexander notes
that an edition of *Le Regale du monde* is currently in preparation by Professor James Laidlaw.

[85] It should be noted that Gessler edits these comments about Frederick and Gherard as if
they were made by another person in response to the first speaker (*Le Livre des Mestiers*, III, 38–9);
there is, however, no evidence in Caxton's print that it should be so (see Oates and Harmer (eds.),
Vocabulary, 33–4).

which the very system he hopes to teach his readers to master continually eludes his own full control.

Equally problematic for this narrator are the women whom he confronts rather uncomfortably in several digressions within his artisanal alphabet. Colombe has 'cursyd' him for trying to kiss her, and he curses her in turn (32 ll. 32–8); Pieryne is the 'shrewest ghyrle' he knows 'on this side the see' (44 ll. 26–8). Even women without a direct connection to the speaker are portrayed, again through detailed stereotyping familiar not only from estates satire but also from much of medieval literature, as either sexually or verbally irrepressible. Clemence has been caught 'wrastlying with a boye' by her irate stepfather (32 l. 39–31 l. 5), Lucie (already a problem because she is a 'bastarde') speaks 'evyll of them / that well have don to her' (41 ll. 8–11), while Xpristine (i.e. Christine) has lodged a complaint against the lover who refuses to acknowledge her child as his own (46 ll. 30–3). Most disturbing of all to the narrator's sense of social order is apparently one Philipote, upon whose theft of ribbons and cloth, subsequent imprisonment, and threat to kill the master from whom she stole he digresses at length before demanding that '[e]veriche kepe his trowthe!' (36 ll. 5–20). While, as we have seen, the speaker does express admiration for some of the female artisans he names, the other townswomen to whom he refers are without exception unruly like Philipote, disabled, ill, and, in one case, dead.[86]

'The Most Noble Craft': Love Letters, Scribal Labour, and the Printed Word

Faced with the twin troubles of artisans in the market and women in the town, the narrator removes himself from both at the end of his alphabet. Calling for pumice, good paper, penknife, and shears, he declares 'I shall write a lettre of love / And shall sende it to my love' (47 ll. 24–5). This unnamed paramour is apparently nothing like the rowdy townswomen; the two other references to her suggest that she is a sophisticated lady of at least the mercantile class, someone to whom Vedast the furrier sold 'a pylche of graye [pelisse of vair] / and of good furres' (46 ll. 19–22) and for whom the narrator ordered 'a forcer', a 'cheste', and a 'scryne' from Ysores the joiner (46 ll. 33–6). In effect, the speaker here replaces business with private pleasure, thereby also connecting himself to the world of aristo-

---

[86] Colombe is lame (32 l. 32), Clare is blind (33 ll. 6–11), someone's unnamed sister is sick (35 ll. 3–8), and Gertrude has just died (39 ll. 14–22).

cratic leisure and aristocratic desire.[87] But he almost immediately returns to thinking of work. The labour he now has in mind, however, is not that of the artisans. 'I am alle wery', he sighs, as he has done before, 'of so many names to name / of so many craftes, so many services'; again, he repeats, 'I wyll reste me' (47 ll. 26–30). Just as he called our attention at the opening to the book's status as a ware 'good to be bouȝt' (4 l. 3), so too does the narrator here remind us again of the labour—his own—that has gone into this book's production.

The narrator's earlier protestation of weariness ('Of thise thinges I am wery, / so that I shall reste me' (22 ll. 12–13)) appears at the end of his long description of the market, where it has seemingly to do with the boundless nature of his topic and the limits of his intellectual energy. These are related difficulties to which the speaker refers several times over throughout the *Dialogues*. In the opening advertisement of his work's lexicographical superiority, for example, he hints that he will be unable to account for all aspects of his topic; rather, his book will provide 'as moche as this writing / shall conteyne and stratche, / for he may not alle comprise' (3 ll. 25–7). Half-way through the text, we find him taking the opportunity to reinforce his readers' appreciation of his hard work and simultaneously excuse his own ignorance. In a passage that strangely undermines his otherwise confident tone about all mercantile matters, the narrator interrupts his list of commodities to declare:

> But how that I
> me entremete
> to make this book
> and I know a partie
> how men name the thinges,
> therfor I ne wote not
> how ne for how moche
> that men selle the goodes:
>
> .   .   .
>
> so that he
> that wyll knowe it,
> he may axe it
> at the marchans,
> whiche well knowe it.

(20 l. 39–21 l. 18)

---

[87] In this way the narrator resembles the reader of Lydgate's 'Dietary', who Sponsler notes is urged to 'retrea[t] into the enclosed space of private consumption whose value rests less on public approbation than on individual health and happiness' ('Eating Lessons', 16).

In this abrupt disavowal of familiarity with market practice and market price, an assertion otherwise given the lie throughout the book, we have what may be a trace of one of the *Livre des Mestiers*' more intellectually inclined redactors.[88] For this protestation of ignorance aligns the voice of the text with those who deal with scholarly rather than practical matters, with those who know how to name things rather than how to sell them and for how much.

But it is worth recalling that intellectual labour was, throughout the Middle Ages, closely intertwined with a marketable skill, the art of writing, and that the weariness topos adopted by the *Dialogues*' narrator had long been connected to scribal practice.[89] It was adopted by Caxton himself, who some ten years before printing the *Dialogues* wrote of both the intellectual and physical fatigue he experienced as translator of the *Recuyell of the Historyes of Troye*, fatigue that led him (or so he claimed) to put the book to press rather than write out more copies.[90] In the *Dialogues*, as his description of Gervays the scrivener at the very centre of the artisanal alphabet reveals, writing is the craft for which the book's narrator has the highest regard. Praising Gervays as a maker of documents who 'can well write chartres, / preuyleges, instrumentis, / dettes, receyttes, / testamentis, copies' (36 ll. 36–9), the narrator then makes the further claim that writing is 'the most noble craft / that is in the world'—without it, he observes, in one of the text's grandest amplifications, 'the law and faith shold perisshe' (37 ll. 10–11; 37 l. 17).[91] A writer of texts himself (if of

---

[88]   In the first version of the text, the narrator says nothing about merchants; rather, he claims that he cannot name 'toutes les choses / qui sont necessaire / a chescun ouvrier' ('all the things necessary to each worker') (*Le Livre des Mestiers*, I, 19). His inabilities here thus have to do exclusively with craft culture and only at some later point were turned into a statement about mercantile knowledge.

[89]   On the trope of writing as labour see Ernst Robert Curtius, *European Literature and the Latin Middle Ages*, trans. William R. Trask (1953; repr. London, 1979), 468. On scribal labour and weariness in English textual culture see Steven Justice, *Writing and Rebellion: England in 1381* (Berkeley, 1994), 24 n. 34. One particularly well-known scribal complaint is that in Thomas Hoccleve's *Regement of Princes* (ll. 1009–15); on that passage see Steven Justice, 'Inquisition, Speech, and Writing: A Case from Norwich', in Rita Copeland (ed.), *Criticism and Dissent in the Middle Ages* (Cambridge, 1996), 289–322, esp. 294–6, and Ethan Knapp, *The Bureaucratic Muse: Thomas Hoccleve and the Literature of Late Medieval England* (University Park, Pa., 2001), 83–93.

[90]   See Kuskin, 'Reading Caxton', 160–4.

[91]   Bradley believed that ll. 8–30, which greatly expand the *Livre des Mestiers* entry for Gervays, were Caxton's addition (*Dialogues*, p. xi), but the same passage appears in the 1501 Anvers edition; since the two books followed a similar original, Bradley's hypothesis is incorrect (see also Gessler (ed.), *Le Livre des Mestiers*, introduction, 46). This passage also contains a remarkable slippage. It clearly means to state that all men 'owe it to knowe' scripture or else 'God . . . shall take of vengeaunce' (37 ll. 23, 25–6) upon them on Judgement Day. But the 'it' that is owed might equally well be read as referring to the art of writing itself.

no others, then at least of this one), the narrator seems almost to compete here for his readers' attention with the other artisans his alphabet depicts. But he goes even further than this: he moves beyond the traditional clerkly encomium of writing to insist that *all* men should learn to write.[92] '[T]her is none so hye / ne so noble', he declares, 'that may hym shame / for to lerne ne for to doo' (37 ll. 12–15).

The narrator in fact makes several remarks throughout the *Dialogues* that indicate the growing cultural significance of writing to a wider population in the later Middle Ages. I have already mentioned several: his comment about the book stretching to cover and contain its subject (3 l. 26), his complaint about bad parchment (47 ll. 14–20), and his observation that 'meke' parchment turns the writing down of words into a potentially infinite task (50 ll. 25–31). In addition, at the beginning of his alphabet he asks one Boneface to make a fire and bring 'the ynche to seethe', and to stir it so that 'it brenne not' (30 ll. 22–6). He further recommends that his readers send their children to school 'to lerne to rede and to write, / that they resemble not bestis' (9 ll. 37–8),[93] and later refers to wax tablets 'in which men teche / the children to write' (20 ll. 28–9). It is in his praise of Gervays, however, that the narrator most definitively removes writing from the realm of specialized skill possessed by the other artisans he surveys, suggesting to his readers in no uncertain terms that they should appropriate this craft for themselves. The ability to write was, of course, first a defining characteristic of, and finally a mandatory qualification for, membership in the merchant class as it rose to prominence in the later Middle Ages. Indeed, somewhat ironically, many merchants may well have learned to write at schools run by scriveners just like Gervays.[94] His skill, which they gradually appropriated as their own, is useful ('a good servise' (37 l. 7)), 'proufitable' (37 l. 6), and above all, empowering. For if we read the narrator's complaint about his overly malleable parchment in this light, we might well find not only mock despair but also real triumph in the observation that this surface 'suffreth on hit to write / whatsomever men wylle' (50 ll. 30–1).

---

[92] On the topos of writing as the mechanism of cultural memory see Curtius, *European Literature*, 476–7.

[93] Where Amos cites these lines as evidence of the mercantile appropriation of noble ideals (' "For Manners Make Man" ', 33), I find them equally relevant to considering the mercantile appropriation of the scribal art. On merchants as readers, see Thrupp, *Merchant Class*, 155–63. Thrupp, who quotes the *Dialogues'* passage about Gervays as evidence of mercantile literacy (p. 155), estimates on the basis of Latin literacy rates that 50 per cent of London lay males could read English by the late fifteenth century (p. 158).

[94] Thrupp, *Merchant Class*, 159–60.

If writing was a craft skill ripe for appropriation by the mercantile class in the later Middle Ages, however, so too was merchandizing a craft that those other than merchants might learn. William Caxton's decision to print the *Dialogues*, writes William Kibbee, 'extended language learning beyond the classroom, creating a new ideal of the pedagogical text'.[95] But it also made the literally 'prouffytable lernynge' (1 l. 2) that the former mercer had discovered in a manuscript more widely available to all who could read. And so, just as the merchant class was able to appropriate noble codes of behaviour through the purchase of conduct literature, so too might literate craftsmen with aspirations have turned to the *Dialogues* for help as they strove to cross the permeable boundary that, as I noted at the beginning of this essay, separated artisans and merchants, makers and sellers.[96] This would have been particularly possible in London, where every citizen had the customary right to trade wholesale, and where many artisans took advantage of the privilege. As Sylvia Thrupp observes, 'any-one whose credit was good might take a plunge'.[97] Caxton's printing of this work encourages the artisans of London to do just that—or, at the very least, to buy the book and practise their lines. In another entry in the 'G' section of his alphabet, the narrator indulges in a lengthy description of George the bookseller's stall in a passage that must have been dear to Caxton's heart. George, the narrator relates,

> hath moo bookes
> than all they of the toune;
>
> .   .   .
>
> He hath doctrinals, catons,
> oures of our lady,
> donettis, partis, accidents,
> sawters well enlumined,
> bounden with claspes of siluer,
> bookes of physike,
> seuen salmes, kalenders;

[95] Kibbee, *For to Speke Frenche Trewely*, 94; see also Hüllen, *English Dictionaries*, 103.

[96] In Michel de Certeau's terms we might think of the book as an object that, in proffering a strategy to the urban mercantile élite, opens itself up to the tactics of artisans seeking to enter that élite. As de Certeau puts it in terms of the modern-day consumer, 'the "strategic" model is . . . transformed, as if defeated by its own success: it was by definition based on the definition of a "proper" distinct from everything else, but now that "proper" has become the whole' (*Practice of Everyday Life*, 40).

[97] Thrupp, *Merchant Class*, 6. See also Martha C. Howell, 'The Spaces of Late Medieval Urbanity', in Marc Boone and Peter Stabel (eds.), *Shaping Urban Identity in Late Medieval Europe* (Leuven-Apeldoorn, 2000), 3–24: 15; Howell suggests that market space itself created a new kind of commercial and even personal freedom for those who entered it.

inke and perchemyn,
pennes of swannes,
pennes of ghees,
good portoses, *breviaries*
which ben worth good money.

(38 l. 31–39 l. 9)[98]

In Caxton's own bookstall, where many of these items were certainly also for sale, the English consumer would have found another book 'worth good money' (or so Caxton hoped), one from which not only merchants, but rather 'one everich / [might] shortly lerne frenssh and englissh' (51 ll. 35–7). For the *Dialogues*, which had entered the world as a Flemish manuscript, was now available in English and could be found, as some of the last lines of the book announce, 'at Westmestre, by London, / in fourmes enprinted' (51 ll. 33–4).[99]

University of Wisconsin-Madison

[98] On this description as an 'exaggeration, or at best an isolated case' in the fourteenth century (as opposed to the later flourishing of a specialized bookseller's trade), see Rudolf Hirsch, *Printing, Selling and Reading 1450–1550* (Wiesbaden, 1974), 61.

[99] For a fascinating analysis of the changing significance of the word 'fourme' in the records of Caxton's own shifting career, see Kuskin, 'Reading Caxton'.

'A Form as Grecian Goldsmiths Make': Enshrining Narrative in Chrétien de Troyes' Cligés and the Stavelot Triptych

Seeta Chaganti

THE PRESENCE of a luxuriously elaborate vision of Byzantine life in Chrétien de Troyes' Arthurian romance *Cligés* is not surprising, given the historical and political backdrop that the twelfth century provides for this text. During this century, crusaders voyaged east and reacted with equal amounts of envy and mistrust upon seeing this new world and the forms of power, protocol, and prestige it contained. But *Cligés* itself, rather than reflecting explicitly the politically antagonistic awareness of the Eastern empire which the West was developing during this period, testifies to an awareness that was aesthetically oriented. The text is preoccupied with the depiction of this culture's artistic productions, such as tombs, shrines, and noble dwellings, and provides us with an alternative to more overtly political perspectives from the twelfth century on the relationship between the Eastern and Western empires.

The Byzantine setting of *Cligés* draws particular attention to what might otherwise be fairly conventional images of enshrined bodies and bodily fragments, from the sacred entombment of the apparently martyred beloved to the treatment of a strand of golden hair as an enshrined relic. In this essay, I shall argue that the act of enshrinement constitutes a poetics in *Cligés*. The features of this poetics are articulated through the devotional and material tradition of the twelfth-century reliquary, an object whose visual language was influenced by the influx of Byzantine culture in the West. *Cligés'* poetics of enshrinement uses the structural conventions of sacred shrines, shared between poem and object, as a model for the incorporation of source material into a narrative structure. Thus *Cligés'* use of source material can be read not through the particular temporality of intertextual reference, but instead through a more multi-faceted and self-enfolding temporality—the temporality of the reliquary.

In espousing this unique poetics, *Cligés* ultimately challenges the boundaries between verbal and visual or material modes of expression.

Proposing a poetics of enshrinement requires at the outset an explanation of the concept of enshrinement itself in the context of the real aesthetic objects of the Middle Ages. In examining body-part reliquaries from a number of points in the Middle Ages, Cynthia Hahn has noted what she calls a 'slippage' between the relic contained and the ornate container. This conflation occurs, she argues, even when these anatomically shaped containers do not reflect the body part that they contain. Instead, both the contained object and the container 'function primarily as metaphor', mutually participating in a symbolic visual and material language.[1] There are other ways as well of understanding the reliquary's subversion of the distinction between container and contained. As Caroline Walker Bynum has demonstrated, the vision of heavenly reintegration expressed in the late-medieval reliquary informed perceptions of the relic's own earthly and fragmented status.[2] Amy Remensnyder offers a related perspective on the relationship between holy relics and the containers that enshrine them—she points out that the language of the reliquary actually endows the relic within with meaning to such a powerful extent that the reliquary is able in some cases to change the meaning of the relic inside it over time, and that the significance of the artefact as a whole can be displaced from the relic to the reliquary.[3] Finally, Ellert Dahl has argued, in analysing statue reliquaries from France, that the materials of a saint's reliquary are meant to gesture symbolically toward the heavenly Jerusalem. The relics within perform a mediating function between the worshipper and the saint, who is ultimately contained within the heavenly Jerusalem, signified as a celestial artefact itself.[4] Enshrining an object thus leads to further layers of enshrinement. These various perspectives on the nature of the reliquary artefact contribute to a broader conception of the enshrined sacred object in the Middle Ages: the act of enshrining a sacred object can give that object meaning, and at the same time the boundaries between the enshrined object and that which enshrines it can

---

[1]   Cynthia Hahn, 'The Voices of the Saints: Speaking Reliquaries', *Gesta*, 36, no. 1 (1997), 20–31: 20, 27–8.

[2]   Caroline Walker Bynum, *The Resurrection of the Body in Western Christianity, 200–1336* (New York, 1995), 327.

[3]   Amy G. Remensnyder, 'Legendary Treasure at Conques: Reliquaries and Imaginative Memory', *Speculum*, 71 (1996), 884–906: 890.

[4]   Ellert Dahl, 'Heavenly Images: The Statue of St. Foy of Conques and the Signification of the Medieval "Cult-Image" in the West', *Acta ad archaeologiam et artium historiam pertinentiae*, 8 (1979), 180–94: 178–9.

be fluid. Most fundamentally, sacred enshrinement represents a dynamic in which everything is both contained and containing.

In *Cligés*, this model provides a framework for understanding the relationship between text and source. Chrétien incorporates the legend of Tristan and Iseut into his text through an act of poetic enshrinement. This reading offers an alternative to traditional perceptions of *Cligés* as embodying several possible moral responses to its precursor text, suggesting instead that the narrative enshrinement of source material is less a form of moral commentary than a unique poetics of the material world. In order to make this case, I shall begin by focusing on the Stavelot triptych, a mid-twelfth-century artefact whose features subvert our sense of what is enshrining and what is enshrined. The triptych enshrines northern European and Byzantine visual elements within each other by means of a complex iconographic programme, and helps to suggest a particular conception of the act of enshrinement in twelfth-century aesthetic practice. I shall then turn to a reading of *Cligés* itself in which we perceive a poetics that also reflects this conception of enshrinement, using a framework of sacred representation to give form to a secular mode of expression. Essentially, *Cligés* enshrines *Tristan*, with all the attendant connotations of the sacred artefact, and in this process offers an understanding of poetic language in this romance as defined by what Michal Kobialka has called the 'representational practice' of the devotional object.[5] The essay's final section moves outward to consider the ways in which *Cligés* suggests the broader possibility that the process of reading a romance text should be made indistinguishable from the process of reading an artefact. This inextricability between the realms of language and object is particularly informed by the Byzantine aesthetic influence present in the romance itself. The Byzantine world alluded to in *Cligés* provides an appropriate aesthetic and ideological context for the romance's own poetics of enshrinement, as the tradition of Byzantine ekphrastic writing—some of whose

---

[5] Kobialka's formulation of the term 'representational practice' refers specifically to the problem of dramatic representations of the sacred from the eleventh to the thirteenth centuries: as he argues, 'representation is a heterogeneous discursive practice, which was defined and redefined, disseminated and erased, and institutionalized and internalized within the dynamic field of the ever-shifting relationships between theological, historical, metaphysical, social, political, and cultural formulations in the Middle Ages' (Michal Kobialka, *This Is My Body: Representational Practices in the Early Middle Ages* (Ann Arbor, 1999), 28). Despite its different generic context, the terms of Kobialka's methodology are useful here for understanding the ways in which we might think about how a site of visual representation operates, and the extent to which those modes of representation shift according to cultural context and the complicated role of the sacred in secular life.

most conventional imagery is suggestively reflected in *Cligés*—provides a methodology for understanding poetic imagery in terms of material and devotional structures.

Cligés' allusions to Byzantine aesthetics and to the construction of sacred shrines can thus ultimately help us to revise our perspectives on the nature of interdisciplinary reading in the visual and verbal arts. Existing interdisciplinary approaches create a fairly wide spectrum of possibilities—at the theoretical level and at culturally specific moments— for conceiving of the correspondences between words and images. At one point on this spectrum of methodologies lies analogy or comparison between the representational techniques which each of these modes employs, as in the perception—familiar to both medieval viewers them- selves and scholars of this age—of the cathedral as a stone rendering of the gospel.[6] At another is the argument of influence, the demonstration that representative artefacts from one field had discernible effects on the pro- ductions of another. An example of this mode of connection is found in the study of the influence of Byzantine rhetorical practice on the visual realm of iconography.[7] What *Cligés* is saying about the relationship between words and material or visual images, however, needs to be ac- commodated by an alternative to such methods of approach, one which allows for the destabilization of some of the boundaries between the visual and the verbal. The work of W. J. T. Mitchell usefully questions the distinctions between traditional categories of imagery such as mental and verbal versus graphic and physical.[8] Mitchell's goal—to show what con-

---

[6] See Brian Stock, citing Ernst Kitzinger, in *The Implications of Literacy: Written Language and Models of Interpretation in the Eleventh and Twelfth Centuries* (Princeton, 1983), 82; see also Emile Mâle on the Gothic cathedral as 'first and foremost a sacred writing of which every artist must learn the characters' (*The Gothic Image: Religious Art in France in the Thirteenth Century*, trans. Dora Nussey (New York, 1958), 1). Arguments about later periods adopt this technique as well, as in the case of Martin Elsky on the analogy between early modern devotional poetry and the mannerist painting of the sixteenth century in 'John Donne's "La Corona": Spatiality and Mannerist Painting', *Modern Language Studies*, 13, no. 2 (1983), 3–11.

[7] In making this argument of influence, Henry Maguire relies on an encompassing definition of the idea of structure, as it pertains to both art and narrative, and his method is an extremely useful one. Making arguments of influence in the reverse direction, however, can prove more difficult, as Maguire himself notes. See Henry Maguire, *Art and Eloquence in Byzantium* (Princeton, 1981), esp. 28.

[8] Mitchell points out that this perspective on the concept of the image in the context of verbal representation has its problematic elements: 'Verbal imagery . . . can involve all the senses, or it may involve no sensory component at all, sometimes suggesting nothing more than a recurrent abstract idea like justice or grace or evil. It is no wonder that literary scholars get very nervous when people start taking the notion of verbal imagery too literally' (W. J. T. Mitchell, *Iconology: Image, Text, Ideology* (Chicago, 1986), 13). But in raising this concern he also exposes a problematic critical tendency to see comparisons between painting and poetry as necessarily

crete forms of imagery have in common with metaphoric or figurative types of imagery—provides a salient model for the present study; I hope to demonstrate here the inseparability of verbal and concrete imagery within the specific context of a moment in medieval history. Chrétien's particular uses of the imagery of the material world, in conjunction with his interest in poetic and narrative structure, open up the possibility that the relationship between verbal and visual art might be understood in other terms besides the inherently metaphorizing techniques of comparison and analogy.

V. A. Kolve has pointed out, in the course of his own interdisciplinary investigations, that 'the best guide to medieval poetic is the practice of poets, closely read and sympathetically imagined'.[9] A sympathetic imagining of Chrétien de Troyes' poetic practice necessarily includes the artistic and material cultures—both Western and Eastern—which surrounded him, and to which he alludes throughout his work. Twelfth-century Continental artistic and devotional practice, exposed as its different levels were to Byzantine aesthetics, provides a culturally grounded space in which to understand the inextricability of material and verbal imagery. In this space, we see that the enshrining structures of sacred artefacts provided Chrétien—and continue to provide his readers—with a means of conceptualizing narrative and poetic structure.

Although the plot of *Cligés* is a familiar one, it may be useful to begin by providing a synopsis that emphasizes the text's different uses of enshrining and enclosing structures, as well as its particular vision of interaction between Eastern and Western worlds. Composed around 1176, *Cligés* links the narratives of a father and son, both of whom travel to Arthur's court from the Eastern empire.[10] It begins with the brothers

hampered by 'inexactness and falsity', as he cites Lessing's *Laocoon*. The problem with this stance, Mitchell contends, is that 'it has tended to conceal from us the figurative basis of our own canons of judgment. We tend to think, in other words, that to compare poetry with painting is to make a metaphor, while to differentiate poetry from painting is to state a literal truth. What I would like to examine here', Mitchell continues, 'is the way in which differences between the arts are instituted by figures—figures of difference, of discrimination, of judgment.' Mitchell ultimately proposes that 'there is no *essential* difference between poetry and painting, no difference, that is, that is given for all time by the inherent natures of the media, the objects they represent, or the laws of the human mind' (p. 49).

[9] V. A. Kolve, 'Rocky Shores and Pleasure Gardens: Poetry vs. Magic in Chaucer's *Franklin's Tale*', in Piero Boitani and Anna Torti (eds.), *Poetics: Theory and Practice in Medieval English Literature* (Rochester, NY, 1991), 165.

[10] The question of *Cligés*' date of composition has been rather heavily contested historically; however, in recent years an overall consensus has been reached—a date of around 1176—with some variant theories. Because the romance appears to refer to a number of somewhat controversial historical events, readers tend to base their judgements about the poem's date upon the likelihood of Chrétien's giving offence to certain politically important figures as a result of his

Alixandre and Alis, the sons of the Byzantine emperor. Alixandre, the eldest, decides that he will achieve more glory if he tests his mettle at King Arthur's court than if he contents himself with being knighted at his Eastern court. He travels west, encounters Arthur at Winchester, and enters into the British king's service. While accompanying Arthur on a military voyage, Alixandre falls in love with the queen's companion, Soredamors. Soredamors gives Alixandre a shirt into which she has secretly woven strands of her hair, and Chrétien compares the shirt enclosing its hair to a holy shrine. Alixandre proves himself in battle against a rebellious count, marries Soredamors (who bears the child Cligés), and travels east with his family, only to discover while in Athens that his younger brother Alis has seized the imperial throne. In order to avoid war, the brothers agree that Alis can keep the throne if he promises not to marry, safeguarding Cligés' eventual inheritance of the empire.

When Alixandre and Soredamors die, however, Alis breaks his word and arranges to marry Fenice, the daughter of the German emperor. Because she has already been promised to the Duke of Saxony, a war breaks out in which Cligés (now an adult) assists his uncle.[11] Cligés falls in love with Fenice, but she refuses to run away with him because she fears comparison to the duplicitous Iseut. She marries Alis, but in order to remain true to Cligés, she and her nurse arrange for Alis to drink a potion which creates in him the misperception that he has consummated his marriage with his wife. Cligés, meanwhile, follows his father's example and travels to the West to participate in tournaments. When his love for Fenice compels him to return to the Byzantine empire, the two finally plot their escape: Fenice will drink a potion to make her appear dead, and Cligés will spirit her away from her tomb, a shrine which Cligés' indentured artisan Jehan tells the emperor Alis he has built in order to enclose the body of a

work. For example, Krijnie Ciggaar places the poem before 1176 as part of a contention that the name Cligés is based on the Turkish sultan Kilidj Arslan, who was on good terms with Byzantium until he destroyed part of their army in 1176 (Krijnie Ciggaar, 'Encore une fois Chrétien de Troyes et la "matière byzantine": la révolution des femmes au palais de Constantinople', *Cahiers de civilisation médiévale*, 38, no. 3 (1995), 267–74: 267); Anthime Fourrier dates it around 1176 (cited in Karl D. Uitti, *Story, Myth, and Celebration in Old French Narrative Poetry: 1050–1200* (Princeton, 1973), 157); but Maurice Halperin places its composition several years earlier—before 1168—because he argues that Chrétien would have been unwilling to offend Henry the Lion, the actual Duke of Saxony, who appears as an unsympathetic character in *Cligés*, after he married Matilda, the daughter of Henry II, in 1168 (Halperin, 'The Duke of Saxony and the Date *ad quem* of *Cligés*', *Romanic Review*, 21 (1930), 239–41: 240–1). Sharon Kinoshita places the romance as late as the 1180s in 'The Poetics of *Translatio*: French-Byzantine Relations in Chrétien de Troyes's *Cligés*', *Exemplaria*, 8, no. 2 (1996), 315–54: 335.

[11]   This event refers to a historical conflict; see n. 14 below.

saint. Three doctors suspect the ruse and try to torture the semi-conscious Fenice into admitting that she is alive during a scene which Chrétien describes as a martyrdom. The deception temporarily succeeds, however, and Fenice escapes and lives with Cligés for a while inside a beautiful tower and walled orchard which Jehan has constructed for them outside Constantinople, and which miraculously conceals all of its own entrances and exits. They are eventually discovered and shamed, but before Alis can catch them and take his vengeance, the artisan confronts the emperor with the fact that the latter broke his original promise not to marry. Eventually, Alis dies traumatized, and Cligés and Fenice rule the Eastern empire legitimately. They are apparently liberated from the spectre of comparison to Tristan and Iseut, except for the fact that Fenice leaves behind her a legacy of mistrust of the Byzantine emperor's wife, who in future generations 'com an prison / Est gardee an Costantinoble'.[12]

The Stavelot Triptych and the Paradox of Enshrinement

Through its imaginative references to artefacts, *Cligés* uses some of the frameworks applicable to the discussion of sacred art in order to create a unique poetics for *Cligés*, one which draws upon the features of sacred shrines and tombs to define the romance as an enshrinement of its Tristanian source material. In order to clarify this perception of enshrinement, and its relationship to the consideration of Byzantine aesthetic influence, I shall consider, before turning in depth to *Cligés* itself, an enshrining object that blends Eastern and Western elements, that was created in a well-known Mosan workshop, and that became an object of pilgrimage during the second half of the twelfth century.[13] This is the

---

[12] Alexandre Micha (ed.), *Cligés*, ii: *Les Romans de Chrétien de Troyes, édités d'après la copie de Guiot (Bibl. nat. fr. 794)* (Paris, 1968), 202, lines 6652–3. All subsequent line numbers will appear in the text. Other editions of Chrétien's work which will be used are Chrétien de Troyes, *Cligés*, ed. Claude A. Luttrell and Stewart Gregory (Rochester, NY, 1993); and Chrétien de Troyes, *Œuvres complètes*, ed. Daniel Poirion *et al.* (Paris, 1994). Line numbers will refer to the Micha edition unless otherwise indicated. Unless otherwise indicated, translations are my own (with some assistance from Burton Raffel's edition (see n. 14)).

[13] According to William Voelkle, 'Although the triptych form had been used in Byzantine devotional ivories and True Cross reliquaries several centuries earlier, the Stavelot Triptych may have helped to further its popularity in the diocese of Liège and beyond' (Helen C. Evans and William D. Wixom (eds.), *The Glory of Byzantium: Art and Culture of the Middle Byzantine Era, A.D. 843–1261* (New York, 1997), 462). On the triptych as a potential pilgrimage object, see Kelly McKay Holbert, 'Mosan Reliquary Triptychs and the Cult of the True Cross in the Twelfth Century' (Ph.D. thesis, Yale University, 1995), 195.

Stavelot triptych, an important Western example of the older Eastern form of the reliquary triptych, commissioned by Abbot Wibald of Stavelot in the Meuse River valley sometime after 1156 (Fig. 1).

As will be immediately clear, the Stavelot triptych's history does bear some provocative connections to the plot of *Cligés*; however, my goal here is not to argue for a scene of explicit influence between object and romance, but instead to point out their shared participation in a larger aesthetics of enshrinement. In representing a developing form in twelfth-century northern Europe, the Stavelot triptych points toward a conception of the material project of enshrinement, and in particular its ability to manipulate narrative temporality through the subversion of distinctions between what contains and what is contained. Although the Stavelot triptych provides an example of the influence of Eastern sacred aesthetic tradition upon Western, the piece ultimately complicates the notion of a straightforward *translatio* from Constantinople to Western Europe. Its Byzantine and Mosan elements fold back upon each other in more ways than one, so that the triptych simultaneously draws the viewer's attention to, and complicates the viewer's understanding of, its origin. The Stavelot triptych creates a symbolic language that enfolds past and present within each other.

In the winter of 1155 and 1156 Abbot Wibald travelled to Constantinople in order to assist in negotiating the marriage of Frederick I Barbarossa to the niece of Manuel I Comnenus, a precursor to the 1171 marriage negotiations of Frederick Barbarossa.[14] On his return to Belgium, Wibald reputedly brought with him two small enamelled triptychs, each of which contained relics of the True Cross. He commissioned a larger reliquary which would incorporate and display these Byzantine pieces, resulting in

---

[14] Frederick Barbarossa attempted in 1171 to negotiate the marriage of his son to the daughter of the Byzantine emperor. See Joseph J. Duggan, afterword to *Chrétien de Troyes: Cligés*, trans. Burton Raffel (New Haven, 1997), 221. Duggan provides a helpful summary of the unsuccessful negotiations surrounding this second marriage and their repercussions: when the negotiations failed, Frederick Barbarossa suspected Henry the Lion, Duke of Saxony, of having conspired with the Eastern emperor to undermine them, and the two became enemies during the 1170s and 1180s. Henry the Liberal at the court of Troyes favoured the German emperor; thus the court would have looked with disapproval upon Henry, Duke of Saxony (p. 222). See also Donald Maddox, who summarizes various arguments about the historical resonances of *Cligés* in 'Critical Trends and Recent Work on the *Cligés* of Chrétien de Troyes', *Neuphilologische Mitteilungen*, 74 (1973), 730–45: 740–1. 'Holer and Fourrier', he says, 'have proposed that *Cligés* reflects the negotiations taking place between Frederick Barbarossa, Emperor of Germany, and the Emperor of Constantinople, Manuel Comnenus, during the 1170s. . . . Henry and Renée Kahane claim that *Cligés* is a portrait of Comnenus' enemy, the Sultan of Iconium, Kilidj Arslan II. . . . The political rivalry between Kilidj and Comnenus would correspond to the rivalry between Cligés and Alis.' Maddox and others discount this latter parallel.

FIG. 1. The Stavelot triptych, full view.

the creation of the Stavelot triptych, one of the most important extant twelfth-century Mosan reliquaries.[15] The Stavelot triptych is the oldest surviving cross reliquary containing scenes of the *Inventio*, and one of a group of five reliquary triptychs thought to be produced during the second half of the twelfth century in the Mosan region.[16] The triptych's style of enamel work indicates its Mosan origin; this section of the Meuse Valley was a popular and prestigious source of both personal and ceremonial reliquaries for many parts of twelfth-century Europe.[17] The two enamel triptych reliquaries which Wibald brought back from the Byzantine empire each use different strategies for framing the cross relics. One of these depicts Christ on the cross, flanked by Mary and Christ's disciple John. The other, larger and placed below the first, displays a fragment of the wood of the cross, in a cross shape and decorated with pearls. On the lower triptych's outer wings, the four Byzantine military saints—George, Procopius, Theodore, and Demetrius—attend the cross. On the cross panel itself, surrounding the wood, appear Constantine, Helena, Gabriel, and Michael (Fig. 2).[18] This pair of Byzantine enamels is set into a central piece, with a wooden core once covered with silver gilt, and a hammered metal border with inlaid stones; two hinged wings flank the central piece, each containing three enamelled roundels illustrating scenes from the finding of the True Cross.[19] The Stavelot triptych locates itself at the

---

[15] On the features of the Stavelot triptych, see Joyce Brodsky, 'The Stavelot Triptych: Notes on a Mosan Work', *Gesta*, 11 (1972), 19–33; Charles Hercules Read, 'On a Triptych of the Twelfth Century from the Abbey of Stavelot in Belgium', *Archaeologia*, 62 (1910), 21–30; and William Voelkle, *The Stavelot Triptych: Mosan Art and the Legend of the True Cross* (New York, 1980). This anecdotal explanation for the presence of the Byzantine pieces in Belgium is generally accepted in art-historical studies of the triptych, despite the lack of direct evidence for Wibald's importation of these Eastern objects.

[16] Voelkle, *Stavelot Triptych*, 11; see Holbert, 'Mosan Reliquary Triptychs', for a comparative discussion of all these reliquary triptychs, of which three, the Stavelot, Guennol, and Ste.-Croix, are attributable to Mosan workshops of this period, and two, the Duduit triptychs, contain significant alterations and restorations dating from the nineteenth century.

[17] See Marie-Madeleine Gauthier, *Émaux du moyen âge occidental* (Fribourg, 1972), 173, on an enamelled altar screen employing the Mosan style and made for Champagne or Lorraine.

[18] The wood of the cross held a particularly important place in the devotional context of France; the establishment of the fair at Lendit in the mid-twelfth century (which Chrétien mentions in his description of Guenever's comb, a reliquary allusion in its own right, during the *Charrete*) focused on the wood of the cross, and France later developed for itself a national identity as the destined receptacle of the relics of the True Cross. See L. Levillain, 'Essai sur les origines du Lendit', *Révue Historique*, 155, fasc. 2 (1927), 254, on processions with a fragment of the True Cross (first recorded in 1145–6) during the public ('in platea') segment of Lendit fair, established in the first half of the twelfth century; and Daniel H. Weiss, 'Architectural Symbolism and the Decoration of the Sainte-Chapelle', *The Art Bulletin*, 77 (1995), 308–20: 308.

[19] Removing the velvet (a modern addition) that now covers the wooden core has revealed that the core's structure confirms that the piece is original in its entirety, and was initially designed to house the two Byzantine enamels (Voelkle, *Stavelot Triptych*, 22).

FIG. 2. The Stavelot triptych, centre panel.

beginning of an important tradition of Western triptych artefacts, whose original influence was Byzantine, that would continue into the thirteenth century and beyond.[20]

The Stavelot triptych speaks through its iconographic programme about the role of time in narrative representation, as well as about the sacred fragment's potential to be made whole again; it makes both these points through its strategic use of a complex and many-layered mechanism of enshrinement. The triptych visually considers different modes of temporality, as it contains both static elements and a sequentially articulated narrative. William Voelkle points out that the construction of the triptych allows it to bring together what he terms 'symbolic representation' with 'narrative mode' in order to contain and authenticate the cross fragments it houses.[21] The iconic Byzantine representations at the centre are juxtaposed with the more explicit act of visual story-telling contained in the Mosan wings with their sequential roundels.[22] But the Stavelot piece as a whole does not simply contrast these two modes with each other. Instead, the enclosing nature of its physical structure creates points of intersection between the two forms of representation, and suggests ways in which each can inform the viewer's perception of the other. The panel on the left side of the triptych depicts, in a series of three roundels, Constantine first receiving the cross vision, then riding into battle against Maxentius with the cross standard held aloft, and finally being baptized (Fig. 3). On the right, the viewer sees in three corresponding roundels a group of Jews telling Helena that Judas knows the location of the cross, Judas himself pointing to its location, and finally the miraculous resurrection of the dead youth by the True Cross (Fig. 4). This last roundel is placed at the same level as the upper central enamel, which portrays the Crucifixion, so that the prospect of resurrection inherent in the Crucifixion itself is reflected in the image to its right (Fig. 1); the triptych aligns these scenes with the baptism on the left as well. The temporal narrative surrounds the static central images of the cross and endows them with

---

[20] Jacqueline Lafontaine-Dosdogne focuses in particular on the influence of the triptych reliquary form on Western devotional artefacts in 'L'influence artistique byzantine dans le région Meuse-Rhin du VIIIe au début du XIIIe siècle', in *Byzantine East, Latin West: Art-Historical Studies in Honor of Kurt Weitzmann*, ed. Christopher Moss and Katherine Keifer, (Princeton, 1995), 185–6.

[21] On the Stavelot triptych's juxtaposition of Eastern and Western liturgical and hagiographic conceptions of Constantine (who was a saint in the East but not in the West), as well as its bringing together of these modes, see Voelkle's commentary in Evans and Wixom (eds.), *Glory of Byzantium*, 463.

[22] On the narrative potential of reliquaries, see Remensnyder, 'Legendary Treasure'.

FIG. 3. The Stavelot triptych, left wing.   FIG. 4. The Stavelot triptych, right wing.

both a history and a future. Specifically, it draws out the narrative of Constantine and Helena which the figures surrounding the lower central cross embody. In one sense, the elaborating temporal narrative prevents the viewer from experiencing the iconic figures as static. At the same time, the object's arrangement of imagery visually draws together, through its enclosing wings, points from different moments of sacred history, undermining the linear nature of this temporality.[23] The resurrection that Saint Helena witnesses, for example, is linked with Christ's own resurrection through the triptych's invocation of the crucifixion at its centre. Thus, while the contrast between the Eastern element's iconic nature and the Western element's visual narrative plays a vital role in the viewer's understanding of the triptych's iconography, it is equally important to recognize that the object's patterns of enshrinement complicate the viewer's sense of division between these two modes of representation.

The triptych's enshrining strategies also contribute to a re-conception of the fragments of the True Cross as emblematic of wholeness.[24] The central panels themselves immediately suggest this reintegration through the crucifix form in which the True Cross relics are presented (Fig. 2). More importantly, however, the enclosing Mosan wings contribute to this process of reintegration by imagining the cross in both its symbolic and its concrete identities. The left panel, which depicts the cross as Constantine perceives it, limits itself to cross images which are small and never centrally placed in the enamel roundels. In fact, both the cross in Constantine's vision and the battle-standard cross are so close to the edge of the enamel that their vertical beams literally push at the roundels' frames (Fig. 5). At this point in the *Inventio*, the cross is not a concrete object but an imagined one, a symbol, appearing as dream and as copy, but not as the

---

[23] Hans Belting articulates some of the problems inherent in thinking about narrative images: 'Images contain moments from a narrative, although they themselves are not narratives. The child on its mother's lap and the dead man on the cross recall the two focal points of a historical life. The differences between them are the outcome of historical factors and consequently make possible remembrance *within* or *through* the image. This image, however, is comprehensible only through being recognized from the Scriptures.' This statement appears in the context of an argument about the primacy of the portrait image over the narrative one, with the portrait exhibiting a 'claim to historicity' of its own (Hans Belting, *Likeness and Presence: A History of the Image before the Era of Art*, trans. Edmund Jephcott (Chicago, 1994), 10).

[24] On the reliquary's participation in the dichotomy of fragmentation and the integrity of resurrection, see Bynum, *The Resurrection of the Body*, esp. chs. 5 and 8. Eugene Vance discusses the reintegrating potential of artefacts in the context of twelfth-century France ('Semiotics and Power: Relics, Icons, and the *Voyage de Charlemagne à Jérusalem et à Constantinople*', *Romanic Review*, 79, no. 1 (1988), 164–83: 172). Christian worshippers in the Middle Ages often believed that the True Cross could withstand an infinite amount of fragmentation by relic hunters seeking a sacred splinter, and yet still remain miraculously whole (Yrjö Hirn, *The Sacred Shrine: A Study of the Poetry and Art of the Catholic Church* (London, 1912), 44).

FIG. 5. The Stavelot triptych, detail of bottom and middle roundels on left wing.

actual wood on which Christ was crucified. The crosses on this side of the triptych hover at the edge of their frames because they are not entirely of the literal world which the roundels portray—they are crosses of vision and imitation, invoking the sacred shape. On the right side of the panel, however, the cross images appear as much larger and more prominent than the ones on the left (Fig. 4). This half of the *Inventio* narrative details the events surrounding the physical cross in Jerusalem, and the size, thickness, and centrality of the crosses on this side, in contrast to their relative obscurity and peripheral placement on the opposite panel, correspond to the right-hand panel's preoccupation with recreating the cross as an integral, tangible object rather than a symbol or an elusive dream. The enamel techniques reinforce this contrast; the cross on the upper right-hand side, a representation of the physical True Cross as unearthed in Jerusalem, is rendered in a translucent enamel backed by foil, so that it receives far more visual emphasis than the crosses on the left side. In addition, the green pigment of this cross representation alludes to the identity of the Cross as the Tree of Life.[25] The Stavelot triptych thus finds an effective iconographic and structural language with which to express the artefact's representation of the cross in a progression from vision to symbol, and finally, to integral object.[26] Its enamel work imagery emphasizes the dichotomy of its concrete and symbolic identities, while at the same time the enfolding triptych form draws the viewer's gaze back towards the central reality of the True Cross, the origin and source—understood as both fragmented and at the same time essentially whole—from which both these versions of its representation derive.

The mechanism of enshrinement allows both the discussion of narrative temporality and the examination of fragmentation and reintegration to take place in the triptych, juxtaposing as it does temporality and stasis, as well as the concrete object and its figurative reimagining. It is therefore important to determine finally what the triptych is communicating about the act of enshrinement itself. The presence of the smaller Byzantine reliquary triptychs at the centre of the piece in one sense stages a clear aesthetic translation, with the larger winged Mosan piece basing itself upon the originating items in the centre. At the same time, the shape of the Mosan triptych frame itself gestures back towards, and symbolically situ-

---

[25] Voelkle, *Stavelot Triptych*, 17.
[26] The reliquary triptych represents an interesting counterpoint to the Augustinian dichotomy of visible figure and invisible truth, *sacramentum* and *res sacramenti*. On the rise of this construct as a 'new sort of symbolism' in the eleventh and twelfth centuries, see Stock, *Implications of Literacy*, 91.

ates itself as part of, the established Eastern tradition that created and disseminated reliquaries of this particular shape and style. In other words, the specific triptych form that characterizes the enclosed Byzantine object reappears in the larger piece as a means of organizing and framing the Western iconographic and decorative material.[27] The triptych-within-triptych format emphasizes the notion that what encloses is also enclosed. As the Stavelot triptych arranges its imagery to fold together a sacred past, present, and future, it also uses enshrinement—understood as a specific strategy of sacred enclosure—as a device to complicate the relationship between the originating form and the newer work that draws upon it. To enshrine something is thus to involve it in several paradoxical dynamics of container and contained, stasis and temporality, original and adaptation. Enshrinement becomes an aesthetic practice relevant to both sacred artefacts and secular narrative.

The Enshrined Beloved in Cligés

The Stavelot triptych uses its programme of sacred and symbolic representation to outline the complexities of enshrinement itself, providing us with a few perspectives on the way in which sacred enshrinement functions. This reading of the triptych can help us to arrive at an understanding of Cligés as a text that enshrines its Tristanian source material, with the specific meaning, outlined above, which is attached to that material notion of sacred enshrinement.[28] Rather than basing itself on a traditional two-part intertextual understanding of Cligés, this interpretation draws

---

[27] It should be acknowledged that this somewhat elaborate reading of the triptych's iconography is vulnerable to the criticism that it relies on what might have been an unrealistic opportunity for detailed examination. At the same time, it seems to me that the convention of enfolding enshrinement, on which this reading depends, would be something apparent to a worshipper familiar with such objects even without microscopic scrutiny. Furthermore, the triptych shape of all these reliquaries meant that the motif of complex states of enclosure played an important role in their definition of enshrining objects even when viewed from some distance, as they were exhibited as folded closed during most of the year, but opened for viewing on certain feast-days (Holbert, 'Mosan Reliquary Triptychs', 260; also p. 227); the Stavelot triptych itself would have been centrally located and displayed in the nave (ibid. 266).

[28] This reading responds to a traditional division between what have been referred to as anti-Tristan and neo-Tristan readings of Cligés, asking if the point of the Tristanian allusion lies not in a moral or aesthetic judgement but in a statement about the nature of romance structure itself. Much of the history of Cligés criticism has consisted of debate over the nature of the moral commentary that Chrétien is making on his source. These arguments imply that Cligés' understanding of its source entails a judgement upon it. Donald Maddox and others also point out that the main source of criticism directed towards Tristan and Iseut in Cligés is Fenice, who does not necessarily reflect Chrétien's own perspective (Maddox, 'Critical Trends', 732).

its motivation from the poem's own overdetermined shrine imagery.[29] Structural arguments about *Cligés* tend to explore the nature of medieval literary influence.[30] They create a linear progression from one part of the romance to the other, originating in the text's Tristanian source. The Stavelot triptych allows us to consider the model of enshrinement, rather than a genealogical and linear pattern of textual influence, as a means of organizing the romance's components. *Cligés* shows how a poem can share with the realm of objects certain conventions of sacred structure. In particular, the treatment of Fenice's body stages this transition from sacred to secular modes. The text uses devotional conventions to create in a secular context a model for relating source material—a vestige of the past—to a narrative of the present.

[29] The interpretation of *Cligés* as a kind of intertextual diptych structure appears in many critical analyses of the poem. See, e.g., Norris J. Lacy, 'Spatial Form in Medieval Romance', *Yale French Studies*, 51 (1974), 160–9; Anthime Fourrier, *Le Courant réaliste dans le roman courtois en France au moyen âge*, *I* (Paris, 1960); and Z. P. Zaddy, *Chrétien Studies: Problems of Form and Meaning in Erec, Yvain, Cligés and the Charrete* (Glasgow, 1973), 81. A number of readings also focus on intertextual and symbolic connections between the first part of *Cligés* and the second. Norris J. Lacy sees a correspondence between Soredamors's hair and the potion which induces Fenice's deathlike sleep: 'Its function as a means to preserve the possibility of their love establishes its relationship to their emotion even more definitely than did the gold hair for his parents.' See Lacy, *The Craft of Chrétien de Troyes: An Essay on Narrative Art* (Leiden, 1980), 83. The potion, however, represents a deceptively complex object in the second half of the narrative, because its correspondence with the other potion, the one which Thessala gives to Alis, must be determined as well. For a discussion of the potion in the Tristan legend as a figure for personal transformation, see R. Howard Bloch, 'Tristan, the Myth of the State and the Language of the Self', *Yale French Studies*, 51 (1974), 61–81: 73. This reading of the meaning of supernatural potions in romances reinforces the argument that the philter does not really provide an effective analogy to the strand of hair, as it connotes the achievement of subjectivity rather than a fragmented state that will be realized as more integral only later in the text.

For a discussion of *Cligés*' use of source in linear terms, see Douglas Kelly, '*Translatio Studii*: Translation, Adaptation, and Allegory in Medieval French Literature', *Philological Quarterly*, 57 (1978), 287–310: 296–303. Kelly defines Chrétien's particular use of the Tristanian source material as an adaptation (or an amalgamation in combination with its other elements), one of the categories he identifies for the medieval concept of *translatio*, which implies not only transmission but also 'the progressive elucidation of the *matière* thus translated'. Michelle A. Freeman argues for a more thematic connection between the sections, proposing that *Cligés* uses a medieval conception of intertextuality in order first to read Tristanian sources and then to 'work itself out similarly as an essentially intertextual operation in which the second part of the narrative derives poetically from the first part' (Michelle A. Freeman, 'Structural Transpositions and Intertextuality: Chrétien's *Cligés*', *Medievalia et Humanistica*, NS, 11 (1982), 149–63: 150; and see *idem, The Poetics of Translatio Studii and Conjointure: Chrétien de Troyes's Cligés* (Lexington, Ky., 1979)). Like A. G. van Hamel, Freeman focuses upon the text's own self-referential characteristics; see van Hamel, 'Cligés et Tristan', *Romania*, 33 (1904), 465–89.

[30] Freeman, e.g., describes predecessor texts as characterized by an open-endedness, like the Guillaume de Lorris section of the *Roman de la Rose*. Romance intertextuality thus involves fulfilment and completion of earlier models, and depends upon these earlier texts presenting themselves in this manner ('Structural Transpositions', 150).

The episodes which connect Soredamors and Fenice to the imagery of enshrinement also implicate the heroines in the imagery of the text's Tristanian source; at times *Cligés* elaborates on certain images introduced in the Tristanian tradition in order to associate them more specifically with the realm of devotional objects, in particular relics and their sacred enclosure. As we shall see, Fenice's martyrdom and sealing inside a tomb represent the culmination of a system of imagery that begins in the first half of the romance, and so return the reader to that opening reference to enshrinement and emphasize its importance in understanding the structure of the romance as whole.

The imagery of the first half of *Cligés* conceives of Soredamors synecdochally, through a fragment of her body which comes to represent her status as worshipped beloved. This fragment is the golden hair which she weaves into Alixandre's shirt. As has often been pointed out, these golden filaments recall the strand of hair that inspires King Mark to seek out Iseut.[31] The Thomas *Tristan*, which represents the most likely analogue to the Tristanian source which Chrétien used, exists only in a number of fragments itself and does not contain the episode of King Mark and the hair. Traditionally, however, the legend incorporates an episode in which King Mark evades pressure from his barons to marry by pointing out a long hair that has fallen from the beak of a swallow in the hall, and declaring that he will marry only the woman to whom the hair belongs.[32] Like the strands of hair on Guenever's comb in the *Chevalier de la Charrete*, the image of the hair in *Tristan* introduces a conflict between the reality of the desired lady's absence and the power of a vestigial and fragmentary object to invoke her presence in the manner of a saint's relic.[33]

---

[31] See Zaddy, *Chrétien Studies*, 175. Zaddy has pointed out this correspondence between the two narratives, but not in the context of the object's associations with relic worship.

[32] Joseph Bédier, *Le Roman de Tristan* (Paris, 1902–5), i. 110.

[33] The description of Guenever's comb in Chrétien's *Chevalier de la Charrete* reflects this tendency to blur distinctions among vestige, image, and person, and suggests that courtly love similarly undermines these distinctions. While the comb is 'd'ivoire doré' (Chrétien de Troyes, *Œuvres complètes*, 540, l. 1357), serving as a reliquary which displays the hair, the hair itself is purer and more precious than gold:

> Ors cent mille foiz esmerez
> Et puis autante foiz recuiz
> Fust plus oscurs que n'est la nuiz
> Contre le plus bel jor d'este
> Qui ait an tot cest an esté,
> Qui l'or et les chevols veïst,
> Si que l'un lez l'autre meïst.

> (ll. 1494–1500)

The floating fragment from *Tristan* becomes a vestigial artefact figuratively enshrined at the beginning of Chrétien's text. *Cligés* develops the Tristanian image through its description of Soredamors's hair woven into the shirt that Alixandre will eventually wear.[34] This moment in the first half of *Cligés* establishes an awareness of the world of devotional objects, and integrates into the narrative an image that represents the enshrinement of both Soredamors and the Tristan myth itself. Alixandre can barely restrain himself from worshipping the shirt threaded with this golden hair as though the entire apparatus constituted a holy artefact:

> Quant cele li conte et devise
> La feiture de la chemise,
> Que a grant poinne se retarde,
> La ou le chevolet regarde,
> Que il ne l'aore et ancline.
>
> (ll. 1611–15)
>
> When she told and described for him
> how the shirt was made,
> it was with great effort that he stopped himself,
> there as he looked upon that hair,
> from falling down and adoring it.

He is tempted to raise it to his eyes and lips, as Lancelot does with Guenever's comb in the *Charrete*, and continues to embrace it alone at night as well. There are a few lines suppressed in the Guiot manuscript, but attested in others, which state that before Alixandre learns the shirt's secret, he would have made a 'saintuaire' (l. 1195 in Luttrell-Gregory) of the shirt, so that he could worship it day and night, had he known that the hair belonged to Soredamors:[35]

> . . . an eschange n'an preïst
> Tot le monde, einçois an feïst

Guenever's hair performs several functions here. As a relic of the actual person, it symbolizes for Lancelot the presence of the queen herself. But it also becomes an artefact associated through the image of gold with the comb which contains it. The hair subverts the distinctions among the person of the queen, the vestige of her hair, and the artistic object connected with both.

[34]   Freeman draws attention to this adaptation of a Tristanian image, but uses it as a means of supporting her analysis of medieval intertextuality; for her, the shirt becomes an image reminiscent of a text—'a text, indeed, that poeticizes its intertextuality' ('Structural Transpositions', 151).

[35]   In their edition of *Cligés*, Luttrell and Gregory speculate that 'la cause de l'omission de ces vers (comme aussi à l'échange dans le ms. [BN fr. 375] de saintuaire contre *une ymage*, vocable moins choquant), semble être le sentiment chez le copiste qu'ils étaient malséants, voire irreligieux' (Chrétien de Troyes, *Cligés*, 258, note to l. 1195–6).

Saintuaire, si con je cuit,
Si l'aorast et jor et nuit.
(ll. 1193–6 in Luttrell-Gregory)

. . . he would not have exchanged it
for all the world; rather he would have made
a relic [*or reliquary*] of it, I believe,
where he would have worshipped it both day and night.

The imagined scene of Alixandre prostrate in adoration before the garment suggests an act of figurative enshrinement for the hair within the shirt; the use of the word 'saintuaire', which signified both relic and reliquary shrine, reinforces this devotional connotation, along with the attendant convention that a significant object or vestige could invoke a desired presence.[36] By connecting the language of sacred shrines to the image, *Cligés* makes explicit the implied potential of the hair in *Tristan* to conjure the presence of the whole beloved through the fragmentary nature of the vestige.

While the worship of Soredamors entails the figurative enshrinement of fragmentary strands of hair, Soredamors' successor Fenice literally reintegrates her entire body—after it has been menaced with violation and torture—in a tomb. Fenice's treatment at the hands of the doctors and her subsequent entombment transform a suggestive metaphor in the first half of Chrétien's narrative into a scene of graphic martyrdom and fragmentation.[37] Of the doctors' attempts to stretch her over a fire, Chrétien says at line 5941 that they made her suffer as a 'martire'.[38] They pour

---

[36] Algirdas Julien Greimas, *Dictionnaire de l'ancien français: le Moyen Âge* (Paris, 1997), s.v. 'saintuaire'. On the ability of the sacred object to invoke a longed-for presence, see Peter Brown, *The Cult of the Saints: Its Rise and Function in Latin Christianity* (Chicago, 1982).

[37] Although our perception of Soredamors is based on figuration, we are asked to eschew metaphor in Fenice's case and focus on the reality of her body in its most literal incarnation. While the language used to describe Soredamors is rich in allusion to other aesthetic media (her throat clearer than crystal at l. 832; her mirrored brow at ll. 800–1), Chrétien employs the device of *praeteritio* in describing Fenice, claiming that no figure of speech can capture her adequately, and that she is God's own work of art:

> Onques Dex qui la façona
> Parole a home ne dona
> Qui de biauté dire seüst
> Tant que cele plus n'an eüst . . .
> Por ce que g'en diroie mains,
> Ne braz ne cors, ne chief, ne mains
> Ne vuel par parole descrivre.
>
> (ll. 2681–4, 2695–7)

[38] Cligés' own actions elsewhere in the narrative, in relation to Alixandre's, form the same arc between symbolic and concrete uses of the body that is described above in the Fenice/Soredamors

lead into her palms, and beat her 'tant que la char li ont ronpue' (l. 5906).[39] Soredamors' lock of hair is only metaphorically a relic, woven into a shirt and imagined as an object of worship through the author's conditional language. But by returning to the realm of the concrete through a painful experience of bodily martyrdom, Fenice herself becomes an enclosed and fragmented object, fulfilling Jehan's deceptive characterization of her as 'molt sainte chose' (l. 6012). Her designation as holy has puzzled critics, but its connection to the themes of fragmentation and reintegration might assist in explaining why Fenice is described this way. Her association with sainthood need not implicate itself in a discussion of moral judgements applied to her; instead it gestures toward Chrétien's narrative poetic technique itself. Fenice in her physical martyrdom embodies the invocation of a sacred convention or framework to represent a secular phenomenon, a technique which Chrétien uses to organize the narrative as a whole in his enshrinement of the Tristan legend.

Her status as a body both enclosed and sanctified appears at first to represent for Fenice the possibility of obliterating her relationship to her

---

narratives. Alixandre deceives his opponents in the first part of the narrative by donning the armour of the slain among them; he is preoccupied with heraldic symbolism as a means to create a ruse. His son, on the other hand, appears in armour that is completely white, bearing a blank ivory shield, during his single combat with the Duke, emphasizing the contrast between the absence of device or symbol in this scene and the focus on painted heraldry that Alixandre's earlier battles display. After killing a Saxon knight, Cligés not only puts on the other knight's armour but also decapitates him and carries the head to the Saxon camp. Because the Duke of Saxony had earlier asked for Cligés' head, Alis and all the Greeks and Germans despair when they see a rider in Saxon arms bearing a severed head, while the Saxons are fooled into wanting to help him: 'Mes les armes toz les desvoient' (l. 3498); 'Nostre chevaliers vient! / An son lance que il tient / Aporte la test Clygés' (ll. 3503-5). In this case, it is the bodily fragment as much as the misleading heraldic devices that assists Cligés in achieving success in battle by creating a false identity. Fenice, in turn, uses the fragmentation of her own body, combined with the artifice of Jehan's tomb, to manufacture successfully her claim as both expired and virtuous. Alixandre and Soredamors begin with symbols and tokens in their self-depictions and their statements about each other, such as the vestige of the golden hair interpreted through Alixandre's worshipful reaction as a symbol of the beloved's presence. Cligés and Fenice instead return us to the realm of the concrete by using the physical body with emphatic literality as means to explore their own representations. On historical precedent for the use of false armour to mislead, see Kinoshita, 'Poetics of *Translatio*', 339 n. 51.

[39] Fenice's use of a sleeping potion to help her to escape an unwanted marriage or other objectionable destiny has its roots in classical tradition. The fourth-century writer Xenophon uses it in the *Ephesiaca*; it continues to appear throughout the Middle Ages and Renaissance, from Masuccio of Salerno in the late fifteenth century to *Romeo and Juliet* (Frank Kermode, introduction to *Romeo and Juliet*, in *The Riverside Shakespeare*, ed. G. Blakemore Evans *et al.* (Boston, 1974), 1055). Freeman points out that every one of Chrétien's romances contains the motif of false death, a 'binary relationship between sleeping and waking', in some form (Freeman, *Poetics of Translatio*, 83-4). Maddox lists several other medieval sources that draw upon the *fausse morte* tradition, including *Eliduc*, *Amadas et Idoire*, the *Roman de Forest*, and the *Marques do Rome*, and says that other versions of the story appear in Slavic, German, and Portuguese (Maddox, 'Critical Trends', 739).

Tristanian predecessor. After her ladies-in-waiting indignantly defenes-
trate the abusive doctors, Fenice's nurse Thessala applies to her body a
precious ointment which will heal her wounds. She is prepared for burial,
wrapped in a white shroud that leaves her face uncovered, and transported to the tomb. Chrétien then carefully demonstrates the sealing of
the sepulchre, saying that Jehan has designed it so cunningly that once he
has closed it, no one else will be able to figure out how to open it without
breaking the seals: [40]

> Bien la seele, et joint, et clot.
> Et lors se poïst bien prisier
> Qui sanz malmetre et sanz brisier
> Ovrir ne desjoindre seüst
> Rien que Jehanz fet i eüst.
>
> (ll. 6074–8)
>
> He sealed it, bolted and closed it well.
> And he who could open anything that Jehan had closed,
> without prying it open, breaking it,
> undoing the seals, could really be proud of himself.

Thus Fenice's body, treated to heal and re-attain its physical integrity,
finds itself enclosed within a structure that reinforces her ideal of integrity
by emphasizing its own. As Peggy McCracken argues, 'The architectural
integrity figures the intact body'.[41] In addition, when Cligés and Jehan
steal her from the tomb in the night, the artisan's ability to preserve the
tomb's physical seamlessness after removing her from it allows Fenice and
her co-conspirators to create the illusion that her tomb is inviolate and
her death real:

> Et Jehanz, au plus tost qu'il pot,
> A la sepolture reclose,
> Si qu'il ne pert a nule chose
> Que l'an i eust atochié.
>
> (ll. 6130–3)
>
> And Jehan, as quickly as he could,
> resealed the tomb,
> so that everything appeared
> just as it had before.

---

[40] On the role of Jehan, and the status of twelfth-century artisans, see Jacques Stiennon,
'Histoire de l'art et fiction poétique dans un épisode de *Cligés* de Chrétien de Troyes', in *Mélanges
offerts à Rita Lejeune* (Gembloux, 1968), 695–708.

[41] Peggy McCracken, 'The Queen's Adulterous Body', in Linda Lomperis and Sarah Stanbury (eds.), *Feminist Approaches to the Body in Medieval Literature* (Philadelphia, 1993), 54.

Chrétien's description of the martyr's shrine which Jehan has constructed demonstrates how in the secular world of art and poetry, the apparent conflict between the authenticating impulse of the reliquary shrine and the privileging of artifice in the construction of the beautiful object is erased, so that other representational strategies associated with the artefact become more important. The combination of her fragmenting martyrdom and her reintegrating entombment seem to prove that Fenice has not consigned herself to the adulterous fate of Iseut. The appearance of her death legitimates her virtue, and the static shrine—beautifully 'taillee' (l. 6006) and an ideal of enclosing artifice—in which she is placed seals her off from the literary legacy which she fears.

At the same time, however, these very devices of fragmentation, reintegration, and entombment undermine Fenice's ability to escape her Tristanian heritage, because they play a significant role in the imagery of the Tristan narrative itself. Before Fenice undergoes her actual martyrdom, she makes a prefiguring statement about it, early in her association with Cligés:

> Mialz voldroie estre desmanbree
> Que de nos deus fust remanbree
> L'amors d'Ysolt et de Tristan.
>
> (ll. 3105–7)
>
> I would much prefer to be dismembered
> rather than that from the two of us be remembered
> the love of Tristan and Iseut.

As McCracken points out, 'Fenice states her refusal to follow Iseut's example in metaphors of dismemberment'; McCracken argues that she undergoes a metaphoric fragmentation in splitting her body between husband and lover.[42] In this passage, Fenice aligns images of fragmentation with her desire to obliterate the memory of her source. But in the very act of juxtaposing through rhyme these concepts of fragmentation and memory, she alludes to the Tristanian past she wishes to obscure. Thomas d'Angleterre's *Tristran* in fact displays a parallel focus on fragmentation and its relationship to memory. In this version, we find Tristan considering a statue of Iseut, speaking to it and reminding it of their past together. As Tristan gazes at the statue, he focuses on Iseut's face, her hand, and the ring that she wears:

---

[42] Peggy McCracken, 'The Queen's Adulterous Body', in Linda Lomperis and Sarah Stanbury (eds.), *Feminist Approaches to the Body in Medieval Literature* (Philadelphia, 1993), 49.

> Quanqu'il pense a l'image dit,
> Poi[s] s'en dessevrë un petit.
> Regardë en la main Ysodt,
> [Qui] l'anel d'or doner li volt,
> Vait la cherë e le senblant
> Qu'au departir fait son amant.
> Menbre lui de la covenance
> Qu'il ot a la deseverance.
>
> (ll. 974–81)

> He would say to the statue whatever came into his mind,
> and then, stepping back a little from it,
> would look at Ysodt's hand
> as it made to offer him the gold ring,
> and see the expression on her face
> as she looked at her lover on their parting.
> He then remembered the pact
> that he made as they parted.[43]

The arrangement of language in this passage associates memory and fragmentation: the phrase 'Menbre lui de la covenance / Qu'il ot a la deseverance' (ll. 980–1) in the last two lines of the passage above ('He then remembered the pact that he made as they parted') juxtaposes 'membrer', 'covenance', and 'deseverance'. Also, 'menbre' derives from the Latin root *memorare*, but it suggests as well the homonymically related *membre* from *membrum*, connoting the limbs of the body. The 'main' on which Tristan focuses as he faces the statue in line 976 represents such a bodily fragment which is implicated in the process of memory and memorial. The gaze of memory is also a fragmenting gaze in this passage, as Tristan's perspective shifts from the 'image' in its entirety to the 'main' to the even smaller vestige of the 'anel' on its finger (ll. 974–7). In the representation of Iseut as an idol or statue in the Thomas *Tristran*, the project of memorial

---

[43] Thomas of Britain, *Tristran*, ed. and trans. Stewart Gregory (New York, 1991), 50, ll. 942–5 and 975–9; all subsequent citations from the Thomas *Tristran* will appear with line numbers in the text, along with Gregory's translations. Lucie Polak reads the 'Hall of Statues' in the Thomas *Tristran* as potentially alluding to the Byzantine marvel of automata: 'Such complex automata were built by Byzantine craftsmen at least since the ninth century. . . . Have we here, then, an exotic conceit like those which adorned the emperor's throne? That such descriptions were popular at the English and continental courts cannot be doubted' (Lucie Polak, 'The Two Caves of Love in the *Tristan* by Thomas', *Journal of the Warburg and Courtauld Institutes*, 33 (1970), 52–69: 60). Polak presents this idea as one of a few potential ways for explaining the significance of the Iseut statue; she ultimately focuses on the ideas of necromancy and pagan idolatry. The Byzantine parallel, however, is suggestive in light of our consideration of Eastern influence on *Cligés* as aesthetic rather than political.

identifies itself as a diminishing focus on smaller and smaller fragments and tokens.[44] Thus when Fenice rhymes memory and fragmentation in her own speech, she invokes and elaborates upon a dichotomy employed in the project of representing her predecessor.

In addition to Fenice's particular reference to the Tristan story as embedded in her own language, *Cligés* contains a more general discussion of source in its prologue. This allusion recalls the paradoxical qualities of enshrinement, showing how Fenice cannot ultimately use her sacred entombment to escape the heritage that encloses her. In the prologue, Chrétien identifies 'un des livres de l'aumaire / Mon seignor saint Pere a Biauvez' (ll. 20–1) ('one of the books from the library of my lord St Peter at Beauvais') as his source.[45] This allusion is somewhat puzzling, seeming to point less to a particular source than to the idea of source in a broader sense. But the reference to St Peter is then repeated near the end of the romance, in the context of Fenice's burial:

> Au mostier mon seignor saint Pere
> Iert anfoïe la defors,
> Ou l'en anfuet les autres cors;
> Car einçois que ele morist,
> Le me pria molt et requist
> Que je la la feïsse metre.
>
> (ll. 6014–19)
>
> At the church of my lord Saint Peter
> she shall be buried outside,
> where the other bodies are buried;
> for before she died,
> she asked and entreated a great deal
> that I have her placed there.

As Daniel Poirion has said, 'cette précision du saint patron de l'église n'est pas sans rappeler l'allusion à l'église Saint-Pierre de Beauvais, au début du roman', where Chrétien locates his precursor text for this romance.[46] By linking the romance's opening and the burial of Fenice, *Cligés* aligns source with images of tombs and graves. Although the locations clearly differ, the allusion to St Peter itself suggestively unites the themes of source and entombment, or even sacred enshrinement, given the status of

---

[44] As we saw in the case of the Stavelot triptych, memorial, narrative, and the fragmented object dynamically align themselves to represent sacred history as well.

[45] See Kinoshita, 'Poetics of *Translatio*', 335, on the burning of St Peter's of Beauvais in 1180.

[46] Chrétien de Troyes, *Œuvres complètes*, 1167.

martyrdom that is accorded Fenice in Jehan's description of her. Source is reformulated as part of a scene of physical memorial; Fenice is to be entombed at a church that is in some sense an analogue for the one that originated her story. Even as her own narrative contains and elaborates upon this source, she finds herself contained finally by the place of origin, specifically through her status as an enshrined body. Like the Tristanian source as represented in *Cligés*, the mysterious textual artefact from the church of St Peter intertwines itself with the imagery of entombment and enshrinement, and causes Fenice to be enshrined by the very past which her own narrative tries to seal off.

This paradox of enshrinement operates in other ways as well. In noting the details of the material realm to which *Cligés* alludes, we find that the world of monuments and shrines, of which Fenice makes use in her project of historical forgetting, at the same time alludes to predecessors and the past. Sarah Kay points out that Fenice's desire for self-entombment gestures toward the *romans antiques*, whose heroes, 'immured within a fabulous and hermetically sealed edifice, elude the historical process'.[47] Kay and McCracken both elucidate the ways in which the act of sealing herself up is aligned with her desire to seal herself from her past and her fate. At the same time, the material reality of entombment in this period also constituted what Linda Seidel calls 'the construction of a narrative' about the one enshrined, that person's history and relationship to the context of his or her burial.[48] Certain actual tombs and reliquaries, as well as the enclosing structures of devotional art from this period, encouraged their viewers to acknowledge the origins, analogues, and associations of the sacred or exalted bodies they contained. We saw, for instance, the way in which the Stavelot triptych's programme draws the viewer's eye back through scenes of origin and discovery—baptism and *Inventio*—to the material of the True Cross itself, even as it elaborates on this material and inserts it in a temporal and historical progression. Seidel, in addition, describes a now-destroyed marble mausoleum shrine from the twelfth century, built to house the remains of Saint-Lazare at Autun. The tomb's sculpted iconography depicted Mary Magdalene, Martha, and Jesus

---

[47] Sarah Kay, *Courtly Contradictions: The Emergence of the Literary Object in the Twelfth Century* (Stanford, Calif., 2001), 242. Kay goes on to argue that Fenice's attempt to imitate her literary models is flawed through her attempt to avoid actually dying—for this reason she momentarily loses control of her plot and 'may thus find herself, if only fleetingly, halted between two deaths' (p. 243).

[48] Linda Seidel, *Legends in Limestone: Lazarus, Gislebertus, and the Cathedral of Autun* (Chicago, 1999), 111.

enacting the resurrection of Lazarus, as well as symbols of the Last Judgement, in order to legitimate the claim that Lazarus was indeed buried
there. The Lazarus shrine 'emphatically positioned itself both as the end
of his story and the point at which access to earlier moments in his narrative could be gained'.[49] Secular places of burial could approximate some
of these functions as well. For instance, the tomb of Henry I, Count of
Champagne, used the rich materials of its construction (copper, gilt,
enamel, precious stones), as well as inscription, iconography, and the representation of the integral body, to comment on the count's power.[50] The
act of sealing a body in a tomb, shrine, or other enclosure constituted an
act of integrating the body into a narrative or a specific heritage, through
sculptural imagery or other signifiers.

For these reasons, the very act of enshrining Fenice in her tomb as a virtuous martyr at the same time ensconces her in some form of legacy. And
in the romance universe of *Cligés*, this legacy is essentially the act of adultery in which her Tristanian precursor is implicated; the gesture of entombment itself, as understood in its material context, reinserts her into
this enfolding and unfolding pattern. The conclusion of the romance
confirms that she has in fact entered herself into this narrative despite her
martyrdom. The final passages of the romance show how that same trope
of enshrinement, which she had tried to use to seal herself off from her
legacy, is in fact the trope that signals her continued implication in this
past. The language of the poem invokes metaphorically the tomb in
which Fenice was sealed, using the motif of enclosure to emphasize the
extent to which the empress's Tristanian heritage still clings not only to
her but to her descendants as well. *Cligés* ends with an ætiological flour-
ish, explaining that Fenice's behaviour has prompted every Byzantine emperor since to keep his empress carefully guarded. Although Fenice herself
was never 'anclose' (l. 6746) by Cligés during her reign,

> . . . com an prison
> Est gardee en Costantinoble,
> Ja n'iert tant haute ne tant noble,
> L'empererriz, quex qu'ele soit:
> L'empereres point ne s'i croit,
> Tant con de celi li remanbre.
> (ll. 6756–61)

---

[49] Seidel, *Legends* 78. On the features of this tomb, see also Claire Wheeler Solt, 'Romanesque
French Reliquaries', *Studies in Medieval and Renaissance History*, 9 (1987), 165–236: 185.
[50] A.-F. Arnaud, *Voyage archéologique et pittoresque dans le département de l'Aube et dans l'ancien diocese de Troyes* (Troyes, 1837), 29–33.

the empress, no matter who she is, or
how high and noble,
is kept in Constantinople like a prisoner:
the emperor doesn't trust her at all,
as he recalls the memory of that other.

As Michelle Freeman points out, Fenice 'does not escape becoming a no-
torious example in her own right'.[51] The specific image of Fenice's enclosure becomes an emblem for the fates of the later empresses who take her
place. Through her successors' confinement, her memory ends up enclosed within the Tristanian legacy of adultery and female deceptiveness,
as embodied in the figure of Iseut. As we observed, the memory of Iseut,
as articulated through the fragment of her hair, was initially enshrined in
the narrative through Alixandre's figurative reliquary of courtly devotion.
Enshrinement becomes the motif and the mechanism that indicates
Fenice's entrapment within her source; it causes the narrative of *Cligés* itself to become enclosed within its Tristanian connotations even as the
narrative structure of *Cligés* tries to contain this same source. Through the
representations of Fenice and Soredamors, the text refers to a particular
world of artefacts in order to make the case that the incorporation
of source is essentially a temporally complex and self-reversing act of
enshrinement.

Word and Image in the Byzantine Bower

It remains for us to determine, however, the real nature of the connection
posited here between material object and text. This final section of the
essay argues that we see in *Cligés* a relationship between visual and verbal
that moves beyond the inevitably indeterminate realm of influence, and
also beyond the limits of a model of analogy. Instead, the Byzantine backdrop of this narrative allows us to think about another kind of interaction
between words and images, in which the very parameters of these two
realms are called into question. *Cligés* shares with certain Byzantine writings its use of the garden as a setting which challenges the defining limits
of art and nature. In *Cligés*, this examination of the boundaries of art and
nature ultimately enables a deeper interconnection between language and
objects. Through its incorporation of Byzantine aesthetics, *Cligés* shows
us how the process of reading a narrative might become indistinguishable

---

[51] Freeman, 'Structural Transpositions', 157.

from the process of reading an artefact, creating a space in which a poetics of the shrine can exist.[52]

The Byzantine allusions in *Cligés* have traditionally been perceived as an expression of medieval Western Europe's knowledge of, fascination with, and anxiety about this sophisticated culture. Some of these allusions might refer to specific events or else to a broader cultural antagonism toward the East. The scene of the angry women who overpower the abusive doctors from Salerno, for instance, has been read as representing an instance of Western awareness of political events in Constantinople—in this case the return of the empress Zoë to the imperial city.[53] In addition, a recent reading of *Cligés* proposes that the text aims to counteract a perception common in twelfth-century France that Constantinople, and Byzantine culture in general, represented a level of sophistication and advancement which the West could only envy. Thus *Cligés* describes a *translatio* in which Eastern characters travel to Western Europe in order to augment their accomplishments and burnish their names.[54] Such studies concentrate on evidence relating to historical chronicle—intermarriages, battles, accounts from Western European crusaders arriving in the imperial city—to explicate *Cligés*' linking of Eastern and Western Christianity.

But despite this demonstrated historical reality of Continental antagonism toward Byzantium, it must be acknowledged that *Cligés* itself does not dwell upon fundamental tensions or differences between the Eastern nobility and their Arthurian counterparts. We might therefore ask about other ways in which this Byzantine material affects Chrétien's narration of this tale, and speculate on its ability to broaden the range of perspectives that *Cligés* espouses on words and images. The tradition of Byzantine ekphrasis introduces the potential for a shared terminology between language and visual images, a less rigidly categorized vision than would develop in Western Europe.[55] As Jean-Claude Schmitt has argued, for

---

[52] In recent years, a number of art historians, influenced in part by the work of Michael Camille, have begun to think about the ways in which visual objects in the Middle Ages could be read, and that the experience of reading an object might have been more a matter of sustained comprehension than immediate apprehension. '[T]he image is not the reflection of some external view of the world but the beginning and foundation of a process of thought' (Michael Camille, 'Before the Gaze: The Internal Senses and Late Medieval Practices of Seeing', in Robert S. Nelson (ed.), *Visuality Before and Beyond the Renaissance: Seeing as Others Saw* (New York, 2000), 216).

[53] Ciggaar, 'Encore une fois', 267.

[54] Kinoshita, 'Poetics of *Translatio*', 319.

[55] Michael Camille suggests as well that the twelfth century was interested in questions about text and image, specifically in the potential malleability of the concept of reading itself. He characterizes decorated initial letters as holding the potential to become 'art objects', because their

example, fundamental distinctions were early established in the shifting relationship between writing and images in spiritual and devotional contexts.[56] The particular conjunction of secular romance narrative, Byzantine aesthetics, and a poetics of the shrine in *Cligés* moves this text beyond some of the limitations placed upon the relationship between text and artefact.

Western Europe in the twelfth century developed its perspective on Byzantium through an influx of artistic styles and contemporary narrative accounts, and through both channels was introduced to Byzantine culture's embedded ideas about the nature of representation itself. Many forms of Byzantine art migrated west before and during the twelfth century.[57] Sicily and southern Europe, for instance, held important mosaics which reflected the Byzantine style, in particular the Palatina mosaics. In the eleventh and twelfth centuries, cultural and artistic centres in France, such as Limoges as well as the Abbey of Cluny, functioned as major centres at which Italo-Byzantine forms were received and disseminated.[58] Thus Eastern iconographic programmes and strategies were becoming familiar to Continental and insular viewers in the twelfth century.

---

textual identity and function differ so radically from that which is dictated by our own processes of reading (Michael Camille, 'Seeing and Reading: Some Visual Implications of Medieval Literacy and Illiteracy', *Art History*, 8 (1985), 26–94: 29). *Cligés* reflects some of these intellectual and artistic concerns as filtered through the unusual lens of Byzantine allusion. In the early modern period in the West, of course, 'The Reformation taught the dominion of the word', as Hans Belting puts it (Belting, *Likeness and Presence*, 465).

[56] Jean-Claude Schmitt, *Le Corps des images: essais sur la culture visuelle au Moyen Âge* (Paris, 2002), 97–140. His argument that 'le rapport de l'écriture et de l'image n'est pas resté stable au cours du Moyen Âge' (p. 131) and that ultimately medieval religious culture was 'de plus en plus une culture chrétienne visuelle' (p. 133), relies upon an understanding of these two categories as fundamentally separate strategies of representation.

[57] On the earlier Carolingian interest in Byzantine art, which was at its height during the reign of Charles the Bald, see Archer St Clair, 'Narrative and Exegesis in the Exodus Illustrations of the San Paolo Bible: Aspects of Byzantine Influence', in Christopher Moss and Katherine Kiefer (eds.), *Byzantine East, Latin West: Art-historical Studies in Honor of Kurt Weitzmann* (Princeton, 1995), 193–202.

[58] Otto Demus, *Byzantine Art and the West* (New York, 1970), 111–12. Demus discusses both the acquisition of Byzantine art objects (p. 20) and the development of a Siculo-Byzantine iconography. He points out that the imagery found in the Palatina mosaics exerted influence in Mosan and insular art (pp. 149–50). Ernst Kitzinger, in 'Norman Sicily as a Source of Byzantine Influence on Western Art in the Twelfth Century', concurs on the importance of these mosaics, but also points out that the Byzantine influence on Western art was complex and many-layered, so that the Gothic style was really an outgrowing rather than a direct descendant of Eastern art (in *Byzantine Art, an European Art: Lectures* (Athens, 1966), 143). On the direct importation of Byzantine artisanal techniques, see Steven Runciman, 'Byzantine Art and Western Medieval Taste', in Demus, *Byzantine Art*, 12.

The Latin account of Odo of Deuil might also provide a way for us to imagine how Eastern perceptions of secular buildings and gardens moved westward in the twelfth century to influence texts such as *Cligés*.[59] In 1149, Odo returned to France with Louis VII after a trip to Constantinople during the Second Crusade, and around 1148 wrote an account which included descriptions of the architectural and landscaping marvels he had seen in the East.[60] Odo's discussion of one of the most famous Byzantine gardens and hunting parks outside the city of Constantinople, the Philopation, describes lairs for game animals, an irrigation system, a circular set of enclosing walls, and splendid resort palaces connected to the parkland. In describing the progress of the German emperor, whose troops preceded Louis' retinue, Odo says:

Before the city stood a spacious and impressive ring of walls enclosing various kinds of game and including canals and ponds. Also, inside were certain hollows and caves which, in lieu of forests, furnished lairs for the animals. In that lovely place certain palaces which the emperors had built as their springtime resort are conspicuous for their splendor. Into this 'Place of Delights', to give it the proper name, the German emperor burst and, destroying practically everything, under the very eyes of the Greeks seized their delights for his own uses, for the imperial palace, the only building which rises above the city walls, is actually directly above that place and affords a view of its inhabitants.[61]

Later Odo mentions that 'From the outside underground conduits flow in, bringing the city an abundance of sweet water'.[62] Odo goes on to mention the interiors of prosperous dwellings: 'All the wealthy people have their own chapels, so adorned with paintings, marble, and lamps that each magnate might justly say, "O Lord, I have cherished the beauty of Thy house", if the light of the true faith shone therein.'[63] He elaborates on the interior of the palace of Plachernae as well: 'Throughout it is decorated elaborately with gold and a great variety of colours, and the floor is marble, paved with cunning workmanship; and I do not know whether

---

[59] We must also bear in mind in using this evidence, however, that Odo's history appears not to have been frequently copied, and also that his description is in fact much more straight-forward and less rhetorically mannered than the Byzantine accounts (Odo de Deuil, *De profectione Ludovici VII in orientem*, ed. and trans. Virginia Gingerick Berry (New York, 1948), p. xxxii).

[60] Ibid. pp. xv–xxiii.

[61] Ibid. 48.

[62] Ibid. 65.

[63] Ibid. 57; this comment is followed by a statement about Byzantine heresies.

the exquisite art or the exceedingly valuable stuff [*materia*] endows it with the more beauty or value.'[64]

Descriptions by Eastern writers of Byzantine gardens and palaces also provide details that seem in one sense to resonate with Chrétien's text. Gardens existed in both urban settings, enclosed as part of a residential structure, and larger suburban landscapes which incorporated hunting parks.[65] These more expansive grounds could also be attached to dwellings outside the city. Byzantine garden descriptions elaborate on complex irrigation systems which organize the gardens and tame them into the service of their human occupants: the Mesokepion, for instance, a well-known garden, 'was irrigated with abundant water. The same water system probably fed two fountains.'[66] There are a few immediately apparent parallels here between *Cligés* and these Byzantine descriptions, creating what might appear to be opportunities to propose a connection between the two. Toward the end of *Cligés*, for instance, when the hero's indentured artisan Jehan shows his master the wondrous tower, Chrétien specifies that the structure Jehan has built is outside the city itself: 'Desoz la vile, en un destor, / Avoit Jehanz feite une tor' (ll. 5487–8) ('Below the city, in a remote spot, Jehan had fashioned a tower').[67] The tower's

---

[64] Ibid. 65. This is a common rhetorical formulation from this period; Chrétien uses it himself in his description of the cup offered by Arthur as a prize for the one who captures the castle in the first part of *Cligés*:

> Molt iert bone et riche la cope,
> Et qui delit avroit de cope,
> Plus la devroit il tenir chiere
> Por l'uevre que por la matière.
>
> (ll.1521–24)

In discussing the golden cup, Freeman speculates that 'the gems in this description correspond, in fact, to the celebrative poeticizations of the romancer's workshop concentrated in the metaphorical descriptions exemplified by the cup and the potion' (Freeman, *Poetics of Translatio*, 153). For the similar inscription on the doors of Saint-Denis see Elizabeth M. Hallam, *Capetian France 978–1328* (New York, 1980), 175. This sentiment is later reflected in Innocent IV's description of the Sainte-Chapelle: *opere superante materiam*. The phrase is derived from the *Metamorphoses'* golden doors, which Vulcan fashions at the opening of Book II (*materiam superabat opus* (II.5)) (Weiss, 'Architectural Symbolism', 308 n. 5).

[65] Steven Runciman, 'The Country and Suburban Palaces', in Angeliki E. Laiou-Thomadakis (ed.), *Charanis Studies: Essays in Honor of Peter Charanis*, (New Brunswick, NJ, 1980), 219–28. Runciman argues that Byzantine rulers maintained palaces and pleasure grounds for themselves outside Constantinople, and were expected to use them (p. 227 n. 28).

[66] Henry Maguire, 'Imperial Gardens and the Rhetoric of Renewal', in Paul Magdalino (ed.), *New Constantines: The Rhythm of Imperial Renewal in Byzantium, 4th–13th Centuries* (Aldershot, 1994), 182.

[67] The tenth-century poet John Geometres composed a poem in which he described a beautiful tower: 'A colossus in height, and cleaving the air, it strives somehow to reach even the sky. It is wide in breadth and in length greater. In both dimensions there is beauty, but how much more!

grounds include a hunting park, where the nobleman Bertrand is riding when he spies Cligés and Fenice. Furthermore, part of the tower's ingenuity is its abundance of running water, nature with an order imposed upon it for human convenience.

Suggestive as they might be, however, the actual meaning of these particular parallels between Chrétien's text and Byzantine representations inevitably limits itself to the realm of speculation. It seems more productive instead to consider some of the more ideological similarities between *Cligés* and these writings about Byzantine settings, as elements of a more generalized influence of Byzantine perspectives on the West. Thinking along these lines, we find in both cases that the garden becomes a site at which to question the border between the natural and the artificial. Masterful artifice plays a role in the creation of both Jehan's imagined garden and the real gardens of Byzantine nobility. When Fenice moves into the tower after her falsified death, she expresses a desire to see the sun and the outdoors, and Chrétien's particular depiction of the orchard Jehan has prepared for her reflects certain aspects of Byzantine landscape descriptions as cunningly contrived:

> Puis est antree an un vergier,
> Qui molt li plest et atalante.
> En mi le vergier ot une ante
> De flors chargiee, et bien foillue,
> Et par dedesoz estandue.
> Ensi estoient li rain duit
> Que par terre panoient tuit
> Et prés de la terre baissoient,
> Fors la cime dom il nessoient.
> La cime aloit contre mont droite
> (Fenice autre leu ne covoite)
> Et desoz l'ante ert li praiax,
> Molt delitables et molt biax,
> Ne ja n'iert tant li solauz chauz
> En esté, quant il est plus hauz,

The stones are beautified by their quadrangular shape, while an admirable and finely (constructed) arrangement (beautifies) the shape of the tower, namely the shape of a delicate honey comb' (Henry Maguire, 'The Beauty of Castles: A Tenth-Century Description of a Tower at Constantinople', in *Rhetoric, Nature and Magic in Byzantine Art* (Brookfield, VT, 1998), 22). Unlike Jehan's tower in *Cligés*, John's is a military fortification rather than a pleasure residence; however, Maguire points out that such towers were meant also to be 'look-out points that were intended to provide aesthetic pleasure' (p. 24).

Que ja rais i puisse passer,
Si le sot Jehanz conpasser
Et les branches mener et duire.

(ll. 6312–29)

Then she entered into an orchard,
which greatly pleased and delighted her.
In the middle of the orchard stood a tree
covered with flowers, and abundantly leaved,
and spread out through the top.
The branches were trained
so that they hung to the ground
and almost touched the earth,
except for the trunk from which they came forth.
The trunk stood up straight
(Fenice longs for no other place)
and below the tree were little meadows
most delightful and beautiful,
the sun was never so hot,
even in the summer, when it is at its height,
that even one ray could pass through,
so skillfully had Jehan known how to arrange it,
and to train and guide the branches.

The tree creates a microcosm of enclosure within the garden wall and tower. In addition, the orchard and its cunningly designed bower identify Jehan's skill at conflating art and nature. The tree has become an object of Jehan's art, grafted and trained in order to provide the most pleasing and functional shape possible, reflecting in its perfectly sealed enclosure Jehan's more explicitly artificial productions, such as the tower.

The Eastern version of this focus on nature as art ultimately reveals that this dichotomy is closely connected to the dichotomy of artefacts and language. A Hellenistic precedent for the Eastern medieval interest in artifice's ability to encroach upon the province of nature is evident in ancient ekphrastic texts; interwoven branches of a tree are referred to with the statement that 'their nature even seemed to be that of art' in *Daphnis and Chloe*.[68] This deliberate confusion between art and nature as a way of creating, emphasizing, or even representing beauty and perfection is a

---

[68] Roderick Beaton, *The Medieval Greek Romance* (New York, 1989), 63. Beaton also points out the importance of the praise of artifice itself in Greek romance from the twelfth century (p. 25).

characteristic of Byzantine garden ekphrasis as well, as shown in the poet
John Geometres' tenth-century account of an estate:

Do you see the multitude of [creatures]: beasts, birds, fishes? It seems to me that
[this multitude], having left every part of the world, has found this place here as
its common home. Or, running together to the beauty of its lord, as formerly to
the melody of Orpheus, they stay here. They sing, and sing in response, the
nightingale, the swan, the cicada, the swallow. . . . Everything rejoices, every
kind of art of the muses gives delight, everything takes delight, everything sings
to its lord and, I think, of its lord.

[In comparison to these] where are the works of Praxiteles, where those of
Phidias, and where those of Lysippos, and where also those of Polykleitos? These
sculptures speak, and are even endowed with voices. And even if they are not talking, yet they speak in their art.[69]

While the things and creatures of the garden in this passage both approximate the perfection of art and surpass it, the nature of their beauty must
still be conveyed in the specific terms of art, artists, and artistic technique.
More striking, however, is the passage's implication that crossing the
boundary between nature and art involves an attendant border crossing
between language and the visual or material image, leading toward a
vision of living sculptures who speak in praise through a non-verbal language of visual art. The ambiguous idea of 'speak[ing] in their art' might
refer explicitly to bird-song, but might also refer more broadly to the idea
of the art object—the natural elements of the garden as artefacts—having
the ability to communicate in a language born of its materiality, its pleasing contrivance and symmetry. For John Geometres, nature becomes art
as part of a continuum on which linguistic expression is transformed into
a language of the artefact.

A related idea is reflected more generally in Byzantine culture through
the examination of the relationship between words and visual images. St
Gregory of Nyssa, for instance, observes that 'painting, even if silent,
knows how to speak from the wall'.[70] As Henry Maguire has pointed out,
'Byzantine authors made numerous references to the connections between verbal eloquence and the visual arts. . . . The word *graphe*, for example, was used for both writing and painting, *historia* could mean either

---

[69] Henry Maguire, 'A Description of the Aretai Palace and its Garden', in *Rhetoric, Nature
and Magic*, 209–13: 211. Maguire elsewhere points out that the passage is somewhat cryptic, since
it is difficult to tell what exactly the description of the sculptures refers to ('Style and Ideology in
Byzantine Imperial Art', *Gesta*, 28, no. 2 (1989), 217–31: 219).
[70] Cyril Mango, *The Art of the Byzantine Empire, 312–1453: Sources and Documents*
(Englewood Cliffs, NJ, 1972), 36–7.

a written history or a picture, whereas *schema* was both a figure of rhetoric and a pose in painting.'[71] John Geometres' text on the pleasure garden asks at one point, 'As for the streams, what streams of words could tell of them?', using rhetorical artfulness to emphasize the way in which the ekphrastic project both requires and at the same time problematizes the distinctions among words, images, and objects.[72] Byzantine aesthetic tradition introduces the possibility of a shared terminology between narrative language, on the one hand, and image and artefact, on the other.

Chrétien's meticulous verbal attention to the Byzantine artisan Jehan's tombs, shrines, gardens, and other significant structures intersects with some of these larger questions about the role of narrative in relation to meaningful objects in the physical world. Chrétien's use of Eastern buildings and artefacts introduces into his own text a conception of poetic language as understood in the same terms as objects. W. J. T. Mitchell has argued that many of the traditional dichotomies that underlie theories of representation are essentially reconfigurations of an ancient but problematic opposition created between visual and verbal modes of expression.[73] His insistence on a critical acknowledgement of certain inherent resistances to thinking about the verbal and visual in the same terms provides a useful basis for thinking about the ekphrasis in *Cligés* as it recalls Byzantine aesthetic traditions. Within the vision of Jehan's orchard, nature itself is transformed into a triumph of artifice, spatially and narratively interlocked with Jehan's aesthetically exquisite tower structure. While in the Byzantine poem streams of words flow into actual streams, in *Cligés* the tower as product of artifice is so perfect that its 'jointure' becomes invisible (l. 5526):

> Par tel engin et par tel art
> Est fez li huis de pierre dure
> Que ja n'i troveroiz jointure.
> (ll. 5524–6)

> By such ingenious skill and by such art,
> the entry in the hard stone has been made
> so that you would never find the joining.

---

[71] Maguire, *Art and Eloquence*, 9. Maguire draws these connections between painting and eloquence as part of an argument that both the 'artist's eloquence' and the rhetorician's persuasive abilities were equally capable, in the Byzantine perspective, of inspiring the faithful to emulate the good deeds of the holy.

[72] Maguire, 'Aretai Palace', 210.

[73] 'Text and image, sign and symbol, symbol and icon, metonymy and metaphor, signifier and signified—all these semiotic oppositions reinstate, I will suggest, versions of the traditional figures of the difference between poetry and painting' (Mitchell, *Iconology*, 50).

Jointure's correspondence with Chrétien's own invocation elsewhere of *conjointure* as narrative compositional technique suggests a use of poetic expression to transform words into material objects. The invisibility of the *jointure*, achieved through perfect artifice, indicates that what is obscured in this ekphrastic passage is not only the seam in the rock but also the textual mechanism of narrative representation itself, so that the line separating verbal and visual worlds fades in the reader's experience of apprehending this artificial paradise. The bower, park, and tower in *Cligés*, oases of ordered nature and refined enclosure, emphasize the artist's ability to challenge the boundaries of the natural world. In achieving this mannered perfection, the world that Jehan creates hides its seams and joints to indicate that the workings of textuality and narrative *conjointure* might similarly disappear. What is left is an image born of words and yet transcending the sequential mechanisms of language and narrative. By privileging the role of artifice in the physical world, *Cligés* identifies a specific interconnection between poetic expression itself and the 'form as Grecian goldsmiths make'.[74] Enshrinement is not simply a metaphor for the structure of *Cligés* but instead part of the reality of the poem's apprehension. If, as Michael Camille has argued, interacting with a visual image constitutes 'the beginning and foundation of a process of thought', rather than simply an immediate response, then *Cligés*' various elements allow it to participate in this type of visual and concrete reading—to be read as an enshrining object.[75] The text's Byzantine setting, alluding to a detailed cultural examination of the relationship between visual and verbal signification, provides an appropriate context for imagining a poetics of enshrinement.

Reading the structure of *Cligés* through the structure of a contemporary artefact, we see a model of incorporating source material which moves outside the temporal chronology required by narrative progression itself. *Cligés*' invocation of the Byzantine world, and the romance's interest in aesthetic and ekphrastic traditions, hints at a unique intellectual environment in which narrative technique and visual image share a set of concepts that describe them, so that the process by which one reads an object is also the process by which one reads a romance text. In such a context, the narrative representation of source material can be construed as participating in the dynamics of an act of enshrinement. It has often been

---

[74] W. B. Yeats, 'Sailing to Byzantium', in *Collected Poems* (New York, 1956), 192.
[75] See n. 52 above for Camille's statement.

remarked that while twelfth-century academic culture engaged in a careful examination of certain aspects of poetic technique, one area which did not figure significantly in these discussions was poetic narrative structure.[76] *Cligés'* structure as an incorporation of source material is filtered through the features of artefact culture, suggesting that the language used to conceptualize romance structure was in fact a visual and material one, with specific ties to artefact culture itself. C. Stephen Jaeger has argued that the textually represented body in twelfth-century romance has instilled within it a charisma that draws upon the vestigial acknowledgement of the charismatic human body.[77] Both the tactile and the textual worlds of twelfth-century France recognized that this worshipped body often articulated its meaning through its own enshrinement. By enshrining its fragments of source as well as its fragmented bodies, *Cligés* offers us a vision of narrative structure as decipherable through its translation into the language of reliquaries.

University of California, Davis

[76] Douglas Kelly points out, for instance, that medieval poetic theories do not expound extensively upon the subject of structure because 'they devote themselves only to the most mechanical aspects of writing. . . . As far as structure is concerned, this can relate only to the question of how to begin and how to end. Beyond that . . . one cannot legislate narrative composition in the same way as oratory or epistolary composition'. See F. Douglas Kelly, *Sens and Conjointure in the* Chevalier de la Charrete (The Hague, 1966), 93.

[77] C. Stephen Jaeger, 'Charismatic Body—Charismatic Text', *Exemplaria*, 9, no. 1 (1997), 117–37: 126.

Between the Old and the Middle of English

Christopher Cannon

> This unified world created by the human Spirit is itself a complete
> entirety, which, in the determinate form of its existence, is objec-
> tively valid, and in essential relation with which every unit of our
> common humanity who is actively engaged with the vital concerns
> of art must infallibly remain.
>
> ——Hegel

'Middle English', it has recently been observed, is a 'rather funny period',
a whole only assembled by a 'very mixed bag' of linguistic criteria, a category wholly vulnerable to the very logic by which it has been confected (as
Roger Lass has shown, a very simple thought experiment can summon up
a past moment when what we now call the 'Middle' was effectively 'Modern' as well as a future moment, sufficiently remote, in which the 'Modern'
will fall squarely in the middle of the past).[1] 'Early Middle English', may
seem, by contrast, a humbler and wiser discrimination, a period brought
into being as an acknowledgement of the subtleties that both the 'Middle'
and the 'Old' lack, a 'transition' (as it is sometimes also called) founded on
the very 'fallacy . . . that there is such a thing as "Middle English", isolable
as such from "Old English" '—as Bennett and Smithers put it in their
defining anthology.[2] In this sense, early Middle English is a period wise
even to its own limits: in so far as it is either an anticipation ('early') or
constituted by change (a 'transition') it requires no firm boundaries for
itself, and yet it acts as a cushion for less subtly defined periods.

What I wish to trace in this essay, however, is the equally funny way
that such wisdom is stripped away from the 'early Middle' in practice,

I am grateful to the three anonymous readers for *New Medieval Literatures* whose comments on
an earlier draft of this essay were invaluable in its revision.

[1] Roger Lass, 'Language Periodization and the Concept "Middle" ', 7–41, in Irma Taavit-
sainen, Terttu Nevalainen, Päivi Pahta, and Matti Rissanen (eds.), *Placing Middle English in
Context*, Topics in English Linguistics, 35 (Berlin and New York, 2000). I quote from pp. 18 and
35. For Lass's thought experiment see p. 11.

[2] J. A. W. Bennett and G. V. Smithers (eds.), *Early Middle English Verse and Prose*, 2nd edn.
(Oxford, 1968), p. xii.

with the strange result that it is rarely taken to be the defining condition of a particular text or texts. As I shall suggest, first, accounts that might describe a text's *language* as early Middle English tend, rather, to treat all the attributes of that text (accidence, grammar, lexis, codicological circumstance, textual affiliation) as separate entities, each of which can then be assigned to a different period. In the second section of this essay I shall describe how such a dissociation is often achieved by elevating the text to the status of *literature*, making it possible to place it in one moment of literary history and a different moment in the history of English. In all of these cases, the attributes of the object which might be called 'early Middle English' are defensibly identified in terms of the 'Old' that they retain or recall, or the 'Middle' that they anticipate or begin, but, by means of disciplinary commitments to the 'Old' and the 'Middle' that are virtually ideological in their self-concealment, texts are often placed in these two periods without it ever being noticed that they have been placed in *both* of them ('we are not aware of this, nevertheless we do it'[3]). It is in part because texts in the 'early Middle' are bound to produce this strange effect that Thomas Hahn has recently suggested that 'historical periodization' is among the many 'foundational and analytical categories' that early Middle English actually 'puts into question'.[4] But Hahn's demonstration of all the modes of coherence which the 'early Middle' unsettles ('race, nation, language of the people, literary writing') is itself, I think, a powerful demonstration of how the 'early Middle' is an epoch distinctive in its very strangeness—and, therefore, a moment in time of sufficient historical interest that period might be the one foundational concept we would be most unwise to relinquish in this case.[5] In fact, what I would like to suggest here is that the general deformation of attempts to describe the 'early Middle' is in fact the effect of a *unifying* complexity and richness which we can only ignore to our cost.

It was Foucault who urged a view of history which could recognize 'distinct totalities' that consisted of 'divisions, limits, differences of level, shifts . . . particular forms of re-handling, possible types of relation', and it may therefore seem perverse that I have begun this attempt to describe a moment so complicated under the sign of Hegel—the philosopher of history who, by contrast, spoke of a period of time as a 'unified world' and

---

[3] Karl Marx, *Capital: A Critique of Political Economy*, i, trans. Samuel Moore and Edward Aveling, ed. Frederick Engels (London, 1954), 78–9.
[4] Thomas Hahn, 'Early Middle English', in David Wallace (ed.), *The Cambridge History of Medieval English Literature* (Cambridge, 1999), 61–91: 61.
[5] Ibid.

a 'complete entirety'.[6] But I also think that the problem which historical description has had in accounting for early Middle English is rooted in a misunderstanding of the 'theoretical problem of periodization', that what often goes awry in our sense of historical period (and certainly in the early Middle English case) is not an overly Hegelian embrace of 'homogeneous continuity', but, rather, a general misunderstanding of the suppleness Hegel attributed to such unities.[7] As Jameson urged historical criticism to recognize some time ago, Hegel insisted that a period was 'all-encompassing' only in so far as it was 'dialectical', various enough in its contours to contain divisions ('the intrinsic and the extrinsic') and determinate differences ('the existential and the historical'), comprehensive enough *as* a whole 'to allow us to feel our way within a single determinate form or moment of history at the same time that we stand outside of it'.[8]

The point is not to use early Middle English to come to some better understanding of Hegel, however, but to suggest that a better understanding of the complexity which Hegel attributed to periods could improve our understanding of how early Middle English actually consists of 'changes' and 'rejuvenescent transitions', that it is a time that may be known by the 'variety of products and formations which it originate[d]'.[9] This essay is, in fact, pendant to a book that details such variety in the particular case of early Middle English literary form, and it is an attempt to state more generally what particulars seem to reveal about the nature of early Middle English as such.[10] For if it can be said (as I argue in this book) that the forms written in such an English always appear to literary history as if standing on their heads—a boldness that looks like eccentricity, a conviction that looks like confusion, a care that looks like carelessness— it can also be said that early Middle English is itself known only by a deft and complete misprision. This means, of course, that the early Middle English period can be most efficiently and pertinently defined by

---

[6] Michel Foucault, *The Archaeology of Knowledge*, trans. A. M. Sheridan Smith (London, 1972), 10. For these phrases (taken from my epigraph) see G. W. F. Hegel, *The Philosophy of Fine Art*, trans. F. P. B. Osmaston, 4 vols. (London, 1920), i. 340. It is in fact the fourth volume of this account that is devoted to the 'art' of 'poetry'. On poetry's complexity as a 'form of knowledge' as well as the 'distinctive variety' it may assume in 'particular epochs' see esp. iv. 25–7.

[7] For the phrase I quote in the text as well as an important example of the presumption that 'Hegelian historical time' is a 'homogeneous continuity' see Louise Althusser, 'The Object of *Capital*', in Louise Althusser and Étienne Balibar, *Reading Capital*, trans. Ben Brewster (London, 1997; first pub. 1970), 71–198: 94–5.

[8] Fredric Jameson, *Marxism and Form: Twentieth-Century Dialectical Theories of Literature* (Princeton, 1971), 330–1.

[9] Georg W. F. Hegel, *The Philosophy of History*, trans. J. Sibree (Amherst, NY, 1991), 73.

[10] The book is *The Grounds of English Literature* (Oxford, 2004).

identifying some of the more glaring omissions in descriptions of some of its texts. But, as I shall also suggest in conclusion, such a critical methodology leads directly to a more positive typology, two general characteristics which can define the early Middle English text as such, by means of, rather than despite, its defining strangeness.

I

Because it is exemplary in its care, as well as the omissions that result from it, a good place to begin such a diagnostic description is the simple comparison which Derek Pearsall offers in *Old English and Middle English Poetry* of early and late versions of 'The Twelve Abuses' (*De Duodecim Abusiuis*), a homily by Ælfric (*c*.955–1012).[11] In order to illustrate the subtle process of 'translation and modernization' that occurred in the latest of these versions Pearsall first quotes from what he calls the 'Old English original':

> Ure Hælend on his jugoðe   wæs gehyrsum his magen,
> & his Heofonlice Fæder   he gehyrsumode oð deað.
> Swa swa þan ealden gedafonigeð   dugende þeawes
> & geripode syfernysse,   swa gerist þan jungan
> þæt he habbe gehyrsumnysse   & underðeodnysse.

[Our Saviour in his youth was obedient to his parents, and obeyed his Heavenly Father unto death. As it is right for the old to have virtuous habits and true faith, so it is right for the young to be obedient and submissive.]

Next to this original he then sets a version of the homily as it survives in the 'thirteenth-century copy' of London, Lambeth Palace MS 487, where it is 'to all intents and purposes in Middle English':

> Vre helend on his ȝuheðe   wes ihersum his cunne.
> and his heouenlich federe   he hersumede to ða deðe.
> Swa swa þan alden bihouað duȝende þewas
> and triwe treofestnesse;   swa biriseð þan ȝungan
> þet he abbe ihersumnesse   and ibuhsumnesse.

---

[11] Derek Pearsall, *Old English and Middle English Poetry* (London, 1977), 81–2. Phrases quoted from Pearsall in the remainder of this and the next paragraph are taken from these pages, as are the texts (although I give slightly shorter quotations), their layout, and their translation. For the editions of these texts from which Pearsall is quoting see (for the first) *Early English Homilies*, ed. Rubie D.-N. Warner, Early English Text Society, os 152 (London, 1917), 12, and, for the second, *Old English Homilies*, 1st ser., ed. Richard Morris, Early English Text Society, os 29, 34 (London, 1868), 109.

Pearsall is of course correct in suggesting that the Lambeth text differs from its 'original' as Old English differs from Middle English: in the second text, diphthongs have been reduced ('ealden' > 'alden'), back vowels fronted ('fæder' > 'feder'), consonants vocalized ('ge-' > 'i-'), and words which have passed out of the language have been replaced ('syfernesse'), just as one would expect in this change.[12] The general point that 'Ælfric's rhythmical alliterative prose had a capacity far more enduring than alliterative verse to survive . . . [such] modernization' is equally well taken. Despite the great quantity of vocabulary that distinguishes these two versions ('magen' > 'cunne', 'gedafonigeð' > 'bihouað', 'gerist' > 'biriseð', 'underðeodnysse' > 'ibuhsumnesse'), alliterative patterns are unchanged and, in one case, alliteration is actually introduced ('geripode syfernysse' > 'triwe treofestnesse').

What Pearsall's description only mentions in a footnote, however, is that Ælfric's 'original' of 'The Twelve Abuses' is quoted from London, British Library, MS Cotton Vespasian D.xiv, and as Pearsall nowhere mentions, this manuscript is only 'original' in the most distant sense, since it has long been dated to the mid-twelfth century.[13] A copy of 'The Twelve Abuses' with a much better claim to being called original survives in Cambridge, Corpus Christi College MS 178 (Ker dates this copy to the first quarter of the eleventh century), and its text could be taken to vindicate Pearsall's description of the Cotton Vespasian text entirely. With the exception of one unlevelled ending ('ʒedafeniað'), its English is no 'older' in the relevant passage:[14]

> Ure hælend on his juʒoðe   wæs ʒehyrsum his maʒon
> & his heofonlican fæder   he ʒehyrsumode oð deað;
> Swa swa þan ealdan ʒedafeniað   duʒende þeawas.
> & ʒeripode syfernyss   swa gerist þan iungan
> þæt he hæbbe ʒehyrsumnysse   & underþeodnysse.[15]

---

[12] On these sound changes see Ferdinand Mossé, *A Handbook of Middle English* (Baltimore, 1952), 16–37 (on vowels) and 40 (on consonants). The word 'sifernesse' is not adduced in English after its appearance in this text. See Hans Kurath *et al.* (eds.), *The Middle English Dictionary* (Ann Arbor, 1954–), s.v. 'sifernesse n.'

[13] N. R. Ker, *Catalogue of Manuscripts Containing Anglo-Saxon* (Oxford, 1957), 271. This manuscript has recently been dated to the second half of the twelfth century in Elaine M. Treharne, 'Production of Manuscripts of Religious Texts', in Mary Swan and Elaine M. Treharne (eds.), *Rewriting Old English in the Twelfth Century* (Cambridge, 2000), 11–39: 35.

[14] Ker, *Catalogue*, 60 (the homily is item 7 in the 'A' portion of this manuscript).

[15] Although he does not specify its source, Richard Morris provides a diplomatic transcription of the homily from this manuscript as Appendix 2 in *Old English Homilies*, 296–304 (for the lines I quote see pp. 299–300). I have silently expanded a few abbreviations. I am grateful to Prof. Malcolm Godden for helping me discover this older version of 'The Twelve Abuses', and for identifying its source, as well as for a very helpful conversation on this whole topic.

On the other hand, by calling the Cotton Vespasian text 'Old' as *well* as 'original', Pearsall's accuracy about language here substitutes for an accuracy about codicological circumstance, and the Vespasian text is consequently displaced by over a century to the time of the Corpus Christi text, in this way neatly deleting the temporal *proximity* of the traits here also separated by their division into 'Old' and 'Middle'. In fact, what Pearsall calls 'Old English' may be much closer in date to what he calls 'transition' than to Ælfric, with the result that what is here described as a substantial change in language over time could just as easily be described (were these facts clear) as two different aspects of a coincident variety.

However implicit this definitional practice may be in such an instance it has effects substantial enough that, where the care taken has been any less than Pearsall's, it is even possible to separate proximate differences by splitting a text in two, as its language is divided up among different periods. This has, in fact, long been the strange fate of an English adaptation of the *Rule of St Benedict*, originally made for a community of women in 961 at the request of Æthelwold. The decomposition is helped along in this case by the re-adaptation of all of the oldest copies of this text into a rule for men (a tell-tale feminine pronoun always betrays their origin).[16] The oldest of these copies is contained in the eleventh-century manuscript which also contains 'The Twelve Abuses' (Cambridge, Corpus Christi College MS 178); the latest, dated to the first quarter of the twelfth century, is London, British Library, MS Cotton Faustina A.x; taken together, with three intervening manuscripts, these texts have also been edited as a single 'Old English' translation of the Benedictine Rule.[17] One version of the translation which is still addressed to women survives, however, in British Library MS Cotton Claudius D.iii; but because of the lateness of its date (the first quarter of the thirteenth century), and its perceived *departure* from the gender of address used in earlier copies (this text is usually called the 'Winteney' version after the community of women for whom it was made), this text has been edited as 'Middle English'.[18]

---

[16] On the history of this translation see R. W. Chambers, *On the Continuity of English Prose from Alfred to More and His School*, Early English Text Society, os 191A (London, 1932), p. xcii.

[17] For this text see Arnold Schröer (ed.), *Die Angelsächsischen Prosabearbeitungen der Benedictinerregel*, 2nd edn. (Darmstadt, 1964; first pub. 1885-8). For a description of these manuscripts see this edition, pp. xix–xxviii, and also Ker, *Catalogue*, 60–4 (Cambridge, Corpus Christi College, MS 178), 194–6 (British Library, Cotton Faustina MS A.x), 262–3 (British Library, Cotton Titus MS A.iv), 430–2 (Oxford, Corpus Christi College MS 197), 464–5 (Wells Cathedral MS).

[18] For the edition of the text see Arnold Schröer (ed.), *Die Winteney-Version der Regula S. Benedicti* (Halle, 1888). For the period classification of the 'Winteney' text see J. B. Severs

This exquisite *hysteron proteron*, whereby the only surviving original of a given text becomes the end-point in its development, is made even more extraordinary by the surprising stability of the text whose various instances have been treated as if so completely different. Here, for example, are a few representative sentences, first from the edition of the 'Old English' text, second, from the 'Middle English' of the 'Winteney' version:

Abbod, ðe ðæs wyrðe sy, þæt he mynsteres wealde, he sceal a ȝemunan, hwæt he ȝecweden is, and þæs ealdorscipes noman mid dædum ȝefyllan. Cristes ȝespelia he is and his note and spelinȝe on mynstre healt; he forþi his aȝenum naman ȝeciȝed is, ȝeseðendum apostole and þus cweðendum: 'ȝe onfenȝon bearna ȝewiscinȝe ȝast, on þæm we clypiað abba, þæt is fæder'.[19]

þeo abbodesse, þe þæs wyrðe sy, þat heo þæs munster wealde, heo sceal a ȝemunan, hwet heo ȝecweden is & þæs ealderscypes naman mid dedum ȝefyllan. Cristes ȝespelia heo is & on þan mynstra Cristes stede healt & forþy his aȝenum naman ȝeciȝed is, swa swa se apostel seȝð þus cweðonde: 'Ge onfengan þane gast bearne ȝewisinȝe, on þan we clypioð abba, þat is fæder, abbodesse, þat is moder ȝenemned'.[20]

[An abbot (abbess) who is worthy to rule a monastery must remember what he (she) is called and fulfil in his (her) deeds the name of such dignity. He (She) is Christ's representative and stands in his (Christ's) place in that monastery (nunnery), and therefore he is called by his own name, as the Apostle said speaking thus: 'You have received the spirit of the adoption of sons, wherefore we cry "Abba" which means "Father" ("Abbodesse" which means "Mother")').]

Some of the forms of the 'Winteney' text show evidence of the kind of vowel fronting ('dædum' > 'dedum') and levelling ('bearna' > 'bearne', 'cweðendum' > cweðonde') that usually marks the difference between Old and Middle English, although most of the more vulnerable forms remain unchanged (e.g. 'ȝemunan', 'ȝespelia', 'fæder'). And Schröer, the editor of these texts, does note the conservatism of the language of the 'Winteney' text, describing it at one point as 'New Anglo-Saxon' ('Neuangelsächsisch'); but this designation obviates rather than provides any opportunity to note that 'Anglo-Saxon' is therefore alive and well as late as the thirteenth century (revised, but also substantially preserved though use); and when Schröer does describe the 'Winteney' text in

et al. (eds.), *A Manual of the Writings in Middle English*, 10 vols. [to date] (New Haven, 1967–), ii. 460–2 and esp. 654 (where it is said that 'OE versions not included' and the 'Winteney' version is the first listed). On the manuscript of this version see Ker, *Catalogue*, p. xix n. 2.

[19] Schröer (ed.), *Prosabearbeitungen der Benedictinerregel*, 10.
[20] Schröer (ed.), *Winteney-Version der Regula S. Benedicti*, 15.

relation to earlier forms he not only describes it as an 'adaptation', but an adaptation in 'Middle English' ('eine "mittelenglische" Umarbeitung'[21]).

In cases such as this (and Pearsall's treatment of 'The Twelve Abuses') it is actually the attention paid to the manuscript record (if not always to manuscript dates) which allows a spatial difference (between book and book) to act like a difference in time (between historical forms of English), and it is a method corrosive enough in the case of early Middle English to decompose even a single manuscript into layers which can then be treated as successive periods of time. This is certainly how the various forms of English which comprise the *Anglo-Saxon Chronicle* in Oxford, Bodleian MS Laud Misc. 636 are usually understood, for this book falls, 'paleographically . . . into three sections', the first copied in a single hand (covering the entries for 449–1121), the second, also 'in the original hand', but with 'frequent changes of ink' and 'variations' in writing style (the entries for 1122–31), and the third, in a single but different hand (the entries for 1132–54).[22] These physical distinctions also correlate quite closely with linguistic distinctions: the text up until 1121 is in 'Old English' or 'Standard Late West-Saxon',[23] the entries from 1122–31 'sho[w] Middle-English trends',[24] and the single long entry from 1132 to 1154 is 'incontrovertibly Middle English'.[25] Because various incidents in the later entries of the text refer particularly to Peterborough, and Peterborough Abbey suffered a catastrophic fire in 1116, a fairly straightforward narrative has always seemed to explain both of these results: this version of the *Chronicle* was begun when the Peterborough monks secured another copy of the *Chronicle* (in 1121); the copyist of this first portion continued the annals yearly until 1131 (a text described, accordingly, as the 'First Continuation'); there was then a gap until 1155, when some other writer (and/or scribe) described the intervening twenty-three years in a single long entry.[26] And, according to this story, the text's divisions have seemed

---

[21] Schröer (ed.), *Winteney-Version der Regula S. Benedicti*, pp. ix and xiv–xv. See also Schröer (ed.), *Prosabearbeitungen der Benedictinerregel*, pp. xxvi–xxvii.

[22] On the various stages of the text's copying see Cecily Clark (ed.), *The Peterborough Chronicle, 1070–1154*, 2nd edn. (Oxford, 1970), pp. xv–xvii.

[23] Ibid., pp. xli–xliv.

[24] In the 'First Continuation' the levelling of vowels in unstressed syllables is 'well-advanced' ('over half the instances of the preterit plural and nearly five-sixths of those of the infinitive have *-en*'), but there is also a marked 'conservatism' in, e.g., the use of a variety of inflected forms of the definite article in this portion of the text ('se', 'þa') (ibid., pp. lii–lxiii).

[25] The 'Final Continuation' exhibits 'drastic simplifications in accidence', and, as a result, 'before our eyes English is beginning to change from a synthetic language to an analytic one' (ibid., pp. lii ('incontrovertibly') and lxiii–lxix (for details of language)).

[26] For discussion of this *Chronicle*'s relation to Peterborough Abbey and the composite nature of the text see John Earle (ed.), *Two of the Saxon Chronicles Parallel (with Supplementary Extracts from the Others)*, rev. Charles Plummer, 2 vols. (Oxford, 1952), ii, pp. xlv–liv.

to distribute themselves 'into two main parts',[27] the copied annals until 1121 forming an instance of the late preservation of 'Old English', the First and Final Continuations collectively forming one of the more important texts of 'early Middle English' (as, for example, Bennett and Smithers anthologize them[28]).

What the parcelling out of times and languages into these various layers obscures, however, is the extent to which the *Peterborough Chronicle* contracts the 'Old' and the 'Middle' into the smallest of spans. Although it is sensible to believe that the Peterborough scribe who copied the annals to 1121 was generally reproducing a language much older than his own, describing these annals as 'copied' and treating them as a single text and time obscures the evidence they give that a 'Standard Late West Saxon' ('notable for the number of obsolescent words it contains') was still being written *anew* in 1116 (in the *Chronicle* that the Peterborough monks borrowed and copied), and that this new 'Old English' was being written only five years before the Peterborough monk's English showed 'trends' toward the 'Middle'.[29] Drawing the line between the 'Standard Late West Saxon' of the copied annals and 'Middle English' (or 'early Middle English') which begins at 1121 also obscures the extent to which this Middle English, however 'new-fangled' (as this *Chronicle*'s editor terms it) has also absorbed a surprising number of 'standard' Old English forms (as this editor also observes).[30] Most of all, however, dividing this text into these layers conceals the general simultaneity of all the varieties of English of which the *Peterborough Chronicle* is comprised: however it was put together, in other words, this single text insists that the temporal distance between a conservative Late West Saxon and an incontrovertible Middle English was only thirty-nine years (from the last entry in the copied annals of 1116 to the writing of the Final Continuation in 1155).

It has of course been widely understood that a great quantity of Old English writing was copied in the twelfth and thirteenth centuries (27 of the 189 manuscripts containing Anglo-Saxon that Ker catalogued were copied after 1100),[31] but it has only recently begun to come clear that works such as London, British Library, MS Cotton Vespasian D.xiv (in which Pearsall found Ælfric's original text) were actually compiled anew

---

[27] Clark (ed.), *Peterborough Chronicle*, p. xviii.
[28] See Bennett and Smithers (eds.), *Early Middle English*, 201–12.
[29] Clark (ed.), *Peterborough Chronicle*, pp. xlv–lxii. Bennett and Smithers say that the 'philological value' of the First Continuation is 'reduced' by 'a slight admixture . . . of forms from the standard written language of late OE' (*Early Middle English*, 374).
[30] Clark (ed.), *Peterborough Chronicle*, pp. lix–lxiii.
[31] See Ker, *Catalogue*, pp. xviii–xix.

in the twelfth century;[32] although it has also long been known that the copying of this old material might affect the later English of those who copied it (as in the *Peterborough* First Continuation), it has also become clear recently that what we blithely term 'Old English' is often a lived aspect of a scribe's linguistic competence (characterized by 'active, sophisticated, and often highly creative . . . participation', and such scribes 'did not hesitate to gloss, translate, rearrange, supplement, diminish, or modernise, their text').[33] Accordingly, even our most generous acknowledgements of the overlap—an informing awareness that there is 'a period . . . in which seemingly advanced and retrograde texts exist side-by-side'—may not go far enough, for inasmuch as we cling to the idea of 'Old English' when describing the circumstances of its 'afterlife', we have lost the variegation and change that characterize such belatedness.[34]

In fact, the very distinction between Old and Middle English is the most compelling and general procedure employed for ignoring the extent to which substantially different kinds of English coincide in the long moment between them. And this is true, even to the extent that we understand this distinction not only as approximate but changeable. Relying strictly on the levelling of inflections in final unstressed syllables, as Henry Sweet did when he first proposed the tripartite division of English into 'Old', 'Middle', and 'Modern', we might show, as Kemp Malone famously did, that the 'Middle' of English includes the major codices of Old English poetry copied in the 'second half of the tenth century'.[35]

---

[32] Susan Irvine, 'The Compilation and Use of Manuscripts Containing Old English in the Twelfth Century', in Swan and Treharne (eds.), *Rewriting Old English*, 41–61: esp. 48–54.

[33] Roy Michael Liuzza, 'Scribal Habit: The Evidence of the Old English Gospels', in *Rewriting Old English*, 143–65: 164.

[34] Seth Lerer, 'Old English and its Afterlife', in Wallace (ed.), *Cambridge History of Medieval English Literature*, 7–34: 9. Lerer is very careful about the 'linguistic indeterminacy' which results from the lateness of what appears to be 'Old', and his chapter offers detailed analysis of a number of the texts which I treat in this essay. As it configures its subject, however (and as it is separate from the *Cambridge History*'s discussion of 'early Middle English'), the subject of this chapter simply presumes that the Old can be distinguished from the Middle.

[35] See Kemp Malone, 'When Did Middle English Begin?', in J. T. Hatfield, W. Leopold, and A. J. F. Ziegelschmidt (eds.), *Curme Volume of Linguistic Studies*, Language Monographs, 7 (Baltimore, 1930), 110–17. For Sweet's original division see Henry Sweet, 'History of English Sounds', *Transactions of the Philological Society* (1873–4), 462–623: 620. Sweet's system was itself a development of the system which Jacob Grimm introduced, with 'Old, Middle, and Modern as terms describing the morphological shifts in time of West Germanic languages in 1819', and it was only because Grimm 'retained the then current German term, *Angelsächsisch*' for what would have been Old English that the division needed to be reinvented by Sweet a half-century later. For this and a compelling narrative of the history of the scholarship which produced 'Middle English' as a category see David Matthews, *The Making of Middle English, 1765–1910* (Minneapolis, 1999), pp. xxviii–xxxi.

Marking the moment, not when levelling began, but when it became 'irrevocable', we might stabilize the division at 1150 but, in this way, draw some of the 'Middle' in, say, the *Peterborough Chronicle* back into the 'Old'.[36] Relying on lexis alone (as its 'Germanic character' gives way to 'Romance elements'), we might even absorb the whole of early Middle English into 'Anglo-Saxon', extending the latter part of the period into the 'late thirteenth' century.[37] But inasmuch as any such distinction makes it possible to locate the 'earliest' Middle English text, as was done, long ago, on the basis of Sweet's designations in the homily called the *Sermo in Festis Sancte Marie Virginis* (because 'the reduction of the vowels of the final syllables, the dropping of the inflectional -*n*, and the monophthongization of diphthongs ha[d] been relatively systematically carried through'), the more complex surround of this text is effectively blocked out.[38] The distinction makes it irrelevant that this homily survives in a manuscript that is separately catalogued as one of those 'containing Anglo-Saxon'.[39] And it makes it all but impossible to point out that this manuscript is London, British Library, MS Cotton Vespasian D.xiv, the book, compiled in the twelfth century, in which Ælfric's 'The Twelve Abuses' can also be found in the 'original' Old English.

II

As David Matthews has shown in his history of Middle English, a historical project that had been under way for some time coalesced as a discipline only at the end of the nineteenth century, when the 'coherence

---

[36] Peter Kitson, 'When did Middle English Begin? Later than You Think!', in Jacek Fisiak (ed.), *Studies in Middle English Linguistics* (Berlin and New York, 1997), 221–69 (esp. p. 223).

[37] Angelika Lutz, 'When did English Begin?' in Teresa Fanego, Belén Méndez-Naya, and Elena Seoane (eds.), *Sounds, Words, Texts and Change: Selected Papers from 11 ICEHL, Santiago de Compostela, 7–11 September 2000*, Amsterdam Studies in the Theory and History of Linguistic Science, 224 (Amsterdam, 2002), 145–71.

[38] Francis P. Magoun, 'Colloquial Old and Middle English', *Harvard Studies and Notes in Philology and Literature*, 19 (1937), 167–73: 171–2, quoting and translating Max Förster, 'Abt Raoul d'Escures und der spätae, "Sermo in festis S. Mariae" ', *Archiv für das Studium der neueren Sprachen*, 162 (1932), 43–8: 47. Since the *Sermo* was a translation of a Latin sermon by Ralph d'Escures (Bishop of Rochester 1108–14, Archbishop of Canterbury 1114–22), bringing such distinctions to this text also made it possible to date the beginning of Middle English textually, to the period 1108–22 (Förster, 'Abt Raoul d'Escures und der spätae', 46–7). Clark calls the *Sermo* 'the text usually classed as the earliest ME one' (*Peterborough Chronicle*, p. lii n. 1).

[39] See Ker, *Catalogue*, 271.

of a linguistic concept' was deployed to convene a 'literary scene', when 'philological certainty' about the kind of English that lay in the 'Middle' was parlayed into a canon of literature.[40] But it is in fact in just such a move (or in such moves) from linguistic certainty to an idea of literature that early Middle English has failed to coalesce. It is, for example, precisely by means of such a manoeuvre that Bennett and Smithers anthologize early Middle English as if their concern were 'literature' (their introduction begins by describing 'the growth of literature in these islands'), but only ever define the 'early Middle' in their volume as a 'language' ('what marks off Middle English from early Middle English?').[41] In the particular case, a text may be carefully described in terms of both literary and linguistic history, but it may be placed in a different period in each one of these respects (part of 'Old English', but written in 'Middle English', say) with the result that every aspect of that text's variety is noted—*except that variety itself.*

One of the texts most vulnerable to such treatment is *Durham*, a poem that sits so conveniently on the customary chronological divide between Old and Middle English (it is datable, by internal evidence, to 1104–9) that that line can be drawn right down the middle of the poem. Because of its 'regular alliterative metre', it can be described as 'the latest of the extant Anglo-Saxon poems', but because its language has changed substantially from the Anglo-Saxon standard (substituting *eo* for *e* ('breome' instead of 'breme'), levelling vowels in end syllables ('steppa' not 'stēape'), simplifying verb endings ('wunað' not 'wuniað'), omitting inflectional final -*n* ('deope') or the whole of the inflectional ending ('eadig' for 'eadigen')) its language can also be placed firmly in the early Middle English (or 'transition') period.[42]

> Is ðeos burch breome geond Breotenrice,
> steppa gestaðolad, stanas ymbutan
> wundrum gewæxen. Weor ymbeornad,
> ea yðum stronge, and ðer inne wunað
> feola fisca kyn on floda gemonge.
> And ðaer gewexen is wudafæstern micel;
> wuniad in ðem wycum wilda deor monige,
> in deope dalum deora ungerim.[43]

---

[40] Matthews, *Making of Middle English*, pp. xxxiii–xxxiv.

[41] Bennett and Smithers (eds.), *Early Middle English*, pp. xi and xxi.

[42] On the poem's date and language see Elliott van Kirk Dobbie (ed.), *The Anglo-Saxon Minor Poems*, Anglo-Saxon Poetic Records, 6 (London, 1942), pp. xliii–xlv.

[43] Ibid., 27 (l. 1–8).

[This city is well known throughout the British kingdom, established on high, the stones on every side raised up wondrously. The Wear encircles it, a stream strong in waves, and many kinds of fish live in the swirling currents. And a great enclosing wood has grown up there; many wild animals dwell in that fastness, innumerable animals in deep dales.]

Despite these different affiliations, however, this poem is always treated as if it were a part of Old English literature because it is so regular in this respect, 'an eloquent survival of traditional techniques of verse-making' or 'an antiquarian *tour de force*'.[44] Not only is its transitional language gathered up into the Anglo-Saxon Poetic Records, but it is there described as 'the only extant example in Anglo-Saxon of the *encomium urbis*'.[45]

According to this same logic, it has also been possible to take great care with the transitional nature of the literary attributes of a particular text, while overlooking the much more stolidly 'Old' attributes of its language. This has tended to happen in descriptions of the poem on the death of Edgar that survive (in the entry for 975) in the two latest copies of the Anglo-Saxon Chronicle, the twelfth-century text usually called the *Worcester Chronicle* (London, British Library, MS Cotton Tiberius B.iv) and the *Peterborough Chronicle*. The lateness of this poem is further emphasized by the poem in 'classical' verse style which can be found at this point in the three older manuscripts of the *Chronicle* (Cambridge, Corpus Christi College MS 173; London, British Library, MS Cotton Tiberius A.vi; and London, British Library, MS Cotton Tiberius B.i), but, even on its own, the later poem seems to manifest the 'dominant forms and rhythms of Middle English verse':[46]

> Cuð wæs þet wide
> geond feola þeoda
> þe aferan Eadmundes
> ofer ganetes bað
> cyningas hine wide
> wurðodon side
> bugon to cyninge
> swa wæs him gecynde.[47]

[It was known widely, throughout many nations, that kings submitted to him, the son of Edmund, far and wide over the sea, as was his birthright.]

---

[44] Lerer, 'Old English and its Afterlife', 8 (for a careful reading of *Durham* see also pp. 18–22).
[45] Dobbie (ed.), *Anglo-Saxon Minor Poems*, p. xlv; emphasis mine.
[46] Pearsall, *Old English and Middle English Poetry*, 70.
[47] Earle (ed.), *Two of the Saxon Chronicles*, i. 121.

Pearsall's description is in this case typically careful, and, in defining such 'Middle English' he suggests that it bestrides two periods, having 'the character of both relic and embryo': 'two-stress phrases dominate', and there are 'some traditional-sounding formulas', but 'the emergent principle is rhyme' (as in the fifth and sixth lines quoted above).[48] Yet the care with which the poem's literary heterogeneity is noticed is itself a method for discounting the regularity of its language, an Old English in which the most vulnerable inflections are intact (e.g. 'feola' and 'þeoda'), and the most commonly dropped prefixes ('ge-' ('gecynde')) and verb endings ('wurðodon') remain because it is that 'Late West Saxon standard' used in all the copied portion of the *Peterborough Chronicle* (and also employed in the *Worcester Chronicle*).[49] It is in this sense strange that the Anglo-Saxon Poetic Records should exclude this poem, since it is 'in' Anglo-Saxon, even though, as is there pointed out, it is also in 'irregular metre'.[50]

Since such divisions are possible only to the extent that the linguistic and the literary are categories which contain the same objects (all the words of a given text), but never actually overlap, it is also possible that descriptions of this kind can assign a text to different periods, but *by turns*, claiming it, now for 'Old English', now for early Middle English (or the 'transition'), but never in *all* its defining variety. This has been the particular fate of *The Rime of King William*, a lament on the death of William the Conqueror that survives in the entry for 1087 in *The Peterborough Chronicle*. In this case the oldness of the poem's language is hard to ignore, because the Late West Saxon prose which surrounds it is also an old-fashioned kind of literature: it makes an 'appeal to emotion' that is 'far from annalistic', adopting a passionate 'homiletic' tone that is 'familiar from . . . Wulfstan' (fl. 996–1023) and 'recalls . . . Ælfric'.[51] Where this surrounding prose is noticed on these grounds (as 'a veritable chrestomathy of Old English discourses'), *The Rime of King William* is emphatically 'in Old English', although it can also be noticed that it 'evoke[s] the short couplets of continental verse' ('the patterns . . . that . . . would crystallize into the first rhymed poetry in Middle English'):[52]

> Castelas he let wyrcean,
> & earme men swiðe swencean.

[48] Pearsall, *Old English and Middle English Poetry*, 71.
[49] On the close relation of the texts of the *Worcester Chronicle* and the copied portion of the *Peterborough Chronicle* see Earle (ed.), *Two Saxon Chronicles*, p. lxiv.
[50] See Dobbie (ed.), *Anglo-Saxon Minor Poems*, p. xxxvi. For the classical poem see pp. 22–4.
[51] Clark (ed.), *Peterborough Chronicle*, pp. lxxv–lxxvii.
[52] Lerer, 'Old English and its Afterlife', 12.

> Se cyng wæs swa swiðe stearc,
> & benam of his underþeoddan manig marc,
> goldes & ma hundred punda seolfres.[53]

[He had castles built and oppressed poor men very much. The king was very stern, and took many marks from his subjects, and many more hundred pounds of silver.]

Where, on the other hand, the prose surround is completely ignored, the *Rime* seems to be on the knife's edge of the 'transition' ('from one point of view . . . the last staggering steps towards dissolution . . . from another . . . contain[ing] the seeds of Laȝamon and the short rhymed couplet of Middle English'), and the Old is barely present as a literary formation (alliteration or two-stress verse) that is 'almost completely decayed'.[54] That its language is standard Late West Saxon is not enough to get this poem even a mention in the Anglo-Saxon Poetic Records ('we may therefore exclude E [*The Peterborough Chronicle*] from further consideration here').[55]

III

To know early Middle English as a period both 'unified' and 'complete', it therefore seems, would be to know it as that moment in which what we are otherwise accustomed to calling the 'Old' and the 'Middle' fully coincide (its beginning would therefore be the beginning of that coincidence, its end the moment that the 'Middle' left the 'Old' entirely behind). It is therefore also some measure of just how hard it is to avoid such a simple idea—how nearly ideological our disciplinary need not to formulate it has been—that it can be found in one of the early Middle English texts to which it ought to be applied, as the very first of the images in what has been described as the 'commonplace content' of *The Poema Morale* (or *Moral Ode*):[56]

> Ich em nu alder þene ich wes awintre and a lare.
> Ich welde mare þene ich dede mi wit ahte bon mare.
> Wel longe ich habbe child ibon a worde and a dede
> þah ich bo a wintre ald to ȝung ich em on rede.[57]

---

[53] Clark (ed.), *Peterborough Chronicle*, 13.
[54] Pearsall, *Old English and Middle English Poetry*, 72.
[55] Dobbie (ed.), *Anglo-Saxon Minor Poems*, p. xxxvi.
[56] Severs *et al.* (eds.), *Manual of the Writings in Middle English*, ix. 3007–8.
[57] *Old English Homilies*, 1st ser., ed. Morris, 159 (ll. 1–4).

[I am now older than I was in winters and in learning; I have more than I did, my skill should be greater. For a long time I have been a child in word and in deed. Although I am too old in years, I am too young in wisdom.]

Although it is never put this way, this poem is almost always understood to combine aspects of the old and the new in the very manner of this speaker: it exhibits traits 'characteristic of the Old English elegiac and penitential tradition', although it is best described as 'a Middle English text'.[58] As Pearsall puts it in this case, the *Poema Morale* 'stands at the junction of two traditions . . . at home in an Anglo-Saxon homiletic collection' but, also, 'rich with rhyme and no trace of alliteration or Old English poetic diction'.[59] But it is also in so far as this combination is seen to be a property of the poem that such observations fail to formulate the idea captured by the poem itself: that a person can be characterized by the co-incidence of age and youth is, in the poem's terms, to stress the real need of the confession it introduces (such a person is supremely out of joint, with much to own up to), but the possibility that there might actually *be* such a person is the poem's warning that many of the attributes we normally depend upon time to dissever (the wisdom that comes with age, for example) have nothing to do with time. What the *Poema Morale* might be said to know according to the logic of its own metaphors, in other words, is that a 'Middle English' with 'Old English' characteristics is not both, but neither. It would not be surprised to learn that its forms stand at the 'junction of two traditions' because such a junction was a tradition of which this poem was only a small and particular part.

A step toward making such wisdom commonplace in linguistic and literary history would consist of a less paradoxical version of the *Poema Morale*'s observations, filled out with the particulars deleted from the kinds of description I have been examining: it would define as 'early Middle English' that period which *appears to combine those attributes we otherwise find separately in 'Old' and 'Middle' English*. It will be yet another measure of the extent to which such a wisdom has been debarred in the past by our separate and separating disciplinary (and near-ideological) commitments to 'Old' and 'Middle' individually that such a definition will seem to be too obvious to require stating ('we are aware of this because we do it'). But appearance is the crucial and qualifying term in

---

[58] For the classification see Joseph Hall (ed.), *Selections from Early Middle English, 1130–1250*, 2 vols. (Oxford, 1920), i. 31–53. For the characterizations I quote see Betty Hill, 'The Twelfth-Century *Conduct of Life*, formerly the *Poema Morale* or *A Moral Ode*', *Leeds Studies in English*, 9 (1976–7), 97–144: 107 and 117.

[59] Pearsall, *Old English and Middle English Poetry*, 90.

the definition I have just given, for the wisdom we have really lacked when looking at the kinds of coincidence exemplified by a poem such as the *Poema Morale*, and fully known in the image that begins it, is that the coincidence of traits thought to be separated by time collapses the separating categories wherever these traits overlap. Early Middle English is not only that period in which attributes otherwise found separately as 'Old' and 'Middle' English coincide, but where, for that reason, *the distinction between 'Old' and 'Middle' is annulled.*

The largest implication of this last point is that all those texts which have come to be described as 'late Old English' or Old English in its 'afterlife', or, most of all, as 'late' copies of Old English 'originals' may have to be redescribed as early Middle English and absorbed into any discussion of this time and its texts. It may no longer be tenable, moreover, to plan a 'linguistic atlas' of early Middle English like the one now in preparation on the presumption that the early Middle English 'period' contains 'two very different types of written English . . . 1) versions of Old English texts and 2) new writings in early Middle English'; it may have to be recognized that, where there is a 'chronological overlap between the two types' (as this plan also acknowledges), it could never be the case that some texts can be seen to be *'clearly* Middle English, rather than Old English productions'.[60] In fact, where 'early Middle' is defined as 'that written between *c.*1150–1300' (as is also the case for this atlas), such an atlas can survey the 'early Middle' only in so far as it considers all the 'Old English' that was 'written' in this period too.[61]

A second attribute of the early Middle English which follows both more subtly and less restrictively from the general definition I have just given is that its texts may be known by the extent to which *they are difficult or impossible to date on the basis of language.* This characteristic has been less clear than it might have been in the foregoing, since I have tended to choose examples from texts that were datable on the basis of source (*Durham*) or codicological circumstance ('The Twelve Abuses' and the 'Winteney' Rule) in order to have a fixed point around which to orient the dizzyingly various attributions of period the texts have been given.

---

[60] Margaret Laing, 'Anchor Texts and Literary Manuscripts in Early Middle English', in Felicity Riddy (ed.), *Regionalism in Late Medieval Manuscripts and Texts* (Cambridge, 1991), 27–52: 36; emphasis mine. In this article Laing describes some of the 'initial problems' discovered in 'a survey of dialectical variation during the early Middle English period' which, it is hoped, will 'in due course . . . produce a linguistic atlas for the period, complementary to *A Linguistic Atlas of Late Mediaeval English*' (p. 27).

[61] Laing, 'Anchor Texts', 27.

Because texts can be firmly dated by such ancillary information, and because that information often attaches in a recoverable form by happenstance, this criterion applies even when the date of a text is clear. But it also means that a text can be known to be in early Middle English simply because it is temporally unmoored. The *Poema Morale* would be gathered into the period, then, not because it could be firmly placed in the period 1150–1300, but because it could *not* be so placed—since it is only *'thought* to be from the twelfth century'.[62]

A more negative implication of both of these characteristics is that it may no longer be possible to say that 'archaism' is the attribute of an early Middle English text, as has become so common, or that any early Middle English writer was motivated by 'antiquarianism sentiments': in an environment where Old English 'originals' are often as new as the 'earliest' of Middle English texts, it could not be possible that a text such as Laȝamon's *Brut* shows 'evidence of linguistic archaizing', despite Stanley's famous and influential claim.[63] This is a point that is also known, in effect, by an omission in our scholarship, and what would necessarily disappear along with such claims is the *scepticism* about such claims that often, so strangely, accompanies them. It may not now be possible to try to date the *Owl and the Nightingale* to the years 1176–8 on the basis of the 'linguistic evidence' of 'earlier' forms (inflected comparatives, numerals, possessives, and adjectives, eight cases of the dual personal pronoun, a neuter pleural, etc.), just as it may no longer be necessary (or sensible) to urge such a redating *while* observing that dating a Middle English poem 'by the dialect is sometimes like trying to tell the hour of day in a room where there are twenty clocks, no two of which keep the same time'.[64] It may not now be possible to support the suggestion that this poem should be dated 'after 1272' with the observations that its language is 'quite forward-looking' and only a few of its forms actually 'appear . . . archaic', and it must also be obvious that to qualify such a claim with the observation that 'it is extremely hard to quantify "archaism" in early Middle English' is also to undermine it completely.[65]

[62] For this dating see Severs *et al.* (eds.), *Manual of the Writings in Middle English*, ix. 3007–8; emphasis mine.

[63] E. G. Stanley, 'Laȝamon's Antiquarian Sentiments', *Medium Ævum*, 38 (1969), 23–37: 25.

[64] Henry B. Hinckley, 'The Date of "The Owl and the Nightingale"', *Modern Philology*, 17 (1919), 63–74: 70–1. For the standard account of the poem's date see Eric Gerald Stanley (ed.), *The Owl and the Nightingale* (Manchester, 1960), 19.

[65] Neil Cartlidge, 'The Date of the *Owl and the Nightingale*', *Medium Ævum*, 65 (1996), 230–47: 236–7.

To eliminate the possibility that the 'Middle' excludes the 'Old' or the 'Old' excludes the 'Middle' in and as the 'early Middle' would expand the canon of early Middle English quite significantly, but its most important accomplishment would be to make the space between Old and Middle English visible to linguistic and literary history in all its defining rarity and conceptual richness; it would put before us, by means of settled criteria, a long moment in time, in which the nature of English writing and its attendant and defining attributes were themselves deeply—and therefore compellingly—*unsettled*. In this sense what was revealed would be more generally tutelary in the variety it could claim for the concept of period, the differences, divisions, and possible forms of relation it would allow even to the more traditional modes of periodization. But, in bringing about all these broad and influential changes, early Middle English would exist as little more than (or only a little more than) the literary scene and canon that have long been convened by an equally rich scholarship and a series of anthologies.[66] For, as I began by saying, it is also my point that what I have said about early Middle English texts and the particular terms of the definitions I have offered have long *existed* in linguistic and literary scholarship—they have just never been *known* to be there.

University of Cambridge

---

[66] In addition to Bennett and Smithers there are Joseph Hall (ed.), *Selections from Early Middle English* (Oxford, 1920), and Bruce Dickins and R. M. Wilson (eds.), *Early Middle English Texts* (London, 1951).

Analytical Survey 7: Actually Existing Anglo-Saxon Studies

Clare A. Lees

ANGLO-SAXON Studies is a thriving discipline, whether we consider the number of books, editions, and articles published each year (which appears to be both steady and increasing) or examine the activity of publication series.[1] The field's self-representation in the form of dedicated journals, newsletters, and professional organizations is lively.[2] Research in the discipline is more securely supported than ever before by the Toronto *Old English Dictionary*, with its on-line corpus, as well as by the two projects on the sources of Anglo-Saxon writing: *Fontes Anglo-Saxonici* and its sister project, the *Sources of Anglo-Saxon Literary Culture* (SASLC).[3] Electronic research ventures with major implications for the field include the *Electronic Beowulf*, the interdisciplinary project on prosopography in Anglo-Saxon England (PASE), and numerous websites, on-line editions,

---

[1] In addition to the major editions recently published under the aegis of the Early English Text Society such as *Ælfric's Catholic Homilies: The First Series Text*, ed. Peter Clemoes, Early English Text Society, ss 17 (Oxford, 1997), and Malcolm Godden (ed.), *Ælfric's Catholic Homilies: Introduction, Commentary and Glossary*, Early English Text Society, ss 18 (Oxford, 2000), see also the collaborative edition of the manuscripts of the *Anglo-Saxon Chronicle*, the most recent of which is David Dumville (ed.), *Anglo-Saxon Chronicle 1 MS F* (Woodbridge, 2003). Boydell and Brewer also publish the series on Anglo-Saxon Texts, which includes David W. Porter (ed.), *Excerptiones de Prisciano: The Sources for Ælfric's Latin-Old English Grammar* (Woodbridge, 2002). Cambridge Studies in Anglo-Saxon England (CASE), published by Cambridge University Press, is another major series which publishes both editions and monographs, but note too a number of smaller ventures now gaining prominence, such as the publications of the Richard Rawlinson Center for Anglo-Saxon Studies and Manuscript Research at Western Michigan University.

[2] Most notably, *Anglo-Saxon England* (published by Cambridge University Press), the *Old English Newsletter* (sponsored by the MLA and published by the Medieval Institute, Western Michigan University), and the International Society of Anglo-Saxonists (ISAS).

[3] For the *Old English Dictionary*, see <http://chass.utoronto.ca/medieval>. For *Fontes Anglo-Saxonici*, see Fontes Anglo-Saxonici Project (ed.), *Fontes Anglo-Saxonici: World Wide Web Register*, <http://fontes.english.ox.ac.uk>; for SASLC, see Fred M. Biggs, Thomas D. Hill, Paul E. Szarmach, and E. Gordon Whatley (eds.), *The Sources of Anglo-Saxon Literary Culture*, i (Kalamazoo, Mich., 2001) and <http://www.wmich.edu/medieval/saslc>.

and teaching tools.[4] The last couple of decades have seen the emergence of the sub-field of Anglo-Latin; and a number of studies have provided us with a much stronger sense of the historical situatedness of the discipline as a whole.[5] The converging interests of historians, art historians, archaeologists, and scholars of literature and culture over a number of common projects and ideas offer an index of interdisciplinary vitality.[6] Institutional support is strong, particularly in North America and in England: to name but a few institutions, in England, the Manchester Centre for Anglo-Saxon Studies (MANCASS), now with its own publication series, provides an important venue for all things Anglo-Saxon; in the United States, the Medieval Institute at Western Michigan University offers a capacious umbrella under which Anglo-Saxon Studies is amply promoted; Canada offers, as already mentioned, the Toronto *Old English Dictionary* and related activities. There are plenty of occasional conferences for Anglo-Saxonists, many sessions sponsored at annual conferences at Leeds, Kalamazoo, and the MLA. And, judging from the number of scholars prominent in the field internationally, there is no reason to be anxious about the future, even granting the tenuous prospects for continuity that any small discipline faces.[7]

Furthermore, Anglo-Saxon Studies is amply furnished with annual bibliographies, both itemized and annotated (in *Anglo-Saxon England* and the *Old English Newsletter*). There is no shortage of state-of-the-field overviews to consult. Indeed, this form of disciplinary introspection seems to go with the territory, although it has been particularly popular since the early 1990s, when Anglo-Saxonists first responded to the challenge of contemporary critical theory.[8] Faced with such levels of analysis,

---

[4] Kevin Kiernan, *Electronic Beowulf* (London and Ann Arbor, 2000). Electronic resources and research are regularly discussed in the *Old English Newsletter*, but see also Patrick W. Conner, 'Beyond the ASPR: Electronic Editions of Old English Poetry', in Sarah Larratt Keefer and Katherine O'Brien O'Keeffe (eds.), *New Approaches to Editing Old English Verse* (Cambridge, 1998), 109–26. For the prosopography project, see <http://www.kcl.ac.uk/humanities/cch/pase>.

[5] For details, see n. 17.

[6] See, e.g., M. O. H. Carver (ed.), *The Age of Sutton Hoo: The Seventh Century in North-Western Europe* (Woodbridge, 2002). See also *Gender and Empire in the Early Medieval World*, ed. Clare A. Lees and Gillian R. Overing, *Journal of Medieval and Early Modern Studies* 34.1 (2004).

[7] Indeed, Bruce Mitchell and Fred C. Robinson's *A Guide to Old English* is now in its sixth edition (Oxford, 2001).

[8] Retrospective analyses of *The Year's Work in Old English Studies* have been offered at ten-year intervals by the *Old English Newsletter, Subsidia* series: after ten years in 1978, ed. Rowland Collins (vol. 2); after twenty years in 1989, ed. Katherine O'Brien O'Keeffe (vol. 15); and after thirty years in 2000, ed. Joseph Trahern (vol. 27). See also the detailed critique of the field by Allen J. Frantzen, *Desire for Origins: New Language, Old English and Teaching the Tradition* (New Brunswick, NJ, 1990).

it would be redundant to offer yet another overview of the field here. The field is thriving, there is ample evidence of sustained research activity, and scholars enough to train the next generation. Yet, as Allen Frantzen has recently argued, while the numbers are up, the perceived value of Anglo-Saxon Studies in the wider arenas of Medieval Studies and English Studies appears to be decreasing.[9] As indexes of the participation of Anglo-Saxonists in these communities, Frantzen points to the falling number of reviews of Anglo-Saxon books, relative to the increasing numbers published, in *Speculum*, as well as, for example, to the infrequent sponsorship of special sessions at the annual MLA conference. Statistical analysis will only get us so far. However, even as the crude tool that it is, Frantzen's analysis points towards a much less confident account of the discipline than the one I have just sketched.[10] Nicholas Howe has also recently advocated caution about the apparent vitality of the field, while T. A. Shippey's quick survey of Anglo-Saxon in popular culture argues that, unlike the Vikings for example, the Anglo-Saxons have rarely seized the popular imagination.[11] Taken together, these studies indicate the extent to which the very success of Anglo-Saxon Studies as a self-contained discipline is a symptom of its weakness as a discipline within the larger fields of Medieval Studies, English Studies, and in popular culture. In this regard, Anglo-Saxon Studies, like the Anglo-Saxons themselves, would seem to be of very minor consequence indeed.

This essay takes these two diverging views of the state of Anglo-Saxon Studies as its subject. If the field is flourishing, independent, and self-regulating, what matter that its participation in and impact on larger fields of knowledge appears to be diminishing? Taking up first the question of Anglo-Saxon Studies as an increasingly irrelevant field, I explore its situation with respect to its closest disciplinary relatives in Middle English, Medieval Studies, and English Studies. I then examine some strategies whereby Anglo-Saxon Studies maintains and promotes scholarship within the discipline itself: by what means and at what intellectual cost does Anglo-Saxon Studies foster its integrity as a discrete, vital field of knowledge? In the final section of this essay, I propose some re-

---

[9] Allen Frantzen, 'By the Numbers: Anglo-Saxon Scholarship at the Century's End', in Phillip Pulsiano and Elaine Treharne (ed.), *A Companion to Anglo-Saxon Literature* (Oxford, 2001), 472–95.

[10] The relevant details are provided by Frantzen, 'By the Numbers', 480–90.

[11] Nicholas Howe, 'The New Millennium', in Pulsiano and Treharne (eds.), *Companion to Anglo-Saxon Literature*, 496–505; T. A. Shippey, 'The Undeveloped Image: Anglo-Saxon in Popular Consciousness from Turner to Tolkien', in Donald Scragg and Carole Weinberg (eds.), *Literary Appropriations of the Anglo-Saxons from the Thirteenth to the Twentieth Centuries* (Cambridge, 2000), 215–36.

mapping of recent scholarship within Anglo-Saxon Studies that might help us move beyond the paradox of disciplinary success on the one hand and diminishing interdisciplinary capital on the other. What intellectual traffic might occur on the roads between the Medieval and the Anglo-Saxon on the map of new medieval literatures? How might more general categories of knowledge such as world, body, and belief be used to step outside familiar disciplinary categories so as to re-map Anglo-Saxon scholarship in ways that connect it to wider fields of knowledge?

Looking Forward, Looking Back

As Anglo-Saxonists work harder to advance knowledge, research, and understanding of this field, as well as to promote it, the field itself and its cultural capital are shrinking. This paradox can be illustrated with reference to *The Cambridge History of Medieval English Literature*, wherein medieval English literature begins after the Anglo-Saxon period.[12] Medievalists are thus encouraged to discard Anglo-Saxon literary culture from the 'backward and forward tracings facilitated by a genuinely diachronic approach' (p. xxii) advocated by David Wallace in his General Preface to the *History*. Yet, by the same token, Anglo-Saxonists have been reluctant to reach out to those later centuries of medieval English literature so thoroughly and innovatively explored by Wallace and his contributors. This parlous state of affairs in literary studies might be usefully contrasted with the ways in which historians handle the same territory. Here the term 'early medieval' serves comfortably (and capaciously) as a discrete category of enquiry that none the less indicates its connections to those subsequent centuries also designated medieval. Early medieval historians are actively concerned to cast their net widely, most notably as they engage the problem of assessing transitions from the late Roman world to an early medieval age that embraces north and south, east and west, in its perspectives.[13] Similarly, scholars of the history of Latin grammar and

---

[12] David Wallace (ed.), *The Cambridge History of Medieval English Literature* (Cambridge, 1999).

[13] As the journal *Early Medieval Europe* amply demonstrates. Even introductory accounts of the early medieval period take a broader cross-cultural approach than used to be the case; see, e.g., Rosamond McKitterick (ed.), *The Early Middle Ages* (Oxford, 2001). For more sophisticated and detailed analyses, see *The New Cambridge Medieval History*, ii: *c.700–c.900*, ed. Rosamond McKitterick (Cambridge, 1995), and iii: *c.900–c.1024*, ed. Timothy Reuter (Cambridge, 1999). See also Frans Theuws and Janet L. Nelson (eds.), *Rituals of Power: From Late Antiquity to the Early Middle Ages* (Leiden, Boston, and Cologne, 2000).

rhetoric, as well as of intellectual history, tend to work across the divides of the late Classical, early medieval, and medieval eras, although with variable results.[14]

The different ways in which literary scholars and historians, grammarians, and intellectual historians (as well as archaeologists) handle periodization do not merely point to the politicized, contingent, and often self-serving nature of disciplinary constructions of the past. Rather, they highlight disparities between theoretical models of historical and cultural change and existing practice. Theoretically, *The Cambridge History of Medieval English Literature* makes a strong case indeed for a dynamic and multivalent diachronic approach to the medieval period that should have profound implications for the study of the early medieval period as well. In practice, however, this approach is limited to the post-Conquest period. *The Cambridge History* is framed by a *grand récit*: medieval English literature begins with 1066 and terminates in 1547—two moments with 'revolutionary effects on all aspects of English writing' (General Preface, p. xxi). Anglo-Saxonists need not balk at this narrative, for we have another one of our own—that which spans from the moment of the conversion of the Anglo-Saxons to Christianity to the end of the period in the eleventh century. In anticipating and rethinking the 'revolution' of 1547, however, our disciplinary cousins in Middle English literary study look forward to the crucially fertile period of the fifteenth and sixteenth centuries—the Early Modern period. Looking back to the early medieval period or to Old English literature has yet to find its place in such a schema.[15] The theoretical case made for focusing the lens of medievalists on the Early Modern period is a historicist one, which aims to re-situate

---

[14] See, e.g., the fine work by Rita Copeland, *Rhetoric, Hermeneutics, and Translation in the Middle Ages* (Cambridge, 1991), and her important argument about diachrony in 'Childhood, Pedagogy, and the Literal Sense: From Late Antiquity to the Lollard Heretical Classroom', *New Medieval Literatures*, 1 (1997), 125–56. See also Martin Irvine, *The Making of Textual Culture: 'Grammatica' and Literary Theory, 350–1100* (Cambridge, 1994). Copeland and Irvine make important gestures toward early medieval vernacular materials, but this could be developed: for the field of pedagogy, e.g., see Scott Gwara (ed.) and David W. Porter (trans.), *Anglo-Saxon Conversations: The Colloquies of Ælfric Bata* (Woodbridge, 1997). See also Mary Carruthers, *The Book of Memory* (Cambridge, 1990) and *idem*, *The Craft of Thought* (Cambridge, 1998), which again deliberately stray only rarely, if fruitfully, into vernacular Anglo-Saxon texts.

[15] Given our increased specialization, it is no surprise that few scholars move either forward or backwards from their own field. Frantzen's work as an Anglo-Saxonist is exemplary in this regard; see, e.g., his *Before the Closet: Same-Sex Love from Beowulf to Angels in America* (Chicago, 1998); rare indeed are those scholars of later medieval literature who work in the earlier medieval period as well, but see Lee Patterson, 'Heroic Laconic Style: Reticence and Meaning from *Beowulf* to the Edwardians', in David Aers (ed.), *Medieval Literature and Historical Inquiry: Essays in Honour of Derek Pearsall* (Cambridge, 2000), 133–57.

synchronic modes of analysis, with their inevitable concentration on the specific and the local, within a newly revitalized diachrony. This is an argument with which few could argue. But this theoretical case, made also by, for example, David Wallace's study of Chaucer and James Simpson's investigations into the 'cultural revolution' of the sixteenth century,[16] has yet to find its practice in a diachrony that would genuinely challenge already existing boundaries between the early medieval period and the Middle Ages.

Where Anglo-Saxon Studies is concerned, discrepancies between theory and praxis take a different form. Studies of the reception of Anglo-Saxon literature in the post-Conquest era take in the eleventh to the twentieth centuries and are complemented by a growing awareness of the history of the discipline itself from the fourteenth century onwards. I think of Frantzen's *Desire for Origins*; *Anglo-Saxonism and the Construction of Social Identity*, edited by Frantzen and John D. Niles; *The Recovery of Old English*, edited by Timothy Graham; *Rewriting Old English in the Twelfth Century*, edited by Mary Swan and Elaine M. Treharne; and *Literary Appropriations of the Anglo-Saxons*, edited by D. G. Scragg and C. Weinberg.[17] These studies can be brought to bear on the theoretical question of when the Anglo-Saxon period ends (a question foreclosed by later medievalists) by providing the evidentiary basis on which the continuities (as well as discontinuities) of Anglo-Saxon culture can be argued. But this theoretical case, with all its implications for rethinking the before-and-after model of periodization, has yet to be fully addressed (although Frantzen's pioneering *Desire for Origins* laid the groundwork).[18] Even given the considerable work in this particular area of Anglo-Saxon scholarship, its practice remains firmly within the boundaries of the discipline.

---

[16] David Wallace, *Chaucerian Polity: Absolutist Lineages and Associational Forms in England and Italy* (Stanford, Calif., 1997), see his remarks on p. xiv and in n. 4 where he signals the relevance of his thinking for early medieval literature. For a similar, sustained argument that questions conventional assumptions about periodization and affirms the 'contingent nature of historical writing', see James Simpson, *Reform and Cultural Revolution*, ii: *1350–1547*, The Oxford English Literary History (Oxford, 2002), 3. Such arguments have a considerable longevity in medieval English scholarship, which makes it even more paradoxical that the early medieval period has yet to feature in them.

[17] Frantzen, *Desire for Origins*; Allen Frantzen and John D. Niles (eds.), *Anglo-Saxonism and the Construction of Social Identity* (Gainesville, Fla., 1997); Timothy Graham (ed.), *The Recovery of Old English: Anglo-Saxon Studies in the Sixteenth and Seventeenth Centuries* (Kalamazoo, Mich., 2000); Mary Swan and Elaine M. Treharne (eds.), *Rewriting Old English in the Twelfth Century* (Cambridge, 2000); and Scragg and Weinberg (eds.), *Literary Appropriations of the Anglo-Saxons*.

[18] See Frantzen's suggestive remarks in *Desire for Origins*, 18–19; see Clare A. Lees and Gillian R. Overing, 'Before History, Before Difference: Bodies, Metaphor and the Church in Anglo-Saxon England', *Yale Journal of Criticism*, 11 (1998), 315–34.

The essays edited by, for example, Swan and Treharne, address, whether to a greater or a lesser extent, the continuing presence of Anglo-Saxon in the post-Conquest period; they provoke a rethinking of the twelfth century more generally that has yet to be taken up. The era of the first European revolution in the eleventh and twelfth centuries, to quote the title of R. I. Moore's recent study,[19] offers a way of reframing analysis of the Anglo-Saxon period as well as the thirteenth century and beyond. Such a possibility is glimpsed in John Frankis's essay on Ælle and the conversion of the English that tracks the reshaping of this legend from Bede to Chaucer and Gower.[20] The same material is used more pointedly by Frantzen in *Before the Closet*, which looks back to Gregory's famous story of the angelic Angles and forward to John Bale's sixteenth-century polemical rewriting of it.[21] The collection of essays edited by Graham advances our historical understanding of Anglo-Saxon scholarship, but not in the context of the related field of Middle English scholarship, with which it might be fruitfully contrasted and compared.[22] In fact, the fifteenth and sixteenth centuries are as crucial an era for understanding the reshaping of Anglo-Saxon culture, the disciplinary history of Anglo-Saxon Studies, and the early publication of Anglo-Saxon texts as they are for the history of Middle English culture, its disciplinary origins, and the early publication of medieval English texts. These centuries offer territory on which Anglo-Saxonists and medievalists can meet to explore our disciplinary connections and differences: a place where we might meet to put our theoretical enquiries into historicist modes into practice. There is, in other words, no reason, theoretical or practical, why we cannot deliver a richer and more inclusive historiography for the medieval period as a whole, save our own limitations.

That we are all limited, both by our disciplinary training as well as our knowledge and abilities, is one of the personal issues that lurks behind our professional scholarship; it points to the need for greater use of collaborative modes than has hitherto been the case. This is one way around the recurrent tension between the two related disciplines of Anglo-Saxon Studies and Middle English Studies, which have never been entirely comfortable with the nature of that relationship. Whether viewed from the

---

[19] R. I. Moore, *The First European Revolution, c.970–1215* (Oxford, 2000).

[20] John Frankis, 'King Ælle and the Conversion of the English: The Development of a Legend from Bede to Chaucer', in Scragg and Weinberg (eds.), *Literary Appropriations of the Anglo-Saxons*, 75–92.

[21] Frantzen, *Before the Closet*, 259–78.

[22] Graham (ed.), *Recovery of Old English*.

perspective of the language or from that of the literary culture, the question of continuity (or discontinuity) between Old and Middle English has been purposefully left unresolved. Purposefully, because there is evidently much to be gained in disciplinary terms from leaving that over-simplified question open. The recent history of both disciplines suggests that English medievalists and Anglo-Saxonists have more to gain from keeping their own counsel than from sharing it in order to work across or, more radically, beyond our disciplines. Nor is it sufficient to invoke competition for cultural capital and limited financial resources by way of explanation for this divisive relationship between Old and Middle English: many other small fields within Medieval Studies (German, Italian, and Portuguese spring to mind) find themselves faced with the same institutional problems. Rather, given the necessity of working under conditions of limited resources with which to deliver distinction and capital, we need to address the reluctance of institutions and individuals, disciplines and sub-disciplines (hence research and enquiry in general), to engage across disciplinary boundaries even as we increasingly invoke the necessity of so doing. Genuine interdisciplinarity is a threat to disciplinarity. Strategies of co-operation and collaboration are thus risky. They are perhaps especially so for disciplines like Anglo-Saxon Studies. Why look forward to medieval English and/or the pre-modern (as it is increasingly termed) when the rewards of an investment of Anglo-Saxon Studies in the early modern, modern, or post-modern are far from self-evident?

As other to modernity in so many regards, Anglo-Saxon Studies has now as little to gain from demystifying its status as an originary discipline as it had in earlier generations. Our 'desire for origins' (to quote Frantzen) continues to play a major role in shaping the field, from both within and without. Installed at the point of origin, rather than merely furnishing one place among many from which to begin, the field acts as a foil both to Middle English Studies as well as, more broadly, to the modernity that some scholars of Middle English view as their ultimate theoretical horizon. Indeed, it is because it is installed as a foil that Anglo-Saxon Studies holds in place the binary opposition between the medieval and the modern that used to characterize relationships between the Middle Ages in general and the Renaissance. In this regard, as Gillian R. Overing and I have argued elsewhere, Anglo-Saxon Studies might be regarded not as pre-medieval or pre-modern, but as a pre-historical discipline.[23] Mystified in this way from both within and without the discipline, it is no

---

[23] Lees and Overing, 'Before History, Before Difference'.

surprise that Anglo-Saxonists appear content to reap the professional rewards of maintaining the inward-looking traditions of our discipline: how often do we invoke our rightful claims to be students of the first European vernacular of any substance, of the origins of literacy, historiography, law, and polity?

It is, of course, Medieval Studies more generally that is supposed to forestall such disciplinary isolation and alienation. Whether by providing an alternative institutional or intellectual home for Anglo-Saxonists, Medieval Studies is a place where we can make use of our field's wider network of affiliations. Here too, however, competition for capital (symbolic or otherwise) between those disciplines that make up Medieval Studies constrains the nurturing of networks of relationships across it. The emergent methodologies of interdisciplinary, comparative, and cross-cultural approaches to this field continue to operate side by side with the more archaic and archaizing constraints of disciplines and fields. Innovative attempts to think across disciplines, cultures, and periods, including the Anglo-Saxon (some of the best of which have been produced under the aegis of feminist medieval studies), amount to the thematizing of connections, as opposed to the rethinking of disciplinarity and the knowledge it produces. This is not to underestimate the many promising signs for the future offered by such thematic studies of, for example, gender and sexuality, but to stress that, once fed back into the discipline of Anglo-Saxon Studies, this work inevitably finds itself compromised. Witness, for example, the prolonged struggle of the *Old English Newsletter* to find a category for feminist, theoretical, or interdisciplinary research in its annual surveys of the *Year's Work*.[24] How disciplinary structures accommodate interdisciplinary work and how interdisciplinary structures accommodate disciplinary work are symptoms of the inevitable tensions between disciplinarity and interdisciplinarity.

There is every reason to surmise that the discrete nature of disciplines such as Anglo-Saxon Studies will be sustained alongside such interdisciplines as Medieval Studies, but it is important to register the asymmetries of these structures even as they seek to complement one another. There are real intellectual losses that derive from the isolation of Anglo-Saxon Studies as a separate, though flourishing, discipline. One is the consequence of the severing of Anglo-Saxon literature from medieval English

---

[24] The varied history of category definition in *The Year's Work in Old English Studies* would require an essay in its own right; suffice it to say here that the category of gender has hardly been stable over the past twenty or so years.

literature, to the mutual impoverishment of both fields. I illustrate this point on the basis of *The Cambridge History of Medieval English Literature,* but I do so not in order to criticize one more time a book that has already had a bad press from Anglo-Saxonists,[25] but because, as I have already argued, the *History* has made a strong theoretical case for the Anglo-Saxon period to be included in its historicist project. In practice, however, the absence of Anglo-Saxon culture from the *History* has a very particular impact on many of its individual chapters as well as on the volume as a whole. Time and again, contributors are put in the position of referring back to the place that is Anglo-Saxon England even though that place has, in fact, no place in the *History* from which to speak. Christopher Cannon acknowledges the problem in his chapter, 'Monastic Productions', which finds itself beginning after the 'so-called monastic centuries' (p. 316), which it has to accommodate in only a page or so of summary (pp. 316–17). A similar problem besets Richard Firth Green's chapter on law, which notes but cannot address the 'great flood of vernacular legal writing in Anglo-Saxon England' (p. 408). To take another example, David Lawton's 'Englishing the Bible' wrestles in vain with the 'long efflorescence of biblical translation and paraphrase in Anglo-Saxon England' (p. 454). Other studies deal with the issue by omission. Aside from Seth Lerer's chapter on Old English (pp. 7–34) that traces an afterlife for a period that here has no life of its own, there is no mention of the important era of tenth-century Anglo-Latin literature in Christopher Baswell's chapter on 'Latinitas', no discussion of the profound importance of vernacularity in the Anglo-Saxon period. Other chapters turn on an implicit and problematic rhetoric of before-and-after (this is especially marked in Andrew Galloway's 'Writing History in England'). Such rhetoric necessarily lacks any critical purchase on the period that comes 'before' (that is, Anglo-Saxon England), and on occasion betrays a worrying ignorance of that period in any case.[26] All this in a history explicitly dedicated to the multiple histories, the mobility, and multivalence of medieval culture in the British Isles.

The Cambridge History of Medieval English Literature, however, does not simply point to some of the intellectual constraints under which a medieval English literature without Anglo-Saxon literature operates; it can also be used to highlight some of the areas of Anglo-Saxon Studies

---

[25] As Frantzen, 'By the Numbers', makes clear.

[26] See Galloway's at best cursory comments on the writing of history in Anglo-Saxon England, in Wallace (ed.), *Cambridge History,* 256–7.

that could most benefit from interdisciplinary exchange. By a profound irony, areas such as monasticism, the law, biblical studies, Latinity, sanctity, and vernacularity—all topics of central concern to Middle English scholarship—are the focus of much important work in Anglo-Saxon Studies during the period just before and just after the publication of *The Cambridge History*. The field of monasticism is, as Christopher Cannon points out, an enormous one for the Anglo-Saxon period, but I note here simply Mechthild Gretsch's important study of the Benedictine reforms, as well as the publication of the major editions of Ælfric and of the anonymous homilists, and major studies of Wulfstan.[27] Patrick Wormald's study of Anglo-Saxon law and literature, Richard Marsden's analysis of the Old Testament, R. M. Liuzza's edition of the West Saxon Gospels, the burgeoning field of Anglo-Latin, and editions of the lives of Margaret by Mary Clayton and Hugh Magennis have not only contributed much to the study of the Bible, Latinity, and sanctity, but have also refined our understanding of the use of English in these domains.[28] Analysis of Anglo-Saxon diplomas, such as charters, has also given us a much stronger sense of the reach of literacy throughout the period.[29] Our intellectual interests are not so different from those of our later medieval colleagues. To the contrary, we share, of course, the same intellectual communities. Historicist modes that emphasize mobility across synchronic and diachronic ways of exploring the past in theory *and* in practice provide the opportunity for better use of the complex networks of critical and cultural affiliations that cross the various fields of Medieval

[27] Mechthild Gretsch, *The Intellectual Foundations of the English Benedictine Reform* (Cambridge, 1999). Two of the most important editions of Ælfric's works are those by Clemoes and Godden (see n. 1 above); see also D. G. Scragg (ed.), *The Vercelli Homilies*, Early English Text Society, os 300 (Oxford, 1992), and for Wulfstan, among other important studies, Jonathan Wilcox, 'The Wolf on Shepherds: Wulfstan, Bishops, and the Context of the *Sermo Lupi ad Anglos*', in Paul E. Szarmach (ed.), *Old English Prose: Basic Readings* (New York and London, 2001), 395–418.

[28] Patrick Wormald, *The Making of English Law: King Alfred to the Twelfth Century*, i (Oxford, 1999); R. Marsden, *The Text of the Old Testament in Anglo-Saxon England* (Cambridge, 1995); Paul G. Remley, *Old English Biblical Verse* (Cambridge, 1996); R. M. Liuzza (ed.), *The Old English Gospels*, i, Early English Text Society, os 304 (Oxford, 1994); ii, Early English Text Society, os 314 (Oxford, 2000); there is as yet no history of Anglo-Latin literature before 1066; but see the general survey by Joseph P. McGowan, 'An Introduction to the Corpus of Anglo-Latin Literature', in Pulsiano and Treharne (eds.), *Companion to Anglo-Saxon Literature*, 11–49. See also Mary Clayton and Hugh Magennis (eds.), *The Old English Lives of St Margaret* (Cambridge, 1994).

[29] Most notably the two essays by Kathryn A. Lowe, 'Lay Literacy in Anglo-Saxon England and the Development of the Chirograph', in Phillip Pulsiano and Elaine Treharne (eds.), *Anglo-Saxon Manuscripts and their Heritage* (Aldershot, 1998), 161–204, and 'The Nature and Effect of the Anglo-Saxon Vernacular Will', *Journal of Legal History*, 19 (1998), 23–61.

Studies such as Old and Middle English. This is one area in which *New Medieval Literatures* must continue to play an important role. Like other publications that offer a home for the multi-disciplinary, the cross-cultural, and the theoretically innovative (such as the *Journal of Medieval and Early Modern Studies* and *Exemplaria*), *New Medieval Literatures* demonstrates the strength of our shared intellectual communities.

If Old English and Middle English Studies need not live out their destiny as uncomfortable neighbours in Medieval Studies, what of our shared affinity with the broader intellectual and institutional arena that is English Studies? From this perspective, Anglo-Saxon Studies would seem to stand on a firmer footing than it did twenty or so years ago. The path-breaking article by Allen Frantzen and Charles Venegoni that offers a convenient point of departure in charting the history of the engagement of Anglo-Saxonists with critical theory was quickly joined by a number of other radical interpretive projects that articulate and explore the field's encounter with critical theory.[30] Such work has made (and continues to make) a space where Anglo-Saxon Studies is one of many interconnected fields engaged on the common project that is English Studies, whether our methodological affinities are with, for example, cultural studies, gender studies, queer theory, or post-colonial studies. And such studies continue to hold out much promise in their creation of a broader symbolic map on which the discipline might be placed. Anglo-Saxon Studies will certainly remain a minority field within English Studies more generally, but it is by no means the only one—take, for example, the situation of Eighteenth-Century Studies. All the (traditionally designated) fields of historical literary study struggle with the diminished sense of the historical and the commodification of the past that is the bequest of late twentieth-century society. Yet in this regard, the astonishing success of Seamus Heaney's translation of *Beowulf,* both in reorienting the status of Old English literature in the canon of English literature as represented by *The Norton Anthology* and as a poem in its own right, offers many ways to think about the work that this old poem performs in contemporary culture.[31] To return to critical theory, there can be little doubt that it has not only facilitated major research in Anglo-Saxon Studies (to the extent that

[30] Allen Frantzen and Charles L. Venegoni, 'The Desire for Origins: An Archaeology of Anglo-Saxon Studies', *Style*, 20 (1986), 142–56. See also Frantzen, *Desire for Origins*, and *idem* (ed.), *Speaking Two Languages: Traditional Disciplines and Contemporary Theory in Medieval Studies* (Albany, NY, 1991), together with, among other fine studies, Gillian R. Overing, *Language, Sign, and Gender in 'Beowulf'* (Carbondale and Edwardsville, Ill., 1990).

[31] Seamus Heaney, *Beowulf: A New Translation* (London, 1999), and also Daniel Donoghue (ed.), *Beowulf: A Verse Translation* (New York and London, 2002).

even the occasional essay in *Anglo-Saxon England* now draws on theoretical models from outside the discipline), but has also deepened perceptions of its affiliation with one of its disciplinary and institutional homes. *Before the Closet*, Frantzen's cross-temporal, cross-disciplinary exploration of queer theory offers in this regard another model for future work in its staging of a complex encounter between queer theory, the Anglo-Saxon past, medieval and Early Modern literature, and the American present wherein the religious, sexual, operatic, and personal find a single voice. Here, then, is an Anglo-Saxon Studies open to the many languages of our disciplinary and intellectual affiliations.

It is not possible, therefore, to consider Anglo-Saxon Studies as a discrete discipline (however much and for whatever reasons we try to do so). The field is not self-contained, coherent, and self-regulating. Rather it is a force-field crossed by various relationships and affinities, with all the tensions, ambivalences, and anxieties that implies. Old, Middle, medieval, modern: these terms point to some of the discipline's relationships that are conceived in terms of temporal divisions. Gender, cultural studies, historicism—these paradigms of intellectual thought are examples of just some of the affinities that cross temporal and disciplinary divisions. Awareness of mobility of place and time fostered by these latter categories of critical theory—that is to say, interdisciplinarity—sits uncomfortably but productively with an awareness of fixed chronological boundaries— that is to say, disciplinarity. An Anglo-Saxon Studies more invested in maintaining and reproducing its disciplinary status than in fostering its multiple interdisciplinary relationships has much to lose in terms of cultural capital and its knowledge. Behind the considerable work of the discipline that I outlined as the successful story of Anglo-Saxon Studies at the beginning of this essay, I detect considerable anxiety.

Traditionality and Disciplinarity

That Anglo-Saxon Studies has been invested in the production of scholarship that both maintains and fosters its traditions, particularly over the last decade or so, is as evident from its enthusiastic support of the large-scale, multi-year, research project as it is from the drift towards the production of numerous introductory companions, encyclopaedias, and anthologies of critical essays that are designed for both beginning students and more established scholars. These are phenomena by no means unique to Anglo-Saxon Studies, although in a field as small and as coherent as this, they do stand out as particularly marked. *Fontes Anglo-Saxonici* has successfully sustained a long-lasting methodology—that of source study—in the face of some not unreasonable criticism from a number of quarters, both within and without Anglo-Saxon Studies.[32] Like its close cousin, the *Sources of Anglo-Saxon Literary Culture* (SASLC), *Fontes* not only shapes the field but tends to promote unexamined 'fantasies of total knowledge' (as Nicholas Howe puts it) that haunt such scholarship.[33] This is not to undermine the significance of these projects, but rather to see that significance for what it is—the production of a research tool that aids analysis, but does not necessarily determine it.

The trend towards recycling and repackaging already established research in the form of critical anthologies, essay collections, companions, and encyclopaedias would appear, on the face of it, to be a different phenomenon altogether. The Basic Readings in Anglo-Saxon England series (BRASE), in which a few new articles find their place alongside earlier reprinted ones, however, does not simply offer a paradigm for a number of other similar anthologies, but exemplifies the ways in which new scholarship is framed by normative expectations of what such scholarship should be. That is to say, like the source projects, this area of endeavour is similarly framed by already established, rarely contested, parameters of genre, form, provenance, and critical convention.[34] Part of the success of BRASE derives from its conception of a multi-tiered audience of students, beginning scholars, teachers, and established scholars. This is certainly an adept marketing technique, but, as even a quick glimpse of the contents of any single volume in the series confirms, one size really does not fit all.

Critical anthologies, like those companions to the field offered by Malcolm Godden and Michael Lapidge (1991), or by Phillip Pulsiano and Elaine Treharne (2001), are similarly multi-functional.[35] They witness to a long-standing, laudable aim of Anglo-Saxon Studies: the dissemination of high-quality research to students (the vast majority of whom will never progress beyond introductory levels), who are thereby provided with a constant stream of textbooks, critical companions, or literary histories.

---

[32] Frantzen includes a convenient summary of the debate in 'By the Numbers', 490–3.

[33] Nicholas Howe, 'The New Millennium', in Pulsiano and Treharne (eds.), *Companion to Anglo-Saxon Literature*, 502.

[34] A good example of this tendency is Szarmach (ed.), *Old English Prose: Basic Readings*, but it is characteristic of all the volumes in this series.

[35] Malcolm Godden and Michael Lapidge (eds.), *The Cambridge Companion to Old English Literature* (Cambridge, 1991); Pulsiano and Treharne (eds.), *Companion to Anglo-Saxon Literature*.

They also offer, therefore, a substantial resource for teachers and more established scholars alike. In consequence, such publications, like BRASE, provide a guaranteed market for their publishers. The market for works of Anglo-Saxon scholarship is not huge, as publishers well know. Brute economies of scale at the various presses that do continue to publish Anglo-Saxon books demand that publishers recoup their costs not only though library sales but by course-book adoption. (Whence the popularity of *Beowulf* critical anthologies.) One consequence of this is that new and often important scholarship has its first airing not in the well-tried format of the article or the monograph, but in the anthology, literary history, or companion to literary studies. The price paid for this compromise is clear: more recent scholarship, methodologies, and ideas are rarely allowed space to develop, remaining instead suggestive and skeletal in form, while more established perspectives are characterized by a high level of redundancy and repetition.

Let me consider the recently published *Companion to Anglo-Saxon Literature*, edited by Pulsiano and Treharne by way of illustration. This is a huge (529 pages) and important survey of the field, aimed at both the beginning and the more established scholar, as was its close relative, predecessor and competitor, *The Cambridge Companion to Old English Literature*, edited by Godden and Lapidge. *A Companion* is also arranged thematically, again like *The Cambridge Companion*, and divided into five parts: Contexts and Perspectives, Readings: Cultural Framework and Heritage; Genres and Modes; Intertextualities: Sources and Influence; and Debates and Issues. Some chapters provide generous and thoughtful introductions to aspects of the discipline that update earlier work from other literary histories, such as the essays on Anglo-Latin literature and Anglo-Latin prose by Joseph McGowan (pp. 9–49 and 296–323), or the rather more rudimentary surveys of religious material pre- and post-Benedictine reform by Susan Irvine, Joyce Hill, or Roy Liuzza.[36] Other essays are similarly pitched at the introductory level, but take on, at least in embryo, more challenging critical concepts—questions of authorship and anonymity, or audience, reception literacy, and manuscript production (as outlined by Mary Swan, Hugh Magennis, and Michelle P. Brown[37]). A third, welcome category of essay reintroduces to the field

[36] Susan Irvine, 'Religious Context: Pre-Benedictine Reform Period', 135–50; Joyce Hill, 'The Benedictine Reform and Beyond', 151–69; and Roy M. Liuzza, 'Religious Prose', 233–50.

[37] Mary Swan, 'Authorship and Anonymity', 71–83; Hugh Magennis, 'Audience(s), Reception, Literacy', 84–101; Michelle P. Brown, 'Anglo-Saxon Manuscript Production: Issues of Making and Using', 102–17.

issues of Continental relations often neglected in recent decades—
Germanic (two essays, by Patricia Lendinara and by Rolf Bremmer[38]) and
Scandinavian (Robert E. Bjork[39])—that find their place alongside analyses of Irish and Patristic traditions (by Thomas Hall and Charles D.
Wright, respectively[40]). But the *Companion* also offers essays that incorporate the introductory with new material and theoretical perspectives:
the essay on religious poetry by Patrick W. Conner (pp. 251–67) asks us to
think (at long last!) about just how the religion in such poetry functions,
while Donald G. Scragg (pp. 268–80) offers an outstanding survey of secular prose (a category often so mixed that it can be used to include anything that cannot be accommodated by other, more familiar categories).
Finally, Part V offers a group of essays on post-Conquest issues of continuity (by Treharne), disciplinary history—both national and international (by Timothy Graham, J. R. Hall, and Hans Sauer[41]), and concludes
with the two more speculative articles on the field at the end of the last
millennium to which I have already referred in this essay (by Frantzen and
Howe[42]). But there is also much repetition of material across chapter and
section divisions: the story of Cædmon and his so-called Hymn does
work, whether in the form of passing reference or more sustained analysis
in nine of the chapters, a third of the total number of chapters; the conversion (and/or *Adventus Saxonum*) surfaces in eight. While the latter
would benefit from a more sustained analysis in its own right, given its
cultural importance, the former—Bede's story of Cædmon—maintains,
by virtue of its repetition, its status as an uncontested originary event for
any understanding of Anglo-Saxon literature.

As this brief survey of its contents suggests, *A Companion to Anglo-
Saxon Literature* combines the introductory and the advanced, the
innovative and the established, with varying degrees of success. It is not
surprising, then, that the *Companion* thus bears marked similarity to earlier literary histories and companions, such as *A New Critical History for
Old English Literature* or *The Cambridge Companion*, edited by Godden

---

[38] Patricia Lendinara, 'The Germanic Background', 121–34, and Rolf Bremmer, 'Continental Germanic Influences', 375–87.

[39] Robert E. Bjork, 'Scandinavian Relations', 388–99.

[40] Thomas Hall, 'Biblical and Patristic Learning', 327–44, and Charles D. Wright, 'The Irish
Tradition', 345–74.

[41] Elaine Treharne, 'English in the Post-Conquest Period', 403–14; Timothy Graham, 'Anglo-
Saxon Studies: Sixteenth to Eighteenth Centuries', 415–33; J. R. Hall, 'Anglo-Saxon Studies in
the Nineteenth Century: England, Denmark and America', 434–54; Hans Sauer, 'Anglo-Saxon
Studies in the Nineteenth Century: Germany, Austria, Switzerland', 455–71.

[42] Frantzen, 'By the Numbers', and Howe, 'The New Millennium'.

and Lapidge.[43] The complementarity of these successive handbooks is entirely to my point—the many connections and themes shared across these books point the reader in the direction of a consensus about just what Anglo-Saxon Studies is. The parameters of the field have broadened but remain safely within established conventions: a high regard for sources, genre, and theme, an emphasis on cultural contact, language, and transmission. That three of the essays in *A Companion to Anglo-Saxon Literature* draw attention to the anxious workings of tradition both in the discipline (Frantzen and Howe) or in the specific genre of religious poetry (Conner) is also germane: traditionality, only now emerging as a topic of concern for Anglo-Saxon Studies, is an important dimension both of the discipline and of the cultural work that much Anglo-Saxon literature itself performs.[44]

It is equally clear from *A Companion to Anglo-Saxon Literature* (as from the earlier *Cambridge Companion*) what the field is not about. Here is found no historicist approach to, or cultural analysis of, gender, the body, ethnicity, race, rank, ideology, the economy, aesthetics, or indeed any sustained encounter with modern critical theory, be it post-colonial, materialist, or post-structuralist. (In this respect, the contrast with *The Cambridge History of Medieval English Literature* is profound.) That there has been much fine recent (and not so recent) work on all of these aspects of the history of the Anglo-Saxon period that has not found its way into these companions is another indication of the extent to which the field has collectively invested in its traditional strengths. Other mappings of Old English criticism have been bolder, while still articulating their concerns firmly within the discrete boundaries of the discipline. Katherine O'Brien O'Keeffe's modestly titled *Reading Old English Texts* (1997) echoes Edward B. Irving Jr's earlier and resonantly titled *A Reading of Beowulf* (1968), but also draws on (in the Introduction) the trope of a conversation between past and present disciplinary concerns.[45] A similar trope structured the collection of essays on Old and Middle English literature entitled *Speaking Two Languages*.[46] Unlike this earlier collection,

---

[43] Stanley B. Greenfield and Daniel G. Calder, *A New Critical History of Old English Literature* (New York and London, 1986), itself the successor to Greenfield's *A Critical History of Old English Literature* (London, 1966).

[44] See also Clare A. Lees, *Tradition and Belief: Religious Writing in Late Anglo-Saxon England* (Minneapolis, 1999).

[45] Katherine O'Brien O'Keeffe (ed.), *Reading Old English Texts* (Cambridge, 1997), 1–19. See also Edward B. Irving, Jr, *A Reading of 'Beowulf'* (New Haven, 1968), and *idem*, *Rereading 'Beowulf'* (Philadelphia, 1989).

[46] As outlined by Frantzen, *Speaking Two Languages*, pp. ix–xv.

however, *Reading Old English Texts* takes Anglo-Saxon Studies alone as its object of scholarly interest and asserts with little qualification the importance of traditional methodologies as the basis for more contemporary theoretical ones. Comparative approaches in Anglo-Saxon Studies are explored by Michael Lapidge without any apparent need to connect them to the dynamic field of contemporary comparatist scholarship; historicist approaches are firmly grounded in Anglo-Saxon disciplinary traditions past and present (by Nicholas Howe); the (inevitable, it would seem) essay on source study (by Scragg) happily ignores any critical challenge to its theoretical basis or methodological apparatus.[47] That methodologies for reading Anglo-Saxon texts are not solely the domain of Anglo-Saxonists is explored in the essays on feminism (by Lees) and post-structuralism (by Carol Braun Pasternack).[48] Overall, however, *Reading Old English Texts* demonstrates how comfortably the critical anthology can be used to assimilate theoretical methodological approaches that actually contest some of the structural principles that traditionally shape the field.

More recent is *Old English Literature*, edited by R. M. Liuzza, an anthology that is entirely comprised of essays first published in the late 1970s to the late 1990s. Like *Old English Texts*, this collection aims to situate its work within the horizon of contemporary theory and methods by offering 'a kind of blueprint for thinking about Old English' (p. xxxiii). This particular blueprint, as far as I am concerned, has already found its way into the classroom as well as the study because of its convenient and canny assembly of well-thumbed articles. Here are offered no fewer than three readings of the Cædmon episode (by Katherine O'Brien O'Keeffe, Kevin S. Kiernan, and Gillian R. Overing and Lees),[49] the last of which makes ample use of the first two, two on *The Battle of Maldon* (by Fred C. Robinson and John D. Niles[50]), and four on the Anglo-Saxon elegies

---

[47] Michael Lapidge, 'The Comparative Approach'; Nicholas Howe, 'Historicist Approaches'; and D. G. Scragg, 'Source Study', in O'Brien O'Keeffe (ed.), *Reading Old English Texts*, 20–38, 79–100, 39–58.

[48] Clare A. Lees, 'At a Crossroads: Old English and Feminist Criticism', and Carol Braun Pasternack, 'Post-Structuralist Theories: The Subject and the Text', in O'Brien O'Keeffe (ed.), *Reading Old English Texts*, 146–69 and 170–222.

[49] Roy M. Liuzza (ed.), *Old English Literature: Critical Essays* (New Haven, 2002), with full publication histories for each essay on pp. vii–ix. Katherine O'Brien O'Keeffe, 'Orality and the Developing Text of Cædmon's *Hymn*', 79–102; Kevin S. Kiernan, 'Reading Cædmon's Hymn with Someone Else's Glosses', 103–24; Clare A. Lees and Gillian R. Overing, 'Birthing Bishops and Fathering Poets: Bede, Hild, and the Relations of Cultural Production', 125–56.

[50] Fred C. Robinson, 'God, Death, and Loyalty in *The Battle of Maldon*', 425–44; John D. Niles, 'Maldon and Mythopoesis', 445–74.

(Bjork, Margrét Gunnársdottir Champion, Peter Orton, and Shari Horner[51]). Also included is such well-known work as Stephanie Hollis's on Wulfstan's *Sermo Lupi*, Godden's on the mind, Carol Braun Pasternack on style in *The Dream of the Rood*, Howe's study of reading, Susan Kelly's analysis of lay literacy, and the glorious 'The Making of *Angelcynn*' by Sarah Foot.[52] The anthology successfully carves out a place for itself by avoiding treading on the toes of other collections (there is virtually no reduplication of essays), and by grounding its territorial claims on Anglo-Saxon literature that is often taught (Ælfric's *Colloquy*, Wulfstan's *Sermo Lupi*, the elegies, *The Battle of Maldon)* but not half as often as is *Beowulf.*[53] That is to say, the rationale for such an anthology is, once again, that of actually existing Anglo-Saxon Studies.

Actually existing Anglo-Saxon Studies, when judged both by the proliferation of anthologies and companions and by the overall confidence of the field, has found a way to thrive by drawing on its disciplinary strengths. The reiteration of traditional paradigms, like traditionality itself, however, is a defence against that which is perceived, whether consciously or (more likely) unconsciously, as a threat. The demon here may well take the face of modern critical theory, but the discipline works hard to contain such challenges. After all, theory (thus invoked and reified) has been accommodated by the discipline as a means of bolstering its boundaries for some time now, as the essay collections edited by O'Brien O'Keeffe, Liuzza, and Pulsiano and Treharne demonstrate. Frantzen's *Desire for Origins* pointed out over ten years ago that contemporary ways of interpreting the past have always structured the discipline, though not necessarily with the conservative, conserving force now evident in the repeated production of companions and introductory guides to the field. We might reasonably ask what lies behind our persistent need to define Anglo-Saxon Studies in such familiar ways. At stake here is the field itself, a fear of change, and the inevitable loss contingent upon such change: the

---

[51] Robert E. Bjork, '*Sundor æt Rune*: The Voluntary Exile of The Wanderer', 315–27; Margrét Gunnarsdóttir Champion, 'From Plaint to Praise: Language as Cure in "The Wanderer"', 328–52; Peter Orton, 'The Form and Structure of *The Seafarer*', 353–80; Shari Horner, 'En/Closed Subjects: *The Wife's Lament* and the Culture of Early Medieval Female Monasticism', 381–91.

[52] Stephanie Hollis, 'The Thematic Structure of the *Sermo Lupi*', 182–203; M. R. Godden, 'Anglo-Saxons on the Mind', 284–314; Carol Braun Pasternack, 'Stylistic Disjunctions in *The Dream of the Rood*', 404–24; Nicholas Howe, 'The Cultural Construction of Reading in Anglo-Saxon England', 1–22; Susan Kelly, 'Anglo-Saxon Lay Society and the Written Word', 23–50; Sarah Foot, 'The Making of *Angelcynn*: English Identity before the Norman Conquest', 51–78.

[53] Katherine O'Brien O'Keeffe's 'Orality and the Developing Text of Cædmon's Hymn', e.g., is also reprinted in Mary P. Richards (ed.), *Anglo-Saxon Manuscripts: Basic Reading* (New York and London, 1994), 221–50.

fear, in sum, that we might compromise the scholarly home we have worked so hard to build and maintain, and in which we believe so deeply. A collective willingness to recognize that responses to change need not only take the form of defensive and anxious assimilation, or that all intellectual growth is won at the cost of loss, is required if and only if we want Anglo-Saxon Studies to have a currency wider than it now has. The stakes are high, I would argue, not only because the field has so much to offer related disciplines and because those disciplines have much to offer us. Beyond actually existing Anglo-Saxon Studies lies another Anglo-Saxon Studies that would offer powerful new ways to think about and respond to the period itself. Such an Anglo-Saxon Studies might offer a place where much of our recent scholarship can be better appreciated for its potential to transform existing fields of knowledge.

World, Body, Belief

World, body and belief: these three words, and the interrelated categories of knowledge that they imply, suggest a way to reposition analytically existing Anglo-Saxon Studies in order to highlight its responsiveness to systems of thought larger, arguably more responsible, and certainly more flexible than those currently offered by the discipline. I use these terms as a way, in short, to look beyond the discipline from the perspective of the discipline itself, and to address concepts of exploration and definition shared with colleagues in related fields.

In contrast to the insularity of existing Anglo-Saxon Studies, Anglo-Saxon England, although geographically insular, was hardly an isolated culture. In recognition of this most obvious fact, issues of world—whether of making, exploring, defining, reckoning, or building worlds—connect the flurry of recent articles that promise a post-colonial Anglo-Saxon Studies to other areas of Anglo-Saxon literature currently under investigation. Articles by Uppinder Mehan and David Townsend, Kathleen Biddick, Kathy Lavezzo, and Kathleen Davis collectively explore colonial and post-colonial ways of staging and thereby reassessing Anglo-Saxon encounters with the old Roman Empire and with the newer *imperium* of Roman Christianity (which are themselves but two worlds that might be examined under the broad category of the new and the old worlds of Anglo-Saxon England).[54] In creating a place in which to think

[54] Uppinder Mehan and David Townsend, ' "Nation" and the Gaze of the Other in Eighth-Century Northumbria', *Comparative Literature*, 53 (2001), 1–26; Kathleen Biddick, 'Bede's

about nation building and Englishness before the advent of the nation state, about the codification of memory in the form of narrative history authorized by king and monk, or about relationships between core and peripheral models of empire and colony, two of these articles (Mehan and Townsend, Lavezzo) have almost obsessively returned to the famous scene of Pope Gregory the Great's vision of the Angles in the slave market of Rome (as recounted by Bede, the earlier anonymous *Life of Gregory*, or the later, tenth-century Ælfrician *Life*).[55] Biddick too makes inventive (and sometimes improbable) use of Bede, while Kathleen Davis takes the much anthologized and discussed Letter (or Preface) to Gregory's *Pastoral Care* by King Alfred as her subject of analysis. In this way we find, rightly perhaps, that dialectical work in a post-colonial Anglo-Saxon Studies can be done in the early, middle, or later periods of the era, and with our most familiar texts and authors.

We can enlarge the territorial reach of this major work, however, by connecting it to other equally important studies that draw on ways of thinking about the world. Early medieval historians offer the path forward here, as in so many other avenues, with studies of the network of international relationships that connect Anglo-Saxon England (from the fourth and fifth centuries to the eleventh) to the Continent, and Continental Europe to those early medieval worlds once conceived as peripheral to Europe itself. Once the mainstay and central focus of any account of the early Middle Ages, French and German history is now more strongly articulated in dynamic relation to the history of the Anglo-Saxon, Scandinavian, Irish, Byzantine, Spanish, and Islamic worlds. There are many ways of thinking about empire and colony in an early medieval world so conceived that would recontextualize a focus on Bede's, Alfred's, or Ælfric's Anglo-Saxon England with their ideas of Rome and Romanness alone.[56] Indeed, Anne Savage's recent article on the Old English poem *Exodus* offers a meditation on the ways in which 'native' Germanic culture colonized scriptural poetry, repositioning the old dichotomy and/or synthesis of the two worlds of Germanic and Christian

---

Blush: Postcards from Bali, Bombay, Palo Alto', in *The Shock of Medievalism* (Durham, NC, and London, 1998), 83–101; Kathy Lavezzo, 'Another Country: Ælfric and the Production of English Identity', *New Medieval Literatures*, 3 (1999), 67–93; and Kathleen Davis, 'National Writing in the Ninth Century: A Reminder for Postcolonial Thinking about the Nation', *Journal of Medieval and Early Modern Studies*, 28 (1998), 611–37.

[55] As does Frantzen, in *Before the Closet*, 259–78.

[56] A good start are the chapters by Ian Wood ('Culture') and Jonathan Shepherd ('Europe and the Wider World') in McKitterick (ed.), *Early Middle Ages*, 167–98 and 201–42, but see also *The New Cambridge Medieval History*, ii and iii.

culture within the broad sweep of colonial studies. Her argument might be pushed further: might we not think that the encounter between the old world of *Germania* and the new world of Latin Christendom was actually created in Anglo-Saxon England, in part by a poetics that collectively and deliberately looked back to the mythic past of an old world?[57] In a similar, though more historical vein, possibilities for exploring Anglo-Saxon identities in place and time are opened up by the emphasis on local and regional studies of the period (many of which have been published by Leicester University Press), which present evidence for local and social, national and international identities; evidence, for example, for the relationship between the Northumbrian and the *Angli*, the Roman Christian and the Irish Christian.[58] Put side by side with Hugh Magennis's survey of concepts of community in Old English literature, notions of the communal, the local, the poetic, and the worldly find new expression.[59] Here, then, are means enough to recalibrate the *longue durée* with the historically specific and local.

Cultural locations of time, place, and self, as suggested by the geographies of space explored by Marijane Osborn and Gillian R. Overing in *Landscapes of Desire,* can reposition the self-reflexive cultural world of *Beowulf,* on the one hand, and the Germanic or English *Beowulf,* on the other.[60] But *Landscapes of Desire* also invites meditation on, and comparison with, the conventions of the natural world as used in Anglo-Saxon poetry, the political dimensions of the pastoral (so close to the nerve-centre of the Carolingian court as well as to readings of that old chestnut of Cædmon and his hymn), or the religious space of the apocryphal (the place of heaven and hell).[61] Cultural geographies are explored in the great historiographical and philosophical genres that underpin so much

---

[57] Anne Savage, 'The Old English *Exodus* and the Colonization of the Promised Land', *New Medieval Literatures,* iv (2001), 39–60.

[58] See, e.g., the collection of essays in William O. Frazier and Andrew Tyrrel (eds.), *Social Identity in Early Medieval Britain* (London and New York, 2000). A study with a more cultural focus is Patrick W. Conner, *Anglo-Saxon Exeter: A Tenth-Century Cultural History* (Woodbridge, 1993).

[59] Hugh Magennis, *Images of Community in Old English Poetry* (Cambridge, 1996).

[60] Marijane Osborn and Gillian R. Overing, *Landscapes of Desire: Partial Stories of the Medieval Scandinavian World* (Minneapolis, 1994). See also John M. Hill, *The Cultural World in 'Beowulf'* (Toronto, 1995).

[61] Jennifer Neville, *Representations of the Natural World in Old English Poetry* (Cambridge, 1999), is the beginning of such a meditation. See also Ananya Kabir, *Paradise, Death and Doomsday in Anglo-Saxon Literature* (Cambridge, 2001), and Catherine Clarke's doctoral dissertation, 'The *locus amoenus* in Old English: *Guthlac A* and its Cultural Context' (King's College London, 2002).

of early medieval knowledge. The ninth-century Old English translations of Orosius and Boethius, for example, are points of entry into a wider understanding of Anglo-Saxon encounters with Graeco-Roman mythologies as much as they are mappings of late antique worlds of thought, belief, and space.[62] Geography, history, and classical mythology can be as firmly connected with the imperial, the clerical, and the kingly as are the Roman and Mosaic undergirdings of Anglo-Saxon law, *Alexander's Letter to Aristotle*, or indeed *The Marvels of the East*. Empires and kings are of course also limned in that oddity of the corpus of short heroic poetry, *Widsith*, making it much more than a mere Germanic, heroic poem; queens and empresses in *Elene* can be productively aligned with Anglo-Saxon discourses of queenship.[63] But what of the imperial dimensions of Latin urban poetry, such as Alcuin's poem on York or the elegiac recall of lost worlds afforded by the material remains of earlier empires instanced, for example, in the Anglo-Saxon poem, *The Ruin*? As *The Ruin* suggests, worlds are reckoned with—measured against—as well as described and reconstructed, and thereby made the object of poetic and clerical knowledge, as the genre of the riddle or the enigma also testifies. John D. Niles rightly points to the riddle as the poetic genre of world-making *par excellence*.[64] But worlds are also counted in less poetic, though no less culturally significant, ways. Take, for example, Stephanie Hollis's exemplary introduction to the phenomenon of *computus* from Bede to Byrhtferth, which is a means both of acquiring practical knowledge of the liturgical calendar and of understanding cosmology—the ways in which God measures, numbers, and orders the world.[65] Or consider how time is structured in the various recensions of the *Anglo-Saxon Chronicle* or in the Old English Bede (according to clerical, monastic, Roman, and social chronologies, for example). Calculus and chronology alike provide plenty of evidence for Anglo-Saxon encounters with worlds past, present, and future. Finally, a series of important studies on textuality offers ways of thinking about the world and the text, which is an important dimension

[62] See, e.g., Michael W. Herren, 'The Transmission and Reception of Graeco-Roman Mythology in Anglo-Saxon England, 670–800', *Anglo-Saxon England*, 27 (1998), 87–103. For a related study of Alfredian translation, see Nicole Guenther Discenza, 'Power, Skill and Virtue in the Old English *Boethius*', *Anglo-Saxon England*, 26 (1997), 65–86.

[63] Stacy S. Klein, 'Reading Queenship in Cynewulf's *Elene*', *Journal of Medieval and Early Modern Studies*, 33 (2003), 47–89.

[64] John D. Niles, 'Exeter Book Riddle 74 and the Play of the Text', *Anglo-Saxon England*, 27 (1998), 169–207.

[65] Stephanie Hollis, 'Scientific and Medical Writings', in Pulsiano and Treharne (eds.), *Companion to Anglo-Saxon Literature*, 188–208.

of the ways in which the written word finds its place within broader systems of knowledge.[66]

Britannia and Europa are abstract concepts of place and time drawn on as much by early medieval writers as by post-medieval thinkers and hovering near the surface of such conceptions are their feminized allegorical figurations. While Bede looks back to Britannia, he does not draw explicitly on such personifications in his History, although the relationship between symbolic geographies and genealogy used by Bede and drawn on by some redactors of the Anglo-Saxon Chronicle, for example, suggests that the link between geography, generation, and gender is firmly in place.[67] More explicit, however, is the gendering of abstract worlds of, for example, vice and virtue (as examined by Catherine Karkov in her study of the Psychomachia manuscripts) or of the many patristic metaphors that undergird early medieval clerical knowledge (as Lees and Overing note), both of which provide evidence for a profound cultural interest in the symbolic relationship between gender, bodies, and world-making.[68] That relationship—to which the Old English and Anglo-Latin riddles also testify—offers a way to connect Katherine O'Brien O'Keeffe's important study of the juridical body, as constructed by Anglo-Saxon law, to other bodies similarly made the object of knowledge through technologies of violence, dismemberment, torture, enclosure, or indeed sin.[69] In an Anglo-Saxon world re-territorialized by Christianity, the body, sexed, gendered, material, and symbolic, is similarly surveyed and mapped. For Hollis, for example, the conversion ushers in new ways of thinking about women, the body, and the erotic.[70] Juridical modes of identifying and comprehending the embodied Anglo-Saxon subject thus find their counterparts in discourses of penance, sanctity, poetry, and medicine. This criss-crossing of discursive domains is, from a critical perspective, powerfully enabling:

[66] See esp. Katherine O'Brien O'Keeffe, Visible Song: Transitional Literacy in Old English Verse (Cambridge, 1990); Carol Braun Pasternack, The Textuality of Old English Poetry (Cambridge, 1995); and Catherine Karkov, Text and Picture in Anglo-Saxon England: Narrative Strategies in the Junius II Manuscript (Cambridge, 2001).

[67] See Craig R. Davis, 'Cultural Assimilation in the Anglo-Saxon Royal Genealogies', Anglo-Saxon England, 21 (1992), 23–36, although Davis does not address the implications of this material for a study of gender.

[68] Catherine Karkov, 'Broken Bodies and Singing Tongues: Gender and Voice in the Cambridge, Corpus Christi College 23 Psychomachia', Anglo-Saxon England, 30 (2001), 115–36. See also Clare A. Lees and Gillian R. Overing, Double Agents: Women and Clerical Culture in Anglo-Saxon England (Philadelphia, 2001), 152–72.

[69] Katherine O'Brien O'Keeffe, 'Body and Law in Late Anglo-Saxon England', Anglo-Saxon England, 27 (1998), 209–32.

[70] Stephanie Hollis, Anglo-Saxon Women and the Church: Sharing a Common Fate (Woodbridge, 1992).

O'Brien O'Keeffe revisits the complex relationship between the legal and the spiritual in her narratives of bodies, punished, dismembered, and miraculously healed as a way to study concepts of Anglo-Saxon subjectivity; Horner takes up the ecclesiastical practice of enclosure of religious women as a point of metaphoric entry into Old English literature—a thematics that might be usefully connected with studies of later medieval religious practices.[71] In another register, the assimilation and use of classical medicinal knowledge—aetiology, diagnostics, and recovery, body part by body part, head to toe—alongside pastoral, 'popular', and liturgical ways of knowing and healing the body, provides evidence of a dynamic repertoire of engagements with textual and material bodies by professional physicians as well as by priests ministering to the laity.[72]

At the risk of stating the obvious, without concepts of the embodied subject which can be ranked, classified, gendered, and ordered, there would in fact be no social, ecclesiastical, or political discourse; no ways of knowing the world. This much is plain from the writings of Wulfstan, at once a lawmaker, homilist, and estates theorist.[73] But, by the same token, as bodies are put into discourse and thereby rendered legible—quite literally in one of the cases explored by O'Brien O'Keeffe—is there a way to recover the material body, to glimpse the 'real' even as it disappears behind the veil of discourse? There are in fact a number of ways of tracking material and discursive bodies throughout the cultural archive: the body disposed in and by liturgical prayers, for example, can seek protection both spiritual and physical through the enumeration of body parts, whether its own or Christ's (as Phillip Pulsiano reminds us[74]); the abstract female body, which is a central site for the production of meaning and metaphor in ecclesiastical discourse to the extent that the 'real' body recedes from view—is hardly an abstraction when the politics of dynastic reproduction and rule are concerned, as is so evident in the histories of Queens Emma and Edith explored by Pauline Stafford;[75] sinful flesh is regulated as much by penitential discourse as by the practices of bodies in

---

[71] Shari Horner, *The Discourse of Enclosure: Representing Women in Old English Literature* (Albany, NY, 2001).

[72] For useful introductions, see Hollis, 'Scientific and Medical Writings', and Phillip Pulsiano, 'Prayers, Glosses and Glossaries', in Pulsiano and Treharne (eds.), *Companion to Anglo-Saxon Literature*, 209–30.

[73] For Wulfstan's most important political treatise, see K. Jost (ed.), *Die* Institutes of Polity, Civil and Ecclesiastical (Berne, 1959).

[74] Pulsiano, 'Prayers, Glosses, and Glossaries', 212.

[75] Pauline Stafford, *Queen Emma and Queen Edith: Queenship and Women's Power in Eleventh-Century England* (Oxford, 1997).

the physical space of the monastery or enclosed convent, as Frantzen demonstrates; and the practices of liturgical ritual more generally order bodies in ecclesiastical space, through worship, procession, and veneration as well as meditation.[76]

Concepts of veneration (both the body venerated and the body that venerates) prompt thoughts of worshipping the dead. In the early Anglo-Saxon period, the elaborate theatre of death suggested by the excavations of Sutton Hoo reveals how much the living invested in their dead in the early period of the conversion. In the post-Christian era, a similar investment takes a different form. As we all know, post-mortem body parts circulate as relics, which are used both discursively and materially to testify to the power of the saintly body to mark spiritual and physical place.[77] Virginia Blanton Whetsell examines the relationship between Ely and its patron saint, Æthelthryth, whose relics and life served long after her death as the focal point for monastic politics;[78] the foundation story of Minster-in-Thanet furnished the textual means by which later communities in Thanet remembered both the woman—Domne Eafe—who originally acquired the land for the monastery and the remarkable family of female religious associated with St Mildred.[79] The saintly body was the place where communities of the living and the dead met; it was also the means by which that place could be identified.[80] Place and sanctity are intimately connected as that familiar phrase *loca sanctorum* reminds us.[81] The body of the saint, in short, is as powerful a means of marking the place of the Church in the world as is the cross. And the cross, as a symbol of Christ, is perhaps the most powerful example of how a body can be materially as well as discursively transformed. If a cross can speak, as in *The Dream of the*

---

[76] Frantzen, *Before the Closet*, 138–83. The importance of liturgical practices is signalled in Christopher A. Jones (ed.), *Ælfric's Letter to the Monks of Eynsham* (Cambridge, 1998). See also Lara Farina, 'Before Affection: *Christ I* and the Social Erotic', *Exemplaria*, 13 (2001), 469–96.

[77] See, e.g., Alan Thacker, '*Membra disjecta*: The Division of the Body and the Diffusion of the Cult', in Clare Stancliffe and Eric Cambridge (eds.), *Oswald: Northumbrian King to European Saint* (Stamford, 1995), 97–127.

[78] Virginia Blanton Whetsell, '*Tota integra, tota incorrupta*: The Shrine of St. Æthelthryth as Symbol of Monastic Autonomy', *Journal of Medieval and Early Modern Studies*, 32 (2002), 227–67.

[79] Stephanie Hollis, 'The Minster-in-Thanet Foundation Story', *Anglo-Saxon England*, 27 (1998), 41–64. See also, more generally, Elisabeth van Houts, *Memory and Gender in Medieval Europe, 900–1200* (Toronto, 1999).

[80] See Catherine Karkov and Kelley Wickham-Crowley (eds.), *Spaces of the Living and the Dead: An Archaeological Dialogue*, American Early Medieval Studies, 3 (London, 1999).

[81] See esp. Alan Thacker and Richard Sharpe (eds.), *Local Saints and Local Churches in the Early Medieval West* (Oxford, 2002).

Rood, then it can also be a monument in place and time, historically specific, contingent, local, and at the same time multi-vocal; the spectre of the cross may in fact haunt our scholarly imagination to the extent that we even see a cross where none might have been originally intended, as Fred Orton's remarkable study of the Ruthwell monument demonstrates.[82]

The saintly body, however, is not the only body put into the world; after all, Beowulf himself testifies to a recurrent Anglo-Saxon fascination with how bodies find their meaning through action: how else do we know Beowulf save by the ways in which he acts in the world? Complementing those ecclesiastical, saintly, and religious bodies are the bodies of the hero and another encounter with death (*Beowulf,* we recall, is framed by two great funerals). The imbrication of the hagiographic and the heroic is a well-worn critical theme; so too are the generic affinities of the romance and the saint's life, although the Anglo-Saxon and Anglo-Latin *Apollonius* still await their readers in this regard.[83] Beowulf wrestles, hand to hand, with Grendel, and their tangled bodies are necessary to our understanding of the emergence of the hero; Apollonius finds his place in the world in part by solving the riddle of incest—that discursive intermingling of bodies must be straightened out. Beowulf, however, fights monsters about whose physicality we are in no doubt: Grendel is a flesh-eater, whose arm is ripped out and whose dead body must be decapitated (much like the saintly Oswald's); his mother, another wrestler, knows well the significance of the body part (she reclaims Grendel's arm), and drips blood; the dragon is emphatically a dragon, a felt presence in the world of the poem that must be killed by a sword. We might then connect (as does the *Beowulf* manuscript) the heroic body with its discursive counterparts—monstrous bodies. The line that divides the wonder-workers of the saints, their fiendish opponents and visionary other worlds, from the monsters in *Beowulf* or those in the *Epistola Alexandri* and the *Liber Monstrorum* is faint indeed. Yet, we have barely begun to think about the representational codes for these monstrous bodies, preferring instead to echo the systems of classification in these works by offering our own—learned, playful, clerical, or moral (as does Andy Orchard in the most detailed study of these works[84]).

---

[82] Fred Orton, 'Rethinking the Ruthwell Cross: Fragments and Critique; Tradition and History; Tongues and Sockets', *Art History,* 21 (1998), 65–106.

[83] See, however, the suggestive comments by Scragg and McGowan in Pulsiano and Traherne (eds.), *A Companion to Anglo-Saxon Literature,* 268–70, 318–19 respectively.

[84] Andy Orchard, *Pride and Prodigies: Studies in the Monsters of the 'Beowulf' Manuscript* (Cambridge, 1995).

The saint's life, like the heroic poem, the romance, the epistolary
tradition, and the marvels of the East, is a pan-European genre—its Old
English and Anglo-Latin instantiations point to the European flavour
of Anglo-Saxon culture (northern as well as Roman) as much as to their
distinctive Englishness.[85] To track the body through these discursive
realms is thus to return to questions of world-making, but also to raise
questions about the nature of knowledge, the beliefs that knowledge
of the world mediates, and the power of language to construct, represent,
and enact those beliefs. Conner's essay on religious poetry (in *A Companion to Anglo-Saxon Literature*) tackles these issues head-on by examining
the cultural space shared by religion and poetry in Anglo-Saxon England.[86] Few critics are so bold, and it is a pity that Conner's is only a preliminary enquiry into the relationship between poetry and belief. With
the exception of Peter Clemoes's book, *Interactions of Thought and Language in Old English Poetry,* which considers poetry and prose, the study
of religious poetry languishes (as any cursory glance at the annual bibliographies confirms).[87] Indeed, the enduring appeal of *Beowulf* indicates
how often, and to what an extent, the modern critical imagination is
drawn to the pagan and heroic, foreclosing exploration of the fact that it
is Christianity that defines the pagan in the first place. In this regard,
Karen Jolly's *Popular Religion in Late Saxon England* is to be celebrated for
finding ways to connect the popular and the poetic (the so-called Anglo-
Saxon charms) with formal official modes of belief (such as the sermon
and the homily) via concepts of syncretism.[88] The work of Conner and
Jolly might be fruitfully extended to the genre of wisdom literature
(which otherwise appears to remain a discrete category in its own right),
but also to religious prose (the recent publication of Patrick P. O'Neill's
edition of Alfred's prose translation of some of the Psalms argues for
studies of this most vital aspect of Alfred's work as royal writer[89]). Cultural
modes of religious expression are also examined in my own study, *Tradition and Belief.*[90] Recent work on religious writing that I mention here is

[85] See, further, the essays in Thacker and Sharpe (eds.), *Local Saints and Local Churches.*
[86] Pulsiano and Traherne (eds.), *Companion to Anglo-Saxon Literature,* 251–67.
[87] Peter Clemoes, *Interactions of Thought and Language in Old English Poetry* (Cambridge, 1995).
[88] Karen Jolly, *Popular Religion in Late Saxon England: The Elf Charms in Context* (Chapel Hill, NC, 1996).
[89] Patrick P. O'Neill (ed.), *King Alfred's Old English Prose Translation of the First Fifty Psalms* (Cambridge, Mass., 2001).
[90] Lees, *Tradition and Belief.*

broadly cultural and/or anthropological: that is, belief itself is taken as an object of enquiry so as to resist more conventional (and divisive) literary classifications that have put, for example, the Anglo-Saxon charms in one camp, poetry in another, and sermons, homilies, and saints' lives in a third.

More generally, the study of religious writing in the Anglo-Saxon period is at long last on the verge of a critical renaissance. The publication of the great editions of Ælfric's works (by Godden, Clemoes, Wilcox, and Jones, for example), the Vercelli homilies (by Scragg), the lives of Margaret (Clayton and Magennis), or the apocrypha (Clayton, Cross), together with the resurgence of interest in Wulfstan (Orchard, Wilcox), for example, testify to precisely this renaissance.[91] In a similar vein, Patrick Wormald's remarkable study of Anglo-Saxon law paves the way for a reconsideration of legislation as literature.[92] Without, however, a more sustained critical investigation into these works as cultural enactments of belief, the workings-out of a vernacular law and theology, and evidence for the vitality of Old English prose as a genre in its own right, this work risks a more limited audience than it deserves. None the less, belief need not be construed only as religious belief (including those alienated from and by orthodox Christian beliefs),[93] polity, or law. As my discussion of the interconnected categories of world, body, and belief suggests, belief can (and should) encompass issues of subjectivity, gender, sexuality,[94] textuality, and sanctity, together with other structures whereby the cultural world of the Anglo-Saxons was negotiated and constructed in English as well as in Latin. Britain was transformed by the religious revolution that was the conversion to Christianity (as was early medieval Europe in general). As we negotiate critically the cultural evidence of this period from the chronological stance of that *grand récit* and

[91] For Godden and Clemoes, see n. 1; for Jones, see n. 76; for Scragg and Wilcox, see n. 27; for Clayton and Magennis, see n. 28. See also Mary Clayton (ed.), *The Apocryphal Gospels of Mary in Anglo-Saxon England* (Cambridge, 1999), and J. E. Cross with Dennis Brealey (eds.), *Two Old English Apocrypha and their Manuscript Source: The Gospel of Nicodemus and the Avenging of the Saviour* (Cambridge, 1996); and Andy Orchard, 'Crying Wolf: Oral Style and the *Sermones Lupi*', *Anglo-Saxon England*, 21 (1992), 239–64.

[92] Wormald, *Making of English Law*, 416–76.

[93] A start is made on this topic by Andrew P. Scheil, 'Anti-Judaism in Ælfric's *Lives of Saints*', *Anglo-Saxon England*, 28 (1999), 65–86.

[94] For a related discussion, see Clare A. Lees and Gillian R. Overing, 'The Clerics and the Critics: Misogyny and the Social Symbolic in Anglo-Saxon England', in Thelma S. Fenster and Clare A. Lees (eds.), *Gender in Debate from the Early Middle Ages to the Renaissance* (New York, 2002), 19–39.

its relation to the temporally local and specific, so too our critical categories need to be flexible enough (theoretically *and* practically) to accommodate both the particular discourse of Anglo-Saxon Studies and the general discourses of Medieval Studies and English Studies, to which it is intimately related.[95]

King's College London

[95] For a similar argument made in the context of thinking about gender in the medieval and Renaissance periods, see the Introduction to Fenster and Lees (eds.), *Gender in Debate*, 1–18.

Postscript

Rita Copeland, David Lawton, and Wendy Scase

THIS, the seventh volume of *New Medieval Literatures*, is also the last with Oxford University Press. The age of seven was, of course, particularly significant in the medieval lifetime; it was the end of one age and the beginning of the next, a time of passage. Just so, the seventh issue of this annual is a fitting time to take stock, to look backwards and forwards. Looking back, the seven volumes, and well over seventy essays, have ranged widely methodologically, chronologically, and culturally. We have featured the work of a large number of the most prominent scholars in the field. We have also included work by many newer authors; one of the privileges and pleasures of editing these volumes has been the opportunity to engage with the work of newer entrants to the profession from across the world. Inevitably, some emphases of content reflect our own interests and profiles. However, it is also the case (and a matter for regret, if not surprise) that submissions from medievalists of many textual disciplines (for example, early medievalists, historians, art historians, historians of ideas, musicologists, and modern linguists) have been greatly outnumbered by those from scholars from the capacious field of late-medieval English Studies.

Taking stock is also an opportunity to express gratitude. We are hugely indebted to a large number of people: to the peer reviewers of the essays, whose painstaking but quite unheralded work has greatly assisted many of our contributors; to the graduate students who have helped us with the *NML* website, indexing, and other matters; to our copy-editors, for outstandingly fast and careful work; to our commissioning editors at Oxford University Press, and to their assistants, for their support for an unorthodox project; to the anonymous readers for the Press (especially the one who suggested that we feature a regular analytical survey); to our essayists, for their creativity, brilliance, and fortitude (especially those who have found that a virtual, unresourced, and unstaffed editorial office variously distributed in cyberspace over two and sometimes three continents is not always the most efficient of organisms); to the authors of the analytical surveys, for heroically undertaking the massive labours needed to produce such powerful pieces; and finally, to the members of our Advisory Board, for support and advocacy of many kinds.

As for the future, in her analytical survey in this volume Clare A. Lees calls for 'better use of the complex networks of critical and cultural affiliations that cross the various fields of Medieval Studies', saying that this 'is one area in which *New Medieval Literatures* must continue to play an important role'. We intend that it should do so. We are pleased to announce that *NML* will be joining the journals list of Brepols Publishers from volume eight. The *NML* website continues to provide information for subscribers, contributors, and readers at http://artsci.wustl.edu/~nml/

Index